Christopher Turner

LONDON Step by Step

The guidebook that *really* guides

A · THOMAS · DUNNE · BOOK

St Martin's Press Inc, New York

Contents

First published 1985 by Pan Books Ltd
Revised 1988 and 1991
This revised edition published 1995
by Thomas Dunne Books,
St Martin's Press Inc, 175 Fifth Avenue, New York, NY10010-7848

ISBN 0-312-13667-6
CIP data available on request
Photoset by Parker Typesetting Service, Leicester
Printed by GraphyGems, Spain

Introduction

I am a manic tourist. When I visit a city I want to see everything that there is to be seen. I want to know each location's history, what is special about its exterior and what is special about its interior. I want to be able to find all these special features without difficulty and I want to learn about them precisely as I reach them. I don't want to get lost and I don't want to go round in circles. When I get to my destination I want to know what else there is of interest nearby and exactly how to get to it.

A personal, qualified guide could help me achieve these aims but he, or she, would certainly charge me a considerable amount of money and, in any case, I prefer not to spend every day with a total stranger, however congenial. So I, like most tourists, have had to resort to guide books.

Although many of them are beautifully produced and entertainingly written, most appear to be intended either to whet the reader's appetite or to serve as an attractive souvenir. None has proved to be of more than limited use to me when I have been standing in a street in Paris, Cairo or Bangkok wondering where to go next.

London Step by Step is a completely new concept in guide books. It treats the visitor to London as someone who, without precise guidance, will get lost and confused. The city is divided into more than six hundred locations which are fully described and linked to form twenty-one itineraries. Each itinerary can be broken into, or left, as desired. Starting and finishing at an Underground station, the visitor is led, literally step by step, around the exterior and, when permitted, the interior of each location. Every major point of interest is referred to precisely as it is reached and directions are then given for walking to the next location.

In other words, *London Step by Step* aims to match, as closely as possible, the services of a personal, knowledgeable guide. It has been written as much for the Londoner who believes he knows London like the back of his hand as for the tourist who is overwhelmed by the size and diversity of this vast city.

Christopher Turner

Acknowledgements: For their kindness and help I should like to thank the numerous librarians, architects, press officers, vicars, clerks, hoteliers and curators who have advised on and checked the contents of this book.
A tremendous amount of valuable time was given by the following in particular: the London Tourist Board; the Historic Buildings and Monuments Commission; the librarians of Westminster Abbey and St Paul's Cathedral; the press officers of Buckingham Palace, the Houses of Parliament and the City of London Corporation; the resident governor of H. M. Tower of London; Frank Bradbeere BA Arch (London) FRSA; David Pelham.
The Buildings of England series and *The London Encyclopaedia* were especially useful sources of information.
London Step by Step was the winner of the London Visitor and Convention Bureau Guide Book of the Year Award.

The development of London

Most of this book is concerned with not one but two cities, which now merge imperceptibly to form central London. They are the cities of London and Westminster.

The City of London
The City of London, usually referred to simply as 'the City', lies to the east of London's centre, not far from the North Sea. It appears to have been established as the major settlement of Londinium after the Romans constructed a wooden bridge across the Thames *c.* AD 43. Almost two centuries later, a defensive wall was built around the city, enclosing approximately one square mile.

Little has been discovered that was built between the departure of the Romans in 410 and the Norman Conquest of 1066; and for part of that long period, known as 'Saxon', the walled city appears to have been abandoned.

Although royal palaces have been built elsewhere, the English Court has officially been established at Westminster since the eleventh century, and Parliament has sat there since the thirteenth century. The function of the City has therefore been not government but trading. The City's financial importance to the Crown has earned it many privileges. After the Norman Conquest, William avoided a battle with the Londoners by allowing their autonomy to continue. This has been confirmed and extended by succeeding monarchs and is expressed by customs and regulations that remain unique to the City.

The Roman wall was repaired and maintained during the Middle Ages but, with one minor exception, the area that it covered was never extended. This is why the City is still referred to as 'the square mile'. However, some building took place outside the wall on land belonging to Westminster Abbey and, in the tenth century, the administrative area of the City was extended westward from Ludgate to the Temple.

The Normans began the building of the Tower of London with the White Tower, which was designed as a palace fortress and guarded the river at London's eastern extremity. Norman buildings, with their massive walls and rounded arches, were essentially a development of the Romanesque style that already existed in Saxon England, and the Conquest, therefore, would have created no great change in London's architectural appearance.

It was not until the twelfth century that this change did occur, when the lighter Gothic style, distinguished by the pointed arch, arrived from France. This, in its three consecutive phases of Early English, Decorated and Perpendicular, remained the dominant style in England until the mid-seventeenth century.

During the reign of Henry VIII the Italian Renaissance at last began to affect English design but its Classical themes were employed only as decoration to what remained basically Gothic forms. The result was an unsophisticated mannerism, which lasted throughout the Elizabethan and Jacobean (James I) periods.

Henry VIII ordered the destruction of numerous monastic buildings at the Reformation, and large areas of London were left in ruins throughout the remainder of the sixteenth century.

The City itself had for centuries been surrounded by convent lands which inhibited its spread; and with the sudden availability of all this land for development the extension of London outside its walls could at last begin. It did so dramatically until Elizabeth I banned further building. Charles I tried to do the same almost a century later but neither monarch could stem the tide.

England's first truly Classical buildings began to appear towards the end of James I's reign, with the advent of the Palladian style introduced by Inigo Jones. Its slow progress, however, was soon to be halted by the Civil War which, after the execution of Charles I, was followed by the Protectorate of Oliver Cromwell (The Commonwealth). During this twenty-year period of strife little was built at all but much was destroyed by puritan iconoclasts. With the Restoration in 1660, building began again; but the Great Plague five years later decimated London's population and in the following autumn the Great Fire of 1666 destroyed most of its buildings. London's medieval appearance disappeared for ever, even though a few Gothic buildings survived outside the area of the fire.

The City was rebuilt, this time in brick rather than combustible timber, and the new houses were designed in the now virtually obligatory Classical style. Grandiose plans for wide new thoroughfares and squares had been submitted to Charles II but all were turned down because of the complexity of land acquisition and redivision. The medieval pattern of narrow winding streets and alleyways was therefore retained with only minor amendments. Regulations on the appearance and dimensions of the new houses were strict, little external decoration being permitted. It was not until Sir Christopher Wren's late work leaned towards the Baroque that this exuberant style, in vogue on the Continent, gained some favour in England. This, however, was soon ended by a reaction in the 1720s led by Lord Burlington who advocated a return to the 'purity' of Palladianism. His many followers created an English Classicism that was based on the tasteful proportions of the temples of antiquity. Again there were few extraneous elements. In spite of a brief flirtation with Neo-Gothic, this style remained dominant until the Victorian era, although its external severity was tempered at a late stage by some decorative features from Adam and Nash.

With the Victorians, the homogeneity of London's appearance disintegrated. This was a wealthy era and residents were gradually pushed out of the City, their houses being replaced with commercial premises. Victorian architecture possessed no single style but adapted those that had been developed in many countries and in various periods, often combining several in a single building. Although much of this work is now regarded with affection, the result was that London gained a varied rather than an imposing townscape. In the second half of the nineteenth century, the Gothic revival became dominant.

The twentieth century continued reviving old styles, with inflated versions of Georgian and Queen Anne now finding favour. The increasingly wealthy City built most of its commercial premises in Portland stone and units became larger. The First World War, with its limited bomb damage, necessitated little rebuilding and after it ended no great change in architectural style occurred.

Modernism, based on new building techniques and materials, was in vogue in other countries but made little impact in England and was not to do so until the second half of this century.

Following the Second World War, much of the City again had to be rebuilt, and once more the medieval street pattern was followed. Modernism now became established as the dominant style, usually in the form of high, steel-framed blocks clad in a variety of factory-made materials. This was soon to be accompanied by Brutalism, a style again developed on the Continent long before the Second World War, with its sinuous horizontal forms cast in concrete. Modernism and Brutalism both proved to be unpopular, partly because neither of them suited London's climate or its existing townscape; and there was a return in the 1980s to smaller units clad with bricks and tiles. This style, known as Post-Modernism, has been followed almost exclusively for the redevelopment of Dockland.

Miraculously, the City's best known sights survived the Second World War and show few obvious signs of the Blitz. Although many of the churches were gutted, most have been lovingly restored and retain many of the seventeenth-century furnishings, fittings and monuments that were salvaged or had been stored elsewhere for safety. Unfortunately, only a handful of the Livery Companies' halls survived the bombing, and their loss was probably London's greatest architectural misfortune in the Second World War.

Apart from the Barbican development, the City is no longer a lived-in area, closing down at night and at weekends. Much of it then appears to be a ghost town and a visit is more enjoyable at other times. In spite of its modern buildings, the City, with its intimate streets and alleyways, retains a strangely medieval atmosphere and for many has an equal although different appeal to that of the West End.

The City of Westminster

Westminster lies immediately to the west of the City, but it was established much later and developed more slowly. The building styles followed have been similar to those already described in the City.

Most of the large area now covered by the City of Westminster was originally owned by the abbey, and its early development almost entirely concerned with Westminster Abbey and the royal palaces of Westminster, Whitehall and St James's.

The ancient village of Charing lay to the north and from the thirteenth century, stately mansions lined the Strand between Charing and the City boundary. Apart from this, most of Westminster remained as open fields or royal hunting parks until the seventeenth century.

It originated on Thorney Island, a swampy triangular piece of land surrounded by rivers. Westminster Abbey, probably its first major building, was allegedly founded in the seventh century but no records pre-date the tenth century.

The Court moved to a new palace nearby, also in the tenth century, and Edward the Confessor soon rebuilt the abbey's church, thus establishing its close link with the Crown which still exists. Parliament has sat either within the abbey's precincts or in the Palace of Westminster since the thirteenth century.

The palace was badly damaged by fire in 1532 and the Court then moved to Henry VIII's recently acquired Whitehall Palace which lay nearby. This itself was almost completely destroyed by a fire in 1693 and the Court migrated to St James's Palace which had also been acquired during the Tudor period by Henry VIII. Although Queen Victoria moved to Buckingham Palace on her accession in 1837, the Court remains officially at St James's.

The Palace of Westminster continued to accommodate Parliament and some courts of law, but a major conflagration in 1834 destroyed most of the complex. Its replacement, the Houses of Parliament, now provides one of London's best known landmarks and did much to encourage the Gothic revival in England during the second half of the nineteenth century.

In 1631, London's first square was built at Covent Garden, and in 1673, St James's Square marked the commencement of the 'West End'. Now building was to continue apace and since land was readily available, Westminster, unlike the City, was laid out with spacious squares and large mansions set in private grounds. It therefore became the popular London address for the nobility, few of whom, in any case, had returned to live in the crowded City of London after the Great Plague. However, with the completion of Belgravia and Pimlico in the early years of Queen Victoria's reign, Westminster's building land was exhausted.

Westminster suffered less than the City in the Second World War and comparatively little of architectural importance was lost. The seventeenth- and eighteenth-century tree-filled squares have all survived, although most of their original houses have long since disappeared and there are no privately occupied mansions apart from the royal palaces. Fortunately, in spite of acquisition by Cromwell and shortage of land, the royal parks have escaped development, and it is still possible to walk for three miles almost entirely on grassland between Whitehall and Kensington.

As with the City, the residential population of Westminster is relatively small but the West End contains London's most important shops, hotels and places of entertainment, so that there is a permanently lively atmosphere. Unlike the City of London, therefore, much of the City of Westminster may be enjoyed at any time.

London's villages

In addition to the two cities, central London now incorporates some areas which, until the nineteenth century, were country villages. The innermost of these, such as Chelsea, Kensington and Lambeth, are included in *London Step by Step*. Although swallowed up by the metropolis, many of them have retained a village atmosphere and make an important contribution to the capital.

Practical information

Accommodation
Visitors who arrive without pre-booking a hotel can receive assistance, for a small fee, from the London Tourist Board's information offices, open daily at Heathrow Airport and Victoria Station, or Concordia, open daily at Gatwick Airport and Victoria Station. Advance bookings can be made by writing six weeks in advance to Accommodation Services, London Tourist Board, 26 Grosvenor Gardens, London SW1.

Transport
The Underground
The quickest and easiest way to travel around London is by Underground – 'the Tube'. (See plan inside back cover.) Unfortunately, the service stops completely around midnight.

Fares are priced on a zonal basis and a change of line within the zone can be made without extra charge. The best value for those staying long enough in the capital is a seven-day Travelcard, which is valid for underground trains and buses. This ticket may be used at any time, the zones selected being dependent primarily on where the visitor is staying: a zone 1 ticket covers every location in this book, but not outer London attractions such as Hampton Court, Kew Gardens or Greenwich. For those with less time available, one-day Travelcards are obtainable for use after 9.30 am; again, these are issued on a zonal basis and are valid for buses (except night buses) and the underground. If more than three underground journeys are to be made in a day, Travelcards will save money. LT Cards are one-day Travelcards which maybe used at any time.

Most underground stations in London have automatic barriers in which all tickets must be inserted, face-up, both on entering and leaving the station. Single tickets for the underground may only be purchased at stations. Travelcards may be purchased at underground stations, bus stations and selected newsagents. A passport-size photograph must be supplied when first purchasing a seven-day travelcard.

DLR Services run through Docklands from Tower Gateway Station.

Buses
Although generally less convenient than the Underground, London's double-decker buses do provide superb views – the approach to St Paul's Cathedral from Fleet Street and Westminster Abbey from Victoria Street being particularly memorable. If using the buses, avoid the rush hour if possible; go to the top of the bus and try to get front seats. Buses are particularly useful for reaching destinations in Fleet Street/Strand as the Underground lines run a fair distance to the north and south of these linked thoroughfares. Unlike the Underground, buses run all night on certain routes. Special sightseeing buses run by London Transport (and several private operators such as Harrods) are particularly useful for making a quick appraisal of the city's layout. There are many boarding points including Marble Arch and Victoria Station.

When boarding a bus at a request stop – indicated by a red sign with 'Request' in white letters – hail the bus by extending an arm. Similarly, when alighting at a request stop, ring the bell once, well in advance. Bus fares, also based on zones, are cheaper than the Underground for very short journeys but no change of route can be made without incurring an extra charge. The driver or conductor will issue and inspect single journey tickets and inspect Travelcards; there is no cancellation machinery on buses. Travelcards are not issued on buses but can be obtained at bus stations.

Check the current situation regarding Travelcards, etc, and obtain free bus and Underground plans at any of the following Underground stations: Heathrow Central, Euston, Kings Cross, Piccadilly Circus, Oxford Circus, St James's Park and Victoria, or ring London Transport Information (222 1234).

Taxis
These are generally, but not always, black vehicles which, if they are free, display an illuminated 'For Hire' notice above the windscreen. A standard additional charge is levied on Saturday and Sunday and daily between 20.00 and 06.00. Minicabs are cheaper for longer journeys but must be hired in advance as they cannot by law be hailed in the street. Their fares are not metred and must be negotiated first.

Waterways
The Thames, once London's 'High Street', now has no public transport but there are excursions from the piers at Westminster, Charing Cross and the Tower. Short trips can be made between them, or further afield to Greenwich and the Thames Barrier, throughout the year. From Easter to October, excursions also run to Kew, Richmond and Hampton Court. For details telephone LTB riverboat information service (730 4812), or the piers direct as follows: Westminster Pier for Greenwich, the Tower and Thames Barrier 930 4097; for Kew, Richmond and Hampton Court 930 8294. Charing Cross Pier for the Tower and Greenwich 709 9697. Excursions on the Regent's Canal are operated in summer by *Jason* 286 3428, *Jenny Wren* 485 4433, *My Fair Lady* 485 6210 and the Zoo Water Bus 286 6101.

Outside London
Other parts of the UK may be reached from London by rail, coach or air. Information can be obtained as follows: British Rail Travel Centre, 4–12 Regent Street (personal callers only), or by telephone: S and SE England 928 5100, E Anglia 928 5100, SW and W England and S Wales 262 6767, Midlands, NW England, N Wales and W Scotland 387 7070, NE England and E Scotland 278 2477; Victoria Coach Station, 164 Buckingham Palace Road 730 0202. Flight information: Heathrow 759 2525 (British Airways) or 759 4321. Gatwick 0293 31299.

Opening times
Specific opening times for locations featured in the book are given in the text. In the City most buildings (including churches and pubs) are closed Saturday, Sunday and bank holidays.

Public buildings
Most close during bank holidays. When an entry charge is made admission is usually refused 30 or even 60 minutes before closing time. Few open before 14.00 on Sunday.

Art dealers/auctioneers
Monday to Friday 09.30–17.00.

Banks (Exchange Service)
Monday to Friday 09.30–15.30. At the time of writing, main

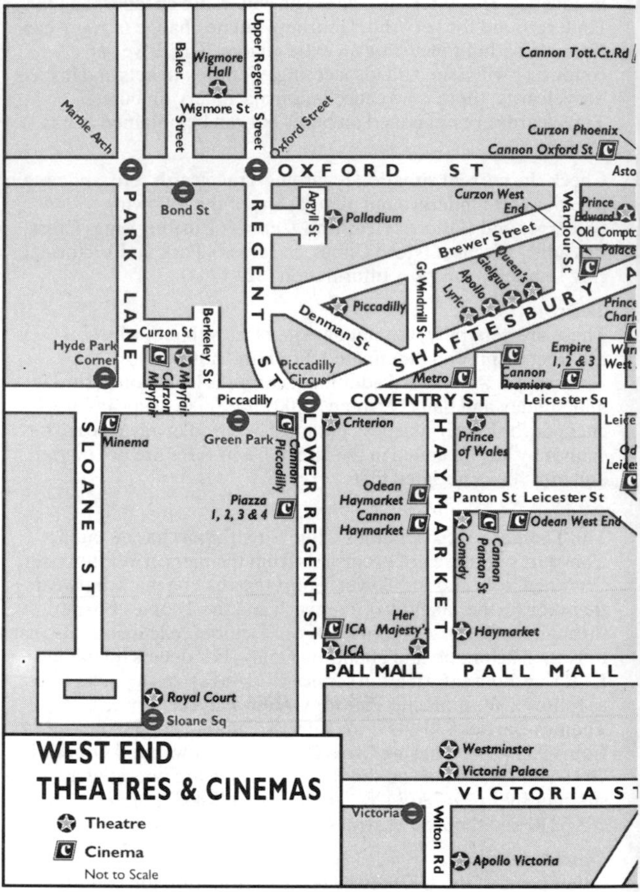
WEST END
THEATRES & CINEMAS
Theatre
Cinema
Not to Scale
Wigmore Hall
Baker Street
Wigmore St
Upper Regent Street
Oxford Street
Marble Arch
OXFORD ST
Cannon Tott.Ct.Rd
Curzon Phoenix
Cannon Oxford St
PARK LANE
Bond St
REGENT ST
Argyll St
Palladium
Curzon West End
Wardour St
Prince Edward
Brewer Street
Queen's
Gielgud
Apollo
Lyric
Gt Windmill St
Piccadilly
Denman St
SHAFTESBURY
Curzon St
Berkeley St
Curzon Mayfair
Mayfair
Hyde Park Corner
Piccadilly Circus
Metro
Cannon Premiere
Empire 1, 2 & 3
Piccadilly
COVENTRY ST
Leicester Sq
SLOANE ST
Minema
Green Park
Cannon Piccadilly
Criterion
HAYMARKET
Prince of Wales
Piazza 1, 2, 3 & 4
LOWER REGENT ST
Odean Haymarket
Cannon Haymarket
Panton St
Leicester St
Odean West End
Comedy
Cannon Panton St
ICA
Her Majesty's
Haymarket
PALL MALL
PALL MALL
Royal Court
Sloane Sq
Westminster
Victoria Palace
VICTORIA ST
Victoria
Wilton Rd
Apollo Victoria

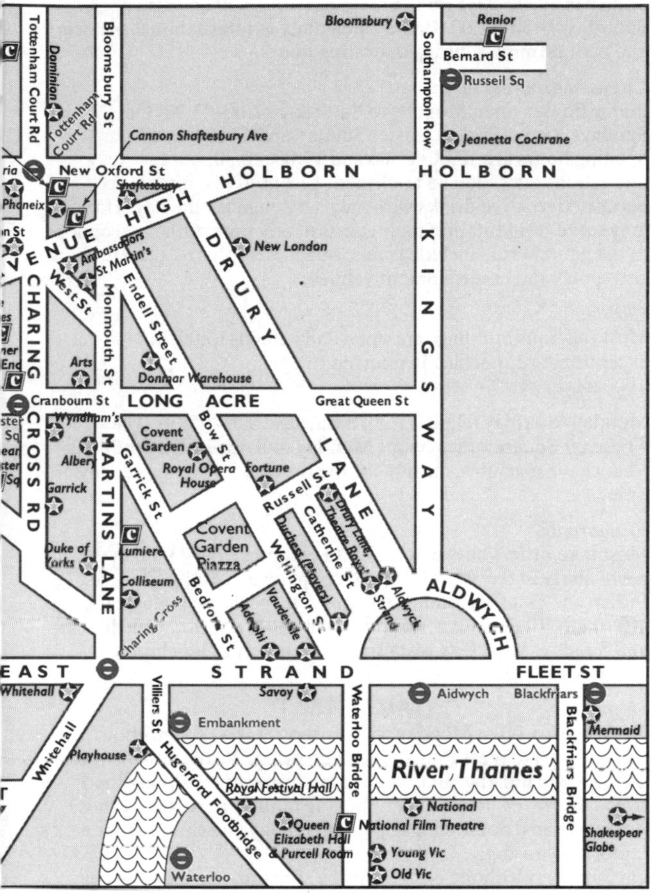

Tottenham Court Rd
Dominion
Tottenham Court Rd
Bloomsbury St
Bloomsbury
Southampton Row
Renior
Bernard St
Russell Sq
Jeanetta Cochrane
Cannon Shaftesbury Ave
New Oxford St
HOLBORN
HOLBORN
Shaftesbury
Phoenix
HIGH
AVENUE
Ambassadors
St Martin's
West St
Monmouth St
Endell Street
DRURY
New London
KINGSWAY
CHARING CROSS RD
Arts
Donmar Warehouse
Cranbourn St
LONG ACRE
Great Queen St
Wyndham's
Covent Garden
Bow St
Albery
Royal Opera House
Fortune
LANE
Garrick
Garrick St
Russell St
Drury Lane, Theatre Royal
Catherine St
Covent Garden Piazza
Duchess (Players)
Wellington St
MARTINS LANE
Lumiere
Duke of Yorks
Colliseum
Bedford St
Charing Cross
Vaudeville
Adelphi
Strand
Aldwych
ALDWYCH
EAST
STRAND
FLEET ST
Whitehall
Savoy
Villiers St
Waterloo Bridge
Aldwych
Blackfriars
Blackfriars Bridge
Embankment
Mermaid
Whitehall
Playhouse
River Thames
Hungerford Footbridge
Royal Festival Hall
National
Queen Elizabeth Hall & Purcell Room
National Film Theatre
Shakespear Globe
Young Vic
Old Vic
Waterloo

branches of Barclays Bank are open until 16.30 and also open Saturday 09.30–12.00. Banks open daily at international airports and boat terminals during operating hours.

Licensed drinking hours
Public houses open Monday to Saturday 11.00–23.00. On Sundays, Good Friday, Easter Sunday and Christmas Day opening hours are 12.00–15.00 and 19.00–22.30, but the restrictions may soon be abolished. Licensed restaurants are permitted to serve drinks with meals throughout the day. Hotels may serve residents and their guests at any time. Other exceptions to the general rule include trains, boats, aeroplanes, private clubs and sports and entertainment venues.

Churches
Most religious buildings are open daily 10.00–16.00, but exceptions are specifically referred to.

Post Offices
Monday to Friday 09.00–17.30, Saturday 09.30–12.30. The Trafalgar Square office opens Monday to Saturday 08.00–20.00. Many have machines outside for the purchase of stamps at any time.

Restaurants
Most take orders between 12.30–14.30 and 19.00–23.00. Some, particularly in the West End, are open longer. Many Chinese, Indian and fast food outlets will provide meals throughout the afternoon. Expensive restaurants may close Saturday lunchtimes and Sunday. Most City restaurants open only at lunchtime Monday to Friday.

Shops
The majority open Monday to Saturday 09.00–17.30 without a midday break. West End and Knightsbridge stores remain open until 20.00 Thursday and Wednesday respectively. Many food stores, however, have longer opening hours – particularly those run by Asians. Some shops open on Sunday and this number is rapidly increasing.
On Sundays alcoholic drinks may be sold only during licensing hours (see above).

Postage
Stamps are generally obtainable only at post offices but some other outlets now also supply them in books. All mail to Europe travels by air automatically. Within the United Kingdom there are two classes of postage, first and second. Second class is usually slower.

Telephones
All locations are in central London. If telephoning central London from outside the area, the prefix 0171 must be dialled. All locations in this book are within the central London area. The prefix for outer London numbers is 0181. Recently introduced competition has led to some reductions in the United Kingdom's horrendous telephone charges. Public telephone booths are operated either by British Telecom (cash or cards) or Mercury (cards only). The cheapest time to call is weekdays before 08.00 and after 18.00, or weekends at any time, when long distance calls in particular are much cheaper. Unlike some countries, local calls are never free nor is time unlimited. Calls made via operators, rather than dialled direct, are even more expensive, and if the call is made from a hotel room the hotel will charge a supplement.

Public telephone booths may contain telephone directories, but as many booths are vandalized these are frequently damaged or missing. Numbers required may be obtained by dialling 142 for addresses in London or 192 for those outside; this service is only free at public booths. Operators will advise on overseas dialling – call 155. The free emergency number for Police, Ambulance or Fire is 999. Most pubs, restaurants, hotels and British Rail stations provide public telephones. Ensure that a good supply of 10p pieces is to hand.

Entertainment

Tickets for London theatres can be obtained by going to the box office during opening hours or by telephoning them and quoting a credit card number. If no tickets are available at the theatre they may still be obtainable from ticket agencies, such as Keith Prowse, who will, however, charge a fee. Half-price tickets for that day's performances are available for many theatres from 12.00 (matinées) and 14.30–18.30 (evenings), Monday to Saturday, at the Leicester Square ticket kiosk. Cash only is accepted and queue well in advance for the most popular shows. Many West End cinemas reduce prices for matinées and all day on Monday. Tickets for all performances are usually available only from the cinema and cannot be reserved. No tipping for services is expected at any entertainment venue.

For up-to-date information consult the London *Evening Standard*, London's evening paper, which is published Monday to Friday, or the weekly *What's On and Where To Go* and *Time Out*. The *Sunday Times* and other 'serious' Sunday newspapers give details of most Sunday entertainments.

Churches/religious buildings

Practically every major church of interest is described, and to guide the visitor with limited time an asterisk appears against the name of a church if its interior, or a major section of it, is of architectural interest, or if some of its furnishings, fittings and monuments are outstanding.

In all churches and chapels, the altar, unless stated otherwise, is situated at the east end. This is a great aid to orientation within the building. For a typical large church layout see the plan of St Paul's Cathedral on page 13.

Roman numerals

Many monuments are inscribed with Roman numerals and therefore the following conversions may be helpful:

1=I, 2=II, 3=III, 4=IV, 5=V, 6=VI, 7=VII, 8=VIII, 9=IX, 10=X
11=XI, 12=XII, 13=XIII, 14=XIV, 15=XV, 16=XVI, 17=XVII, 18=XVIII, 19=XIX,
20=XX, 30=XXX, 40=XL, 50=L, 60=LX, 70=LXX, 80=LXXX, 90=XC, 100=C,
200=CC, 300=CCC, 400=CD, 500=D, 600=DC, 700=DCC, 800=DCCC, 900=CM, 1000=M,
1500=MD, 1900=MCM, 2000=MM

Toilet facilities

Public toilets in central London are better maintained than in most cities. Some in the West End now charge for entry, but those in large hotels, pubs and stores are, of course, free. No tipping is necessary. There are always facilities at mainline railway stations, but few on the Underground.

Public holidays

In England these are known as bank holidays and are as follows: 1 January, Good Friday, Easter Monday, the first and last Mondays in May, the last Monday in August, Christmas Day and Boxing Day (26 December). Practically everything closes.

Tourist information services

The National Information Centre run by the London Tourist Board is at Victoria Station (730 3488) and opens daily. Other LTB centres are at: Heathrow Airport; Harrods, Knightsbridge (fourth floor); Selfridges, Oxford Street (basement); and the Tower of London (April–October). The City of London Information Centre is located at St Paul's Churchyard (606 3030).

Daily events in London are listed in *The Times* newspaper – particularly those attended by members of the royal family. Details can also be obtained by telephoning 246 8041 (Teletourist). London's weather forecasts are available from 246 8091.

By appointment only

To view the following locations featured in this book it is necessary to write in advance, giving as much notice as possible. The itinerary and location numbers are shown in brackets.

Clermont Club (13/22) The Secretary, Clermont Club, 44 Berkeley Square, London W1
Custom House (11/16) Lower Thames Street, London EC3
Houses of Parliament (for guided tours, or reserved seats for either house in session) (7/20) Write to an MP, a peer of the realm or, if a foreigner, the embassy in London
Lambeth Palace (8/9) Palace Secretary, The Archbishop's Palace, Lambeth
Mansion House (4/7) Mansion House, London EC4
Old Admiralty (7/2) Old Admiralty, Spring Gardens, London SW1
Scottish Office (7/12) Dover House, Whitehall, London SW1
Theatre Royal, Drury Lane (10/12) The Historian, Theatre Royal Drury Lane, Catherine Street, London WC2
Tower of London (Ceremony of the Keys) (3/4) The Resident Governor, HM Tower of London
Westminster School (6/13) The Librarian, Ashburnham House, Little Deans Yard, London SW1
Whitefriar's Crypt (1/21) Premises Manager, Freshfields, Whitefriars, 65 Fleet Street, London EC4Y 1HS

For visits to City Livery Companies (changed annually) write to:
City of London Information Centre
St Paul's Churchyard
London EC4

1

St Paul's Cathedral, Fleet Street and the Temple

St Paul's Cathedral is unquestionably the most impressive Classical building in London. It is reached via Fleet Street, with its many courtyards which include the complex of the Temple, one of London's three ancient centres of the legal profession.

Timing: Monday to Friday mornings are preferable.

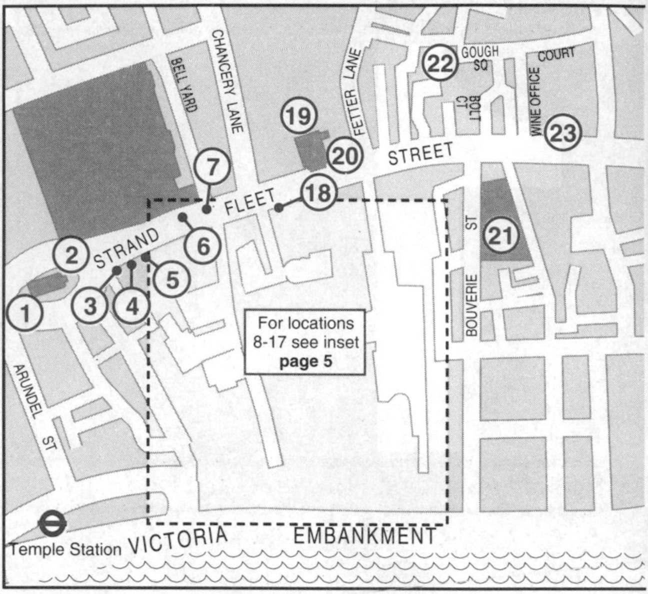

Locations

1 St Clement Danes
2 Royal Courts of Justice
3 Twining's
4 Lloyds Bank
5 Wig and Pen Club
6 Temple Bar Monument
7 Fleet Street
8 Middle Temple Gateway
9 The Temple
10 Middle Temple Lane
11 Brick Court/Essex Court
12 New Court
13 Middle Temple Hall
14 Temple Church of St Mary
15 Kings Bench Walk
16 The Buttery
17 Inner Temple Gateway
18 Prince Henry's Room
19 St Dunstan-in-the-West
20 'Sweeney Todd's'
21 Whitefriar's Crypt
22 Doctor Johnson's House
23 Ye Olde Cheshire Cheese
24 St Bride
25 St Martin-within-Ludgate
26 Queen Anne Statue
27 St Paul's Cathedral
28 College of Arms
29 St Benet's Welsh Church
30 St Andrew-by-the-Wardrobe
31 The Black Friar

Start *Temple Station, Circle and District Lines. Leave the station by the exit immediately ahead. Turn L and ascend the steps to Arundel St ahead. Third R Strand. Cross to St Clement's in the centre of the road.*

Location 1 — **ST CLEMENT DANES** *Wren 1682*

Strand

A colony of Danes settled around this area in the 9C; the first St Clement's church was built for them and named after the patron saint of Danish sailors. It was partly rebuilt in the 15C and again in 1640. The present St Clement's implies that it is the 'Oranges and Lemons' church of the nursery song as its bells play the tune on the hour every three hours 9.00–18.00. However, St Clement Eastcheap in the City more believably claims this distinction.

The masonry of the lower part of the tower is 15C, although completely encased by Wren. Everything from the clock level upwards was added by *Gibbs* in 1719.

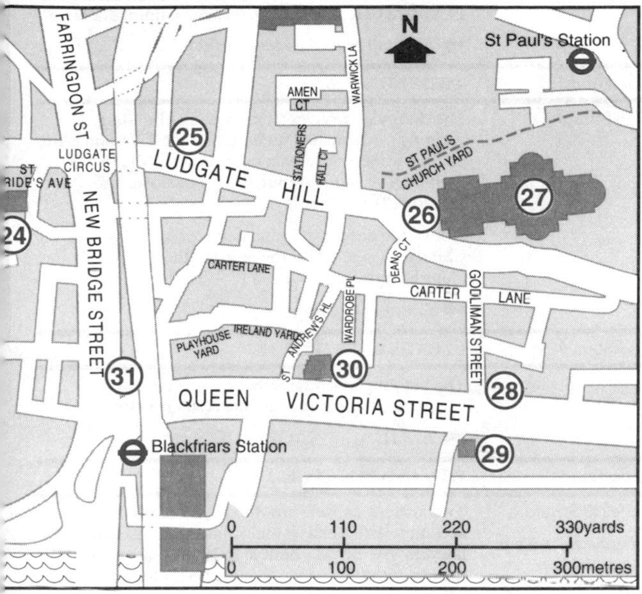

Enter from the west front.

St Clement's interior was restored after being gutted by bombs in the Second World War. The church has been adopted by the Royal Air Force and there are many slate badges commemorating their squadrons.

At the east end of the nave is a chair dedicated to Thelma Bader. This commemorates the wife of Douglas Bader, the pilot who flew in the Battle of Britain after losing both legs. His ashes were brought to the church in 1982.

The pulpit by *Gibbons* (?) is original.

The two bishop's thrones in the sanctuary are embroidered with 15C Florentine silk.

The altar painting is by *Ruskin Spear*.

Exit R and cross to the north side of the road. Proceed eastward.

From here it can be appreciated that St Clement's, unlike St Mary-le-Strand further west, was not originally designed for its island site. The north facade was obscured by other buildings and there is, therefore, no Baroque carving here as there is on the south side.

Standing outside the east apse of the church is the monument to Dr Johnson by *Fitzgerald* 1910.

Continue ahead.

Location 2

ROYAL COURTS OF JUSTICE *Street 1882*

Strand

The Great Hall is open Monday–Saturday 10.30–16.30.

The 'Law Courts' were built for the hearing of civil cases previously tried in Westminster Hall or Lincoln's Inn. The building was designed in 13C. Gothic style.

Enter the Great Hall by the main entrance.

Examples of legal dress are displayed immediately R.

Exit and cross the road.

Location 3	**TWINING'S** *1787*
216 Strand	The doorway survives from an earlier building. Twining's established premises here in 1716 and is the oldest business to remain on its original site in Britain. The shop is reputedly the narrowest in London (?). Above the door, the Chinamen represent Twining's China tea trade whilst the lion was the company's identification mark. *Continue eastward.*

Location 4	**LLOYDS BANK** *1890*
222–225 Strand	The building was originally a restaurant and its vestibule contains outstanding ceramic work. *Exit R.*

Location 5	**WIG AND PEN CLUB** *17C*
229/230 Strand *Restaurant open to non-members. Closed Saturday lunchtime and Sunday.*	Two ancient houses, now linked internally, accommodate a club founded for journalists and lawyers. No 229 was built in 1625 and was at one time the headquarters of the Temple Bar gatekeeper. No 230 is late 17C. Internally, only the staircase is original. *Exit R. The Temple Bar Monument stands in the centre of the road.*

Location 6	**TEMPLE BAR MONUMENT** *H. Jones 1880*
Strand	This monument marks the boundary between the cities of Westminster and London and records the position of the old Temple Bar. On entering the City at this point, the sovereign requests permission to proceed from the Lord Mayor of London who then symbolically presents the Pearl Sword. Initially, the bar was a simple chain across the road but later, elaborate structures were built. Wren's gateway was the last physical barrier. It stood here from 1672 until 1878, when it became too much of an obstacle for traffic. The arch, illustrated on the east side of the memorial, was dismantled and re-erected in Theobalds Park, Herts where it remains at present. *Continue eastward.*

Location 7	**FLEET STREET**
	Fleet Street, for long the centre of the newspaper industry, was named after one of London's several 'lost' rivers that now flow underground in sewers or conduits. The newspapers have, in recent years, relocated mostly to Docklands. The Anglo-Saxon word *fleet* meant a tidal inlet. The river runs north-west to south-east from Hampstead to Blackfriars. *Proceed ahead to the Middle Temple Gateway (first R).* This is one of three entrances to the Temple from Strand.

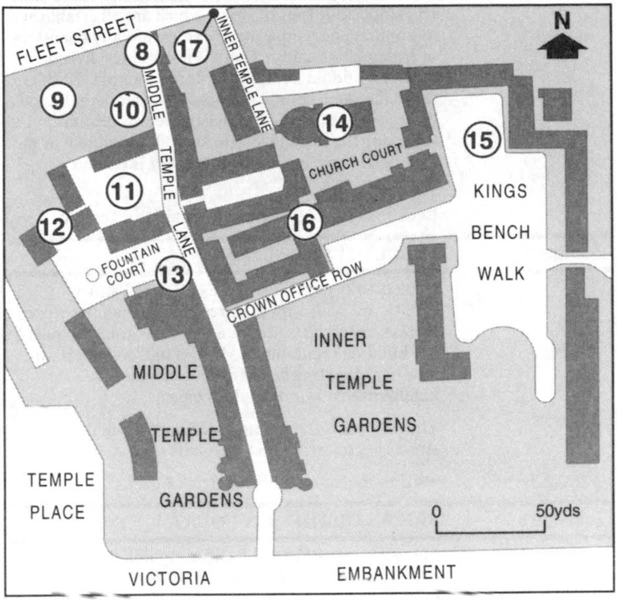

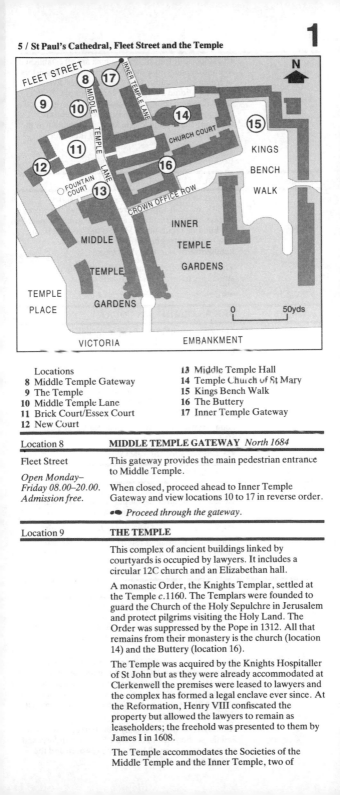

Locations
- **8** Middle Temple Gateway
- **9** The Temple
- **10** Middle Temple Lane
- **11** Brick Court/Essex Court
- **12** New Court
- **13** Middle Temple Hall
- **14** Temple Church of St Mary
- **15** Kings Bench Walk
- **16** The Buttery
- **17** Inner Temple Gateway

Location 8 — **MIDDLE TEMPLE GATEWAY** *North 1684*

Fleet Street

Open Monday–Friday 08.00–20.00. Admission free.

This gateway provides the main pedestrian entrance to Middle Temple.

When closed, proceed ahead to Inner Temple Gateway and view locations 10 to 17 in reverse order.

Proceed through the gateway.

Location 9 — **THE TEMPLE**

This complex of ancient buildings linked by courtyards is occupied by lawyers. It includes a circular 12C church and an Elizabethan hall.

A monastic Order, the Knights Templar, settled at the Temple *c.*1160. The Templars were founded to guard the Church of the Holy Sepulchre in Jerusalem and protect pilgrims visiting the Holy Land. The Order was suppressed by the Pope in 1312. All that remains from their monastery is the church (location 14) and the Buttery (location 16).

The Temple was acquired by the Knights Hospitaller of St John but as they were already accommodated at Clerkenwell the premises were leased to lawyers and the complex has formed a legal enclave ever since. At the Reformation, Henry VIII confiscated the property but allowed the lawyers to remain as leaseholders; the freehold was presented to them by James I in 1608.

The Temple accommodates the Societies of the Middle Temple and the Inner Temple, two of

England's four Inns of Court which are all established in London and whose members are already barristers or training to qualify. There is no obvious division between Middle Temple and Inner Temple. Both share the same church but possess separate halls and libraries. Most of the Inner Temple was rebuilt following the Second World War. The emblem of the Middle Temple is a lamb and that of the Inner Temple a winged horse.

Locations 10–17 are situated within the Temple.

Location 10

MIDDLE TEMPLE LANE

Immediately past the gateway, Nos 1, 2 and 3, *c.*1693, are built with picturesque overhanging upper storeys, an architectural feature that broke the post-fire building regulations. Most of the 'chambers' are now occupied by barristers whose names are handwritten around the doorways.

The Temple is the last area of London where the streets are lit by gas and manually operated.

Proceed ahead. First R Brick Court.

Location 11

BRICK COURT/ESSEX COURT

Many courts within the Temple are linked by alleyways which, although private, may be freely used by the public.

Before the Second World War, Brick and Essex Courts were divided by a range which was bombed and has not been rebuilt; the two courts now appear as one. The block ahead, facing Middle Temple Lane, is dated 1677.

John Evelyn, the diarist, lived at No 1 Essex Court in 1640.

Proceed ahead to New Court.

Location 12

NEW COURT

This court was built over the garden of old Essex House by a wealthy developer, Dr Barbon, in 1667. The buildings are original and dated.

Turn L. Descend the steps to Fountain Court.

The central fountain is referred to by Dickens in *Martin Chuzzlewitt.*

Turn L.

Location 13

MIDDLE TEMPLE HALL *1573*

Open Monday–Friday 10.00–12.00 and 15.00–16.30. Admission free. To ensure entry, telephone in advance, particularly during August (353 4355).

In this hall, students, on passing their final examinations, are 'called to the Bar', i.e. they become barristers. Lunch and dinner are served in the hall and students must dine here on at least twenty-four occasions.

Shakespeare's *Twelfth Night* is recorded as being performed here in 1601, possibly with the author himself in the cast (?). Apart from the rebuilt Grays Inn Hall this is the only existing venue in London where a Shakespeare play was certainly performed in the author's lifetime.

Although the hall is basically Elizabethan, the tower and the section east of this are 19C. The windows and the buttresses have all been much restored and the lantern on the roof renewed.

Enter the north porch.

The carved double doors to the hall were added c.1670.

Immediately behind the visitor, at the east end of the hall, is an Elizabethan screen which was painstakingly reassembled after bombs had shattered it.

The roof of the hall is a rare double hammerbeam structure.

The 29–foot Bench Table at the west end is believed to have been presented by Elizabeth I. A four-foot extension was added in 1928.

The small cupboard table in front of this has an oak top which, reputedly, formed the hatch of Sir Francis Drake's ship *Golden Hind* (?) Its modern protective top can be removed to reveal the original.

In the south-west bay, adjacent stained glass windows record two of the Society's 'readers', Mr Jekyll and Mr Hyde. Robert Louis Stevenson was inspired to adopt their names for the title of his book.

The coats of arms in stained glass commemorate important members from the 16C to the 19C. Most of the suits of armour displayed beneath them are Tudor.

Exit R.

Between the hall and the river are Temple Gardens where Shakespeare, in *Henry VI,* set the scene for the historic plucking of the roses that began the War of the Roses.

L Middle Temple Lane. Second R pass through Pump Court. Continue ahead through the cloister to the church.

Location 14

TEMPLE CHURCH OF ST MARY*

Open 09.30–16.00. Closed throughout August and most of September.

The 12C nave of this church is the only circular example in London. Although situated within the precincts of the Inner Temple, the church, built by the Knights Templar, serves both Inns. It is, like Westminster Abbey, a 'Royal Peculiar', i.e. directly responsible to the sovereign.

The **nave,** 'The Round', was built 1160–1185 in a circular form to emulate the Church of the Holy Sepulchre in Jerusalem. It marks the transition between the Norman and Gothic styles and is one of the earliest buildings in England to employ the pointed arch. Romanesque details are few.

Proceed clockwise to the west porch.

Although renewed externally in the 19C., the rib-vaulting within the Gothic porch is original. Behind this, the semi-circular entrance portal, built at the same time, is typically Norman.

Return to the south side and continue eastward to view the exterior of the chancel.

The rectangular **chancel** 'The Oblong' was added in 1240 and is entirely Early English in style. It replaced the original chancel of 1185.

Enter the south porch.

The chancel roof, Purbeck marble columns,

stonework and woodwork (apart from the reredos) were completely renewed after the Second World War.

•➡ *Turn immediately L.*

The tomb chest of a Recorder of London, Richard Martin, d.1615, is at the west end of the chancel.

•➡ *Return eastward and proceed anti-clockwise.*

At the east end of the south wall is a Purbeck marble effigy, believed to have come from the tomb of Bishop Silvester de Evedon of Carlisle, d.1256 (?). The Bishop died at the Temple after falling from his horse during a visit. It is believed that he had been entertained too well (?).

Above L is the 13C double piscina.

The Classical reredos behind the altar by *W. Emmett* 1682 formed part of Wren's heavy restoration work.

The east windows by *Carl Edwards* 1958 contain what is judged to be some of London's best modern stained glass.

At the west end of the north wall is the tomb of Edmund Plowden, d.1584. He was the Treasurer responsible for building Middle Temple Hall.

The door R opens to a stairway which leads to a penitents cell and the triforium passage. (Apply to the verger who will arrange entry whenever possible.)

Immediately L behind the door are two niches where food and drink would be left for the penitent.

•➡ *Ascend the stairs to the cell and the triforium passage.*

The floor of the triforium passage is covered by tiles made in 1842 which were first laid on the floor of the church below.

•➡ *Descend to the chancel R. Proceed to the nave.*

Internally, the Gothic style predominates in the **nave** but most of the detailing is the 19C work of *R. and S. Smirke.*

The triforium passage above the aisles is an early English example of a blind arcade in the French style.

All the Purbeck marble columns were replaced in 1843.

Some of the medieval effigies of knights were made in the 12C and are the oldest known English statues to survive. Only the most southerly example, a member of the Ros family, escaped damage in the war.

Ahead is a 19C copy of a Norman font.

•➡ *Return to the south porch and descend the steps R to the* **undercroft.**

This was built below the original chancel. There is a piscina and a bench.

•➡ *Exit from the church L. Pass through the arch ahead to Kings Bench Walk. Cross the road.*

Location 15

KINGS BENCH WALK

The present houses replaced the offices of the Kings Bench which burnt down in the 17C. Nos 1–7 on the east side by *Wren* 1678 have been much restored. No 1 has been rebuilt and the front of No 3 renewed.

From No 7 cross the road. Turn R. First L Crown Office Row. Cross to the north side turn L and follow Inner Temple Hall to its west end. The stone Buttery adjoins this.

Location 16

THE BUTTERY

This two-storey 14C (?) building was originally part of the monastic refectory and probably served as a provisions store.

Pass the Buttery. Turn R. First R, ascend the steps and proceed northward through the cloister towards the west end of the church. Continue ahead past the west porch and Dr Johnson's Buildings to Inner Temple Lane. Pass beneath Inner Temple Gateway.

Location 17

INNER TEMPLE GATEWAY *1610*

17 Fleet Street

All the Jacobean woodwork had to be renewed in 1906, except for the carved panels between the windows. The stone arch was rebuilt in 1748.

Enter the doorway next to the shop on the east side of the arch. Ascend the stairs to the first floor.

Location 18

PRINCE HENRY'S ROOM *1610*

17 Fleet Street

Open Monday Saturday 11.00–14.00. Admission free.

The ceiling with 'PH' and the Prince of Wales's feathers commemorates the investiture of Henry, eldest son of James I, as Prince of Wales in 1610. It is unlikely that the royal family were connected with the building as has been alleged, because the ground floor immediately served as the Prince's Arms tavern.

The Jacobean panelling on the west wall is a London rarity. That on the south and east walls, including the fire surround, is 18C.

Mementoes of the diarist Samuel Pepys include an original letter to Charles II.

Exit R. Cross the road.

Location 19

ST DUNSTAN-IN-THE-WEST *John Shaw 1833*

Fleet Street

Open Tuesday and Thursday, other days irregularly.

The statues that embellish the exterior of St Dunstan's are its greatest historic attraction.

St Dunstan's, first recorded in 1185, is dedicated to a 10C Bishop of London who later became Archbishop of Canterbury. The previous building just escaped the Great Fire which stopped a few yards away but it eventually had to be rebuilt.

Shaw based his design of the tower on All Souls Pavement in York.

The clock was the first public example in London to include a minute hand. It was made for the previous church in 1671 as a thanks offering for its escape from the Great Fire. The two savages, possibly Gog and Magog (?), who strike the bells on the quarter hour, are part of the clock. Below is a memorial to newspaper baron, Lord Northcliffe by *Lutyens* 1930. The bust was made by *Lady Hilton Young*.
The statues of most interest, however, came from old Ludgate, once the most important western entrance to the City. The gate was rebuilt in the Elizabethan period and stood until 1760. 'Lud' in Old English meant the back or postern. Above the

small east porch, Elizabeth I *Kerwin* 1586, from the gate's west side, is the oldest public statue of an English monarch. The inscription below is modern.

•● *Enter the east porch via the gate to the courtyard.*

Within L are 16C (?) statues of the mythical King Lud and his two sons, from the gate's east side.

•● *Return to Fleet St R and enter the church from the west porch. Proceed clockwise.*

Unusually, the High Altar is at the north end. Some chapels are reserved for Orthodox worship.

Most of the monuments came from the previous church.

In the second bay L the monument above the door is to Hobson Judkin Esq, 'The Honest Solicitor'.

The 19C icon screen was brought from Antim Monastery in Bucharest, Romania in 1966.

The 17C reredos is Flemish.

The iron Lord Mayor's sword rest facing the pulpit was presented to the church in 1785 to celebrate the English victory over the Scots at Culloden.

•● *Exit L and proceed to the adjacent building.*

Location 20

'SWEENEY TODD'S'

186 Fleet Street

This is the favourite candidate for the site of the barber shop owned by Sweeney Todd, the mythical (?) 'Demon barber of Fleet Street', who murdered his clients and disposed of their bodies to a pie-maker established on the other side of St Dunstan's.

•● *Exit L. If viewing Whitefriar's Crypt (by appointment) continue eastward. Fourth R Bouverie St. Cross the road.*

•● *Alternatively proceed to Location 22.*

Location 21

WHITEFRIAR'S CRYPT

Freshfields,
Whitefriars,
65 Fleet Street

Open by appointment only. Admission free.

This small 14C crypt from the Carmelite Whitefriars monastery was excavated in 1927. Above it, the old News of the World building has been demolished for an office development, but the crypt has been preserved and may now be viewed.

•● *Return to Fleet St R. First L Bolt Court. First R follow the passage to Gough Square.*

Location 22

DR JOHNSON'S HOUSE

17 Gough Square

Open May–September, Monday–Saturday 11.00–17.30, October–April 11.00–17.00. Admission charge.

This house was occupied by Doctor Samuel Johnson 1748–59 and here he completed his dictionary. Mementoes of Johnson are exhibited together with 18C furniture.

•● *Exit ahead and proceed beneath the arch. First R Wine Office Court.*

Location 23

YE OLDE CHESHIRE CHEESE *1667*

Wine Office Court
(353 6170)
Open Monday–Saturday.

Allegedly patronized by Dr Johnson, this is one of London's oldest and least-altered pubs. Its ground floor bar retains an open fire. Similarly atmospheric is the Chop Room restaurant opposite.

•● *Exit L to Fleet St L. Third R St Bride's Avenue.*

Location 24 | **ST BRIDE** *Wren 1678*

St Bride's Avenue

St Bride's possesses the highest of all Wren's spires. It suggested to a local baker the tiered design for wedding cakes which remains popular. Seven churches have been recorded on the site since Saxon times. Samuel Pepys, the diarist, was baptized here in 1632.

Enter the church from the north porch ahead.

The interior of this, the journalists' church, was completely rebuilt after the bombing and all the furnishings are modern. Facing the entrance are models of St Bride's Charity School Children *c.*1711.

Descend the steps R to the crypt.

The burial crypt was re-opened in 1953 and now houses a museum illustrating the history of St Bride's. A Roman pavement is preserved *in situ.*

Exit and return to Fleet St R. Continue ahead and cross Ludgate Circus. Proceed beneath the railway bridge to Ludgate Hill. Cross the road to St Martin's.

Location 25 | **ST MARTIN-WITHIN-LUDGATE*** *Wren 1684*

Ludgate Hill

This Wren church, dedicated to St Martin of Tours, is renowned for its dark 17C woodwork. St Martin's is first recorded in the 8C. King Cadwalla was buried within. The church was rebuilt in 1223 and 1437. Captain William Penn, founder of Pennsylvania, USA, was married in the previous building in 1643.

St Martin's stood just within London's wall against the old Ludgate and a plaque L commemorates this.

Wren designed the slender spire as a visual foil to the dome of St Paul's Cathedral further up the hill.

Enter the vestibule and turn L. to the nave.

The font, ahead, was made in 1673. Above this, in the west gallery, is the organ made by *Schmidt* in 1684 but rebuilt. Most of the woodwork, including the pulpit, altar rails, reredos and lectern, is original.

At the east end of the church, on the south side, is a churchwarden's double chair of 1690.

The three doorcases beneath the south gallery are outstanding and possibly carved by *Gibbons.*

Exit L and continue to St Paul's Churchyard.

Location 26 | **QUEEN ANNE STATUE** *Belt 1886*

St Paul's Churchyard

The statue, a copy of *Bird*'s original, stands in front of the main entrance to the cathedral which was completed in Anne's reign. As the Queen's statue looked away from the cathedral a contemporary satirist, referring to her indulgence, wrote: 'Brandy Nan, Brandy Nan, you're left in the lurch. Your face to the gin shop, your back to the church.'

Proceed to the west front of St Paul's.

Location 27

ST PAUL'S CATHEDRAL* *Wren 1710*

St Paul's Cathedral, founded in 604, surmounts Ludgate Hill, the second highest point in the City. The first building burnt down in 1087 and its Norman replacement, extended in the 13C, was destroyed by the Great Fire of London in 1666. Wren's building is, therefore, the third on the site, but nothing structural survives from its predecessors.

During the 17C, Old St Paul's, like many other churches, was neglected and became dilapidated. Shortly before the Great Fire, Wren proposed replacing the tower with a dome. John Evelyn records in his diary that Wren's plans were approved just six days before the fire struck.

The cathedral is open to visitors daily, 08.30–16.00. Admission charge to the cathedral and its crypt (galleries extra).

Guided 'Super Tours' Monday–Saturday 13.30 and 14.00. These include visits to the crypt, ambulatory, geometrical staircase, choir and Chapel of St Michael and St George. Admission charge.

After the fire, many wanted to repair the building and services were actually held amidst the ruins. However, following the collapse of a column, Wren was at last commissioned to design a completely new cathedral and the remnants of the old building were demolished. A coal tax had been levied to pay towards the cost of rebuilding London and one third of the revenue was allocated to St Paul's.

None of Wren's drawings or models were ever fully accepted, but, with Charles II's approval, he proceeded with the 'Warrant Design' of 1673. The King gave Wren permission to amend ornamental detail as he felt fit and the architect interpreted 'ornamental' liberally, to produce more or less what he wanted. Work began at the east end, the foundation stone was laid in 1675 and the cap stone positioned on the lantern by Wren's son in 1708.

Due to the efforts of the St Paul's fire-watch during the Second World War, the cathedral survived, whilst most surrounding buildings were destroyed, and it became the symbol of British resistance.

St Paul's, like all the major Gothic churches, has a Latin cross plan, but its appearance is Classical and there is much Baroque detailing.

The dome is the second largest in the world, after St Peter's in the Vatican. Although, this appears to be a single structure, it in fact comprises three separate elements, an inner dome, an outer dome and a central cone.

Portland stone, never before used structurally in London, was selected for the exterior.

Wren originally designed the portico to be supported by one range of massive columns but the quarry could not provide them and eventually two tiers had to be employed. The carving on the pediment, by *Bird,* illustrates the conversion of St Paul.

The bell towers are the cathedral's most Baroque feature. The south-west clock tower houses three old bells. 'Great Tom', the hour bell, was recast from Big Ben's predecessor at the Palace of Westminster.

To view the exterior proceed clockwise around the building keeping initially to the paved area outside the railings.

Alternatively, enter the cathedral by the door, L.

The upper storey of the north facade wall is false. It was designed, both here and on the south facade, to

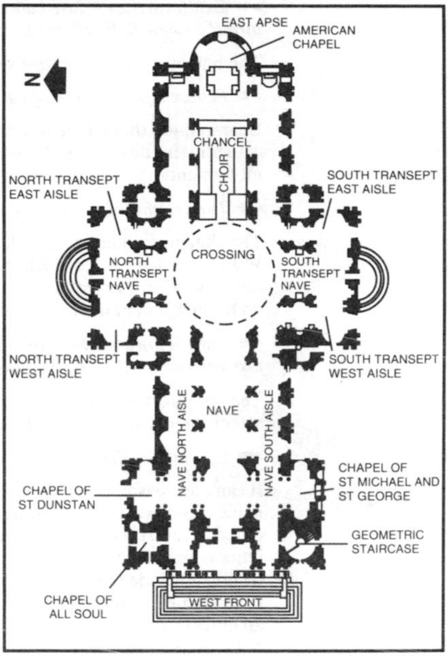

increase the apparent size of the building and thus permit the large dome to be built without appearing unduly voluminous. Additionally, it screens the Gothic-style flying buttresses that support the weight of the dome, and which Wren wanted to hide. The balustrade that runs along the top was forced on Wren who had specified a solid parapet. 'Ladies think nothing well without an edging,' was his wry comment.

Most of the carved panels beneath the ground floor windows are by *Gibbons*.

Pass the restored Chapter House L Wren *1714 and enter the enclosed section of the churchyard through the second gate R opposite the north transept.*

The railings were made in 1714 and are an early example of cast-ironwork.

The Stuart arms on the north transept's pediment are by *Gibbons*.

Turn L.

The monument ahead by *R. T. Blomfield* 1910 commemorates the medieval Paul's Cross which stood nearby until demolished by Cromwell in 1643. It was a wooden, lead-covered pulpit from which speakers delivered sermons, royal proclamations and political orations.

At the monument turn R and follow the path towards the cathedral's apse.

A stone slab on the ground marks the original site of Paul's Cross.

The modern Choir School L incorporates the tower of St Augustine, by *Wren*, 1683, the only part of the church that survived the Second World War.

Exit from the enclosed area. Cross the road and turn R to view St Paul's south facade.

The phoenix on the transept's pediment is by *Cibber*.

Proceed to the west front and enter the cathedral.

Bear in mind that all the tombs are situated below the cathedral in the crypt and not beneath the monuments.

Turn L immediately to the **Chapel of All Souls.**

The chapel, frequently closed, commemorates First World War leader, Lord Kitchener, who appeared on the 'Your Country Needs You' posters. The statues on his monument were carved by *Reid Dick* in 1925.

Turn R towards the shop and then turn L and proceed eastward along the nave.

The clerestory windows, hidden externally by the screen wall, can now be seen below the nave's roof.

Continue to the **crossing.**

It can most easily be appreciated from here that the **dome** comprises three separate elements: an inner dome, a central cone and an outer dome. Both the inner dome and central cone are built of brick and completely hide the outer dome which is made up from lead-encased timber beams. Wren decided that an inner dome was necessary as the height of the outer dome would appear excessive from within.

Painted on the inner dome are monochrome frescoes of scenes from St Paul's life by *Thornhill* 1719. These were not approved of by Wren who wanted mosaics.

The mosaics in the crossing (and the chancel) by *Watts, Stevens* and *Richmond,* were added *c.*1900.

The gilded keystones above the crossing arches were carved by *Cibber.*

In the centre of the floor, the circular inscription in Latin includes Wren's epitaph composed by his son: *Si monumentum requiris, circumspice,* 'If you seek my monument look around you.'

The floor tablet ahead marks where Churchill's catafalque rested during his funeral service in 1965.

The eagle lectern was carved by *Jacob Sutton* in 1720.

The **choir** is entered only on a Super Tour, when the finely carved stalls may be approached more closely. *Gibbons,* the carver, was half-Flemish, born in Belgium, and *Tijou,* the ironsmith, was a French Huguenot. However, all their known work is in England.

The low choir screen by *Tijou* formed the original communion rail and was then situated at the east end of the cathedral in front of the apse. The organ, in two sections, above L and R, is by *Schmidt.* Its case by *Gibbons* is original.

The contents and layout of the choir are no longer as Wren knew them. Originally, most of the service could be heard but not seen by the congregation in the nave. To overcome this, *c.*1870, the organ with its casing was divided, the choir screen and organ gallery removed and the choir stalls brought forward. Much of the fine woodwork and ironwork were re-used.

Turn R and proceed to the east of the crossing.

The canopied pulpit was designed by *Mottistone* in 1964 in 17C style.

No monuments existed in St Paul's for eighty-five years and most are judged to have little artistic value. The earliest was to the prison reformer John Howard by *Bacon the Elder* 1795 in the south-east corner of the crossing.

Continue to the **south transept east aisle.**

Against the south wall ahead, is the monument to Collingwood d.1810, by *Westmacott.*

South transept nave. The monument to Generals Packenham and Gibbs, d.1815, by *Westmacott* stands L of the door.

The doorcase was constructed *c.*1870 from the unwanted 17C choir screen and gallery by *Gibbons.*

Against the pillar R is the monument to Nelson by *Flaxman* 1818. This was first erected in front of the choir in the north bay now occupied by the organ.

South transept west aisle. Against the west wall is the monument to General Abercromby, d.1801, by *Westmacott.*

Continue to the **nave**. *Turn L.*

On the second pillar L in the **south aisle** is a copy by *Holman Hunt* of his painting 'The Light of the World'.

Continue ahead to the chapel in the last bay L.

Chapel of The Order of St Michael and St George. This chapel is entered only on a Super Tour. The screen was carved by *Jonathan Maine* in 1706.

If on a Super Tour proceed, with guide, to the south entrance door to view the south-west clock tower's **geometrical staircase**.

The balustrade is by *Tijou.*

Cross to the north aisle opposite.

Chapel of St Dunstan. The screen is by *Maine* 1698.

Proceed eastward.

North aisle. The Wellington monument, in the central bay R, is the cathedral's largest. It was begun by *Alfred Stevens* in 1857 but only completed after fifty-five years by *John Tweed* 1912. The monument stood in the Chapel of St Michael and St George until moved here in 1892.

Continue ahead and turn L to the **north transept, west aisle**.

Immediately L is the monument to Reynolds by *Flaxman* 1813.

The marble font by *Bird* 1723 was briefly housed in the Chapel of St Michael and St George when it served as a baptistery 1892–1902.

Continue eastward towards the ambulatory screen.

L of the gate is the monument to Dr Samuel Johnson by *Bacon the Elder* 1795.

Enter the **ambulatory.**

All the ironwork referred to is by *Tijou* unless stated. The aisle screen at the entrance was brought forward in the 19C rearrangement.

A close view of the rear of the choir stalls by *Gibbons* may now be had.

The double gates, at the east end of the ambulatory R, incorporate part of the old choir screen and were formed by adding gilded pilasters and crestings specially made in 1890.

Opposite, is the sculpture 'Mother and Child' by *Henry Moore,* presented by its creator in 1984.

The single gate ahead R is in its original position.

The baldacchino (canopied altar) is a memorial to Commonwealth citizens killed in both World Wars. It replaced the Victorian reredos destroyed by bombs. The baldacchino's design was suggested by Wren's unused drawings and dedicated in 1958.

The **American Chapel** in the apse commemorates the 28,000 US citizens based in Britain who were killed during the Second World War. It was formerly the Jesus Chapel and rebuilt after bomb damage.

The next single gate ahead is in its original position.

Immediately L of this is the cathedral's original altar table by *Wren.* It originally stood in the apse and St Paul's had no grand altarpiece for many years.

The double gates R were made up, similarly to those opposite, from the old choir screen.

Against the third pillar L is the monument to John Donne by *Stone* 1631. Donne was a poet and Dean of St Paul's and his monument was the only intact example saved from the old cathedral.

The screen ahead was moved forward in the 19C.

Exit from the ambulatory. Turn immediately L to the north aisle of the south transept. Descend the steps L to the crypt.

The **crypt** stretches beneath the entire cathedral and is the largest in the world. Some monuments commemorate those buried elsewhere.

At the bottom of the steps turn L, R and first L.

Immediately ahead are the tombs of First World War admirals Jellicoe and Beatty.

Descend the steps and proceed ahead.

Nelson lies in the black marble sarcophagus made in Italy for Cardinal Wolsey *Benedetto da Rovezzano* 1529, but by tradition confiscated by Henry VIII.

Continue ahead beneath the central arch.

The model of Old St Paul's includes the wooden spire that was destroyed by lightning in 1561. It was 150 feet higher than the present dome. Display panels describe the evolution of the cathedral's design.

Return towards Nelson's tomb but turn R just before the steps which lead down to it.

The bust of poet W. E. Henley, d.1903, against the second pillar L, is by *Rodin.*

Turn L and proceed ahead.

Against the third pillar R (facing Nelson) is the bust of Lawrence of Arabia, d.1935, by *Kennington.*

Turn L, R and R again.

Wren's death mask and a copy of his bust, originally carved by *Bird* in 1673, are displayed in a case against the wall L.

The damaged effigy R, of William Cokain, d.1626, came from Old St Paul's.

Turn L and first L to the **Treasury of the Diocese.**

Plate and vestments belonging to St Paul's and other churches in the diocese are exhibited.

Turn L.

Another damaged effigy R, rescued from Old St Paul's, commemorates Nicholas Bacon, d.1579.

Continue ahead. Turn R and First L.

Wellington's sarcophagus is surrounded by plaques commemorating Second World War field marshalls.

Proceed ahead to the OBE Chapel.

The **Order of the British Empire (OBE) Chapel** was originally St Faith's Chapel. It was re-designed by *Mottistone* and adopted by the OBE in 1960.

Turn R and second L. Proceed to the end of the aisle. Turn R to **Artists Corner.**

Wren and his family are buried here. Below Wren's black tombstone lies the foundation stone of the cathedral. Above, on the wall, the architect's epitaph is repeated.

The English painters Turner, Millais and Reynolds, together with the American artist Benjamin West, are buried in front of Wren.

Return to the west end of the chapel and exit. Immediately L of the gates ascend the steps and return to the south transept. Proceed R to the crossing and first L to the south aisle of the nave. Immediately L is the entrance to the galleries.

There are 527 steps to the very top, however, they are broken by galleries at three levels.

The **Whispering Gallery** is reached first. Its name refers to the unusual acoustics whereby words whispered against the wall can be heard by someone else who presses an ear to any other part of the wall.

From the **Stone Gallery** that runs outside the drum of the cathedral dome, can be seen the buttresses below.

The **Golden Gallery** gives an impressive bird's-eye panorama of the City.

Descend to the nave. Turn L and exit from the cathedral L. Cross St Paul's Churchyard. Turn L. First R Godliman St. Third L Queen Victoria St.

Location 28

COLLEGE OF ARMS *1688*

Queen Victoria Street
Court Room open Monday–Friday 10.00–16.00. Admission free.

The College, originally known as the College of Heralds, was probably established by Edward I in the 13C. It received its first Charter from Richard III in 1484. Heraldic functions include the preservation of state ceremonial procedure, the examination and recording of pedigrees and the designing and granting of new coats of arms. Members are appointed by the Earl Marshall, the Duke of Norfolk, and retain their ancient titles e.g. Garter King of Arms.

The 18C (?) iron gates which came from Goodrich Court, Herts, were presented to the College in 1956.

Derby House, a mansion originally belonging to Lord Derby, was given to the College by Mary I in 1555 when she renewed its Charter. This was rebuilt, forming an open quadrangle, by *M. Emmett* and *F. Sandford* in 1688.

Proceed through the courtyard.

The 17C central block survives but has lost its original pediment. Its two wings, which also had pediments, were shortened in 1867 for the creation of Queen Victoria Street.

Ascend the steps to the central door.

The **Court Room** is entered immediately. The internal woodwork is by *W. Emmett*. Behind the Earl Marshall's throne is a carved early 18C 'reredos'.

The adjoining waiting room R retains its 17C panelling and chimneypiece.

Exit from the courtyard R. Remain on the north side to view St Benet's opposite.

Location 29

ST BENET'S WELSH CHURCH *Wren 1683*

Queen Victoria Street (723 3104)

Open for Sunday services, otherwise by appointment only.

St Benet's has been adopted as the Metropolitan Welsh church and services are held in the Welsh language. Inigo Jones, the father of English Classical architecture, was buried in the previous building. The brick exterior is an early London example of the Dutch style. Internally, the church is little altered, even retaining its galleries. Practically all the furnishings and fittings are 17C. Outstanding are the carved arms of Charles II.

Continue westward.

Location 30

ST ANDREW-BY-THE-WARDROBE *Wren 1695*

Queen Victoria Street

The church was gutted during the Second World War and only the walls and tower were saved. Its interior has been entirely renewed.

'Wardrobe' refers to the Great Wardrobe where many of the monarch's possessions were stored and which stood behind the church from the 14C until destroyed by the Great Fire.

Exit R. Proceed beneath the bridge to the Black Friar R.

Location 31

THE BLACK FRIAR *Fuller Clark 1897*

Queen Victoria Street

The Black Friar is a unique, Art and Crafts pub. The ground floor was rebuilt in 1905 and the snack bar added in 1924. The marble, mosaics and bronze friezes are mostly by *Henry Poole*.

Leave by the Queen Victoria St exit. Turn R and continue ahead to Blackfriars Station, Circle and District lines.

Alternatively, if continuing with Itinerary 2, leave by the Queen Victoria St exit L. First L Blackfriars Lane. Continue ahead past the Playhouse Yard junction. (First R.) Proceed to the archway R.

Itinerary 2

2

St Bartholomew-the-Great and the Charterhouse

Due mainly to the Great Fire, little has survived from the medieval City of London. This itinerary includes the area outside the north-west section of London's wall where the fire stopped. Here, in spite of heavy bombing during the Second World War, the greatest concentration of ancient buildings is to be found.

Timing: The Charterhouse is open from April to July but only on Wednesdays at 14.15. A special visit is recommended, or begin the itinerary mid-morning to ensure arriving in time. St John's Gate and Priory Church are open Tuesday, Friday and Saturday but may also be seen by appointment on other days when convenient.

Start *Blackfriars Station, Circle and District Lines. From the station follow the subway and exit second R. R Queen Victoria St. First L Blackfriars Lane. Continue ahead past the Playhouse Yard junction (first R) and proceed to the archway R.*

Alternatively, continue from itinerary 1.

Location 1 — **APOTHECARIES HALL** *Locke 1671*

Blackfriars Lane

Only the courtyard may be entered.

This is one of the few 17C livery halls to survive the Second World War. The Apothecaries Society, which is still closely connected with the medical profession, broke away from the Grocers Company and received its Charter in 1617. When the present site was acquired by the Apothecaries in 1632, their hall was adapted from the original 13C guesthouse of the

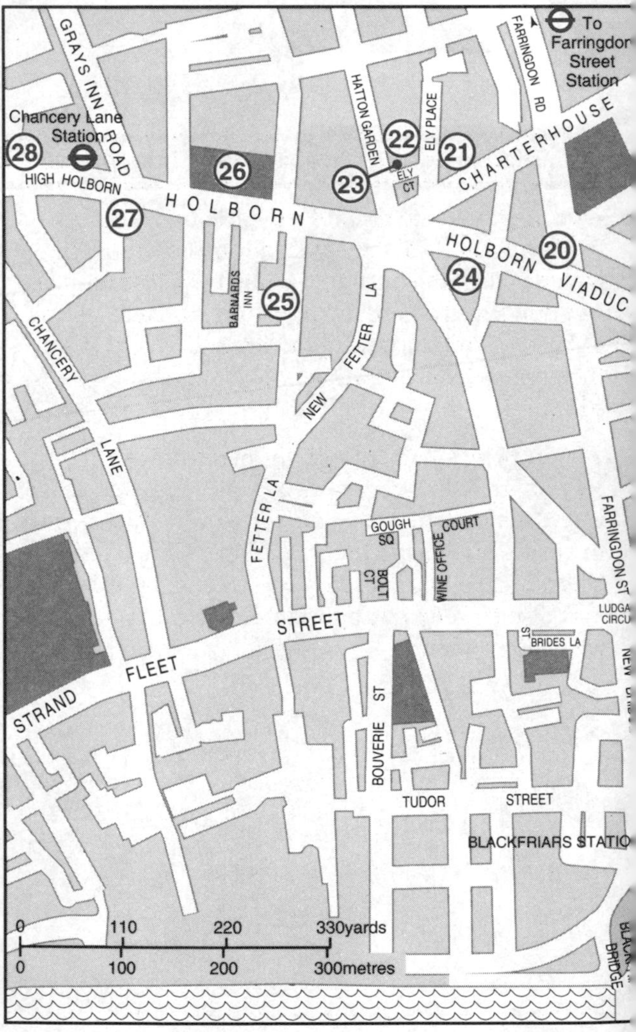

21 / St Bartholomew-the-Great and the Charterhouse

2

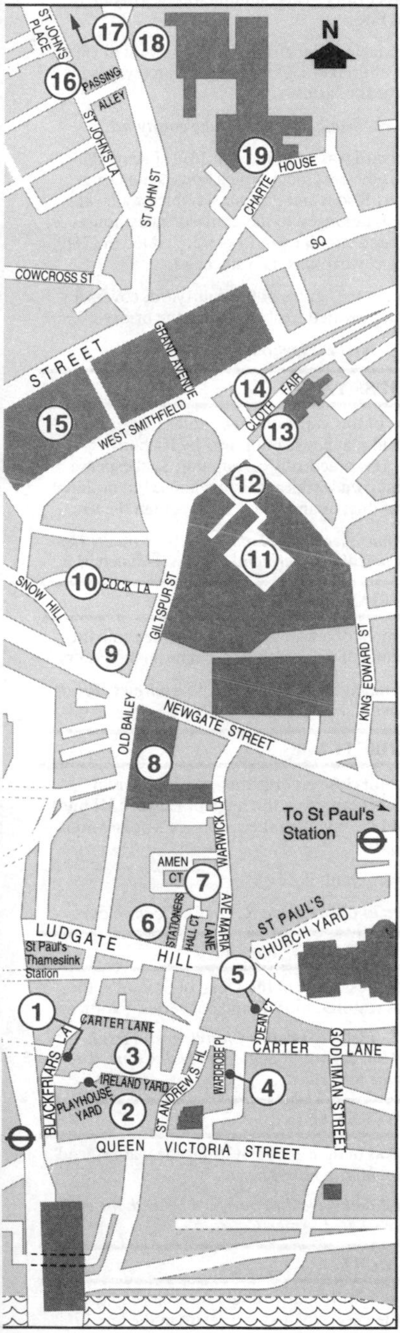

Locations

1 Apothecaries Hall
2 Playhouse Yard
3 Blackfriars Priory
4 Wardrobe Place
5 The Old Deanery
6 Stationers Hall
7 Amen Court
8 Central Criminal Court, 'Old Bailey'
9 St Sepulchre-without-Newgate
10 Cock Lane
11 St Bartholomew's Hospital
12 St Bartholomew-the-Less
13 St Bartholomew-the-Great
14 Nos 41 and 42 Cloth Fair
15 Smithfield Market
16 St John's Gate
17 Priory Church of St John
18 The House of Detention
19 Sutton's Hospital in the Charterhouse
20 Holborn Viaduct
21 Ely Place
22 St Etheldreda
23 Ye Old Mitre
24 St Andrew Holborn
25 Barnards Inn
26 Prudential Assurance
27 Staple Inn
28 The Cittie of Yorke

Blackfriars Priory. This building was destroyed by the Great Fire.

The block facing Blackfriars Lane was built in 1684 but much altered in 1779. Above the archway is the Society's coat of arms.

Proceed through the arch to the courtyard.

The courtyard was completed in 1671. Facing the entrance is the east block which houses the Great Hall, Court Room and Parlour. Its thick walls, at lower level, belonged to the monastic guesthouse. A pediment and circular windows were added in 1786 and the brickwork was then stuccoed.

The lamp, in the centre of the courtyard, covers a well which provided fresh water for the priory.

Exit L. First L Playhouse Yard.

Location 2

PLAYHOUSE YARD

The name of this yard commemorates the Elizabethan playhouse built here by Richard Burbage. It is practically certain that Shakespeare acted in his own works at the playhouse but nothing survives of this, or any other, Elizabethan theatre.

Continue ahead to Ireland Yard. Ascend the steps L to the small churchyard and turn immediately R.

Location 3

BLACKFRIARS PRIORY

Ireland Yard

This fragment of a wall is the only visible remnant above ground of the great 13C Dominican monastery.

Descend the steps L. Third L St Andrews Hill. R Carter Lane. First R Wardrobe Place.

Location 4

WARDROBE PLACE

The peaceful close records the site of the Great Wardrobe where, from the reign of Edward III until the Great Fire, many of the sovereign's possessions were stored.

Nos 3–5 were built in 1710.

Return to Carter Lane R. First L Deans Court.

Location 5

THE OLD DEANERY *Wren 1670*

Deans Court

Built as the residence of the Dean of St Paul's, the house was restored in 1983 and converted to offices.

Exit L. First L St Paul's Churchyard. First L Ludgate Hill. Second R Stationers Hall Court. The hall is on the west side.

Location 6

STATIONERS HALL

Stationers Hall Court

The hall was built in 1670 but its facade was refaced in stone by *McIntyre* 1800.

Only the courtyard may be entered.

Turn R and leave the courtyard beneath the arch immediately left. L Amen Court.

Location 7

AMEN COURT

This forms another surprisingly rural close in the heart of the City. Nos 1–3 were built in the late 17C.

Follow the path to the secluded gardens at the rear.

The old London wall lay just beyond the present garden wall.

Exit through the gate. L Warwick Lane. Second L Newgate St. Proceed ahead to the Central Criminal Court. The first door L leads to Courts 1–4 (major trials). Ring the bell for entry. For other courts proceed ahead. First L Old Bailey (the street). Enter the last door L.

Location 8 — CENTRAL CRIMINAL COURT, 'OLD BAILEY'

Newgate Street/
Old Bailey

Courts are open free to the public (over 14 years old) when in session 10.30–13.00 and 14.00–16.15. Be early to queue for important cases.

The name 'Old Bailey' derives from the bailey which once stood nearby as a defensive rampart outside London's ancient wall. A Sessions House was first built here in 1549 adjoining Newgate Prison which was also referred to as Old Bailey. Public hangings took place outside from 1783–1868 after they had ceased at Tyburn and, as can still be seen, the road here was widened to accommodate the spectators. Famous trials held in the present building include those of Dr Crippen, Christie, and recently Peter Sutcliffe, the 'Yorkshire Ripper'.

The main building by *Mountford* 1907 incorporated the site of Newgate Prison which was demolished for its construction. Surmounting the building is a gilded figure holding scales that represents Justice.

Exit L from courts 1–4 and proceed ahead to Holborn Viaduct. Cross the road. From other courts exit R. First L Holborn Viaduct. Cross the road.

Location 9 — ST SEPULCHRE-WITHOUT-NEWGATE

Holborn Viaduct

St Sepulchre is the largest parish church in the City and, although damaged by the Great Fire, its 15C Gothic tower, porch, and external walls remain. A church has been recorded here since the 12C 'without Newgate', i.e. built outside the wall.

St Sepulchre's bells, the 'Bells of Old Bailey', are featured in the 'Oranges and Lemons' nursery song. One of them tolled when Newgate prisoners were about to be executed. Previously, when the gallows were at Tyburn, the condemned were taken there from the prison in an open cart (hence the expression 'in the cart' meaning trouble) and they were handed a nosegay as they passed St Sepulchre's.

St Sepulchre's windows, which had been altered in 1790, were mostly restored to their Gothic form in 1878. At the same time, the porch was partly rebuilt and refaced and the pinnacles on the tower enlarged.

Enter the **south porch.**

The 15C vaulting of the porch is original.

Immediately L of the entrance to the nave is a font cover *c.*1690 which was bravely rescued by a postman, from Christ Church nearby, whilst the building was ablaze following a bombing raid.

Enter the **nave.**

Some 17C pews remain on both sides of the entrance but most were removed at the same time as the galleries in 1878.

Following the Great Fire, the interior was restored and all the walls refaced but the architect is unknown. The coffered ceiling was added in 1834.

Proceed to the **north chapel.**

This, formerly the Stephen Harding Chapel, becar

the Musicians Chapel in 1955. The ashes of conductor Sir Henry Wood were interred here in 1940. He had been an assistant organist at the church and later gained fame as the founder of the Promenade Concerts. He is commemorated in the central window. The first window L commemorates the composer John Ireland. Dame Nellie Melba's window, R of Henry Wood's, includes peaches in the lower corner R. These refer to 'Peach Melba' the dessert created for the Australian soprano by Escoffier at London's Savoy Hotel.

Below Melba's window is a 16C recess which probably served as an Easter Sepulchre (?).

Exit from the chapel L.

Although the organ case dates from 1671, the original organ by *Harris* has been replaced.

Once twin pulpits, the matching lectern L and pulpit R, both shortened, were made in 1854.

The ornate reredos was made *c.*1670.

Proceed to the column in the south aisle that faces the pulpit.

The hand-bell, displayed in a glass case on the column, was rung by St Sepulchre's clerk at midnight outside the condemned prisoner's cell in Newgate Prison to announce his day of execution. This was considered a charitable act which was paid for by the will of Robert Dowe.

On the other side of the same column is an early 18C Lord Mayor's sword rest.

Proceed to the plaque at the rear of the south choir stall.

The plaque commemorates the burial in the church of Captain John Smith. Whilst in America, he was captured by Cherokees but saved by the chief's daughter, Pocahontas, who pleaded for his life.

Opposite, on the south wall, is a 15C piscina.

Proceed to the west end of the aisle.

The font and its cover were made in 1670.

Exit L. First L Giltspur St. Proceed to the Cock Lane corner (first L).

Location 10

COCK LANE

It is believed that the lane gained its name from birds that were bred here for cock fighting in the 12C (?).

This was the only thoroughfare in the City to be licensed for prostitution in medieval times. Cock Lane was 'haunted' in the 18C by a famous ghost known as 'Scratching Fanny' and the Duke of York and Dr Johnson were amongst those who attended her 'visitations'.

On the Giltspur Street corner, inset in the wall at first floor level, is the gilded statue of a 'Fat Boy', once an inn sign. Traditionally, but erroneously, this marks where the Great Fire stopped.

Continue along Giltspur St. First R West Smithfield. Proceed to the gatehouse.

Location 11

ST BARTHOLOMEW'S HOSPITAL *Gibbs 1769*

West Smithfield
(600 9000)

Stairway and hall open Monday–Friday 09.00–17.00. Admission free.

The 18C Great Hall and staircase with *Hogarth* paintings are the grandest in a London hospital.

The hospital's **gatehouse,** dated 1702, was rebuilt by *Philip Hardwick* in 1834, and rooms added for residential use. Above the arch is London's only statue of Henry VIII by *Bird* 1702.

Pass through the gatehouse.

St Bartholomew's (St Bart's) is the oldest hospital in London to occupy its original site. It was founded by Rahere at the same time as his Augustinian monastery in 1123 but became independent in 1170. Harvey, the discoverer of blood circulation, was a physician at this hospital in the 17C.

Continue beneath the arch ahead to the courtyard.

This was built by *Gibbs* 1730–69 but the original Bath stone facing wore badly and the buildings were refaced with Portland stone in 1851. The block ahead was rebuilt in 1937.

Turn L and enter the first door L.

The paintings 'The Pool of Bethesda' and 'The Good Samaritan' on the **staircase** are by *Hogarth* 1737.

Ascend to the **Great Hall** *on the first floor.*

The coffered ceiling and panelling are original.

A stained-glass window illustrates Henry VIII giving the hospital its charter in 1546. This was made *c.*1664 and installed here in the 18C.

Return towards the gatehouse as far as the church R.

Location 12

ST BARTHOLOMEW-THE-LESS

This, the hospital's own church, was founded in the 12C and rebuilt in the 15C. The present building was designed by *Dance the Younger* in 1793 but rebuilt by *T. Hardwick* in 1823 as a replica. Much of the tower and the vestry L survives from the 15C church.

Turn the L handle to the left, push hard and enter.

The tower retains some Perpendicular features. Although the church is basically octagonal it is squared-up by chapels.

Exit from the hospital grounds R and proceed to the timbered gatehouse of St Bartholomew-the-Great.

Location 13

ST BARTHOLOMEW-THE-GREAT*

West Smithfield

The church is famed for its Norman chancel, only matched in London by the Chapel of St John in the Tower of London.

The restored 13C stone porch of the **gatehouse** originally led directly into the church. Its timber super-structure, much renovated, was added in the 16C and served as the rectory.

Proceed through the gatehouse to the churchyar

The path follows the approximate position of the south aisle of the long nave which once stretched the road. A low wall R is all that remains of the Norman south wall of this aisle.

Rahere, a courtier of Henry I, recovered from

fever, and in gratitude erected a church and hospital dedicated to St Bartholomew in 1123. The church formed part of the small Augustinian Priory of St Bartholomew and Rahere became its first prior. Only the chancel and ambulatory were completed by Rahere. The transepts and crossing were added in the mid 12C and the nave completed in 1240. Miraculous healings were reported and on 24 August, St Bartholomew's Day, the church was filled with sick people. At the Reformation, the long nave was almost entirely demolished, together with the transepts and only the crossing, Lady Chapel, and one bay of the nave were reprieved to provide the parish church.

Although St Bartholomew's escaped the Great Fire, by the 18C it had become run down and was occupied by industrial squatters. Much restoration and rebuilding was carried out by *Aston Webb* in the late 19C. The church was undamaged by bombs.

The brick tower with its lantern dates from 1628. The west porch is entirely the work of *Webb* 1893.

Enter the chapel.

The interior was originally painted throughout with red and yellow zig-zag stripes, a characteristic Norman motif. Much of the stonework was damaged in the 18C as a forge stood where the north transept had been.

The **nave** is entered directly but only one bay remains.

Turn immediately L and R through the choir screen to the **crossing.**

The choir screen was decorated by *Frank Beresford* in 1932.

The pointed north and south arches of the crossing are believed to be mid-12C and may therefore represent the earliest known appearance of the Gothic style in London (?).

Continue ahead through the **chancel.**

Massive, typically Norman piers support a gallery. The clerestory windows above were remodelled in Perpendicular style in 1406.

The wall monument R commemorates Percival Smallpace, d.1568, and his wife, d.1588.

Facing this is the monument to Sir Robert Chamberlayne, d.1615.
The oriel window, protruding from the gallery, was built for Prior Bolton in 1515. His punning rebus (emblem) on the stonework depicts an arrow or bolt piercing a barrel or tun.

The decorative tomb of Rahere, the founder, stands L of the altar. Although Rahere died in 1144 his present tomb was made *c.*1500.

At the gallery level, the arches at the east end are blind in the manner of a triforium. They had been mostly demolished in 1406 when this wall was rebuilt but were restored in the 19C.

Turn L and follow the ambulatory clockwise to the **Lady Chapel** *behind the altar.*

This was added to the church in 1331 but heavily restored by *Webb* in 1897. A printer set up his press in this chapel and in 1724 employed Benjamin Franklin, later to become the renowned American statesman. Only the windows at the extreme east end of the north and south walls are original. The sill of the latter formed a sedilia (priest's seat).

Continue around the ambulatory.

Two wall monuments in the **south ambulatory** commemorate James Rivers, d.1641, and Edward Cooke, d.1652. The Cooke statue originally 'wept' in damp weather, due to condensation.

The large monument to Sir Walter Mildmay, d.1589, and his wife, commemorates an Elizabethan Chancellor of the Exchequer.

Proceed to the **south transept.**

Like the north transept, this was rebuilt by Webb in the late 19C. Both were originally much longer.

Turn immediately L.

The early 15C font in which the painter Hogarth was baptized in 1697 is the only medieval example in a City church but its cover is probably 17C (?).

On the east wall is a small monument to Elizabeth Freshwater, d.1627.

Continue ahead to the 13C door L at the west end of the church. This leads to the **cloister.**

The restored east cloister was rebuilt in 1406, and is all that remains of the original four.

Proceed ahead towards the south end.

The blocked 15C door L originally led to the monastic Chapter House. At the end L is a 13C doorway.

Exit from the church. R West Smithfield. First R Cloth Fair. Proceed ahead to view the exterior of the church.

This north facade of St Bartholomew's is its most interesting. First seen are traces of Norman and 13C work. *Webb*'s 19C north transept is followed by the low wall of the chancel's aisle which Webb also rebuilt. Most of the church has been refaced with flint.

The upper level brickwork is 17C but the brick house with its turret is 16C.

Some buttresses supporting the Lady Chapel at the east end of the church are 14C.

First R St Bartholomew Lane passes the east end of the Lady Chapel. First R follow the south facade as far as possible. Return to Cloth Fair.

Location 14

NOS 41 AND 42 CLOTH FAIR *c.1670*

These rare London examples of houses built immediately after the Great Fire have protrudir bays and overlook the churchyard. The name street commemorates the cloth fair held at Sr in the Middle Ages.

Return to West Smithfield R. Second F Avenue leads through Smithfield Market

Location 15

SMITHFIELD MARKET *H. Jones 1868*

Operates in the early morning. Some local pubs also open then to serve the porters.

Smithfield Market, covering ten acres, is the largest meat market in the world.

'Smithfield' derives from smooth field. The field became a venue for jousting tournaments, public executions and the burning of heretics. The annual Fair of St Bartholomew, which lasted up to fourteen days, was held in the field from 1133 to 1855.

Wat Tyler, with his rebels, confronted the boy king Richard II at Smithfield in 1381 and was stabbed by the Lord Mayor William Walworth. Before the buildings for the butchers were constructed, livestock were driven through the surrounding streets to the cattle market in what was then an open square.

•• *Continue ahead to St John St. Third L Passing Alley (a polite re-christening of Pissing Alley). R St John's Lane.*

Location 16

MUSEUM OF THE ORDER OF ST JOHN

St John's Gate
St John's Lane (253 6644)

Open Monday–Friday 10.00–17.00, Saturday 10.00–16.00. Admission free. Guided tours Tuesday, Friday and Saturday at 11.00 and 14.30. The one-hour tour includes the nearby St John's Church.

St John's Gate provided the entrance to the Priory of the Order of St John, founded in Jerusalem in the late 11C to care for the sick and pilgrims; in the 12C its knights took a military part in the crusades. Their priory was established here by 1110. The Order was suppressed at the Reformation but revived in the 19C.

The present Tudor gatehouse of 1504 replaced an earlier structure and after the priory was dissolved, accommodated respectively: Elizabeth I's Master of Revels, *The Gentleman's Magazine* (Dr Johnson worked here for its publishers), the parish Watch House and The Old Jerusalem tavern.

•• *To view the interior of the gatehouse enter the modern building R. Proceed to the museum.*

In the east tower of the gatehouse is the Old Chancery.

The Council Chamber is situated above the arch. The west tower accommodates the library and a room displaying a collection of paintings and furnishings.

•• *Exit with the guide and proceed northward through the arch.*

Location 17

PRIORY CHURCH OF ST JOHN

St John's Square

Open as for the gatehouse.

The nave of the original 12C church was circular, like those of the Knights Templar, but this was rebuilt in the 14C.

The church was remodelled and restored in 1956. Its crypt, partly Norman and partly Early English, is of greatest interest.

An outstanding 16C alabaster effigy of a Spanish knight lies at the east end of the crypt.

•• *Exit from the church right and continue northward to Clerkenwell Green. Seckforde Street, ahead, stretches north-eastward from the green, first left St James's Walk. Left Sans Walk. First right Clerkenwell Green.*

Location 18 | **HOUSE OF DETENTION**

Clerkenwell Green

Open daily 10.00–18.00. Admission charge.

A 'Bridewell' prison was first built on the site in 1616; this later became a debtor's prison, but was rebuilt as the Clerkenwell House of Detention in 1845 to accommodate more than 100,000 prisoners a year, most of them on remand. This substantial, multi-storey complex only survived 45 years, when all except its basement level was demolished and replaced by the present school buildings. During both world wars, part of the basement was reopened to provide air raid shelters.

Visitors are conducted via the wash room, kitchen and ventilation corridors to the cells, each of which has been allocated a 'prisoner'. By means of earphones, one hears a prisoner describe his or her 'crime' and the conditions in the house of detention. The cases are based on actual records which have survived. Talking was forbidden, and those who ignored this regulation were punisheds with solitary confinement and a diet of bread and water.

Exit left and return to St John's Lane, continuing to its end at Smithfield Market. Left Charterhouse Street. First Left Charterhouse Square (via the gate). The gateway left is the entrance to Sutton's Hospital in Charterhouse.

Location 19 | **SUTTON'S HOSPITAL IN CHARTERHOUSE**

Charterhouse Square

Open only for one-hour guided tours April to July Wednesday 14.15 (not following public holidays). Admission charge.

After seizing monastic estates at the Reformation, Henry VIII sold many of them for adaptation as private mansions. This is London's only remaining example.

Visitors assemble at the outer gatehouse to await the guide. The archway and oak doors are 15C but the house above was added in 1718. An arm of the last prior, John Houghton, executed by Henry VIII, was fixed to one of the doors as an incentive to the monks to accept the King as head of the church.

The Charterhouse was founded as a Carthusian priory by Sir Walter de Manny in 1371 and building work was supervised by *Yevele,* master mason of Edward III. Sir Edward North acquired the monastic buildings and adapted them to form his mansion in 1545. The Duke of Norfolk purchased the estate in 1565 and made several alterations, mostly internal. Thomas Sutton, reputedly the prototype of Jonson's *Volpone* (?), bought the Charterhouse in 1611 and adapted the buildings to provide the Hospital of King James. This served as a home for eighty male pensioners and a school for forty-five boys. Pensioners remain but the school was moved to Godalming in 1872. Extensive restoration, following the Second World War, revealed some features that later work had covered.

Much of the stonework in **Masters Court** is original.

The 16C **Great Hall** was built by *North* with materials from the monks' church that he had demolished. Its hammerbeam roof and screen survive.

The **library** was originally the monks refectory and then incorporated the Great Chamber above. The separating floor was added in the 16C.

The **Great Cloister** represents only a fraction of the 14C cloisters. A section of the monastic wall, including a hatch and entrance to a monk's cell can be seen.

Elizabeth I was entertained in the **Great Chamber** shortly before her death in 1603. Later that year James I created 133 knights in this room whilst staying at the Charterhouse early in his reign.

The **chapel** was converted from the 14C Chapter House by *Sutton* early in the 17C when the north aisle was added and the screen and pulpit made.

Sutton's monument was carved by *Stone* and *Jansen* in 1615.

The **tower** once housed the monks' treasury. Its first two storeys are 14C but the top storey, with cupola above, was added in the 17C. Original 14C floor tiles remain on the first floor. From the 'squint' the monks could view the high altar in the church. Below this, the grave of Manny, the founder of the Charterhouse, was discovered in 1947.

Buildings in **Wash House Court** originally served as outbuildings to the priory. Much of the brickwork is 15C and the stonework 14C.

The other Tudor style buildings at the Charterhouse are the 19C work of *Blore*.

Exit from the Charterhouse R. Proceed through the gate to Charterhouse St. Continue ahead to the Farringdon Rd junction. Holborn Viaduct runs above L.

Location 20

HOLBORN VIADUCT *Heywood 1869*

Holborn Viaduct was built to avoid the steep valley of the Fleet River, here known as the Holbourne (stream in the hollow), which had to be crossed to reach the City from the west. Its painted and gilded motifs make this one of the most decorative of London's bridges.

Proceed ahead. Second R Ely Place.

Location 21

ELY PLACE *Cole 1773*

Ely Place, a private thoroughfare of 18C houses, occupies much of the site of Ely House the late 13C London residence of the Bishops of Ely. John of Gaunt moved to Ely House when his Savoy Palace was destroyed by Wat Tyler's rebels in 1381 and died there in 1399. Christopher Hatton, a favourite of Elizabeth I, acquired much of the estate in the 16C when the house and its famous gardens were divided, by order of the Queen, between him and the Bishop.

Two of Shakespeare's plays refer to Ely House. John of Gaunt makes his famous 'This sceptred isle' speech here in *Richard II* and in *Richard III* the Duke of Gloucester requests strawberries from the gardens. The house became the Spanish Embassy in the 17C but was demolished in 1772. All that remains is St Etheldreda Church, built as the bishops' chapel.

Proceed along the west side of Ely Place to the church.

Location 22

ST ETHELDREDA* *c.1300*

Ely Place

The church is a rare London example of the Decorated style and its window tracery is exceptional. St Etheldreda's, dedicated to the Saxon Queen who founded Ely Abbey, is Britain's oldest existing Catholic church, reverting to the faith in 1879. Roman masonry has been found in the fabric and traditionally a 3C church stood nearby.

The east gable is dominated by the intricate, early Decorated window tracery. Originally, there were pinnacles on either side.

Enter the church through the porch of the adjoining house L. (Ring the bell if the door is closed.)

The corridor was once an open cloister. Here, by tradition, Henry VIII was introduced to Thomas Cranmer whom he later appointed Archbishop of Canterbury.

At the end of the corridor descend the steps R to the **undercroft.**

The windows have been renewed but at the east end L are blocked 13C examples. All the piers were renewed in the 19C.

Ascend the steps and turn R. Ascend further steps to the upper church.

On the wall L is the Stuart coat of arms.

Enter through the door R to the upper church.

The church was much restored by *George Gilbert Scott* in 1874 and again, following the Second World War. Its early Decorated window tracery has been judged some of the finest in existence. The stained glass is modern.

Exit from the church R. First R Ely Court (unnamed at this end).

Location 23 — **YE OLD MITRE** *late 18C*

Ely Court

The date, 1546, displayed outside, refers to the establishment of the inn by Bishop Goodrich for his servants. Ye Old Mitre's secluded position is its main attraction.

Exit R. First L Hatton Garden. Cross Holborn Viaduct to St Andrew's.

Location 24 — **ST ANDREW HOLBORN** *Wren 1690*

Holborn Viaduct

St Andrew's is the largest of Wren's parish churches.

A Saxon church on the site is recorded *c.*900. The later building of 1485 was mostly destroyed in the Great Fire but the lower section of its tower was retained and refaced.

The statues of schoolchildren at the base of the tower came from the parish school nearby.

Enter from the north porch. Turn R and L to the **chancel.**

The 18C pulpit, organ and font were brought here from the Foundling Hospital at Berkhampstead. T organ had been a gift from the composer Handel the original hospital.

The reredos *c.*1730 came from St Luke Old S

Return to the west end of the nave, pass

In a niche R, is the tomb of Thomas Cora the Foundling Hospital.

Continue ahead.

Some 15C vaulting remains within th

Exit from the church L and proceed to Holborn. Fourth L a tiled passage, opposite the Prudential Assurance building, leads to Barnards Inn. Proceed ahead through the archway dated 1770. Turn R.

Location 25

BARNARDS INN HALL *late 14C*

Barnards Inn Hall

Now occupied by Gresham College, the hall is no longer open to visitors.

Barnards Inn Hall retains its original roof lantern, a unique 14C survivor. This hall was built as part of the London mansion of John Markworth, Dean of Lincoln. The entire property was then briefly occupied by Lionel Barnard until he leased it to legal students of Grays Inn nearby and the complex became an Inn of Chancery. The Mercers Company acquired Barnards Inn in 1907 and soon replaced most of the ancient buildings with a new school. Fortunately, the hall itself was retained, but in 1933 this had to be dismantled due to major timber decay. It was reconstructed as a replica, using much of the original material.

Return to Holborn L. Cross the road.

Location 26

PRUDENTIAL ASSURANCE *Waterhouse late 19C*

Holborn

These offices, in High Victorian Gothic style, were begun at their west end in 1879 but this section was rebuilt in 1932. The remainder was constructed 1899–1906. The main entrance hall is decorated with glazed tiling.

Exit R. Proceed ahead to the Holborn and Grays Inn Rd junction. From here the best view is obtained of Staple Inn opposite. Cross Holborn.

Location 27

STAPLE INN

Holborn

This is London's only surviving half-timbered terrace. Its much restored Elizabethan facade dates from 1589 but the interiors have been completely rebuilt. A hostel and market place were established here in the 14C for traders in wool, known as staplers, and this is how the Inn acquired its name. Staple Inn remained an Inn of Chancery until the 19C but the buildings now accommodate offices and shops.

Proceed through the arch to the courtyard.

This courtyard was completely rebuilt after the Second World War, including the mid 16C hall of the inn. The hall does, however, retain some of its original materials, including the glass in the windows that had been stored for safety.

Exit L and cross High Holborn.

Location 28

THE CITTIE OF YORKE *1890*

High Holborn

This pub, on the site of a 15C tavern, belonged, until recently, to Henekeys.

Pass through the front bar to the Long Bar at the rear.

In the famous Long Bar are great vats, a high trussed roof and intimate mahogany-partitioned seating areas. The restored coal stove of 1815 came from the hall of Gray's Inn nearby.

Exit L to High Holborn and Chancery Lane Station, Central line.

3

Tower of London

The fabulous Crown Jewels are displayed in the Tower of London, which, together with Tower Bridge, provides one of the capital's best known vistas. St Katharine's Dock nearby has recently been remodelled to provide a boat marina. The last of the Royal Navy's 'big ships', HMS *Belfast*, is moored opposite the Tower.

Timing: Monday to Saturday with an early morning start is recommended. There are many new attractions in the area including entry to the high Tower Bridge walkway, and a visit to every location will require a whole day.

The Tower of London is also open Sunday mornings (not August) for services in the Chapel of St Peter-ad-Vincula and every evening, by appointment, for the Ceremony of the Keys. No refreshments are available within the Tower but exit passes are given and there are snack bar facilities on Tower Wharf.

3

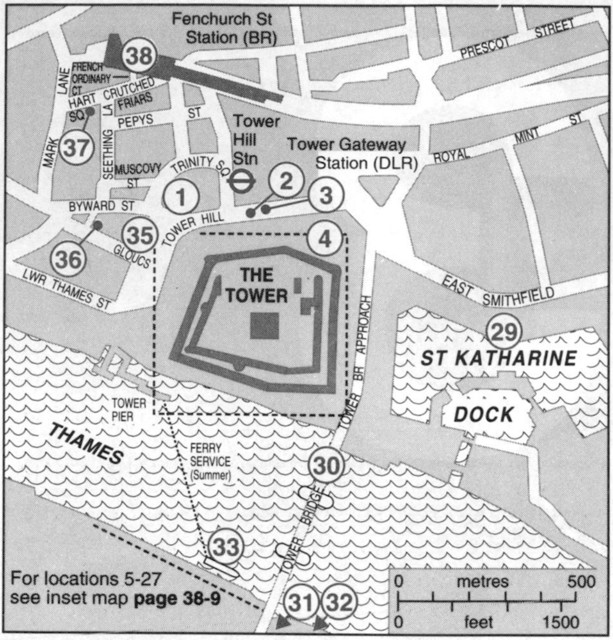

Locations

1 Tower Hill Scaffold Memorial
2 London Wall
3 Postern Gate
4 Tower of London
5 Middle Tower
6 Moat
7 Byward Tower
8 Bell Tower
9 St Thomas's Tower, 'Traitors Gate'
10 Wakefield Tower
11 Bloody Tower
12 Wardrobe Tower
13 White Tower
14 Jewel House
15 Martin Tower
16 Fusiliers Regiment Museum
17 Bowyer Tower
18 Devereux Tower
19 Chapel of St Peter-ad-Vincula
20 Tower Green
21 Beauchamp Tower
22 Queens House
23 Old Palace Wall
24 Ravens' Cages
25 Roman Riverside Wall
26 History Gallery
27 New Armoury
28 Tower Wharf
29 St Katharine Dock
30 Tower Bridge
31 Design Museum
32 Tea and Coffee Museum
33 HMS *Belfast*
34 Tower Hill Terrace
35 Tower Hill Pageant
36 All Hallows-by-the-Tower
37 St Olave
38 French Ordinary Court

Start *Tower Hill Station, Circle and District lines. Exit from the station L. First R follow the path through Trinity Square Gardens. Turn R and proceed to the south-west end of the gardens.*

Alternatively, take the boat from Westminster Pier (Westminster Station) or Charing Cross Pier (Embankment Station). Both stations are on the Circle and District lines. Proceed directly to the Tower (location 4) and view locations 1–3 later.

Location 1 **TOWER HILL SCAFFOLD MEMORIAL**

The chained area marks the site of the Tower Hill scaffold where 125 eminent people are known to have been officially executed between 1347 and 1747. Victims included Sir Thomas More, Thomas Cromwell, Archbishop Laud and the Duke of

Monmouth. The eighty-year-old Simon, Lord Lovat was the last person to be axed in England. At his execution, in 1747 some of the specially erected seating collapsed killing twelve spectators.

Return through the garden, and continue ahead passing the south side of the station. Proceed along the terrace and descend the steps R towards a remnant of the London wall L.

Location 2

LONDON WALL

The sunken garden, in which the wall stands, marks the ground level in Roman times. Roman work is approximately 10 feet high whilst the 15 foot section above is medieval.

In front of the wall is a 19C composite bronze statue purporting to represent the Roman Emperor Trajan. The body of one of the originals belonged to Augustus and the head of the other to Trajan; neither came from Roman London.

On the modern wall L is a replica of an inscription from the tomb of Gaius Classicianus the humane Roman Procurator of London who died *c.* AD65.

Descend the steps to the subway.

Location 3

POSTERN GATE *late 13C (?)*

These remnants of a medieval postern (rear) gate in the London wall are passed L.

Continue along the path R to the ticket office and the adjoining book kiosk.

Location 4

TOWER OF LONDON

Open March–October, Monday–Saturday 09.00–18.00, Sunday 10.00–18.00. November–February, Monday–Saturday 09.00–17.00. Sunday 10.00–17.00. Admission charge.

Changing of the Guard on Tower Green 11.30 daily in summer, on alternate days in winter.

Ceremony of the Keys, by appointment only, every evening at 22.00. Admission free.

Guided tours are given free by Yeomen Warders.

Last tours 15.00 (14.30 winter).

The Tower of London, begun more than nine hundred years ago, is the most important castle in England and its keep is the oldest, continuously occupied, fortified building in Europe. Restoration and remodelling have continued throughout the centuries and much of what is seen, particularly externally, is relatively modern work. There are a total of twenty towers within the 18-acre complex.

Following the Norman Conquest in 1066, William I 'The Conqueror' built a wooden fort overlooking the river and just within the eastern section of London's Roman wall. This was soon replaced by a large stone keep intended to overawe rebellious Londoners and deter upstream attackers. Work began *c.* 1078 but William died before its completion. The White Tower, as it is now called, stood in splendid isolation as a palace fortress for one hundred years and this is why the entire complex that evolved is still known as the Tower of London, rather than the Castle of London, which it effectively is.

To strengthen the defences, a wall with bastion towers was begun by Richard I 'Coeur de Lion' in the late 12C, continued by Henry III in the early 13C and completed by Edward I in the late 13C.

The outer wall, also with bastion towers but surrounded by a moat, was almost entirely built during the reign of Edward I 1272–1307.

In addition to serving as a fortified royal palace until the 17C the Tower has in its time accommodated a mint, observatory, arsenal, menagerie and public records. It has also served as a state prison, but there are not known to have been any dungeons within the Tower, most prisoners being kept in upper rooms.

In spite of its apparent strength, at least forty prisoners have made successful escapes.

The Royal Armoury (part) and Crown Jewels remain guarded and displayed within its precincts.

Much of the exterior has recently been cleaned and selected rooms decorated. The Tower now, therefore, more closely matches its earlier appearance, when the stonework gleamed and most rooms were comfortably furnished and decorated.

Locations 5–29 are within the Tower of London.

Proceed towards the iron gates where the Bulwark Tower originally stood.

The gentlemen in picturesque Tudor uniforms are **Yeomen Warders**: Yeomen have guarded the Tower since it was built and became the King's Bodyguard of the Yeomen of the Guard Extraordinary in 1485. There are forty-one of them and their task is to guard the Tower and guide its visitors. Their unofficial nickname 'Beefeaters' probably refers to their former meat allocation from the Crown.

Pass through the gates and proceed ahead.

Beneath the path, immediately after entering the main gates, can be seen part of the pit for the outer drawbridge and remains of the original causeway.

The path and road to the main entrance both cross the site of an outer moat which was filled in the 19C.

Proceed to the Middle Tower.

Location 5

MIDDLE TOWER *1280 (partly rebuilt 1717)*

This is now the main entrance to the Tower. It originally possessed a drawbridge. Carved above the arch are the arms of George I 1717. The Lion Tower, since demolished, once faced it to the west and was almost entirely surrounded by water. It housed the royal menagerie from the 13C. The animals were transferred to the new Regent's Park Zoo in 1834.

Assemble by the clock L for guided tours by a warder.

Alternatively, cross the moat.

Location 6

MOAT *late 13C/early 14C*

This was drained by the Duke of Wellington, whilst Constable of the Tower, in 1834 due to outbreaks of typhoid caused by its insanitary condition. It was briefly filled by the freak Thames tidal wave of 1928.

Proceed to the Byward Tower.

Location 7

BYWARD TOWER *1280*

Open for research by appointment only.

This tower was named Byward as it stood by-the-ward i.e. the outer area or ward of the Tower. Once three drawbridges had to be passed before the Tower could be entered at this point.

On the first floor is the original portcullis with its winch, and 14C wall paintings, discovered in 1953.

Pass through the arch.

The timber-framed superstructures seen from this side were added in the 14C and 16C.

Continue ahead.

Location 8

BELL TOWER *1200*

The Bell Tower is the first of the inner range of towers to be passed. Its upper storey can only be reached from the staircase in Queens House with which it is linked. London's oldest curfew bell is rung twice daily from its turret. Both the Duke of Monmouth and Sir Thomas More were held within.

By tradition, Princess Elizabeth, the future Elizabeth I, stayed for two months in its upper storey (?) whilst imprisoned in the Tower by her half-sister Mary I in 1554. She is also believed to have exercised between here and the Beauchamp Tower on the battlements above (?), known as Elizabeth's Walk.

Against the outer wall of the tower are the Casemates where many of the warders live. Most of the houses were built in the 19C.

Proceed ahead to 'Traitors Gate' R.

Location 9

ST THOMAS'S TOWER, 'TRAITORS GATE' *1276 (partly rebuilt 19C)*

The white stone steps which originally led down to the river have been replaced, but traces remain on both sides of the present flight.

This tower gained its name from an oratory chapel, dedicated to St Thomas à Becket which was situated in a turret that still faces the river. For one year, prior to his appointment as Archbishop of Canterbury in 1162, à Becket had been Constable of the Tower.

Sir Roger Casement was briefly imprisoned here during the First World War.

Traitors Gate became the main river entrance to the Tower after the Thames had been pushed back and the outer walls built. Its name commemorates the many 'traitors' who passed through it, usually to face imprisonment and execution. There is no longer a portcullis.

The timber-framed wall of the upper storey is a remodelling of 1532.

Enter the tower by the stairs R.

Rooms in this tower and the upper floor of the Wakefield Tower, with which it is linked, have been restored and decorated to give the impression of a Medieval Palace during the reign of Edward I (1272–1307), who was responsible for building St Thomas's Tower.

The first room seen, the Magna Camera, has been only partly restored, so that visitors can see the traces of Edward's fireplace and garderobe which have survived. Both the ceiling and the brick/timber wall date from Henry VIII's reign. A small exhibition in the adjoining room explains the conversion work.

The first completely recreated room, the Aula, may have served as Edward's dining hall. In the turret, facing the river, is the oratory chapel dedicated to St Thomas à Becket, after whom the tower is named; i was here that Edward frequently heard Mass.

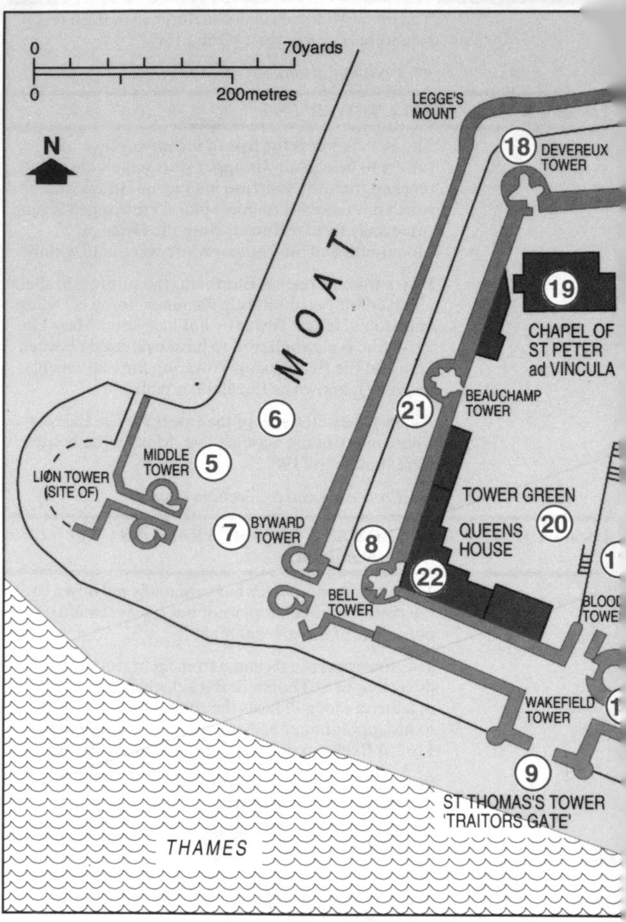

Visitors enter the upper floor of the Wakefield Tower via the 19C link building by *Salvin*. Built in 1235, this tower was an important part of the palace of Henry III.

The Throne Room was originally Henry's Royal Presence Chamber, and it is probable that Edward also received members of the court and important visitors here, seated on a throne. The design of the present throne, which is modern, is based on the Coronation Chair in Westminster Abbey, made for Edward in 1300. There is no evidence that the room was ever lit by a Corona chandelier; the present example is a modern copy of a contemporary piece in Hildesheim Cathedral, Germany.

Behind the 13C style screen is the oratory in which it has been alleged that Henry VI was assassinated while at prayer in 1471. However, state documents were stored in this tower from 1360 until 1869, and during this period it was known as the Records Tower, hardly a suitable venue for worship, even by a deposed king. The Crown Jewels were kept in this chamber from 1869 until they were moved to the basement of the former Waterloo Barracks in 1967. The exterior and

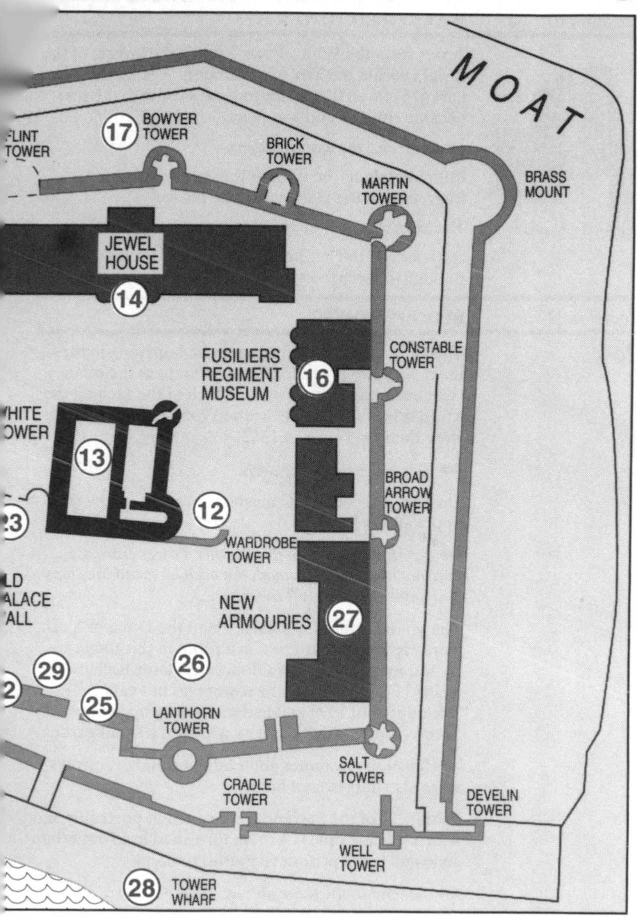

lower floor of the Wakefield Tower are described later.

A wall walk leads through the Lanthorn Tower before steps descend to ground level. The walk continues further, via the Salt Tower, but reopening of this stretch is uncertain at the time of writing.

Set against the outer wall are artists impressions of how the Tower looked during its major stages of development.

Genuine 13C articles are exhibited in the Lanthorn Tower's display, *Life in The Palace of Edward*. This tower, together with the stretch of wall that follows it, was destroyed by fire in 1788 and rebuilt, slightly further north, in 1883.

Descend and return westward towards Traitors Gate Opposite, just before this is reached, stands the Wakefield Tower, the upper rooms of which have already been seen (the linking stairway between t[illegible] is no longer open).

Location 10

WAKEFIELD TOWER 1225

Apart from the White Tower, this is the largest of the towers within the Tower of London. It is the only part of Henry III's palace to have survived; the rest became ruinous and was demolished in the 17C.

•● *Descend the wooden steps.*

Immediately to the right of the entrance are fragments of the staircase to the palace.

The huge chamber entered served as the Guard Room.

Steps ascend to The Bloody Tower, left. Proceed through the arch to its south side (facing Traitors Gate).

Location 11

BLOODY TOWER

Open.

This originated in 1225 as an arched opening in the inner wall and preceded Traitors Gate as the main river entrance to the Tower. Much of the arch on the south side is 13C but its vaulted roof and floor above were built by *Yevele* in 1362.

•● *Return through the arch.*

On the north side, 14C masonry remains below the upper storey level.

•● *Continue ahead to the Bloody Tower entrance, approached first L beneath the arch. Ascend the steps and enter the Bloody Tower.*

The young princes, Edward V and the Duke of York, were reputedly murdered in a room in this tower by their uncle the Duke of Gloucester, later Richard III, in 1483 (?). However, the tower was not called 'Bloody' until 1579 and had previously been known as the Garden Tower as it overlooked a small garden.

Archbishops Cranmer and Laud and Judge Jeffreys were also imprisoned here.

Within, R of the entrance, is an ancient portcullis and winch. Facing this, is a room furnished in Elizabethan style and some prisoners' graffiti remains.

•● *Ascend to the floor above. Turn R.*

The bedroom furniture is from Raleigh's period. Raleigh wrote *History of the World* in the Bloody Tower during his thirteen years' imprisonment. Released in 1616, he was again briefly imprisoned by James I elsewhere in the Tower before his execution outside Westminster Palace in 1618.

In the next room a display illustrates the colonization of Virginia.

•● *Exit from the tower and proceed north-eastward to the remnants of the Wardrobe Tower, at the south-east corner of the White Tower.*

Location 12

WARDROBE TOWER

Fragments of the Roman wall and one of its bastions survive behind the remnant of this late 12C tower which housed the monarch's more valuable possessions. The Crown Jewels were first kept here when they were transferred to the Tower from Westminster Abbey in 1303. They were removed to the Jewel Tower (demolished) which was built nearby in the 14C.

•● *Follow the path ahead to the White Tower.*

Location 13 **WHITE TOWER** *1097*

Open.

This was the first stone structure to be built at the Tower of London and formed the nucleus of the complex. The White Tower remains the largest and most important building within the castle. It housed the royal apartments until Henry III built a new palace, to its south, in the 13C.

William the Conqueror commenced the work in 1078 as a replacement for the earlier wooden keep and his son William II 'Rufus', completed it in 1097. The builder was *Gundulf*, a Norman monk who later became Bishop of Rochester. The tower is called 'White' not from the colour of the stone but because both the exterior and many of the internal chambers were white-washed for Henry III in 1240.

The White Tower, originally surrounded by its own moat, is known as a hall keep, a type only built in England and confined to the early Norman period.

The walls, 15 feet thick in places, are of Kentish ragstone and Caen stone brought from Normandy.

Three of the corner turrets are square but the north-east example is circular and houses the tower's spiral staircase. From its top floor Flamsteed briefly operated the Royal Observatory in the 17C.

The four onion-shaped (ogee) cupolas, surmounting the turrets, were originally conical and probably remained so until the 16C (?).

The curved apse of the chapel's four levels protrudes from the south-east corner turret of the tower.

All the walls were refaced and most of the windows in the White Tower were altered and enlarged by *Wren* in the early 18C but four of the original small examples remain on the south side at the upper level.

Ascend the wooden steps to the entrance.

The present entrance was once reached by stone steps and when these were removed in the 17C a box containing children's bones was discovered. They were almost certainly the remains of the 'Princes in the Tower' who had disappeared in 1483. The bones were transferred to the Henry VII Chapel in Westminster Abbey.

Enter at first floor level (described as ground floor).

Each of the four floors of the White Tower is divided into three chambers by stone walls. Situated in the south-east corner are the four levels of St John's Chapel. The original function of many of the other chambers is uncertain. Displayed within them is the national collection of arms and armaments begun by Henry VIII and displayed by Charles II as England's first public museum.

Proceed clockwise, passing the **Sporting Galler**

Weapons and armour used for jousting are exhib in the **Tournament Gallery.**

Continue to the crypt of St John's Chapel.

The crypt now accommodates a shop.

•• *Leave the crypt. Turn first L beneath the arch. Turn L and ascend the stairs ahead to the first floor. Entered immediately is the* **Chapel of St John.**

This Chapel Royal is London's most impressive example of early Norman architecture. It is massive, severe and has been little altered since the 11C. This was, at one time, the chapel of the Knights of the Bath, an appointment founded by Henry IV at his coronation in 1399 when he created forty-six knights. On his initiation, it is believed that each knight bathed in forty-six separate baths in the chamber next to the chapel and the king symbolically made the sign of the cross on his back.

After spending the night here at prayer, the new monarch would proceed from the Tower to Westminster Abbey for the coronation ceremony, a custom that was initiated by Henry III in 1216 and last followed by Charles II in 1661.

It was in this chapel that Archbishop Sudbury was seized by Wat Tyler's rebels and summarily executed on Tower Hill in 1381. Here also, Mary I married Philip II of Spain by proxy in 1554.

The nave possesses a rare English example of tunnel-vaulting. Its aisles form an ambulatory around the chapel and a gallery runs above. White Caen stone was used exclusively for the interior.

•• *Exit and proceed ahead.*

The next two rooms on this, the most important floor, originally incorporated the floor above. They were probably divided in the 17C. The first room entered, now the **Medieval Gallery,** is believed to have been the Great Chamber (?). Between this and the next chamber are two original garderobes (toilets). Surprisingly, many rooms in the Tower had private toilets.

The **16C Gallery** was originally the Banqueting Hall.

•• *Ascend the stairs to the second floor.*

Facing the entrance to the **Tudor Gallery** is Henry VIII's massive suit of armour, made in 1535 when he had become corpulent. The king's armour was kept at Greenwich.

At the far end of the chamber is a painting of Charles I as a youth. He was rarely portrayed clean-shaven.

Before the floor was added, the gallery beneath the windows was used to observe the chamber below. From here it was possible to fire arrows through the windows at an aggressor. The four small windows on the south side, R of the Charles I painting, are the only surviving Norman examples.

•• *Proceed to the* **17C Gallery.**
Suits of armour from the Stuart period are displayed.

•• *Descend the stairs directly to the basement.*

Much of this floor housed prisoners in the 16C and 17C. However, the tradition that Guy Fawkes was racked here is unproven.

Displayed in the **Mortar Room** are 16C and 18C exhibits. A terrorist bomb exploded here in 1974 killing one person and injuring thirty-five. A plaque on the floor marks the spot. It is believed that at one period the passage between this and the adjacent

Lion Room had a door on both sides and formed a small prison cell (?). The remaining door is allegedly 11C and the oldest in the Tower.

The **Lion Room** is a sub-crypt of St John's Chapel. Its gilded Venetian lion was brought from Corfu in 1809.

An open well in the **Second Cannon Room** indicates that it may once have been used as a kitchen.

•• *Exit from the White Tower and cross the path to the central entrance to the Jewel House ahead.*

Location 14

JEWEL HOUSE
(Former Waterloo Barracks) *Salvin 1845*

Open as for the Tower throughout the year at no additional charge. Photography is not permitted within the building.

A completely new display of the Crown Jewels, transferred from part of the basement to the entire ground floot of the same building, was opened in 1994. The west wing, seen first, provides an introduction to the display, while the east wing accommodates the jewels. Long queues, formerly a problem, have virtually been eliminated.

The exhibition in the west wing explains the significance of each item of the regalia used in the coronation ceremony. A **Line of Kings** is formed by oak stalls representing every sovereign from William the Conqueror to Elizabeth II; their Gothic design was inspired by the stalls in St George's Chapel, Windsor.

In the next chamber the **Coronation Cinema** exhibits, on a tryptych of screens, colour film of the coronation ceremony at Westminster Abbey of Elizabeth II in 1953.

The **Crown Jewels Cinema** utilises modern techniques including, for the first time in a British Museum, high definition television. It is divided into two viewing areas, each with two screens; the first illustrates close-ups of individual jewels, the second shows entire pieces.

Occupying the east wing, the **Treasury** exhibits the Crown Jewels in the same order as they are utilized in coronation ceremonies. Royal maces and swords in the **Processional Way** corridor form an introduction to the jewels themselves.

Separate cases display swords of state, the Ampulla and Spoon, and the Imperial Mantle, Supertunica and Stole. The **Ampulla** and **Spoon** are the only pieces of the regalia that, in essence, predate Charles II's coronation of 1661. Charles I pawned most of the jewels and Cromwell, on the assumption that there would never be another coronation, disposed of the remainder. Some precious stones, however, were recovered and have been incorporated in the present regalia.

The Spoon is believed to be 12C work and part of the Ampulla, which was remodelled in 1661, almost certainly predates the 14C.

Parallel, slowly moving walkways flank the display o the most valuable jewels. All crowns face the entrance hall, not the viewer.

For some reason, Cromwell did not dispose of **St Edward's Crown**, which is worn only during the coronation ceremony. However, it was remod and enlarged for Charles II.

The Sovereign's **Sceptre** and **Orb** follow. Also ma for Charles II, the Sceptre was embellished for Edward VII in 1908 by the incorporation of the largest cut diamond in the world, the Star of Africa, formerly part of the Cullinan Diamond.

Queen Elizabeth the Queen Mother's Crown (among the regalia of the Queen's Consort) was made for the coronation of 1937. It incorporates the Koh-i-Noor Diamond, formerly in the gem collection of India's Great Mogul rulers.

Crowns of the Prince of Wales precede the **Imperial State Crown**, which is surmounted by the sapphire formerly set in the coronation ring of Edward the Confessor. Below it, set in descending order on the face of the crown, are the Black Prince's ruby and the second Star of Africa, which was also cut from the Cullinan Diamond. Allegedly, the two pendant pearls were once Elizabeth I's earrings; the Stuart Sapphire is set in the back. Made for the coronation of Queen Victoria in 1838, this crown is worn by sovereigns on major state occasions, including the opening of parliament. Neither the Imperial State Crown nor the Crown of St Edward may leave the country.

Ending the display are **Altar and Banqueting Plate**, **Royal Christening Fonts** and the **Delha Coronation Durbar Crown** of 1911 made for George V to wear.

The original **armlet** setting for the Koh-i-Noor Diamond is inset with a reproduction of the gem as it was before being recut, and thereby reduced in size, for Queen Victoria.

Leave the Jewel House from the north-east exit of the building, which faces the Brick Tower. Immediately right of this is the Martin Tower.

Location 15

MARTIN TOWER

When the entire Wall Walk is reopened, visitors may descend once more at this tower, which now accommodates the Jewel House Shop.

The Crown Jewels of Charles II were kept on the ground floor of the Martin Tower until they were removed to the Wakefield Tower in 1869 and it was from here that Colonel Blood stole them in 1671. He was caught, but surprisingly pardoned by Charles II. There was suspicion of collusion between them, as the King needed money and could hardly sell the jewels himself.

Partial reconstruction of the interior to its 17C appearance had been effected. External detailing from the Stuart period includes the tower's brickwork, which other towers lost through 19C remodelling.

Behind the Martin Tower, on the north-east corner of the outer wall stands **Brass Mount**, one of two bastions built for Henry VIII to provide a solid base for cannon. **Legge's Mount**, on the north-west corner, also survives.

Exit left to the Fusiliers Regiment Museum ahead.

ocation 16

FUSILIERS REGIMENT MUSEUM

en. Additional ission charge.

This mid 19C building originally provided officers' quarters. It now displays regimental mementoes, including a prototype of the Victoria Cross.

Exit R. Return to and pass Martin Tower. Continue ahead, passing Brick Tower.

Location 17 **BOWYER TOWER** *13C*

Open.

The tower was probably named Bowyer because bows were made there (?). The Duke of Clarence is believed to have been drowned here in a butt of Malmsey wine (?) in 1478, as described by Shakespeare in *Richard III.* Displayed within are torture instruments, a gibbet, Lord Lovat's block, and an executioner's axe.

Exit R and pass the rebuilt **Flint Tower.**

Location 18 **DEVEREUX TOWER** *13C.*

Elizabeth I's erstwhile favourite, Robert Devereux, Earl of Essex was imprisoned here prior to his execution. The tower is named to commemorate him.

The Armouries and Mint once stood behind this tower against the outer wall.

Proceed ahead to the Chapel of St Peter ad Vincula.

Location 19 **CHAPEL OF ST PETER-AD-VINCULA** *W. Vertue (?) 1512*

Open to visitors until 16.00 but a party conducted by a Yeoman Warder must be joined.

Also open to the public for Sunday services 09.15 and 11.00 (except August).

This is the third chapel to be built on the site. Before the extension of the Tower in the late 12C it stood outside the complex and served as the parish church. The first church was probably built early in the 12C by Henry I (?). It was rebuilt in the late 13C by Edward I and the north wall of this building survives. St Peter's was then much larger. *Ad vincula* is Latin for 'in chains'. Its name derives from the church of San Pietro in Vincoli, Rome, where St Peter's chains are displayed on 1 April, the day that this chapel was consecrated. St Peter's became a Chapel Royal in 1966.

Enter from the north porch (with guide).

The tie-beam roof is original.

The 15C canopied tomb of John Holland, L of the entrance, originally stood in the chapel of St Katharine's Hospital nearby which was demolished in 1827.

Important prisoners executed on both Tower Green and Tower Hill were buried in unmarked graves beneath the altar. The sanctuary floor tiles which illustrate some of the victims' crests were laid in 1876.

Exit and proceed to the paved centre of Tower Green.

Location 20 **TOWER GREEN**

A granite-paved square marks the site of the execution block. Only six people are known to have been executed here, with the advantage of semi-privacy. They were the cousins Anne Boleyn and Katherine Howard (second and fifth wives of Henry VIII), Jane Grey (queen for nine days), the Earl of Essex, the Countess of Salisbury and the Countess of Rochford. Lord Hastings was executed nearby.

The ceremonial appointment of the new Constable o[f] the Tower is held on the green every five years. The Constable represents the sovereign but does not reside within the complex. His deputy, originally t[he] Lieutenant, took over the effective management [in] 1189 but the Tower is now the responsibility of th[e] resident Governor.

Proceed to the west side of the green.

Location 21 **BEAUCHAMP TOWER** *1200*

Open.

When built, this was the only landward entrance to the Tower. It is named after a 14C prisoner. Thomas Beauchamp, Earl of Warwick. The large window was added in the 19C.

Enter and ascend the steps.

Important prisoners were housed within, and the Tower's best examples of graffiti are seen. Some of it, however, was brought from other towers. The Dudley Coat of Arms incorporating a bear and a lion, is believed to have been cut by Jane Grey's imprisoned husband Guildford Dudley. Two small inscriptions 'Jane' were also probably cut by him *c.*1554.

Exit and look to the south-west corner of the green.

Location 22 **QUEENS HOUSE** *1540*

Queen's House is the finest example of a Tudor domestic building in London. It was originally the Lieutenants Lodgings but is now the Governor's residence and, since 1880, has been known as either Queens House or Kings House, depending on the reigning monarch. The house replaced an earlier building in which it is believed Anne Boleyn was lodged immediately preceding her execution in 1536.

All state prisoners were taken, on arrival, to Queens House where they were registered and searched.

The double windows on the top floor of the south range look out from the Council Chamber where Guy Fawkes was first interrogated. Hitler's deputy, Hess, was imprisoned here for four days in 1941.

Queens House was also the scene of the Tower's most famous escape; by Lord Nithsdale in 1716. His wife and her lady friends smuggled him out with the aid of a spare cloak and the couple eventually reached the Continent and freedom.

The Tower of London is locked up every night during the Ceremony of the Keys and the keys are then taken to Queens House. The ceremony is open to the public by appointment only.

The adjacent brick range, on the north side, was built in the early 17C and now forms part of the Governor's private accommodation.

Proceed towards the White Tower. Descend the steps R. Continue southward towards the Bloody Tower. Immediately L is the old palace wall.

Location 23 **OLD PALACE WALL** *13C*

This stone fragment formed part of the bailey wall that enclosed Henry III's royal palace. The wall was linked with the White Tower by the Coldharbour Tower, which no longer exists.

Pass through the Bloody Tower gateway. Turn L past the Wakefield Tower. Proceed L through the arch. Turn L. The ravens' cages are against the inner wall.

Location 24 **RAVENS' CAGES**

The large, black birds that hop around within the inner ward of the Tower of London are ravens, a type of crow. They were once common, together with kites, as scavengers in London's medieval streets but, with better sanitation, their services were no longer needed and in the 18C they were destroyed – except for those in the Tower. Traditionally, if the ravens leave the Tower it will fall. Although six is the minimum requirement, eight are kept for safety. The present ravens were adopted as fledglings and their wings are clipped. They may live for forty years; in 1990, for the first time, ravens bred within the Tower.

The birds are returned here nightly but may occasionally be seen resting within.

Return and proceed ahead passing the arch.

Location 25 **ROMAN RIVERSIDE WALL**

This forms a section of the 4C Roman wall. No other part of London's riverside defence remains visible and probably only the Tower's stretch was renewed in medieval times.

Cross to the display opposite.

Location 26 **HISTORY GALLERY**

An informative display describes the Tower's history.

Immediately to the east is the New Armouries

Location 27 **NEW ARMOURIES** *1664*

Open.

Formerly known as the Horse Armoury. The doorway was renewed in 1950. Small arms provided by the Board of Ordnance from *c.*1600 to 1855 are displayed. The 17C Great Storehouse, which occupied the site of the Wellington Barracks, burnt down in 1841. Its huge pediment, reputedly carved by *Gibbons* (?), was saved and is exhibited in this gallery.

Exit and proceed westward. Pass through the archway in the walk and exit from the Tower L.

Location 28 **TOWER WHARF**

Open Monday–Saturday 07.00–18.30 or later. Sunday 10.00–18.30 or later. Admission free

Historic cannons facing the river are supplemented, on state occasions, by four modern guns and a royal salute is fired.

Continue beneath the Tower Bridge approach road and pass the Tower Hotel by the riverside walkway. Cross the drawbridge ahead.

Location 29 **ST KATHARINE DOCK**

This man-made 'pool' was originally excavated as part of London's dockyard system by *Telford* 1827. The demise of London as a port led to the dock's recent conversion to a boat marina surrounded by warehouses which have been adapted to other uses. There are two hundred moorings. Occupants include the London Trade Centre, shops, restaurants and the Dickens Inn created from a 19C warehouse.

Return past the Tower Hotel. Ascend the steps of the arch ahead to Tower Bridge. Proceed to the main north tower.

Location 30	**TOWER BRIDGE** *Wolfe Barry* and *H. Jones 1894*

(403 3761)
The towers and high level walkway are open daily, April–October 10.00–18.30, November–March 10.00–16.45. Admission charge.

Many visitors confuse this with London Bridge which is the next bridge upstream. Although the bridge is constructed of iron, its four towers were stone clad to harmonize with the adjacent Tower of London.

Both sections of this suspension bridge weigh over 1,000 tons each but can be fully raised in under two minutes. On the busiest recorded day they were raised and lowered sixty-four times but the average is now just five times a week. In 1952 a bus passed the stop signal but successfully 'leapt' the widening gap.

The two main towers and high level walkways, recently enclosed, were opened to the public in 1982 after being shut since 1909 due to lack of use. In addition to the unique views there are five displays.

•● *Enter the main north tower from its west side and take the to lift the second floor.*

An exhibition illustrates the design of the bridge and explains its mechanism.

•● *Cross the east walkway for downstream views then return along the west walkway for upstream views. Return to the south tower.*

Displays explain the history of the City's bridges.

•● *Descend to the floor below.*

A model of Tower Bridge is exhibited and displays describe its history.

•● *Descend by lift and exit from the main tower. Proceed southward. Descend the steps beside the small south Tower and enter the museum.*

Displayed are the original steam engines that drove the opening and closing mechanism of the bridge until the change was made to electricity in 1976.

•● *Exit and proceed to the south side of the bridge. Descend from the east side of Tower Bridge to Shad Thames and continue ahead to the Maguire Street corner (fourth right).*

Location 31	**DESIGN MUSEUM**

Shad Thames

Open Monday–Friday 11.30–18.00, Saturday and Sunday 12.00–18.00 Admission charges.

When opened in 1989, this museum, on three floors, became the first in the world exclusively devoted to contemporary design of consumer products. The **Review Gallery**, approached by stairs from the foyer, accommodates temporary exhibitions devoted to a specific theme. Above, the museum's permanent exhibits are displayed in the second floor's Collection Gallery.

Apart from nostalgia, many find that the items of greatest interest are futuristic designs, some of them prototypes that can be seen nowhere else.

•● *Exit left and follow Maguire Street southward.*

Location 32	**BRAMAH TEA AND COFFEE MUSEUM**

Maguire Street

Open daily 10.00–18.00. Admission charge.

This surprisingly large museum explains the history and development of drinking tea, England's favourite beverage, and coffee, the popularity of which has always lagged well behind (in continental Europe the reverse is the case). One learns that coffee, however, was the first to appear in England (1637), tea arriving 20 years later. Edward Bramah's collection includes 1,000 teapots and coffee-makers, and features amusing novelty pots produced in the 1930s – Mickey Mouse, Santa Claus etc. Weighing 89 lb empty, the Bramah Teapot, made in 1957, is the world's largest – although completely unusable. Earl Grey's own teapot, a star of the collection, was stolen from the museum in 1994.

Exit right and return to Tower Bridge. Follow the riverside walkway westward. Signs lead to HMS Belfast.

Location 33

HMS *BELFAST*

Tooley Street (off). (407 6434)
Open daily, April–October, 10.00–18.00, November–March 10.00–16.30. Admission charge.

This cruiser is Europe's largest preserved warship. Visits are not recommended for the infirm or very young as there are many steps to climb.

A ferry service runs between the ship and Tower Pier in summer at an additional charge.

Permanently moored here since 1971 as a floating museum, this battle cruiser, launched in 1938, is the Royal Navy's last remaining 'big ship'. Its only sister ship, HMS *Edinburgh,* was sunk in the Second World War with a cargo of Russian gold which was partly salvaged in 1981.

Belfast played a key role in the sinking of the German *Scharnhorst* in 1943 and did not end her active career until 1963. Most of the cruiser has been preserved so that little has changed since it was on active service. Yellow arrows guide visitors through the seven decks. Of particular interest are the Operations Room, Engine Room and Boiler Room.

Return by ferry (summer only) or by foot to Tower Pier. Proceed past the Tower's main entrance gate. Second L Gloucester Court. Ascend the steps R to the Tower Hill terrace.

Location 34

TOWER HILL TERRACE

Public speakers: Monday to Friday 12.30–14.00.

This terrace is mistakenly believed by many to be the site of the Tower Hill scaffold. A plaque commemorates that Lord Soper has been speaking to the public from here for many years.

Location 35

TOWER HILL PAGEANT

1 Tower Hill Terrace

Open daily 09.30–17.30 (16.30 November–March) Admission charge.

Tableaux illustrating major stages in the 2000-year-old history of the City of London are viewed from computer-controlled 'dark ride' cars, which take 15 minutes to complete the circuit. Sound, movement and aromas help to recreate the past.

Displayed at upper level, in association with the Museum of London, are recent discoveries made during the excavation of London's new Thameside buildings 1972–90. Due to land reclamation, the modern river wall of the City now extends 100m from the natural bank of Roman times.

The damp earth has acted as an effective preserver of wood, and framework for bridges and warehouses, together with sections of boats, are included among the expected pottery, coins and jewellery.

Proceed westward through the paved seating area towards the church ahead. L Byward St. Continue ahead to the north side of All Hallows.

Location 36

ALL HALLOWS-BY-THE-TOWER*

Byward Street

Although gutted by bombs, much of interest remains within this ancient church. There is Roman and Saxon work and one of London's most beautiful pieces of carving – attributed to Grinling Gibbons.

All Hallows was first built by the Saxons in the 7C, shortly after the foundation of Barking Abbey in Essex with which it was closely connected. Traces of Roman buildings existed on the site and some of their bricks and tiles were used. Aisles, added in the 11C, were rebuilt in the 15C. The chancel was renewed in the 14C.

An earlier tower was destroyed by the blast from an explosion in a nearby ships' chandlers' premises in 1649. It was reconstructed in 1659 and represents the only new building work in a London church during the Commonwealth. The steeple by *Mottistone* 1958 was the first newly designed example in the City for two hundred years.

Enter from the late 19C porch. Proceed ahead and turn R beneath the organ to the Brass Rubbing Centre.

Remains of a Saxon wall L, from the original 7C church, were discovered after the bombing. Roman tiles were incorporated in the top of the arch but the red brickwork dates from the 17C. The church possesses outstanding medieval brasses and rubbings may be made. Ask here for details.

Leave the Brass Rubbing Centre R and proceed to the baptistry R in the south-west corner of the church.

Viewed behind a glass screen is the prize possession of All Hallows, its font cover, almost certainly carved by *Gibbons* in 1682. This is judged to be one of the most exquisite pieces of carving in London.

Return to the south aisle. Turn L and proceed R along the nave.

Three 18C Lord Mayor's sword rests stand in the bays.

Medieval wooden statues of saints are fixed to piers on either side of the nave.

The founder of the Toc H Christian Association, 'Tubby' Clayton, was for many years the vicar of All Hallows. He is buried in a tomb chest L that bears his bronze effigy.

The pulpit *c.*1670 came from St Swithin's church.

Cross to the **Mariners' Chapel** *in the south aisle.*

The lectern 1613, with rails of Sussex iron, was rescued from the rubble and restored.

At the east end of the chapel the ivory figure of Christ is believed to have been taken from a ship of the 16C Spanish Armada.

Cross to the north aisle **Lady Chapel**. *Turn R.*

On the north wall is the restored tomb chest of Alderman Croke, d.1477.

In the centre of this chapel are the four Tate panels, a 15C altar-piece painted originally in five sections. They disappeared from the Royal Chantry Chapel (now demolished) in 1547 and were rediscovered in the 18C but with the central panel missing. The kneeling figure depicts Sir Robert Tate.

Ask to visit the crypt. Descend the steps with the guide.

The **crypt** was only formed when the foundations of All Hallows were strengthened in 1926. Two Roman tesellated pavements are displayed and a detailed model of Roman London is exhibited. The three Saxon crosses discovered after the Second World War, are London's most important Saxon finds.

Exit from the north door of the church. Cross the road. Proceed ahead along Seething Lane. Enter St Olave's churchyard L facing Pepys St.

Location 37

ST OLAVE* *c.1450*

Hart Street

This rare example of a medieval City church escaped the Great Fire. In spite of bomb damage, much of the interior and its monuments survived.

The churchyard's macabre entrance arch of 1658 is decorated with skulls and gained for St Olave's Charles Dickens's description as 'The church of St Ghastly Grim'.

There was an 11C church on the site which was rebuilt in the 13C and again *c.*1450.

The brickwork of the top section of the tower was added in 1732. Its turret and weathervane were renewed in 1954.

A plaque on the south wall ahead commemorates the now-blocked direct entrance to the old Navy Pew which was at gallery level and approached by an external covered wooden staircase. The 17C Navy Office stood nearby in Seething Lane.

Enter from the churchyard by the door in the modern porch.

Immediately ahead, the Norwegian flag commemorates King Haakon who worshipped here whilst in exile during the Second World War. St Olave, to whom the church is dedicated, was a compatriot.

The two arcaded walls partly survived the bombing but the light oak woodwork is modern.

Proceed along the north aisle.

On the north wall L, is the monument to Sir Andrew Riccard, d.1672. He was a chairman of the East India Company. Peter Cappone, d.1582, a Florentine merchant, is commemorated on the south wall of the north aisle.

Proceed to the **chancel.**

The pulpit *Gibbons* (?), from St Benet Gracechurch Street, and the carved communion rail are late 17C.

Four 18C sword rests stand in front of the altar.

On the wall L is the monument to Elizabeth Pepys, wife of diarist Samuel, d.1669, by *Bushnell.*

Below is the monument to the Bayninge brothers, both aldermen. Andrew, d.1610, and Paul, d.1616.

There are two fragments from a large tomb on the wall R of the altar. Sir John Radcliffe, d.1568, and below, his wife, Lady Ann, d.1583.

Proceed R to the south aisle.

In the south-east corner R, a 15C door leads to the vestry built in 1662. Request permission to view the interior which retains its original plaster ceiling decorated with a large angel.

The 17C painting above the overmantel is believed to be by *De Witte* (?).

Exit from the vestry.

Above the vestry door, the monument to Sir James Deane, d.1608, commemorates a wealthy merchant adventurer.

In the centre of the south wall is the memorial to the diarist Samuel Pepys, d.1703, by *A. W. Blomfield* 1884. The position of the bust marks the old entrance to the Navy Pew where Pepys who was secretary to the admiralty, worshipped. Both Pepys and his wife are buried in St Olave's but there are no tombstones.

The crypt survives from the 13C church and is entered from the west end of the south aisle (the Baptistery). There is an ancient well.

Exit from the churchyard. L Seething Lane. R Crutched Friars. First L French Ordinary Court.

Location 38

FRENCH ORDINARY COURT

This dark, cavernous passage runs beneath Fenchurch Street Station and conjures up images of Jack the Ripper. No 42 Crutched Friars, L of its entrance, is one of London's finest early 18C houses.

Return to Seething Lane L. First L Muscovy Street. L Trinity Square and Tower Hill Station, Circle and District lines.

Alternatively, return to Tower Pier for the boat to Charing Cross or Westminster Piers.

4

The Financial City

The major financial and administrative buildings in the City are visited, together with the Barbican Arts Centre and some of Wren's loveliest churches.

Timing: Monday to Friday is preferable, allowing a whole day to complete the itinerary which, if preferred, may conveniently be terminated at the Museum of London (location 26).

Remains of a Roman fort can be seen within the Museum of London on the first Tuesday and the third Friday of each month.

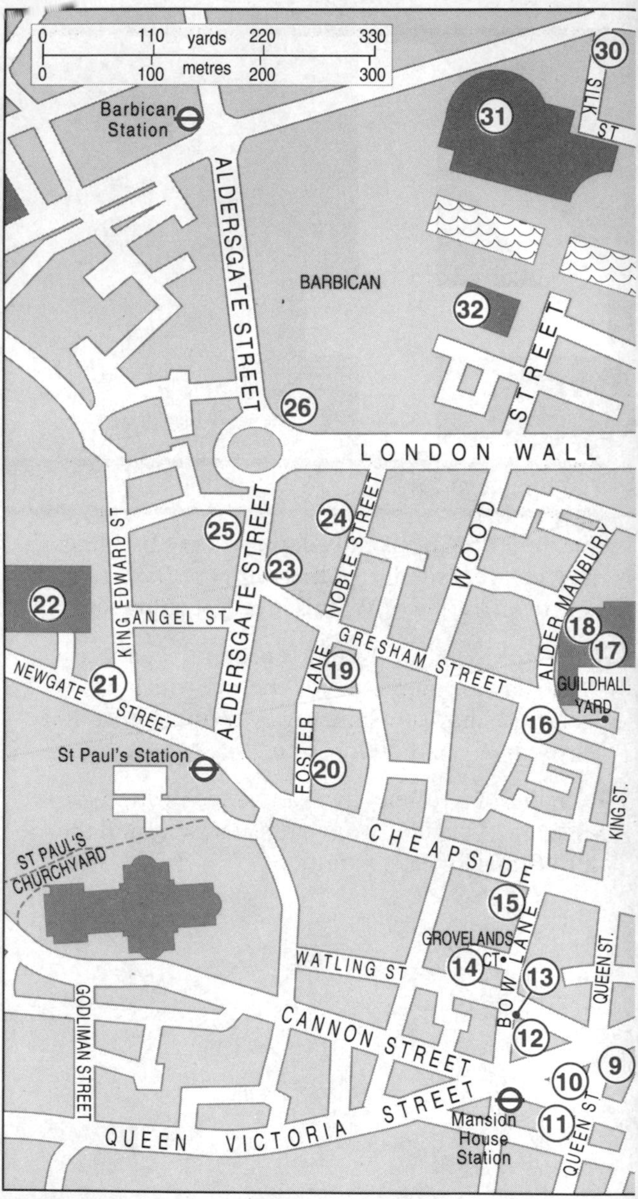

Locations
1 Bank of England
2 Royal Exchange
3 Stock Exchange
4 City of London Club
5 Merchant Taylors Hall
6 St Margaret Lothbury
7 Mansion House
8 St Stephen Walbrook
9 Temple of Mithras (Mithraeum)
10 Sweetings
11 No 28 Queen Street
12 St Mary Aldermary
13 Ye Olde Watling
14 Williamson's
15 St Mary-le-Bow
16 St Lawrence Jewry

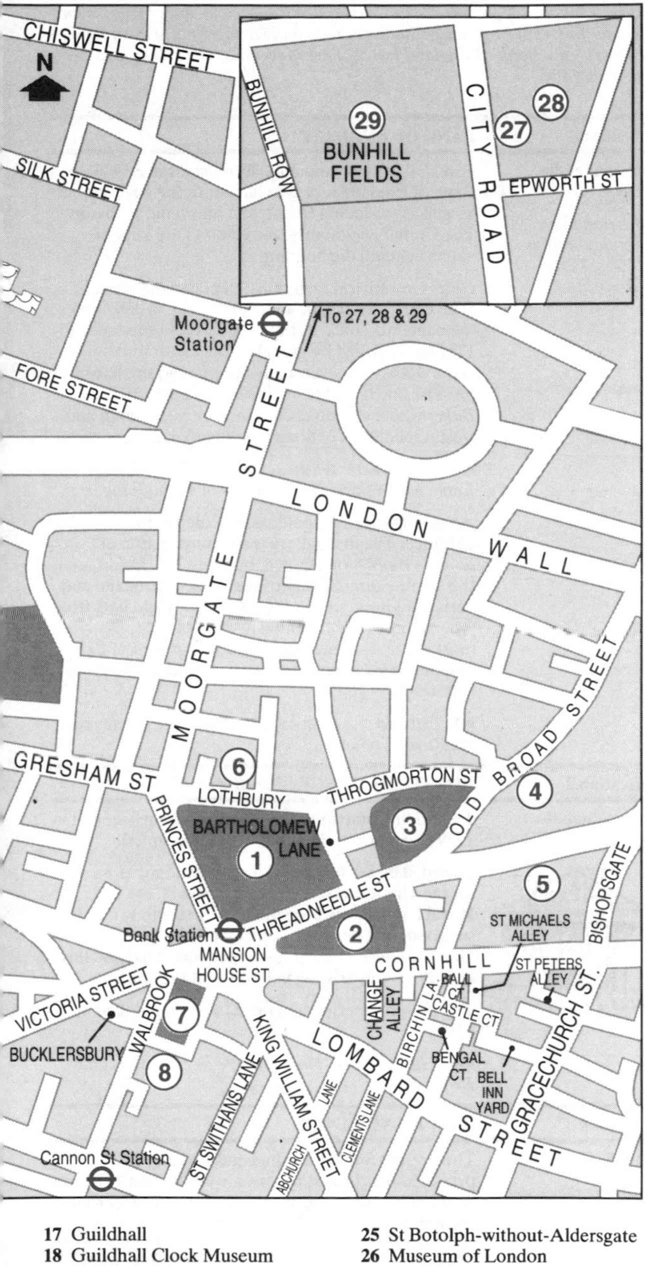

17 Guildhall
18 Guildhall Clock Museum
19 Goldsmiths Hall
20 St Vedast
21 Christ Church (tower)
22 National Postal Museum
23 St Anne and St Agnes
24 London Wall
25 St Botolph-without-Aldersgate
26 Museum of London
27 Wesley's House
28 Wesley's Chapel
29 Bunhill Fields
30 Whitbreads Old Brewery
31 Barbican Centre
32 St Giles-without-Cripplegate

Start *Bank Station, Central, Northern and Waterloo/City lines. There is an elevator link with Monument Station, Circle and District lines. Leave Bank Station by the Bank of England exit. L Threadneedle St. The Bank occupies the corner site.*

Location 1	**BANK OF ENGLAND**

Threadneedle Street

Museum open Monday–Friday 10.00–17.00. Admission free.

Founded in 1694, and publicly owned since 1946, the Bank of England serves as banker to the government as well as to leading British and international banks. The United Kingdom's gold reserves are kept in vaults beneath the building.

Gillray, a satirical cartoonist, depicted the Bank as 'The Old Lady of Threadneedle Street' in 1797 and the name has stuck. A building was commissioned in 1732 but replaced by a single-storey structure by *Soane* 1808. This eventually became too small for its purpose and was almost entirely rebuilt in 1939 by *Baker* who insensitively retained only the south and west screen walls of Soane's masterpiece.

Visitors enter the museum from Bartholomew Lane, which skirts the north side of the building.

An informative free guide is provided at the entrance. The first gallery is a reconstruction of *Soane*'s Bank Stock Office, built in 1793. In this area, the architectural history of the Bank of England and early banking systems, are described. Gold bars from Roman times are exhibited in the Rotunda, *Baker*'s most impressive interior. The development of British banknotes from hand-written examples to the present is traced.

Exit and cross Threadneedle St to the portico of the Royal Exchange.

Location 2	**ROYAL EXCHANGE** *Tite 1844*

Threadneedle Street

The trading function of the Royal Exchange ended in 1939 and much of the building is unoccupied.

Founded by Sir Thomas Gresham in 1566, as a venue for merchants to conduct their business, the first Royal Exchange was opened by Elizabeth I. Its 17C successor was destroyed by fire in 1838 but Gresham's crest of a grasshopper was saved and this surmounts the existing bell tower at the rear.

The present interior (not open) was remodelled in 1982.

Exit R. First R Threadneedle St. Second L Old Broad St.

Location 3	**STOCK EXCHANGE**

Old Broad Street

Public gallery open Monday–Friday 10.30–15.15. Admission free.

The present Stock Exchange has had many predecessors. Its first premises were built in 1773 and dealings in stocks and shares were then transferred from the overcrowded Royal Exchange.

Enter from Old Broad Street and ascend the stairs L of the main entrance to the public gallery.

Jobbers can be seen negotiating with brokers.

Exit L. Pass the Throgmorton St junction (first L). Cross the road.

Location 4	**CITY OF LONDON CLUB** *Philip Hardwick 1834*

19 Old Broad Street

This stuccoed building, a rare City survivor from the Regency period (technically William IV), was destined for destruction when the Nat West Tower was planned but reprieved at the last moment. It is reputedly London's most expensive club.

Return southward. First L Threadneedle St. Cross the road. Enter Merchant Taylors Hall from Threadneedle St and await the guide.

Location 5	**MERCHANT TAYLORS HALL**

30 Threadneedle Street

Open by appointment only. Admission free.

This is the only Livery Hall that retains traces of its medieval origin. The City Livery Companies began as crafts guilds and were first recorded in England in 1180. They had monopoly powers in the Middle Ages, controlling prices, quality, wages, employees and working conditions. The guilds became known as Livery Companies due to the distinctive clothing, or 'livery', worn by their members. Twelve, pre-eminent in medieval times, still exist and are known as 'Great Companies', the others are 'Minor'. A Master and one or two Wardens preside. Today, the Companies only rarely play a trading role, charitable and educational work being their chief functions.

The Merchant Taylors is one of the twelve Great Livery Companies. A Royal Charter was granted in 1327, but it had been established even earlier. A famous dispute with the Skinners Company, as to which should be given precedence, was settled by the Lord Mayor in 1484. He decided that each would rank sixth and seventh respectively on alternate years. Hence the expression, 'at sixes and sevens', meaning confused.

Until the Second World War, the 14C **livery hall** was the only surviving example in London to pre-date the Great Fire. It was bombed, however, and rebuilt by *Richardson* in 1959. Reputedly, the national anthem 'God Save the King' was first sung in this hall under the direction of its author John Bull (?). Some of the fabric remains and in the south-west corner is a concealed 14C bay (buffet), with blocked windows. Sections of the 14C clay floor and the stone floor of 1675 have survived.

Completely destroyed by bombs, the **parlour** has been rebuilt as a replica of the 17C original.

Situated on the first floor, directly above the parlour, the **drawing room** was similarly destroyed.

Much of the **kitchen** dates from the 15C and some Perpendicular arches remain. It is a unique London survivor of a medieval kitchen.

The 14C **crypt** ran beneath the Company's chapel which was demolished in the 16C. There are now only two bays but the crypt was originally much longer and probably used for storage (?).

The enclosed **cloister** and **gallery** were added by *Baker* in 1927. Displayed are two funeral palls (hearse covers) of 1490 and 1520.

Exit L. Second R Bartholomew Lane. L Lothbury. Enter St Margaret's.

Location 6

ST MARGARET LOTHBURY *Wren 1690*

Lothbury

St Margaret's, first recorded in 1197, was rebuilt in 1440.

Proceed towards the screen.

The carved screen *c.* 1689 is one of only two examples contemporary with Wren that have survived. This, together with the canopied pulpit, came from All-Hallows-the-Great.

The reredos and altar rails are from St Olave Old Jewry. The arms of William and Mary surmount the reredos. There are two late 18C sword rests.

In the north aisle is the bust of Sir Peter Le Maire by *Le Sueur* (?) 1631.

Flanking the door in the south aisle are two busts: Alderman Boydel by *Banks* and *F. W. Smith* 1791 and Mrs Simpson by *Nollekens* 1795.

By tradition, the late 17C font is by *Gibbons*.

Exit R. First L Princes St. R Mansion House St. Cross immediately to the Mansion House ahead.

Location 7

MANSION HOUSE *Dance the Elder 1752*

Mansion House Street

Open for group tours and by appointment only. Admission free.

Every Lord Mayor of London must reside in the Mansion House throughout his year of office. This was the first residence to be built specifically for the City's Lord Mayors.

Proceed westward past the portico. First L Walbrook. Enter the Mansion House from Walbrook. Visitors await a guide in the entrance hall and proceed to the first floor and the State Apartments.

The courtyard, originally sited here, proved to be impracticable and when it rained water seeped from it into the building. It was, therefore, roofed over in 1794 to provide the **Saloon**.

The 19C crystal chandeliers, part of a set of sixteen, were the first in the City to be electrified.

The thrones for the Lord Mayor and Mayoress were made in 1860.

All the tapestries are Victorian.

The twenty-four dining chairs were made to commemorate Nelson's victory at the Battle of the Nile in 1797.

Once the Lord Mayor's dining room, the **Long Parlour** is now used as a Council Chamber. Its coffered ceiling is unique in the house.

The **Egyptian Hall** originally had a clerestory, in the 'Egyptian' style, which was replaced by the present barrel-vaulted ceiling by *Dance the Younger* 1795.

The radical John Wilkes was Lord Mayor in 1775 and the **State Drawing Room** was known for many years as Wilkes's Dining Parlour.

A chest which allegedly belonged to Sir Walter Raleigh (?) is displayed in the **stairway passage**.

Items of interest in the **Gold Vaults** include: The Pearl Sword, given to the City by Elizabeth I in 1571, and still symbolically presented by the Lord Mayor when the sovereign enters the City at Temple Bar.

The Lord Mayor's 16C chain once belonged to Sir Thomas More. Due to its delicacy, a replica is now worn.

Exit L. First L Walbrook.

Location 8

ST STEPHEN WALBROOK *Wren 1679*

Walbrook

This is Wren's major City church and seemingly, with its dome, possibly England's first, was a rehearsal for St Paul's Cathedral. The Samaritans organization was established in the crypt in 1953. Reopened in 1987, St Stephen's retains the original altar-rail, reredos, font and pulpit. Dominating the interior, however, is the controversial circular altar made by *Henry Moore* in 1972.

Exit R. First L Bucklersbury. First L Queen Victoria St. Proceed ahead to the Mithras Temple which has been re-sited outside the Temple Court office block. Ascend the steps to the viewing platform.

Location 9

TEMPLE OF MITHRAS (MITHRAEUM)

Queen Victoria Street

These remains of a 2C Roman temple to Mithras, god of light, were discovered during excavation work for nearby Bucklersbury House and transferred here in 1954. Originally the temple lay 18 feet below the present street level by the Walbrook stream. The worship of Mithras was popular amongst legionnaires.

Exit L. Pass Queen St (first L). On the corner L is Sweetings Restaurant.

Location 10

SWEETINGS

39 Queen Victoria Street

Open for lunch only, Monday–Friday 11.45–15.00.

Sweetings, London's oldest fish restaurant, was established at Islington in 1830 and relocated in the present building in 1906. Marble counters and high ceilings maintain an Edwardian atmosphere.

Exit R Queen Victoria St. First R Queen St. Pass Cannon Street (first R). R is No 28 Queen Street.

Location 11

NO 28 QUEEN STREET

Two Georgian houses, rare survivors in the City, have been linked to provide offices.

Exit L. First L Cannon St. First R Queen Victoria St. Cross the road to St Mary Aldermary.

Location 12

ST MARY ALDERMARY * *Wren 1682*

Queen Victoria Street

A Norman church, recorded *c.*1080, was rebuilt in the 16C. 'Aldermary' means the old church of St Mary. John Milton, the poet, married his third wife here in 1663.

Only the tower remains from the medieval building. It is part 1511 and part 1629 but the top section with its pinnacles is by *Wren* 1704. After the Great Fire, the rest of the church was rebuilt on the old foundations but why Wren decided to retain the Gothic style remains a mystery.

Proceed ahead through the short alley. First R Bow Lane. Enter the church.

The carved doorcase within by *Gibbons* (?) came from St Antholin.

Immediately L is is the original font.

The 'fan-vaults' in the nave and aisles are of plaster.

Most of the 17C furnishings were replaced in 1868 but the original pulpit and a rare 17C wooden sword rest, attached to the third column from the east, remain.

Exit R Bow Lane.

Location 13	**YE OLDE WATLING** *1688*
39 Bow Lane	This inn was reputedly frequented by workmen constructing St Paul's Cathedral (?). Its beamed interior was restored in 1901 and again in 1947.

Exit R Bow Lane. Second L Grovelands Court.

Location 14	**WILLIAMSON'S**
1–3 Grovelands Court	Williamson's, first licensed as a tavern in 1851, was built on the site of a manor house which had once been the residence of Sir John Oldcastle, the prototype of Shakespeare's Falstaff. The present inn was reconstructed *c.* 1900.

Proceed to the end of the court.

The iron gates, with the 'W and M' monogram, were reputedly presented in the 17C to the owner of the manor house by William and Mary (?).

Return to Bow Lane L. Third L Cheapside.

Location 15	**ST MARY-LE-BOW** *Wren 1680*
Cheapside	St Mary's possesses London's most famous church bells and what is judged to be Wren's finest steeple.

A Saxon church on the site burnt down and was rebuilt as St Mary New Church in 1087. The Norman crypt from this building survives and its arches 'bows' gave the church its present name. St Mary's was rebuilt several times but destroyed in the Great Fire.

Only the walls, tower and steeple escaped the bombing. The steeple is judged Wren's proudest and was certainly his costliest. Its design was inspired by the Basilica of Maxentius in Rome. As the tower was found to be unsafe, following the Second World War, it was taken down and rebuilt stone by stone.

By tradition, a 'Cockney' is defined as anyone born within the sound of Bow Bells. Allegedly, 'Cockney', like 'cock-eyed', derives from *cokeney* meaning a cock's egg (?) and implied that a person was misshapen or a simpleton. It is now, however, virtually a term of endearment. Bow Bells are referred to in the 'Oranges and Lemons' nursery song and in the 15C they are said to have 'called' Dick Whittington to return to the City from Highgate (?). From the 14C until 1847 Bow Bells rang at 21.00 (originally for the curfew) and again at 05.45 to rouse sleeping Londoners. The bells were shattered in the Second World War but recast.

Above the north and west doors of the tower are Baroque carvings of cherubs' heads.

Enter the church.

To many, the interior is a disappointment. It was unsympathetically rebuilt after the war and the furnishings are neo-Georgian. Art exhibitions are held.

Descend the steps to the **crypt.**

Here can be seen the rounded Norman arches, or

'bows'. The refectory leads to the Court of Arches, once the Archbishop of Canterbury's court.

Exit from the church R. Second L King St. Second L Gresham St.

Location 16

ST LAWRENCE JEWRY *Wren 1687*

Gresham Street

Gutted by bombs, only the tower and walls of this church survived. The steeple is a replica. Internally the restoration is of a high standard.

Exit R. Pass the west wall of the church to Guildhall Yard behind.

Location 17

GUILDHALL *Croxton c.1440*

Guildhall Yard

Open Monday–Saturday 10.00–17.00, Sunday also May–September 14.00–17.00. The undercroft is closed 12.00–14.00. Admission free.

The Guildhall, always the City's most important secular building, has stood on or near its present site since the 11C. The City is administered from here by the Court of Common Council which developed from the ancient Court of Hustings.

The first mayor was installed at an earlier Guildhall in 1192 and King John, by charter, gave the citizens of London the right to elect a mayor in 1215. The title 'Lord Mayor' (Dominus Major) was first recorded in 1283 and then used from time to time until it became standard in 1545. The title, however, is unofficial.

The present building by *Croxton* was constructed *c.*1440. Much of this was destroyed in the Great Fire but the porch, walls, undercroft and some of the internal stone-panelling survived.

Due to fires and bombing, the roof, with its lantern, has been restored several times.

The porch front was reconstructed following the Great Fire and later remodelled in Portland stone to provide the present front *Dance the Younger* 1789.

Enter via the modern ambulatory L of the hall.

The interior has been gutted by fire on several occasions but much of the 15C decorative stone-panelling survives. All the woodwork and the roof are the work of *Giles Gilbert Scott* 1954.

Immediately above, flanking the entrance, stand, Gog and Magog, 1953 replacements of two 18C figures destroyed in the Second World War. Earlier versions of these mythical giants are recorded from the 15C. Their original names, Gogmagog and Corineus, were too much of a mouthful for Londoners.

Proceed clockwise.

Monuments line the walls as follows: Churchill by *Nemon* 1958, Nelson by *J. Smith* 1810, Wellington by *Bell* 1857, Pitt the Elder by *Bacon* 1782, Pitt the Younger by *Bubb* 1813, Beckford (Lord Mayor) by *Moore* 1770, Royal Fusiliers Regiment by *Pomeroy* *c.*1903.

The lower window, R of the Royal Fusiliers monument, is the only 15C example to survive.

Exit from the hall L and ask an attendant for permission to visit the porch and the undercroft.

The **porch** retains 15C blind tracery and vaulting.

Proceed ahead and descend the steps L.

The wall ahead gives an indication of the original appearance of the Guildhall's exterior which was similarly clad with carved stone panels.

●● *Enter the undercroft*

The **undercroft**, built at 15C ground level, is the largest medieval example in London. The 15C east section, seen first, retains its original Purbeck marble columns. The west section is believed to have been built in the 13C (?), i.e. before the present Guildhall. Its vaults were destroyed in the Great Fire and this area was then filled in. It was opened up in 1973 and the vaults were rebuilt.

●● *Exit from Guildhall R and proceed to the south-west corner of the yard. Pass beneath the arch of the modern extension. R Aldermanbury. Proceed to the second door R.*

Location 18

GUILDHALL CLOCK MUSEUM

Aldermanbury

Open Monday–Friday 09.30–17.00. Admission free.

Clocks and watches dating from the 15C to the 20C are exhibited. Of particular interest is a 19C clock with a rolling ball replacing the pendulum. Early playing cards are also displayed.

●● *Exit L. First R Gresham St. Fourth L Foster Lane. Goldsmiths Hall is the corner building.*

Location 19

GOLDSMITHS HALL *Philip Hardwick 1835*

Foster Lane

Open for some exhibitions or by appointment only when there is an admission charge. The vestibule and stairway may generally be viewed.

The Goldsmiths are one of the twelve Great Livery Companies and their present hall replaced a 17C building that had been damaged in the Great Fire. A million items of gold and silver are assayed and hallmarked here monthly. The Trial of the Pyx, when sample coins are checked for accuracy, has been held annually in Goldsmiths Hall since 1871. It had previously been held at Westminster since the 13C.

Goldsmiths Hall's external carvings are by *Nixon*.

●● *Enter the vestibule.*

Displayed is a wooden statue of St Dunstan preserved from the Company's 17C barge.

●● *Ascend the stairs with the guide.*

The **Livery Hall** was redecorated in 1871 but the original furniture, designed by the hall's architect *Philip Hardwick*, remains.

The panelling and ceiling of the **Court Room** are original. Exhibited is a small Roman altar to the goddess Diana found beneath the building. The fireplace by *Roubiliac* (?) came from Canons Park.

The **Drawing Room** was rebuilt and decorated in Louis XVI style after the bombing.

Some panelling in the **Library Ante-room** is 17C and came from East Acton Manor House.

Items of gold and silver, dating from the 15C, are displayed in the **Exhibition Room.** Elizabeth I drank from the Bowes Cup at her coronation banquet.

●● *Exit L.*

Location 20

ST VEDAST *Wren 1673*

Foster Lane

St Vedast's medieval predecessor was gutted by the Great Fire but the walls, the base of the tower and the 17C doors of the west porch survived.

The interior of the church and its furnishings were completely destroyed in the Second World War. Its present 17C furnishings were all brought from other churches and include the font, reredos and pulpit.

The organ case and communion rail are 18C.

Exit L. R Cheapside. Proceed ahead to Newgate St. First R King Edward St. Cross the road.

Location 21 | **CHRIST CHURCH (TOWER)** *Wren 1687*

Newgate Street

Only the tower with its steeple, and sections of the walls survived the Second World War bombing. The steeple resembles that of St Mary-le-Bow.

Proceed along King Edward St. Pass the drive-in and enter the first door L.

Location 22 | **NATIONAL POSTAL MUSEUM**

King Edward Street (239 5420)

Open Monday–Friday 09.30–16.30. Admission free. Research and library by appointment.

Exhibited permanently is the Phillips collection which created the museum when it was donated in 1965. A large display is devoted to the evolution of the world's first postage stamp the 'Penny Black'.

Exit L. First R Angel St. L Aldersgate St. First R Gresham St.

Location 23 | **ST ANNE AND ST AGNES** *Wren 1680*

Gresham Street

Open only for Sunday Lutheran services and occasional concerts.

The short tower by *Colin* was added *c.*1714.

Gutted by bombs and rebuilt, the church's unusual plan of a vaulted square within a square is similar to that of Nieuwe Kerk, Haarlem in Holland.

The original west doorcase and reredos survive.

Exit L. First L Noble St.

Location 24 | **LONDON WALL**

Noble Street

Much of the structure in Noble Street represents the south-west section of a Roman fort *c.*100. The wall itself, which later encircled London and linked the forts, was built in the 2C. It fell into disrepair after the Roman exodus in the 5C but was mostly reconstructed in the Middle Ages. The last known rebuilding was in 1476, but after this the wall deteriorated and all seven of its ancient gateways were demolished for road widening in the 18C.

Continue ahead. L London Wall (the street). L Aldersgate. Cross the road.

Location 25 | **ST BOTOLPH-WITHOUT-ALDERSGATE*** *N. Wright 1791*

Aldersgate

Open Thursday 13.00–14.00 but more frequently in summer depending on staff availability.

The church is renowned for its virtually complete late 18C interior. St Botolph's, founded in the 13C, like several other London churches sited near the old gates was dedicated to the English patron saint of travellers. It was completely rebuilt in 1791 but the east end was remodelled by *J. W. Griffith* (?) in 1831.

Enter the church from Aldersgate.

Against the wall, immediately R, is the bust of Elizabeth Richardson, d.1699. The Lord Mayor's sword rest is late 18C.

All the pews are Victorian but the pulpit is late 18C. The east window's 'Agony in the Garden' was painted by *James Pearson* in 1788. Other windows are late 19C.

Baroque plasterwork decorates the ceiling which is coffered above both apses.

St Botolph's three galleries are original and the organ case above the west gallery is by *Green* 1778.

•• *Proceed to the south aisle.*

On the east wall is the tomb of Ann Packington, d.1563.

•• *Exit L. At the roundabout continue L. Ascend the stairway ahead to the bridge which crosses the road. The Museum of London is signposted.*

Location 26 — **MUSEUM OF LONDON** *Powell* and *Moya 1978.*

London Wall

Open Tuesday–Saturday and Bank Holiday Mondays 10.00–18.00, Sunday 12.00–18.00. Admission charge, but free after 16.30. Remains of a Roman fort may be seen on the first Tuesday in each month 10.30–12.00 and the third Friday in each month 14.30–16.00. Admission free.

The museum traces London's history from Roman times to the present in chronological order. The period before 1666 is dealt with on the ground floor and after 1666 on the lower ground floor.

The Pre-History Gallery is a recent addition.

Popular exhibits on the ground floor include: Tableau of the Great Fire. Roman Mithras temple findings. Panels from the 13C Eleanor Cross at Cheapside. The 14C porch from St Ethelburga Church. Statues from the Guildhall's 15C porch. A model of Whitehall Palace. On the lower floor may be seen: Old London shop fronts. The Lord Mayor's coach.

Ask at reception to see the **Roman fort** (see left for times) which is entered, with a guide, from the museum's car park. Much of this 2C fort discovered in 1956, lies beneath the London Wall street level. Displayed is a model of the fort as it would have appeared in Roman times.

•• *Exit from the museum L. Descend the steps to London Wall L. From the bus stop (request) take bus No 141 to Wesley's Chapel, City Rd (also a request stop). Cross the road.*

•• *Alternatively, return to London Wall R. Second L Aldersgate St and St Paul's Station, Central line.*

Location 27 — **WESLEY'S HOUSE** *c.1770*

47 City Road

Open Monday–Saturday 10.00–16.00, Sunday 12.00–14.00. Admission charge.

John Wesley, founder of Methodism, lived in this house from 1778 until his death in 1791. His study, bedroom and prayer room 'The Power House of Methodism' are on the first floor. Wesley's furniture and many personal items are exhibited.

•• *Exit R and proceed to the east side of the court.*

Location 28 — **WESLEY'S CHAPEL**

47 City Road

The original chapel of 1778 was restored after fire in 1880. Furnishings from the earlier building include Wesley's pulpit (shortened), the communion rail and the communion table.

The Adam style ceiling is a replica of the original.

In the crypt is the Museum of Methodism.

Wesley's monument, above his burial vault, stands in the churchyard behind the apse of the chapel.

•• *Exit and cross the road.*

Location 29	**BUNHILL FIELDS**
City Road	Bunhill Fields was once much larger and approximately 120,000 were buried here between 1315 and 1854. It became the recognized burial ground for Non-Conformists in 1695. ●● *Follow the path ahead. Take the first path R.* The tombs of Daniel Defoe the author of *Robinson Crusoe*, and William Blake, poet and artist, overlook the path. ●● *Return to the junction with the main path.* The tomb of John Bunyan, author of *Pilgrim's Progress*, lies ahead. ●● *Exit from Bunhill Fields R. First R Chiswell St.*

Location 30	**WHITBREAD'S OLD BREWERY**
Chiswell Street (606 4455) *Open Monday–Friday 10.00–17.00*	Whitbread's opened here in 1749 and many of the brewery's early 18C buildings remain. ●● *Enter the courtyard* Displayed is the coach in which the Speaker of the House of Commons rides on state occasions. It was made in Holland for William III in 1698. ●● *Exit L. First L Whitecross St. Continue ahead to Silk St and the Barbican Centre. Proceed R below the arch to the Concourse at Level 5.*

Location 31	**BARBICAN CENTRE** *1982*
Silk Street (Box Office 628 8795) *The Centre is open daily, 10.00–22.00. Admission free.*	The Barbican Arts Centre, is the centrepiece of a large, basically residential scheme. A fortified, medieval watch-tower outside London's wall, known as a Barbican, was situated nearby and gives its name to this modern development in 'Brutalist' style. The site of thirty-five acres, made available through Second World War bombing, provides residential accommodation for 6,000 people in addition to the Arts Centre. The most important features of the Arts Centre are its theatre and hall. The Barbican Theatre (1,160 seats) is the permanent London home of the Royal Shakespeare Company whilst the Barbican Hall (2,026 seats) acts similarly for the London Symphony Orchestra. Access to both the hall and the theatre is from various levels. There are nine altogether but visitors will find the following of most interest: **Level 5:** the Concourse on this level houses exhibitions. ●● *Turn L and descend the stairs.* The Waterside Café with its outside Terrace overlooks the lake and fountains. ●● *Take the lift and ascend to Level 8.* **Level 8:** on this level are the Conservatory, Art Gallery and Sculpture Court. ●● *Ascend the stairs to Level 9. (There is no lift to this level).* **Level 9:** Conservatory Terrace. ●● *Descend the stairs to Level 7.* **Level 7:** 'The Cut Above' Restaurant, Library, and Advance Booking Office are on this level. From here there is access to the high level walkway.

•▬ *To exit from the Barbican Centre proceed along the high level walkway. Cross the lake, pass Gilbert House and descend the steps to St Giles's.*

•▬ *Alternatively, visitors possessing Agency tickets (which must be exchanged for house tickets at the Barbican), or seeking tickets for the day's performance should descend by lift to the Box Office on Level 3.*

Location 32

ST GILES-WITHOUT-CRIPPLEGATE *c. 1550*

The Barbican

This 16C church escaped the Great Fire and much of the building, together with its monuments, also survived the Second World War bombing.

St Giles stood outside Cripplegate, the oldest known gate in London's wall. A 'cripple' (covered way) is believed to have run from this gate to the Barbican watch tower (?). The church was founded in the 11C, rebuilt in 1537 and again in 1550 following a fire.

Edward, the illegitimate son of Shakespeare's brother Edmond, was baptized in St Giles in 1606. He only lived for a short time and was buried here in 1607. Oliver Comwell married in the church in 1620.

Most of the tower is 15C but the brick upper section, together with its cupola, replaced a spire in 1682.

•▬ *Enter by the north door facing the lake. Proceed towards the chancel.*

The interior has been restored following the bombing.

The stone corbels which support the shafts of the clerestory windows are carved to depict musicians.

On the floor in front of the communion rail a tablet records the burial place of poet John Milton, d.1674.

The chancel originally stretched further east but has been shortened and its east window renewed. In the south-east corner is a medieval sedilia and piscina. The floor was raised in 1888.

•▬ *Proceed to the south aisle where there are four monuments of interest.*

Margaret Lucy, d.1634, was the grand-daughter of the Sir Thomas Lucy who reputedly threatened Shakespeare with prosecution for stealing his deer (?). Lucy is also believed to have been the prototype of Justice Shallow in Shakespeare's *The Merry Wives of Windsor* (?).

John Speed, d. 1629, historian and map maker.

The statue of Milton was carved in 1904 and originally stood in the churchyard. It is based on a contemporary bust carved in 1654.

The adjacent bust, also of the poet, is by *Bacon the Elder* 1793.

•▬ *Exit from the church R.*

Remains of London's wall can be seen.

•▬ *Pass the foot of the stairs which lead to the upper walkway. L Fore St. Proceed ahead to Moorgate and Moorgate Station, Circle, Metropolitan and Northern lines.*

Alternatively, R Fore St. Continue ahead to Wood St. Third R Cheapside. Proceed to St Paul's Station, Central line.

Itinerary 5

5

The Royal Palaces

London's most important royal palaces are seen, together with St James's Park and the Roman Catholic Westminster Cathedral (not the Abbey).

Timing: Fine weather is essential as few interiors can be seen. The day chosen depends on preferences, because many of the locations are open only at specific times as follows:

Institute of Directors, Monday–Friday by appointment. Queen's Chapel, Sunday morning service in summer. Chapel Royal, Sunday morning service in winter. Queen's Gallery, Tuesday–Saturday. Royal Mews, Wednesday and Thursday afternoons.

Changing of the Guard at Buckingham Palace takes place daily in summer at 11.30. Every other day from September to March. Always dependant on the weather.

Buckingham Palace's State Apartments may be entered in Summer (variable dates) until 1998.

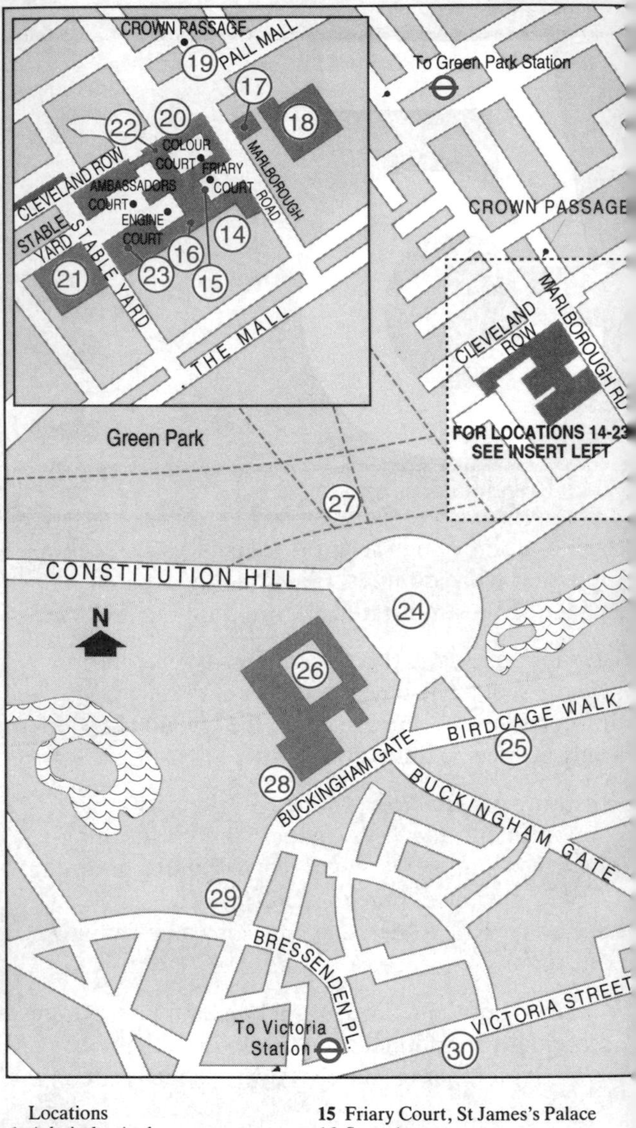

Locations
1 Admiralty Arch
2 The Mall
3 The Citadel
4 Carlton House Terrace
5 Duke of York Monument
6 Giro Tombstone
7 Athenaeum Club
8 Institute of Directors
9 Pall Mall
10 Travellers Club
11 Reform Club
12 Carlton Gardens
13 St James's Park
14 St James's Palace
15 Friary Court, St James's Palace
16 State Apartments, St James's Palace
17 The Queen's Chapel at St James's
18 Marlborough House
19 Crown Passage
20 Gatehouse, St James's Palace
21 Lancaster House
22 The Chapel Royal, St James's Palace
23 Clarence House
24 Queen Victoria Memorial
25 Guards' Museum
26 Buckingham Palace

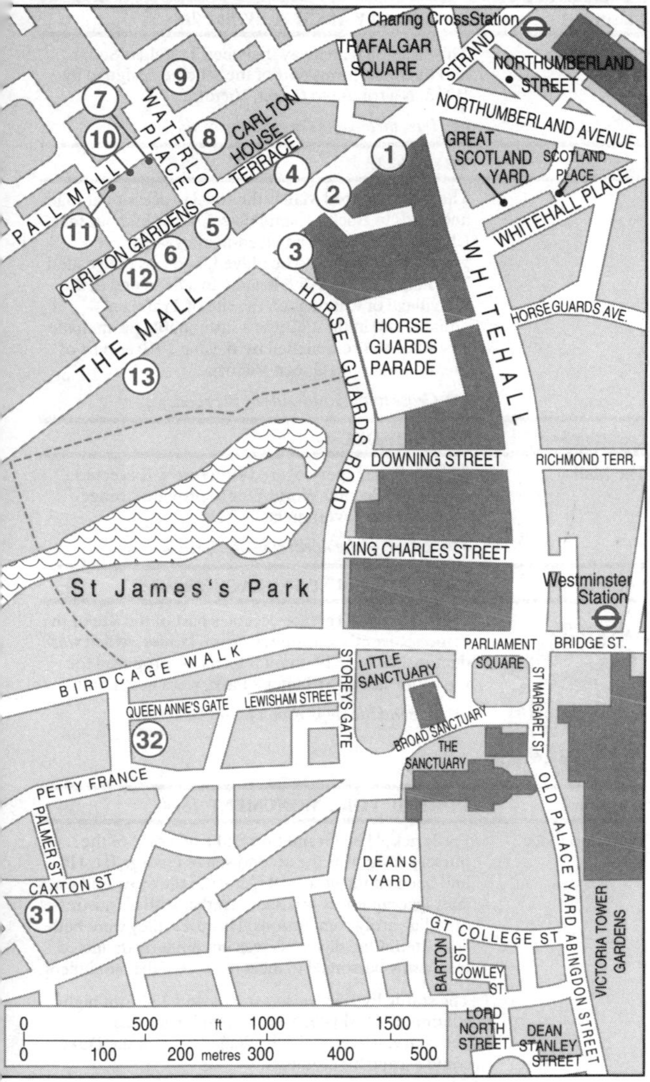

27 Green Park
28 The Queen's Gallery
29 The Royal Mews
30 Westminster Cathedral
31 Blewcoat School
32 Queen Anne's Gate

Start *Charing Cross Station, Bakerloo, Jubilee and Northern lines. From the Bakerloo line turn L at the barrier. Leave by the Cockspur Street/Mall exit. Turn L. First R the Mall and Admiralty Arch. From the Jubilee and Northern lines exit ahead to Strand (South). Turn L and proceed to Trafalgar Square. Admiralty Arch is directly ahead.*

Alternatively, continue from itinerary 6.

Location 1 | **ADMIRALTY ARCH** *A. Webb 1917*

The Mall

This triumphal archway, between Trafalgar Square and the Mall, forms part of the scheme designed by *Webb* as a tribute to Queen Victoria.

Pass through the arch to the Mall.

Location 2 | **THE MALL**

The pink-surfaced Mall is the royal processional road and leads to Buckingham Palace. It was laid out for Charles II in 1632 as a fenced-in alleyway for the game 'paille maille' to be played, and was then called The Pall Mall. Initially, it came to a dead end at the old village of Charing, on the site of Trafalgar Square, and in the 18C was a fashionable promenade. The Mall was remodelled by *Webb c.*1910 as part of the monument to Queen Victoria.

Cross to the south side of the road.

Location 3 | **THE CITADEL**

The Mall

This plain, creeper-covered structure was erected during the Second World War to provide storage space for the government.

Return to the north side of the road.

Location 4 | **CARLTON HOUSE TERRACE** *Nash 1832*

Carlton House Terrace occupies part of the site of the Prince Regent's mansion, Carlton House, which was demolished in 1829. Similar terraces, proposed for the south side of St James's Park, were never built.

Ascend the steps R that bisect the terrace.

Location 5 | **DUKE OF YORK MONUMENT** *1834*

Waterloo Place

Frederick, 'The Grand Old Duke of York' of the nursery song, was the second son of George III. He had been an unsuccessful C-in-C of the army and was later ignominiously accused, together with his mistress, of selling army commissions. However, they were both acquitted. One day's pay was unpopularly deducted from army personnel to meet the cost of the monument.

The statue by *Westmacott* stands on a 124-foot high column *B. D. Wyatt.* Such a great height was necessary, it was cynically alleged, so that the Duke could escape his creditors.

Pass through the gate L of the column and turn immediately L. In front of the tree is a tombstone.

Location 6 | **GIRO TOMBSTONE**

Carlton House Terrace

This is London's only Nazi monument and relates to the German Embassy that occupied Nos 7–9 Carlton House Terrace before the Second World War. Beneath the stone, Hitler's ambassador, Leopold von Hoesch, predecessor of von Ribbentrop, buried his dog Giro in 1934.

Proceed northward to Waterloo Place.

In the centre of the road is an equestrian statue of Edward VII by *MacKennal* 1922.

Proceed to the Athenaeum Club on the corner L.

Location 7

ATHENAEUM CLUB *D. Burton 1830*

Waterloo Place

The Athenaeum is one of London's most elegant gentlemen's clubs and occupies part of the site of the Prince Regent's Carlton House. Its upper storey was added in 1899. Above the porch, the gilded statue by *Baily* represents Pallas Athena.

Although the Athenaeum is only open to members, the hall with its original light fittings may be seen.

Exit L and cross the road to the Institute of Directors. Turn L.

Location 8

INSTITUTE OF DIRECTORS *Nash 1828*

116–119 Pall Mall

Open by appointment only. Admission free.

The United Service Club that commissioned the building, had been founded in 1815 for British officers from the Napoleonic wars and this was the first building in London to be designed as a club.

Originally, only No 116 was built, but when the adjoining No 117 was acquired in 1858 the two buildings were linked. *Decimus Burton*, the architect who carried out the new work, had previously designed the Athenaeum Club opposite. He remodelled the exterior, adding the frieze, cornice and balustrade and removing columns from the Waterloo Place frontage. Nos 118 and 119 were acquired in 1912, and the United Service Club occupied the entire premises until 1974.

First R Pall Mall. Enter the building and request permission to view the ground floor public areas.

In the **Forum Restaurant**, a plaque records the 'Norwegian Corner' where King Haakon of Norway and his officers met in exile during the Second World War.

The 15–foot high chandelier, above the stairwell, was presented by George IV to commemorate the Battle of Waterloo.

Exit L and proceed along Pall Mall to the Travellers Club (adjoining the Athenaeum).

Location 9

PALL MALL

Pall Mall, together with St James's Street at its west end, accommodates the majority of London's gentlemen's clubs. It was named after the French game paille maille, a 17C version of croquet, first played in London along a tree-lined avenue on the north side of Pall Mall.

Pall Mall became, in 1807, London's first gas-lit street.

Continue ahead.

Location 10

TRAVELLERS CLUB *C. Barry 1832*

106 Pall Mall

The Travellers Club, built in Italian Renaissance style, was founded by Lord Castlereagh in 1814 to encourage renewed European contacts following the Napoleonic wars. Members still only need to prove having travelled five hundred miles from London – once considered a great distance.

Proceed to the next building.

Location 11 | **REFORM CLUB** *C. Barry 1841*

104 Pall Mall

The Reform Club was established by the Whig party at the time of the Reform Bill of 1832. Its name has been immortalized by the dish Lamb Cutlets Reform, which was invented by the club's 19C chef Alexis Soyer and is still served in the restaurant.

It can be seen that the building, although more ambitious, is similar in style to the same architect's adjoining Travellers Club.

Continue ahead. First L Carlton Gardens. First R Carlton House Terrace which leads again to Carlton Gardens. Proceed to the corner building L.

Location 12 | **CARLTON GARDENS**

No 4 was occupied by the Free French during the Second World War. A wall plaque records General de Gaulle's message to his countrymen.

Turn L.

At the west end of Carlton Gardens a bronze statue of **Charles de Gaulle** was erected in 1994.

The monument to **George VI** by *Macmillan* 1955 overlooks the Mall.

Descend the steps. Cross The Mall to St James's Park. Continue ahead across the grass to the lake.

Location 13 | **ST JAMES'S PARK**

This is London's oldest royal park and, although small, is judged to be its most attractive. St James's Park was created by Henry VIII *c.*1532 when he seized the land from Westminster Abbey. A Russian ambassador presented Charles II with pelicans for the royal menagerie, established here by James I, and pelicans have been amongst the exotic wildfowl ever since. In the 17C, Charles II ranged a series of aviaries along an avenue on the south side. To commemorate this, the road that took its place was named Birdcage Walk. It was also this monarch who, at the Restoration, gave the public access to the grounds of a royal palace for the first time. From the 17C to the mid 19C St James's Park was the main London venue for licensed milk sellers, accompanied by their cows.

The present picturesque layout, with its serpentine lake that replaced the formal canal, is by *Nash* 1828. Refreshments are available at the east end. No swimming or boating is allowed.

Follow the lakeside path R and turn L at the bridge. Proceed to the centre.

The views towards both Whitehall and Buckingham Palace from the centre of the lake's modern bridge are some of London's most romantic.

Return across the bridge and proceed ahead to the exit gate. Cross the Mall to Marlborough Rd ahead. First L Friary Court, St James's Palace.

Location 14 | **ST JAMES'S PALACE**

The palace, commissioned by Henry VIII as a manor house for Anne Boleyn, was built by *Molton c.*1532. St James's Leper Hospital for Women had previously occupied the site and its name was adopted for the palace. After the fire at Whitehall Palace in 1698 the Court was relocated here and St James's remained the sovereign's premier London residence until Queen Victoria occupied the remodelled Buckingham Palace on her accession in 1837. However, St James's is still the statutory seat of the Court and ambassadors are accredited to it.

Some Tudor work remains, denoted by small red bricks, but the palace has been extensively rebuilt at various periods. The complex, which is built around four courts: Friary, Ambassadors, Engine and Colour, now provides official residences and 'grace and favour' homes. Locations 15, 16, 17, and 19 are within the palace.

Location 15

FRIARY COURT, ST JAMES'S PALACE

Changing of the guard daily, 11.00. At other times the courtyard may be entered.

From the balcony in this courtyard, which is partly Tudor, every new sovereign is officially proclaimed. Friary Court was once much larger and enclosed by an east range which included a chapel built for Queen Anne. This range was destroyed by fire in 1809.

Exit from Friary Court L.

Alternatively, if the State Apartments are open, proceed to the north-east corner.

Location 16

STATE APARTMENTS, ST JAMES'S PALACE

The State Apartments may only be entered on special occasions, usually when royal gifts are displayed. There are always long queues.

The castellated range housing most of these apartments was built on the south side of the palace for Queen Anne by *Wren* (?) in the early 18C and links with Clarence House.

Enter by the door in the north-east corner of Friary Court.

The stairway by *Wren* (?) leads to the **Armoury** and **Tapestry Rooms**, Tudor apartments which retain their original fireplaces but were redecorated by *William Morris* in 1867. In the latter, the cyphers of Henry VIII and Anne Boleyn are seen above the fireplace. The 17C tapestries were woven for Charles II. The doorcases in the other rooms are the 18C work of *Kent* but the interiors are mainly 19C.

The **Throne Room** overmantel was carved by *Gibbons*.

It is believed that Charles I spent his last night before execution in the Tudor **Guard Room**.

Exit to Friary Court. L Marlborough Road. Cross the road.

Location 17

THE QUEEN'S CHAPEL AT ST JAMES'S
Inigo Jones 1627

Marlborough Road

Open for services from Easter Day until the end of July, Sunday 10.45 (service at 11.15). Alternatively, the chapel interior is included in the Marlborough House tour (location 18).

This was the first ecclesiastical building in England to be designed in the Classical style. The Queen's Chapel belongs to the Chapel Royal which is not a building but an establishment, founded in Saxon times to serve the spiritual needs of the sovereign. The Chapel Royal is regarded as the cradle of English church music, and its organists have included the composers Tallis, Byrd and Purcell.

Inigo Jones designed the Queen's Chapel in Palladian style for Roman Catholic worship by the Spanish Infanta, the intended bride of the future Charles I. Although Charles eventually married Henrietta

Maria instead, she was also a Catholic and this became her chapel.

Enter from Marlborough Rd for Sunday services or from the side door, with guide, when part of the Marlborough House tour.

The coffered ceiling and communion rail are original. The west gallery is also original and served as the Royal Pew. It cannot be visited, but the chimney piece by *Inigo Jones* can be partially seen. His Venetian window is believed to be the earliest example of its type in England.

The chapel was remodelled for Charles II's consort, Catherine of Braganza, by *Wren* in 1661. His work included the panelling, stalls, lectern and reredos carved by *Gibbons*. The reredos was altered in 1938 to incorporate the painting by *Carraci*.

Exit R. First R Pall Mall. Enter the Marlborough House courtyard first R.

Alternatively, if the chapel has been seen as part of the Marlborough House tour, proceed to Pall Mall L. Cross the road. First R Crown Passage (location 19).

Location 18

MARLBOROUGH HOUSE *Wren c. 1710*

Pall Mall

Marlborough House was built for Queen Anne's Mistress of the Bedchamber, Sarah, Duchess of Marlborough, wife of the first Duke. The Duchess had a capacity for making enemies in high places and eventually fell out with both Queen Anne and Prime Minister Robert Walpole. Walpole denied Sarah a frontage to her new house from Pall Mall by acquiring the land between; the present insignificant entranceway was only obtained after bitter negotiations. The Crown acquired the property in 1817. Edward VII lived here whilst Prince of Wales, George V was born in the house, and Queen Mary, his consort, was the last royal occupant.

Wren's original building was two storeys high and appeared very different from today. The upper storeys, porch, balustrade and north range were added by *Pennethorne* in 1863.

The interior is no longer open to the public, as the building is occupied by the Commonwealth Secretariat

Return to Pall Mall. Cross the road and proceed ahead to Crown Passage.

Location 19

CROWN PASSAGE

This passage includes several refreshment establishments, rare in the immediate vicinity of the royal palaces.

Return to Pall Mall R. Cross the road.

Location 20

GATEHOUSE, ST JAMES'S PALACE

Pall Mall

This original Tudor gatehouse is the main entrance to the palace but the public may no longer pass through. Immediately R, the windows with Tudor stone mullions belong to the Chapel Royal (location 22).

•• *Continue along Cleveland Row. First L Stable Yard.*

The arcade R was designed by *Hawksmoor* but recently rebuilt.

•• *Proceed to Lancaster House on the south side of the yard.*

Location 21

Stable Yard

LANCASTER HOUSE *c. 1833*

Lancaster House possesses some of the most sumptuous interiors in London. It was commissioned by Frederick, Duke of York in 1820. However, George IV disliked the designs of the architect *R. Smirke* and he was replaced by *B. D. Wyatt* in 1825. After the death of the Duke of York, the building, known as York House, was purchased by the Marquess of Stafford and eventually became a centre for fashionable gatherings. Queen Victoria reputedly told its new owner, the Duchess of Sutherland, 'I have come from my house (Buckingham Palace) to your palace.' (?)

The exterior is of Bath stone.

The interior is not open to the public.

•• *Proceed ahead through Ambassadors Court (only permitted if attending a service at the Chapel Royal, which lies in the north-east corner).*

•• *Alternatively, first R Stable Yard Rd.*

Location 22

Ambassadors Court

Open for services only, from October to Good Friday, Sunday 10.45 (Service at 11.15)

THE CHAPEL ROYAL, ST JAMES'S PALACE

The chapel was built for Henry VIII c. 1532 and most of its fabric is original. Internally, however, the ceiling (part) is the only feature to survive from the Tudor period. Charles I, while briefly imprisoned in the palace, took Holy Communion here on the morning of his execution 30 January 1649. Queen Victoria married Prince Albert in the Chapel Royal in 1840 and the future George V married Princess Mary of Teck here in 1893.

The chapel was extended by *R. Smirke* 1836 and most of the interior is his work. The ceiling is of greatest interest. Its main section to the east by *Holbein* (?) is in the Italian Renaissance style and decorated with cyphers commemorating Henry VIII's short marriage to Anne of Cleves. One panel, however, incorporates the arms of Katherine Howard, Anne's successor and Henry's fifth wife, who was soon to be executed. The smaller west section of the ceiling was designed in the 19C to match the style of the existing Tudor work. It is decorated with the cyphers of William IV and Adelaide.

•• *Exit from Ambassadors Court L.*

Location 23

Stable Yard Road

Clarence House became the residence of Queen Elizabeth The Queen Mother in 1952 and is never open to the public.

CLARENCE HOUSE *Nash 1827*

The painted, stuccoed house was built for the Duke of Clarence who continued to live here when he became William IV, as the remodelling of Buckingham Palace had not been completed.

The top storey was added in 1873 and at the same time, to give greater privacy, the entrance to the house was moved from the west side beneath the balcony, to the south where a new porch was built.

Proceed ahead through the gates to the Mall R. Continue to the Queen Victoria Memorial in front of Buckingham Palace. Here, the roundabout is called Queens Gardens.

Location 24

QUEEN VICTORIA MEMORIAL
A. Webb and *Brock (sculptor) 1911*

Queens Gardens

The memorial is part of Webb's scheme that commemorates Queen Victoria.

From the memorial proceed southward to Birdcage Walk and enter the gateway to Wellington Barracks.

Location 25

GUARDS MUSEUM

Wellington Barracks, Birdcage Walk

Open Saturday–Thursday 10.00–16.00. Admission charge.

More than three centuries of the Foot Guards' history is described by displays, uniforms and medals.

Exit and cross to the east facade of Buckingham Palace.

Location 26

BUCKINGHAM PALACE

The Mall
(930 4832)

Changing of the Guard. April to August, daily 11.30 in the forecourt, dependent on weather. September to March, alternate days only. The palace is open to the public annually for most of August and September until 1998, daily 09.30–17.30, but check these times. The Queen's Gallery and the Royal Mews are within the grounds and may be visited throughout the year (locations 27 and 28).

Buckingham Palace is the principal residence of the British sovereign. Although much of the building is early 19C the stonework of the east facade,seen from the Mall, only dates from 1913.

The palace stands near the site of a Jacobean mansion, Goring House, which burnt down and was rebuilt as Arlington House in the late 17C. The estate, to which an old mulberry garden had been added, was acquired by John Sheffield who demolished Arlington House and built a new brick residence. Sheffield had once paid court to Queen Anne and she appointed him first Duke of Buckingham – unrelated to the Villiers dynasty. The mansion then became known as Buckingham House. George III purchased this for Queen Charlotte in 1762 and renamed the building Queen's House.

George IV commissioned *Nash* in 1826 to remodel and extend Buckingham House as 'a simple pied-a-terre'. As work proceeded, the residence became increasingly palatial and budgets were greatly exceeded. Newly built sections were demolished and the project became the most notorious architectural scandal of the time. In 1830 George IV died, Nash was dismissed, and the work was continued by *Blore*. Not until 1837 was the building ready for occupation and Queen Victoria became the first monarch to reside there.

The Marble Arch was erected to provide the triumphal entrance in front of what was then, a huge open courtyard. It remained there from 1833 until 1847 when it was dismantled because the east range, which faces the Mall, was added to the palace by *Blore*. It was not too narrow for the state coach to pass through as is often alleged. The archway was re-erected on its present site in 1851 (itinerary 15).

The east range was refaced with Portland stone by *A. Webb* in 1913 and this facade, which incorporates the famous balcony, now provides the best known view of the palace. The Royal Standard flies when the monarch is in residence.

•● *Proceed R to the north-east corner.*

Facing the forecourt can be seen the Bath stone garden screen with the royal coat of arms by *Nash*.

The Royal Family's private apartments are in the north range overlooking Green Park.

The west range to the rear by *Nash* is hidden from public view by the later buildings but, when the trees in the palace gardens are bare, its west facade, built in Bath stone, can be glimpsed from tops of buses passing down Grosvenor Place. The State Apartments are on the first floor and some of Nash's interiors (1828–30) remain.

•● *Visitors to the State Apartments proceed to the kiosk in St James's Park, which faces the Mall – queues can be long. Admission is from the the Ambassador's Entrance on the Buckingham Gate side of the complex.*

On entering the **Quadrangle**, note that the range right by *Blore*, is faced, as originally, with Caen stone, never having been remodelled in Portland stone as was its balcony facade, on the east side.

Immediately right of the palace entrance, the **Grand hall** survives structurally from the original Buckingham House.

Artistically, the most important of the ten portraits which line the **Grand Staircase**, is William IV, by *Lawrence*.

Those expecting to discover a wealth of Georgian and Regency furniture within the State Apartments will be surprised to discover that most specimens are French, from the 18C and early 19C. It was probably felt that the more exotic French designs, with emphasis on inlay, veneers and ormolu, would blend more easily with the rich mouldings and gilded surfaces of the apartments than their more restrained English equivalents.

At the top of the stairs, the **Guard Room** leads to the **Green Drawing Room**, where guests to Investitures and State Banquets assemble. On display is a mid-18C vase of Sèvres porcelain, which belonged to Madame de Pompadour, mistress of Louis XV.

Thrones on the dais in the **Throne Room** were made for use of Elizabeth II and Prince Philip during the coronation ceremony at Westminster Abbey in 1953 and are still occupied by them on certain formal occasions.

The **Picture Gallery**, like the Grand Staircase and the rooms already seen, was designed by *Nash*, but its original heavy doorcases and Neo-Gothic ceiling were simplified in 1914 in order to increase the natural lighting. The most important paintings in the palace are displayed here and include:
East wall left, up to central door. 'Tavern Interior', *Jan Steen*. 'The Passage Boat', *Cuyp*. 'Christ and Mary Magdalene at the Tomb', *Rembrandt*. 'Portrait of a Man', *Hals*. 'The Shipbuilder and his Wife', *Rembrandt*. 'Agatha Bas', *Rembrandt*.

West wall right, up to central door. 'Assumption of the Virgin', *Rubens*. 'The Mystic Marriage of St Catherine', *Van Dyck*. 'Courtyard at Delft', *Pieter* *de Hooch*. 'Yacht under Sail', *Willem van de Velde*.

East wall left, beyond central door. 'Charles I and Henrietta Maria with two of their children'. *Van Dyck*. Landscape with St George and the Dragon', *Rubens*. 'Rape of Europa', *Lorrain*.
West wall right, beyond central door. 'Charles I with M. de St Antoine', *Van Dyck*. 'Landscape with a Negro Page', *Cuyp*.

The **Silk Tapestry Room** was created in the mid 19C to link the **Picture Gallery** with the **East Gellery**, which was remodelled at the same time to connect with the new **Ballroom**, added by *Pennethorne* in 1859 (not open to visitors), and where State Banquets are now held.

A short **Cross Gallery** leads to Pennethorne's **West Gallery** of 1853, constructed to link the Ballroom with the **State Dining Room** designed by *Nash*, and now used for less formal banquets. Originally serving as a Music Room, this was completed by *Blore c*. 1845.

The next three rooms, all designed by *Nash*, comprise the **Blue Dining Room**, with a porcelain table made for Napoleon, the **Music Room**, used for royal christenings in recent years, and the White Dining Room, where members of the royal family assemble prior to state occasions.

Visitors descend the **Ministers' Staircase**, built by *Blore c*. 1853, to the **Marble Hall** and **Bow Room**, which is the main feature of *Nash*'s garden front.

From the terrace, follow the south path of the garden to the **Souvenir Shop** and the Grosvenor Gate exit.

Return to the east front of Buckingham Palace and proceed northward to Green Park.

Alternatively, proceed to location 27 as indicated.

Location 27

GREEN PARK

This, alone of central London's royal parks, possesses no lake. It was added to St James's Park by Charles II in 1667 who regularly walked through it in the early morning from St James's Palace along a pathway. To commemorate this, the road which replaced the path and runs immediately north of the palace grounds, was named Constitution Hill.

Return to Buckingham Palace and continue southward following its east facade. First R Buckingham Gate. Follow the south facade of the palace. Proceed to the end of the railings where a sign R indicates the Queen's Gallery.

Location 28

THE QUEEN'S GALLERY *Nash c.1830*

Buckingham Gate

Open Tuesday–Saturday 10.00–17.00. Sunday 14.00–17.00. Admission charge.

This gallery was built as a conservatory, but heightened and converted to a chapel in 1893. The building was again remodelled to provide an art gallery in 1963. Paintings from the vast royal collection are displayed and periodically changed.

Exit R and follow the palace wall to the last entrance R. A sign indicates the Royal Mews.

Location 29

THE ROYAL MEWS *Nash 1825*

Buckingham Palace Road (930 4832)

Open Wednesday and Thursday 14.00–16.00. Closed in June during Ascot week. Admission charge.

The buildings form a quadrangle and were constructed before conversion work began on Buckingham House itself. Royal processional horses are stabled here and the coaches on display include the Queen's State Coach made in 1761. Saddlery and harnesses are also on view.

Exit R. First L Bressenden Place. Continue to the end. L Victoria St. Proceed first R to the piazza that faces Westminster Cathedral.

Location 30

WESTMINSTER CATHEDRAL *Bentley 1903*

Victoria Street

Open daily 07.00–20.00. Closes at 19.00 Monday–Friday in winter. A lift to the top of the tower operates daily, Easter to September 09.00–17.00 or dusk. From October–March weekends only (charge for the lift).

This is England's principal Roman Catholic cathedral and is the seat of the Archbishop of Westminster.

Westminster Cathedral was designed in Byzantine style, partly to avoid comparison with the Gothic Westminster Abbey nearby. Its campanile is reminiscent of Siena Cathedral in Italy.

Enter from the north side.

The internal wall linings of marble, gradually being extended as funds permit, are judged to be the finest examples in London. Westminster Cathedral's nave is the widest of any church in England. Reliefs at the Stations of the Cross were designed by *Gill* in 1918.

Exit and return to Victoria St R. Second L Buckingham Gate. First R Caxton St.

Location 31

BLEWCOAT SCHOOL *1709*

23 Caxton Street

Open Monday-Friday 10.00–17.30. Thursday closes at 19.00. Admission free.

The school, which now accommodates the National Trust shop, is not connected with the famous Christ's Hospital Bluecoat School. It was founded nearby in 1688, and transferred to the present site in 1709 when the building was completed. The school remained in use by infants until 1926. Above the door is an 18C statue of a Blewcoat Boy. On the south facade, the painting of a Blewcoat Boy was renewed in 1979.

Enter the building.

Internally, the school consisted of one panelled room with a basement below. The 18C chandelier came from Bruerne Abbey and was hung in 1974.

Exit R. First L Palmer St. First R Petty France. First L Queen Anne's Gate.

Location 32

QUEEN ANNE'S GATE

The central section of this quiet street is judged a fine example in London of early 18C domestic architecture. Queen Anne's Gate was laid out in an 'L' shape in 1704 and first named Queen Square.

Proceed ahead to the bend in the road R.

Here can be seen the earlier houses, with No 17, in the corner, least altered. All were originally built three storeys high with steep-pitched roofs.

Proceed ahead.

The statue of Queen Anne by *Bird* (?) 1705 stands outside No 15. Originally, a low wall ran across the road from here, thus creating a self-contained close. The statue stood against its centre, facing west, and is recorded as being in position by 1708. Assertions that it was made for the portico of St Mary-le-Strand would, therefore, seem to be untrue as St Mary's was not begun until 1714.

A separate close on the other side of the wall was laid out in 1773 and named Park Street, but the wall was demolished in 1873 and the thoroughfares united.

Proceed ahead to Lewisham St. R Storeys Gate. L The Sanctuary. Cross the road to Westminster Abbey (itinerary 6). If not viewing the abbey, proceed ahead to Parliament Square. Second L St Margaret St. First R Bridge St and Westminster Station, Circle and District lines.

6

Westminster Abbey and its Precinct

The medieval Westminster Abbey may well be considered England's most important building. It is both the coronation church and a royal mausoleum. Together with its Precinct, Westminster Abbey forms a monastic survival that is unique in Britain.

Binoculars are invaluable as much of the fine detailing within the abbey is at a high level.

Timing: Any weekday is suitable but allow half a day to explore thoroughly. On Sunday the chapels are closed. A return visit on a Wednesday evening is recommended when entry to the chapels is free, they are lit and only then can they be photographed. The Chapter Library is open on Wednesday afternoons in summer.
The College Garden and all of Little Cloister are open every Tuesday and Thursday (except Maundy Thursday).

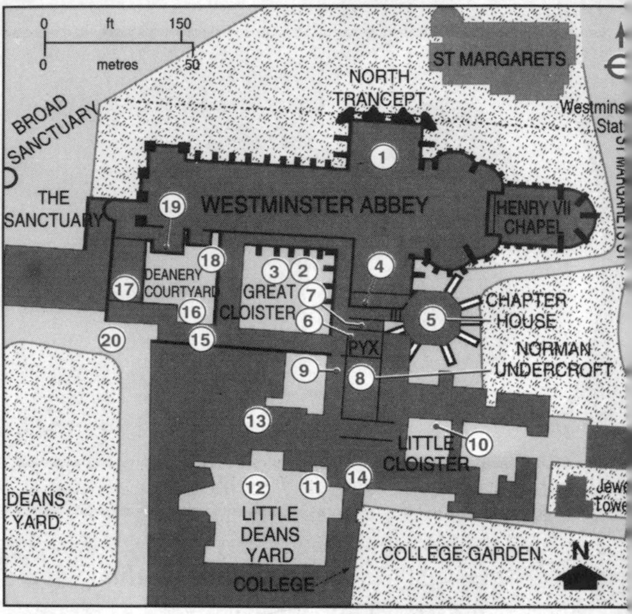

Locations
1 Westminster Abbey
2 Precinct
3 Great Cloister
4 Chapter House Vestibule
5 Chapter House
6 Pyx Chamber
7 Chapter Library
8 Abbey Museum
9 Dark Cloister
10 Little Cloister and College Garden
11 Westminster School
12 Little Deans Yard
13 Ashburnham House
14 Great Hall of Westminster School
15 Parlour
16 Deanery Courtyard
17 College Hall
18 The Deanery
19 Jericho Parlour/Jerusalem Chamber
20 Deans Yard

Start *Westminster Station, Circle and District lines. Leave by the subway L which leads to the exit indicated for Westminster Abbey. Ahead Bridge St. First L Parliament Square. Follow the west facade of the Houses of Parliament (itinerary 7) to St Margaret St. Cross the road at the pedestrian crossing. Proceed L passing the east end of St Margaret's. Continue to the Henry VII Chapel R which protrudes from the east end of the abbey.*

Alternatively, continue from itinerary 5 or 7.

Location 1 — **WESTMINSTER ABBEY***

222 7110

A Benedictine monastery at Westminster is first recorded *c.*970 although by tradition the abbey was founded in the 7C (?). The devout Anglo-Saxon king, Edward the Confessor, who was half-Norman, rebuilt much of the abbey, including a completely new church, in the Norman style. Its completion just pre-dated the Conquest. The new abbey church was consecrated in 1066 but within a few days Edward died and became the first English king to be buried at Westminster. On Christmas Day, 1066, William I 'The Conqueror' was crowned in the same church, predecessor of the present building. This was the first coronation ceremony to be held at Westminster.

The nave, aisles and Precinct are open daily 08.00–18.00 (Wednesday until 20.00). Admission free.

The ambulatory, transepts and chapels are open Monday to Friday 09.20–16.45, Saturday 09.20–14.45 and 15.45–17.45. Admission charge. They are also open Wednesday 18.00–19.45 when admission is free (only then is photography of the chapels allowed). NB last admission is 45 minutes before closing time.

Super Tours: *Guided 1½ hours (25 people maximum). April to October, Monday to Friday 10.00; 10.30; 11.00; 14.00; 14.30; 15.00 (not Friday), Saturday 10.00, 11.00; 12.30. November to March, Monday to Friday: 10.00; 11.00; 14.00; 15.00 (not Friday), Saturday 10.00; 11.00; 12.30 (subject to demand and Westminster Abbey being open to visitors). Admission charge. Bookings: at the reception desk in the south aisle of the nave or reserve by telephone or by letter to Super-Tours, 20 Deans Yard, London London SW1P 3PA. The tour includes the chapels and, when possible, the Jericho Parlour and Jerusalem Chamber – both can only be entered on a Super-Tour.*

The building history of the present church began in 1245 when it was commissioned by Henry III to house a magnificent new shrine for Edward the Confessor, canonized in 1161.

Westminster Abbey was one of the great monasteries dissolved by Henry VIII in 1540. The church then became a cathedral, but in 1556 the Catholic Mary I revived the monastery and its status was briefly restored. The next monarch, Elizabeth I, again dissolved the monastery, and decreed in 1560 that its church should be known as the Collegiate Church of St Peter in Westminster, still the official name.

The dean is directly responsible to the sovereign, and Westminster Abbey is, therefore, a 'royal peculiar'. Every monarch is crowned here and most kings and queens of England are buried here.

Henry VII Chapel *Vertue brothers* (?) 1512. This long chapel, with its polygonal apse, protrudes at the east end of the abbey and replaced a Lady Chapel that Henry III had added in 1220 before starting the rebuilding of the 'Norman' church. The outward appearance of the chapel has been little altered.

Continue ahead. First R enter the gate and follow the path. (The 'No Entry' sign refers to the church not the grounds.) Immediately behind the Henry VII Chapel is the apse of the church.

Apse *Henry of Reyns* (?) c.1252. Work on Henry III's abbey began here. Westminster Abbey is similar in appearance to contemporary French examples at Amiens and Rheims and was probably designed by the King's master mason, Henry of Reyns (from Rheims ?). After his death this was continued by John of Gloucester and Robert of Beverley. The style adopted is now known as Early English Gothic. Reigate stone was quarried as the base material and the more malleable Caen stone imported from Normandy for windows and doorways. The 'Norman' building was demolished as work proceeded westward. Two apsidal chapels, **St Nicholas's** and **St Edmund's**, protrude on this side.

Continue ahead to the door in the east wall of the south transept (no extrance).

South transept *Henry of Reyns* (?) c.1252. The doorway was reputedly the sovereign's private entrance.

A plaque R of the door commemorates England's first printing press that was set up next to the Chapter House by Caxton in 1476.

The Chapter House L lies south of the transept.

Chapter House *Henry of Reyns* (?) c.1252. This octagonal building replaced the monks' earlier chapter house (meeting place). It was built at the same time as the chancel and transepts. The roof, which was originally flat, was rebuilt in the 19C.

The grassed area east of the Chapter House was the monks' burial ground and once much larger.

Return towards St Margaret's Church. Pass through the first gate L and proceed along the path that runs between Westminster Abbey and St Margaret's.

Passed on this side are the apsidal chapels of **St Paul** and **St John the Baptist**.

North transept *John of Gloucester c.*1258. This provides the most important facade of Westminster Abbey but practically all detailing is the 19C work of *George Gilbert Scott* and *J. L. Pearson*. Wren had already remodelled this transept in the 18C but is believed to have kept the tracery pattern of the 13C rose window. Scott redesigned it completely.

In the vaulted roof of the third porch is a 13C boss, all that remains of the transept's original carving.

Crossing. It is believed it was originally intended to erect a tower above the crossing and in the 18C Wren produced a model for a tower and spire; they were never built.

Nave (east section) *Robert of Beverley c.*1269 (**west section**) *Yevele* 14C. Only the first bay of the nave was completed before Robert of Beverley's appointment. At the fifth bay from the east there is a change in the design of the window tracery. This is where building work stopped *c.*1269 until 1375 when, surprisingly, the new master mason, *Yevele*, continued in the Early English, instead of the then fashionable Perpendicular, style. Most of the church, therefore, appears to have been built during one period.

All the statues were added in the 19C.

Continue towards the west front.

West front *Yevele* 14C and *Hawksmoor* 1745. Yevele did adopt the Perpendicular style for this facade but his twin towers ended at parapet level.

The parapet was added and the towers completed by *Hawksmoor* 1745.

Jerusalem Chamber 14C. This castellated stone building, immediately behind the 19C Abbey Book Shop, forms part of the Dean's Lodgings.

Enter the abbey by the west door.

In medieval times, the abbey's walls were painted white, with red lines and rosettes, the carvings were brightly decorated and the windows filled with vivid stained glass. There were few monuments. Now only traces of the decoration remain and most of the medieval stained glass has been replaced. The Purbeck marble piers, however, are unchanged. Monuments have proliferated since the 16C, particularly in the aisles, which now resemble sculpture galleries. As in St Paul's Cathedral, there are some post–17C monuments to those buried elsewhere, but unlike St Paul's, the church has no crypt (except for a low, vaulted area beneath the Henry VII Chapel) and the dead are buried in tomb chests or beneath the floor.

Only selected monuments are described here, based on artistic value or the importance of the person commemorated. Visitors may neither descend nor ascend to any part of the church.

The **nave** is the highest (103 feet) in an English church. An open gallery runs above the aisles in the English style rather than a triforium (blind arcaded passage) as the French, by that time, preferred.

Immediately R, against the second pier, is a painting of Richard II *c.*1390. It is the first known contemporary painting of an English monarch.

Proceed L to the centre of the nave.

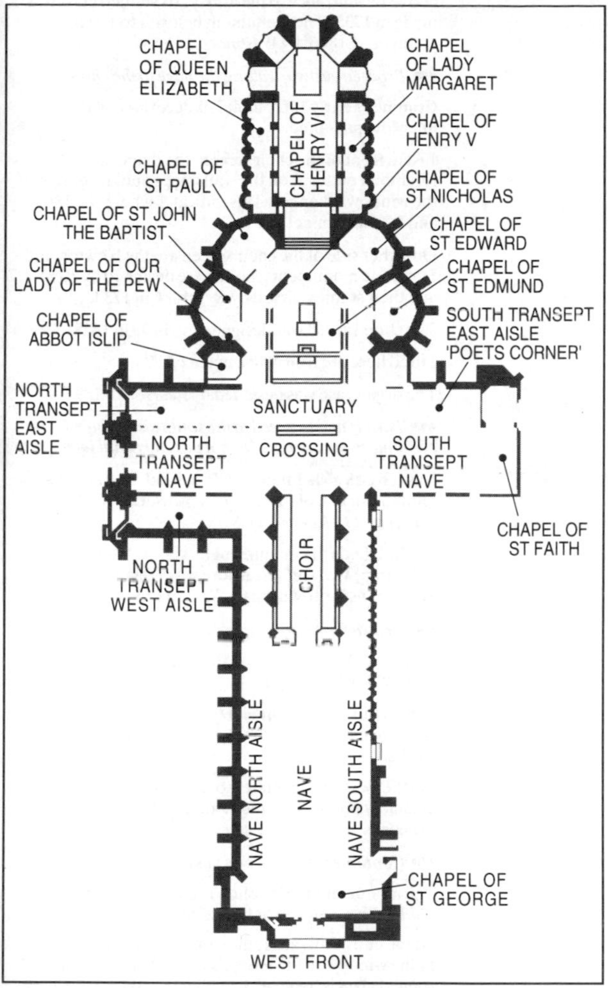

Churchill's green marble commemorative tablet is on the floor immediately facing the entrance. He is buried at Bladon, Oxfordshire.

Beyond, the black marble floor stone marks the grave of the 'Unknown Warrior'. His anonymous body was brought from France in 1920 to represent all British servicemen killed in the First World War.

Behind this, a beige floor tablet denotes where George Peabody, the philanthropist, was buried in 1869. He is the only American citizen to have been interred in the abbey but now lies in Massachusetts.

Proceed to the pier immediately north of the Unknown Warrior's grave.

The Congressional Medal of Honour attached to this pier was posthumously awarded to the Unknown Warrior by the United States Congress in 1921.

From here can be seen the renewed west window

above the entrance to the abbey. Its stained glass was made in 1735. The monument below is to Pitt the younger, d.1806, by *Westmacott*.

•➨ *Proceed eastward along the nave to the choir.*

Cranmer's early 16C pulpit L is decorated with linenfold panelling.

Just in front of the choir screen, the diapering (diamond pattern) on the walls stops and the design of the windows changes. This indicates where the 13C and 14C walls meet.

On either side of the choir screen are the Newton and Stanhope monuments; both were designed by *Kent* and their statues carved by *Rysbrack* in 1733.

The choir screen was designed by *Blore* in 1828.

Fitted here are iron gates, made *c.*1725.

The organ case was designed by *Pearson* in 1897.

•➨ *Turn R and proceed to the south aisle. Turn L and continue to the barrier. Do not pass this until later.*

Nave, south aisle Immediately behind the barrier is the monument to Colonel Roger Townshend by *Adam, Carter and Eckstein c.*1759.

Behind this is the monument to Major André by *Adam* and *Van Gelder*. André was executed by the Americans for spying in the War of Independence.

•➨ *Return westward.*

Just west of the barrier, on the south wall, is the bust of Sidney, Earl Godolphin by *Bird* 1712.

Above this, the monument to General Hargrave by *Roubiliac* 1757 is one of the sculptor's most famous works.

Further west, immediately before the Super Tour assembly point, is the monument to Dean Joseph Wilcocks, d.1756 by *Cheere*.

•➨ *Continue westward and pass the next door L.*

The monument to Dr John Freind was designed by *Gibbs*. The sculpture is by *Rysbrack*.

At the end of this aisle, the stone screen is early 16C. In the window of St George's Chapel behind, the 15C stained glass is believed to depict the Black Prince as St George (?).

The memorial tablet to President Franklin Roosevelt is on the west wall L of the abbey's west door.

Immediately R is the monument to Thomas Hardy, d.1732, by *Cheere*.

•➨ *Cross to the north aisle. Turn R and proceed to the second bay.*

Nave, north aisle The monument by *Westmacott* 1815 between the first pillar and the north wall commemorates Charles Fox.

Stained glass in the west window, depicting a large figure, is 14C.

•➨ *Proceed eastward.*

The small wall plaque touching the floor in the fourth bay commemorates the playwright Ben Jonson and includes a famous mis-spelling 'O rare Ben Johnson'. In the next bay is the oldest monument in the nave,

Mrs Jane Hill (née Stotevill), d.1631. Above her effigy are a shrouded skeleton and the tree of life.

From the north aisle barrier proceed ahead towards the north transept.

Alternatively, and preferably when possible, proceed through the choir from the south aisle barrier.

The choir stalls, like the screen, were designed by *Blore* in 1828.

At the east end of the choir, turn L and L again to the north aisle of the nave.

Nave, north aisle On the north wall, immediately west of the north transept, is the monument to Philip de Sausmarez by *Cheere* 1747.

Proceed to the north transept.

North transept, west aisle. The Elizabeth Warren monument by *Westmacott* 1816, against the second pier R, depicts a beggar girl holding her baby.

In the roof of the aisle are exceptional 13C bosses.

North transept, nave. Although the rose window tracery is the 19C work of *Scott* and *Pearson*, the 18C stained glass by *Thornhill* was retained but had to be cut to fit which is why the figures have no feet.

Below the rose window, in the corners on either side (spandrels), are two 13C angels.

R of the door is the Newcastle monument. The statue is by *Bird* and the frame by *Gibbs* 1723.

Numerous monuments to prime ministers stand here. They are all 19C apart from Pitt the Elder.

Proceed to the crossing.

Sanctuary (Presbytery). For coronations, the chair is brought here from Edward the Confessor's Chapel and placed in front of the high altar. The abbey's close connection with the Crown as both coronation church and royal mausoleum was the chief reason why it was spared by Henry VIII.

The Sanctuary's floor is of 13C Roman Cosmati mosaic.

The gilded pulpit is basically early 17C but its pedestal and sounding board were added in 1935.

Three ancient tomb chests stand in line on the north side as follows: Aveline, d.1273, Countess of Lancaster and wife of Edmund (Crouchback).

Aymer de Valence, d.1324, Earl of Pembroke and cousin of Edward I.

Edmund (Crouchback), d.1296, Earl of Lancaster and son of Henry II.

The gilded reredos is by *George Gilbert Scott* 1867.

The 14C sedilia (priest's seat) is seen R of the altar. Above the seat are early 14C paintings by *Thomas of Durham* (?).

In front of the 16C tapestry is a 15C Madonna and Child triptych by *Bicci di Lorenzo*, presented to the abbey in 1948.

Anne of Cleves, d.1557, was Henry VIII's fourth wife and is the only one to lie in the abbey. The lower part of her tomb chest remains beneath the triptych.

Henry divorced 'the mare of Flanders' but they remained on good terms. Anne was converted to Catholicism and the approving Mary I decreed that she should be buried in the abbey. (Henry VIII is buried at St George's Chapel, Windsor, in the same grave as Charles I).

The lectern was made in 1949.

Return to the north transept.

North transept, east aisle. This aisle may only be visited by prior arrangement. Its entrance is partly blocked by the monument to General Wolfe of Quebec by *Wilton* 1772.

Behind Wolfe's monument is the tomb of Sir Francis Vere, d. 1609, by *Colt* (?). His armour is laid out on the slab carried by four knights.

The famous Nightingale monument by *Roubiliac* 1761 stands below the first window R. Mr Nightingale is depicted trying to fight death (the skeleton) from his wife.

Exit from the aisle and turn L.

The tomb chests of Aymer de Valence and Edmund (Crouchback) are passed R. Facing Edmund's tomb chest L is the Islip Chapel.

Islip Chapel 16C. Abbot Islip was the last but one abbot at Westminster. His double-punning rebus is carved on the cornice above the door and windows: an eye with a branch or slip of a tree and a man slipping from a tree.

Proceed to the next two chapels that interlink.

Chapels of Our Lady of the Pew and of St John the Baptist. In the Chapel of St John, the monument to Hunsdon, d.1596, is the tallest in the abbey.

Exit L.

Tomb chests of Edward I, Henry III and Eleanor of Castile are passed. These are seen again in Edward the Confessor's Chapel and are described later.

Proceed to **St Paul's Chapel** *opposite Eleanor's tomb chest.*

Immediately L of the entrance is the monument to William Pulteney, Earl of Bath, d.1764, by *Wilton*.

Within the chapel, on the east wall, is the Cottington monument by *Le Sueur* (part) *c.1635*.

On the north wall, the monument by *Stone* 1640 commemorates Dudley Carleton, Viscount Dorchester.

Exit L and ascend the steps ahead. Turn L.

Henry VII Chapel, north aisle (Queen Elizabeth's Chapel). The Henry VII chapel, built in late Perpendicular style 1503–19, is one of England's most highly acclaimed architectural works. It is believed to have been commenced by *Robert Vertue* (?) and completed by his brother *William Vertue* (?). Henry VII commissioned this, the abbey's Lady Chapel, as a memorial to Henry VI, whom he wrongly expected would be canonized. However, when completed, it was dedicated by Henry VIII to his father instead.

There is a central nave and chancel with aisles on both sides. The vaulted ceilings throughout are judged to be amongst the finest in England. Both this aisle and the south aisle, seen later, are fan-vaulted.

The canopied tomb of Elizabeth I by *Colt* 1606 was commissioned by James I. Also buried within is Elizabeth's half-sister and predecessor as Queen, Mary I, d.1558.

Against the end wall, shown in her cradle, is Princess Sophia by *Colt* 1606. She was a daughter of James I and died when three days old.

Next is the monument to another daughter of James I, Princess Mary, d.1607, who lived for two years.

Between them, inset in the wall, is an urn containing the bones of two boys, discovered in the Tower of London in 1674. They are believed to be the remains of Edward V and Richard Duke of York, the young 'princes in the Tower', who disappeared, presumed murdered, in 1483.

Exit and turn L.

Henry VII Chapel, nave and chancel. Immediately L of the door, the marble 15C font was altered in the 17C and a new cover added in 1872.

This part of the chapel was adopted by the Order of the Bath when it was founded by George I in 1725. The ceremony in which Knights Grand Cross of the Order are installed, terminated in 1812 but was revived in 1913 and held nominally every four years. The banners, crests and mantels of many of the knights hang above their stalls.

The wooden stalls were made *c.1520*. Their seats have carved misericords (mercy seats) on which infirm monks could partially rest.

In the nave of the chapel, the groin-vaulted roof is designed to appear as fan-vaulting.

Below the windows and within the apsidal chapels is a unique group of 16C statues of saints. Most of the original hundred survive but are no longer decorated.

The canopied altar by *Tapper* 1935 incorporates two white marble pillars (partly covered by the cloth) which come from the chapel's original altar by *Torrigiani c.*1522. Edward VI, d.1553, is buried here.

On the floor, immediately L, a slab marks the surprisingly undisturbed burial place of Oliver Cromwell's daughter, Elizabeth Claypole, d.1658.

Behind the Gothic grille by *Imber c.*1510 is the tomb of Henry VII, the founder of the chapel, and his wife Elizabeth of York by *Torrigiani* 1518. Torrigiani was an Italian Renaissance sculptor who had studied under Ghirlandaio and in a fight broke the nose of fellow student Michelangelo. James I, d. 1625, was buried later in the same grave.

Opposite, in the chapel on the north side, is the tomb of George Villiers, first Duke of Buckingham by *Le Sueur*. The Duke was assassinated at Portsmouth in 1628. He was James I's favourite and his proximity to the King is unlikely to be a coincidence.

In the next chapel is the monument of another, but unrelated, Duke of Buckingham, John Sheffield, d.1721, by *Plumière, Scheemakers and Delvaux*. It was for this duke that Buckingham House, later to become Buckingham Palace, was first built.

Proceed to the apse.

In front of the **RAF Chapel**, with its Battle of Britain window, is a floor slab that marks the original burial place of Oliver Cromwell, d.1658. At the Restoration, Cromwell's remains were symbolically hanged at Tyburn and reburied in a pit.

Proceed to the second chapel L.

The monument commemorates Ludovic Stuart, Duke of Lennox and Richmond, d.1624, by *Le Sueur*.

Exit from the Henry VII Chapel and cross the modern bridge.

Henry V Chapel. Henry V, d.1422, planned his own two-storey chantry chapel, which was completed in 1450. The King's tomb chest is seen L, just before entering St Edward's Shrine. The body was originally covered with gilt-plated silver and the head was of solid silver but all the precious metal was removed in 1546. The present head of polyester resin was added in 1971.

Proceed ahead and enter St Edward's Chapel.

The gates passed were made in 1431; their iron tracery is the oldest known example in England.

Henry V's French wife, Catherine de Valois, is buried within the altar, which stands in the upper storey of the Henry V Chapel. This can be reached from St Edward's Chapel by narrow stairs, entered on either side of the entrance, but is only open to the public for the annual services that commemorate Henry's death, 31 August, and St Crispin's Day (the battle of Agincourt), 25 October.

Continue ahead.

Edward the Confessor's Chapel (Retrochoir, St Edward's Chapel, Shrine or Feretory). Henry III commissioned the central shrine for Edward the Confessor, the builder of the previous abbey church. Edward had died in 1066 and Henry brought his remains here from the old church in 1269. Originally, the shrine was surmounted by a coffer of gold but this was removed at the Reformation. The 13C base of the shrine is of Purbeck marble and traces of Cosmati mosaic work remain.

Ancient tomb chests within this chapel are passed R as follows: Eleanor of Castile, d.1291, by *Torel*. Eleanor was the wife of Edward I who erected twelve large stone crosses (the Eleanor Crosses) where her coffin rested on its route to Westminster from Hanby near Lincoln where she died.

Elizabeth Tudor, d.1495, daughter of Henry VII.

Henry III, builder of the abbey, d.1272. The gilded bronze effigy is by *Torel* 1291.

Edward I, d.1307. Edward, the first monarch to be crowned in the present church, was 6 feet 2 inches tall and known as 'Longshanks' hence the large tomb.

The **Coronation Chair** was made for Edward I by *Master Walter* in 1300. Since the coronation of Edward II, every English monarch, apart from Edward V, Edward VIII (and Lady Jane Gray), has been crowned seated on this chair. It was specifically designed to incorporate the Stone of Scone, which had served as the Scottish throne since the 9C. This stone, traditionally the original 'Jacob's Pillow' (?), had been captured by Edward I, the 'Hammer of the

Scots', in 1297 and lies beneath the wooden seat. It was stolen from the abbey in 1950 by Scottish nationalists but recovered the following year.

The chair, made of English oak, was originally brightly coloured. Its gilded lions were added, probably in the 16C.

The reredos was carved in 1441. Its frieze depicts scenes from the life of Edward the Confessor.

Further tomb chests are passed as follows: Richard II, d.1399, by *Yevele* and *Lot* (effigies by *Nicholas Booker* and *Godfrey Prest*). The King is buried with his first consort, Anne of Bohemia, d.1394.

Margaret of York, d.1472, daughter of Edward IV.

Edward III, d.1377, by *Yevele.*

Queen Philippa of Hainault, d.1369, by *Hennequin de Liège*. Philippa pleaded with her husband, Edward III, to spare the Burghers of Calais.

Exit from the chapel and cross the bridge to the south aisle of the Henry VII Chapel.

Henry VII Chapel, south aisle (Lady Margaret's Chapel). The fan-vaulted roof matches that in the north aisle.

Three royal tombs are passed: Countess of Lennox, d.1578, grandmother of James I.

Mary Queen of Scots, by *Cornelius Cure*, 1612. Mary was executed at Fotheringay in 1587, by order of Elizabeth 1, and first buried at Peterborough Cathedral. Although cousins, the two Queens never met. Mary's son, James I, brought her remains here and commissioned the tomb. Buried in the same grave is Lady Arabella Stuart, cousin of James I.

Lady Margaret Beaufort, mother of Henry VII, by *Torrigiani*, 1513. This, England's first Renaissance work, is judged to be the finest tomb at Westminster.

Four late-Stuart monarchs, Anne, William III, Mary II and Charles II are buried beneath the altar. Each has several memorial stones but no monuments.

Exit from the chapel and descend the steps. Proceed ahead.

South ambulatory. Below the tomb chest of Philippa of Hainault R, is a painted, late 13C retable (altarpiece). It is damaged but extremely rare.

Enter the **Chapel of St Nicholas** opposite.

Immediately R, within the chapel, is the monument to the Duchess of Northumberland, d.1766, by *Adam* and *Read.*

Exit L and continue westward.

The rear of Edward III's tomb R retains bronzes by *Orchard* (?) depicting six of his children, including the Black Prince. Further examples on the reverse side have disappeared.

Enter the **Chapel of St Edmund** *opposite.*

The three 13C coats of arms in the window are the oldest pieces of stained glass remaining in the church.

The tomb chest R is that of William de Valence, d.1296, half brother of Henry III. This is the only tomb in England decorated with Limoges enamel work.

Exit L and pass the rear of Richard II's tomb.

The tomb beneath the rear of the sedilia R, is believed to be that of Sebert (?), d. 616. By tradition, this East-Saxon king founded Westminster Abbey. A legend claims that the church was consecrated by St Peter.

Proceed ahead to the south transept.

South transept, east aisle, 'Poets' Corner'. The second monument R is to Dr Richard Busby by *Bird* 1703. Busby was a headmaster of Westminster School, famed for his heavy hand with the birch.

Turn L and proceed southward.

Immediately L is Dryden's bust by *Scheemakers* 1731.

Geoffrey Chaucer, d.1400, poet and author of *The Canterbury Tales*, is believed to have been buried in the altar chest on the east wall (?). The monument was erected in its present position in 1556 but is probably of an earlier date (?). Chaucer lived in a house on part of the site of the Henry VII Chapel.

On the floor, in front of Chaucer's tomb, are many stones commemorating famous authors.

The monument on the south wall to Ben Jonson by *Gibbs and Rysbrack c.*1737 repeats the mis-spelling.

On the west wall is the monument to Matthew Prior, d.1721, *Gibbs* and *Rysbrack*.

South transept, nave. Against the second pillar from the north is the bust of painter and poet William Blake by *Epstein* 1957.

In the centre of the floor is Thomas Parr's white burial stone. It is claimed that he lived from 1483 to 1635, i.e. 152 years (?).

On the east wall, the monument to Shakespeare, d.1616, was designed by *Kent* in 1731. The effigy is a copy of the original, carved by *Scheemakers* for actor David Garrick. The 'immortal bard' is buried at Stratford-upon-Avon.

On the south wall are 13C murals with St Thomas and St Christopher; they were discovered in 1936.

The rose window tracery was renewed in the 19C and its stained glass made in 1902.

Below this window are 13C sculptures. In the corners (spandrels) the two censing angels are carved in the slender French style and are judged to be the finest sculptures in the abbey. Between them are damaged statues of St Edward and the Pilgrim.

On the same wall R, the monument to John, Duke of Argyll by *Roubiliac* 1749 is judged to be the sculptor's finest work.

On the west wall is the monument to the composer Handel by *Roubiliac 1761*.

Below this is a memorial plaque to singer Jenny Lind 'The Swedish Nightingale', d.1887.

On the floor are the burial stones of Handel, d.1759, and two writers, Charles Dickens, d.1870, and Rudyard Kipling, d.1936.

At the north end of the west wall, the monument to David Garrick by *Webber* 1797 depicts the actor parting the curtains for his final bow.

Above the west wall, in effect lying on the roof of the

east cloister, is the Muniments Room (not open). This is where the abbey's official records are kept. It is believed to have once been the royal pew. There is a wall painting of Richard II's white hart emblem.

Return to the transept's south wall and enter the central door to **St Faith's Chapel.**

This well-preserved chapel c.1249 originally served as the monks' vestry. The painting of St Faith is believed to be 13C (?).

The carved heads on the stone corbels are original and judged to be the best examples in the abbey. Some 13C floor tiles remain in front of the altar.

Along the west wall, the monks' nocturnal passage leads to what was originally their dormitory but is now the Chapter Library. Its entrance to the south transept is blocked.

Return to the south transept and turn L to the south aisle of the nave.

Nave, south aisle. Facing the door to the cloister is the black marble monument to Sir Thomas Richardson, d.1635, by *Le Sueur*.

Further west, beneath the organ, the monument to Thomas Thynn by *Quellin* illustrates the scene of his assassination in Pall Mall by hired killers in 1682.

Return towards the crossing and exit from the church R to the Precinct beginning at Great Cloister.

The doorway from the abbey to the east cloister is one of the best 13C examples at Westminster.

Location 2

PRECINCT

Although the public were allowed to worship in the abbey church, the other buildings which make up the Precinct, were out of bounds and a surrounding wall protected the monks' privacy. Much of the south section of this wall remains. The establishment of the Benedictine Abbey of St Peter's consisted of an abbot, a prior and approximately fifty monks, plus servants and lay members of the Order. As with the church, extensions, rebuilding and remodelling continued at various periods but much survives. The north side of the Precinct remains mostly church property although the Chapter House and Pyx Chamber have for long been in the possession of the Crown. Many of the buildings further south belong to Westminster School.

Locations 3–20 lie within the Precinct.

Location 3

GREAT CLOISTER

The monks studied, taught and worked in these cloisters which were begun at this north-east corner in the mid 13C, but not completed until the mid-14C.

Proceed ahead.

East cloister (from the church to the Chapter House). The first two bays were built in the 13C but the fragments of medieval stained glass came from various windows in the abbey and were assembled in the present century.

It is believed that the monks' bookcase stood on the bench in the first bay R.

Against the wall opposite, is one of the simplest, but most touching memorials in the abbey, to 'Jane Lister dear childe'.

From the stone bench in the second bay R, the abbot washed the monks' feet every Maundy Thursday.

The change in the design of the cloister that follows denotes 14C work. In the bay of the arcade R, facing the outer vestibule of the Chapter House, is a restored example of intricate Decorated tracery c.1350, rare in London.

•● *Return to the* **north cloister**.

All of this cloister was completed in the 13C. Here, for a fee, brass rubbings may be made.

•● *Proceed westward.*

At the end of the north cloister R, circular indentations in the benches were made in the 14C by novice monks for a game called 'Nine Men's Morris'.

The 14C door R, leads to the south aisle of the nave.

•● *Turn L.*

West cloister was built entirely in the mid-14C, and the vaulted roof is lower. It has been much restored.

Seen from the first bay of the arcade, across the garth (central green) and above the south cloister's roof, is a ruined 14C wall of the refectory. This was the monks' dining hall and, like the Chapter House, provided a venue for the House of Commons.

•● *Proceed ahead.*

On the wall R, at the end of this cloister, are two stone corbels with carved effigies.

The blocked arch between them originally led to the lavatorium where the monks washed their hands prior to dining in the refectory.

•● *Turn L.*

South cloister is also basically mid-14C but again much restored.

The door ahead, now leads to the Song School but was originally the entrance to the refectory.

At the end of this cloister, a black slab on the floor, 'Long Meg', is believed to cover the tomb of twenty-six monks who died from the Black Death in 1349 (?).

Above the arched entrance to Dark Cloister is a stone bracket set in the wall. A lamp once stood on this which the monks lit from the small blocked window.

•● *Turn L.*

East cloister (from Dark Cloister to the Chapter House). The iron gate was made c.1750.

The 14C arcade was restored in 1835.

The two doors passed, lead respectively to the Pyx Chamber (location 6) and the Library (location 7).

•● *Proceed R to the outer vestibule of the Chapter House.*

Location 4

CHAPTER HOUSE VESTIBULE

The outer vestibule was formed in the mid-13C by demolishing half a bay of the undercroft. The old dormitory runs above, which is why the roof is low.

Dilapidated 13C statues of the Virgin and Child, flanked by angels, survive above the entrance.

At the rear of the ticket office is an 11C door, behind which lies the Pyx Chamber. In 1303, with the connivance of some of the monks, Richard Podelicote broke into the Pyx Chamber from here and stole royal treasure. He was captured and executed and, by tradition, his skin was fixed to the inside of this door as a warning to future robbers (?). Only fragments, of what may be skin (?) now remain.

Proceed ahead.

Higher vaulting creates a dramatic approach.

The arch above the Chapter House entrance is 13C but its central figure of Christ was unfortunately added by *George Gilbert Scott* in the 19C.

Location 5

CHAPTER HOUSE *c.1257*

Open daily 09.30–18.00. Closes 16.00 October–March. Admission charge. Combined ticket to Pyx Chamber and Abbey Museum sold when they are open.

The Chapter House served as the monks' meeting place from *c.*1257 until the Reformation, when it became the property of the Crown. The first assembly of Parliament's predecessor, the Great Council, was held here in 1257 and, from *c.* 1352–95 the Chapter House served as Parliament House for the House of Commons. The building was restored in 1872, after serving since 1540 as a records office, by *George Gilbert Scott* who renewed the central pier, vaulted roof and windows. The stained glass is 19C and later.

Flanking the entrance are outstanding 13C statues of the Angel Gabriel and the Virgin Mary

The 13C floor tiles are well preserved. Those around the perimeter illustrate the original rose window tracery in the north transept of the church.

The murals are late 14C and *c.* 1500 (birds and beasts).

Facing the entrance is what was once the abbot's seat.

Beneath the window immediately R of this, supporting one of the pillars, is a crisply carved wyvern – a mythical beast.

Leave the outer vestibule of the Chapter House L and enter the Pyx Chamber (second door L).

Location 6

PYX CHAMBER *c.1070*

Open daily 10.30–16.00. Admission charge. Tickets from the Chapter House.

It is not easily appreciated that the Pyx Chamber forms a small part of one long, two-storey building which is the oldest in the abbey. It was probably divided from the remainder of the undercroft in the mid 12C, when the floor was lowered by fifteen inches and, shortly afterwards, the capitals of some of the columns were carved. The monks lost their vestry at some stage during the rebuilding of the abbey church and it is probable that the chamber was then briefly used for this purpose (?). If so, the stone altar *c.*1240, the oldest in the abbey, would have been installed then. When St Faith's Chapel was completed *c.*1249, Henry III exchanged it with the monks for this chamber which he wanted for a treasury; it has remained under the Crown's jurisdiction ever since. The treasures, which were kept here until seized by Oliver Cromwell in 1649, were stored in chests, or pyxes, that gave the chamber its present name.

The 'Trial of the Pyx' was inaugurated *c.* 1281 to ensure that newly-minted currency contained the standard amount of gold or silver. Later, samples of coins were deposited in one of the pyxes and tested, probably at Westminster Palace (?). The testing equipment was kept here until 1871 when it was transferred to Goldsmiths Hall where the annual trial has taken place ever since.

The roof is barrel vaulted.

Some of the floor tiles are similar to those in the Chapter House but inferior; they were laid *c.* 1260. The black tiling dates from 1291.

Following the robbery of 1303, the north wall was partly rebuilt, its doorway filled and the present door fitted in the wall facing the cloister, from where the chamber could be observed more easily.

A medieval cope chest, with a 17C gold cloth cope, is displayed.

Since 1968, abbey plate has been exhibited.

•● *Exit R. Proceed to the door first R (only on Wednesdays in summer), ring the bell and ascend the stairs to the Chapter Library.*

•● *Alternatively, exit L. Enter the first door L to the Undercroft Museum (location 8).*

Location 7

CHAPTER LIBRARY *c. 1070*

Open May–September, Wednesday 11.00–15.00. Admission free.

A stairway was first constructed here in the mid 13C to give the monks direct access from the Great Cloister to their dormitory. It has since been rebuilt to a different design.

The library runs above the outer vestibule of the Chapter House and all of the Pyx Chamber. It now occupies approximately one-third of what was the monks' dormitory but originally continued past the south wall as one long, undivided room. The fabric of the outer walls is 11C but no Norman details survive.

The plain hammerbeam roof was added *c.* 1450 (?) after a monk had accidentally caused a fire.

Although the dividing wall lies immediately above the part late-12C north wall of the Pyx Chamber it is not certain when it was built.

Many of the library furnishings were installed in 1624.

The door in the north wall leads to the monks' nocturnal passageway.

•● *Descend the stairs. Turn L and proceed ahead. Enter the second door L to the Undercroft Museum.*

Location 8

ABBEY MUSEUM *c. 1070*

Open daily 10.30–16.00. Admission charge. Tickets from the Chapter House.

This is the most important Norman survivor in the Precinct. The undercroft lies directly beneath the section of the dormitory that is now the Great Hall of Westminster School. When built, it almost certainly incorporated the rest of the undercroft, including the Pyx Chamber. The undercroft probably housed the abbey's common room (?) which was the only area where the monks were permitted to light a fire in winter. The monastic chamberlain's department was also likely to have been here; his rooms would have included a tailor's shop and a shaving area.

Massive, typically Norman piers support the roof.

Display cases partly obscure features on the north side. In the first bay, facing the entrance wall, are the jambs of a blocked 16C window. It is believed that there was originally a door here that led to a small garden (?).

The second bay's arch has the only remaining example (restored) of the abbey's 12C zig-zag decoration. This arch originally led to the Chapel of St Dunstan, no trace of which remains.

In the last bay is a blocked 11C window.

Return to the entrance and proceed clockwise.

Chief exhibits are death masks and effigies of monarchs, generally made for lying-in-state or funeral processions. In the 18C many of these models were placed beside monuments in the abbey.

Against the north wall stands a Roman sarcophagus, discovered in the abbey's churchyard. Re-used by the Saxons for a Christian burial, its lid dates from that time. The chair, made for Mary II's coronation in 1689, was only used on that occasion. Duplicate coronation regalia, with substitutes for the precious metals and jewels, is used for rehearsals of the ceremony. The death mask of Edward III, d. 1327, is the oldest to survive in Europe; the drooping mouth indicates his stroke. Its nose was replaced following bomb damage and the wig and beard have long disappeared. Armour (achievements), borne at Henry V's funeral procession in 1422, was originally exhibited above the king's chantry chapel in the abbey. The arrow, with its head and slot for feathers, is the only complete medieval example to survive. Nelson's effigy was acquired early in the 19th century to attract visitors away from St Paul's Cathedral, where he had recently been buried. The bronze roundel commemorating Sir Thomas Lovell, d. 1504, by *Torrigiani* is one of England's earliest Renaissance works. For many years this was displayed in the south aisle of Henry VII's chapel; its wooden frame is later. Panels of 13C stained glass, the oldest in the abbey to survive, are displayed on the south wall. They came from various windows in the church, but until recently were fitted in the Jerusalem Chamber's north window. Facing them is a carved Norman capital, c. 1120, from the cloister of The Confessor's earlier abbey; the Judgement of Solomon is depicted. In a cabinet against the south wall is displayed the Essex Ring, allegedly given by Elizabeth I to Robert Devereux, Earl of Essex, when still her favourite. Later the Queen ordered his execution and it is said that if Essex had been able to return the ring to her, he would have been pardoned. A plaster cast of a 13C angel from the south transept has been painted to indicate its original appearance. Funeral effigies in the centre of the chamber: Frances, Duchess of Richmond and Lennox, d. 1702 (central display L) was the model for Britannia on the English coinage and is shown with her parrot, the oldest known stuffed bird in England. Charles II (centred display R) wears his original Order of the Garter robes.

Exit L to Dark Cloister.

Location 9

DARK CLOISTER

This 11C passage ran between the undercroft and the refectory.

First L follow the short 11C passage to Little Cloister. Its west cloister is entered.

Location 10

LITTLE CLOISTER AND COLLEGE GARDEN

All the Cloister is open April–September, Tuesday and Thursday 10.00–18.00. October–March, Tuesday and Thursday (closed Maundy Thursday) 10.00–16.00. Admission charge.

The monastery's 12C infirmary (hospital) originally stood in the centre. The arcades were first built *c.*1681 but, except for east cloister and part of north cloister, were rebuilt after the Second World War. The walls are basically 14C but there are traces of earlier work. Their doors once led to separate chambers occupied by infirm monks.

Turn R. (Thursday only).

Alternatively, return to Dark Cloister L. Proceed to Little Deans Yard (location 13).

West cloister (south section). At the south end R, the small rounded window is a detail in the east wall surviving from the 11C reredorter (latrine block).

Proceed to the end of the south cloister and enter College Garden R.

College Garden. This nine-hundred-year-old garden is the oldest established example in London and probably in England (?).

On the west side R is 'College' built as Westminster School's dormitory in Oxfordshire stone by *Burlington c.*1723.

The long wall enclosing the garden on the south side is part of the abbey's wall. It was built *c.*1372.

Return to Little Cloister and proceed ahead following its east cloister.

East cloister. The wall incorporates remnants of the Infirmarers Hall.

The 14C central doorway led to the infirmary's chapel *c.*1170, dedicated to St Katherine. Part of the chapel's south wall can be seen R.

Continue through the north and along the west cloisters. Turn R and return to Dark Cloister. First L proceed to the entrance to Little Deans Yard (Westminster School).

Location 11

WESTMINSTER SCHOOL

The Benedictine monks were a teaching order and a monastic school probably existed within the abbey by the end of the 12C (?). Following the Reformation, this became the King's Grammar School and was refounded by Elizabeth I in 1560. The School's premises are mostly divided between Little Deans Yard and Deans Yard.

Location 12

LITTLE DEANS YARD

Privacy is requested.

The yard was originally much smaller as domestic buildings stood here until 1758.

Turn immediately R.

Location 13

ASHBURNHAM HOUSE *J. Webb (?) 1665*

Little Deans Yard

Open Easter week or by appointment only. Admission free.

Ashburnham House accommodates the school's library. Although much altered externally, it has been judged to possess London's finest 17C domestic interiors. The house was the Churchill Club for American officers 1942–5.

External stonework on the west facade originally formed part of the wall of the Prior's House and there are other remnants within.

A second floor was added in the 19C. The west wing was built in 1930 to give the house a symmetrical appearance.

Enter the second door R. Ascend the modern stairs to the librarian's office and await the guide.

The **drawing room** is decorated with 17C plasterwork. From here, a door leads to the **stairway** *c.*1665 with its cupola and lantern.

In the garden can be seen the ruined north and east walls of the monastic refectory. Some work is Norman.

Exit L and proceed to the east side of the yard.

Location 14

GREAT HALL OF WESTMINSTER SCHOOL

Little Deans Yard

Open by appointment only. Admission free.

The stone archway L by *Burlington* 1734 is carved with elegant graffiti which was paid for by schoolboys who employed abbey masons to record their names.

Ascend the stairs (with the guide) to the vestibule.

The oak door to the hall, although in Jacobean style, was evidently carved *c.*1669.

This hall, built *c.*1070, was originally the southern continuation of the monks' dormitory. From 1591 to 1884 the whole of Westminster School was taught here and the hall is still referred to as 'School'.

Second World War bombing destroyed the 15C hammerbeam roof which, when built, continued from the adjacent Chapter Library.

Some 11C detailing remains in the walls.

Exit R. Return along Dark Cloister. First L proceed along south cloister and continue to the passage ahead.

On the wall R, the monument to Captain Cornewall, d.1743, by *R. Taylor* was brought here from the west end of the nave and cut down. It was England's first monument to a naval hero.

Location 15

PARLOUR

14C visitors were received in this vestibule.

Continue ahead. First R a short passage leads to Deanery Courtyard.

Location 16

DEANERY COURTYARD

The buildings make up the dean's (originally the abbot's) lodging and form the best example of a medieval house in London.

A 14C oak door guards the courtyard.

The bosses in the vaulted ceiling of the entrance passage are removable. They were so designed to enable defenders to fire arrows or pour boiling liquid on to an invader.

The south wall of the court immediately L is 13C.

On the west side L is College Hall.

Location 17

COLLEGE HALL *Yevele (?) 1376*

Deanery Courtyard

Open by appointment only

This hall, where the abbot once dined, is now used by Westminster School as a dining room.

The timber roof is probably by *Hugh Herland* (?), the carpenter responsible for the roof of Westminster

Hall. Corbels supporting the roof are carved and decorated.

The windows have been mostly renewed.

The screen, gallery and oak tables are 16C.

•➡ *On the east side of the courtyard is The Deanery.*

Location 18	**THE DEANERY**
Deanery Court Yard	This is now the Dean's residence. Some 17C and 18C work remains but most was rebuilt after bombing.
	•➡ *Cross the court to the north side (if on a Super Tour).*

Location 19	**JERICHO PARLOUR/JERUSALEM CHAMBER**
Deanery Courtyard	The 16C Jericho Parlour leads directly to the 14C Jerusalem Chamber, located immediately behind.
Entrance by Super Tour only.	The chamber's name possibly derives from tapestries or wall paintings with which it was once decorated (?). Henry IV reputedly died here in 1413 (?).
	Most of the tie-beam roof is original. 17C Flemish tapestries are hung.
	The fire surround incorporates Elizabethan work.
	•➡ *Exit from Deanery Courtyard R to Deans Yard L.*

Location 20	**DEANS YARD**

Much of this yard was originally occupied by farm buildings. Its 14C east range forms the oldest medieval domestic terrace in London.

•➡ *Adjoining the Parlour, immediately L, is the* **Cellarers Building**, *the first house in the east range.*

The top storey of the 14C Cellarers Building, much remodelled, once provided the abbey's Guest House. It became 'School' from 1461–1561 and the entire Westminster School, then much smaller, was taught within.

•➡ *Continue to the first arch L and the* **Blackstole Tower.**

The 14C archway originally formed the entrance to the monks' kitchen but the tower, which surmounted it, has been demolished.

•➡ *Proceed to the next arch and the* **Tower of the Monk Bailiff.**

Most of this 14C tower has also been demolished.

•➡ *The arch beneath leads to Little Deans Yard but continue ahead to* **No 17**.

This late 18C Georgian house is the residence of the headmaster of Westminster School.

•➡ *Return to the north side of the yard, turn L and exit R beneath the arch to the Sanctuary. R Broad Sanctuary. Follow the path between the abbey and St Margaret's. First L St Margaret Street. Cross the road. First R Bridge Street and Westminster Station, Circle and District lines.*

•➡ *Alternatively, if continuing with itinerary 8, commence at St Margaret's.*

•➡ *Alternatively, if continuing with itinerary 5, exit from the Sanctuary. L Victoria St. Cross the road and proceed to the second bus stop. Take bus 11,24 or 29 to the Horse Guards stop in Whitehall. Continue ahead. First L the Mall.*

7

Houses of Parliament and Whitehall

This itinerary covers the area once wholly occupied by the ancient royal palaces of Whitehall and Westminster. What remains of them is described but most buildings on this itinerary are devoted to government administration. They include the Prime Minister's residence at number 10 Downing Street and the Houses of Parliament, with their great clock's famous bell, 'Big Ben'.

Timing: Tuesday to Saturday with a mid-morning start is recommended. Since 1982, tours of the Houses of Parliament, the most important location, can only be made by appointment. Mounting of the guard at Horse Guards is at 11.00 (12.00 Sunday).

7

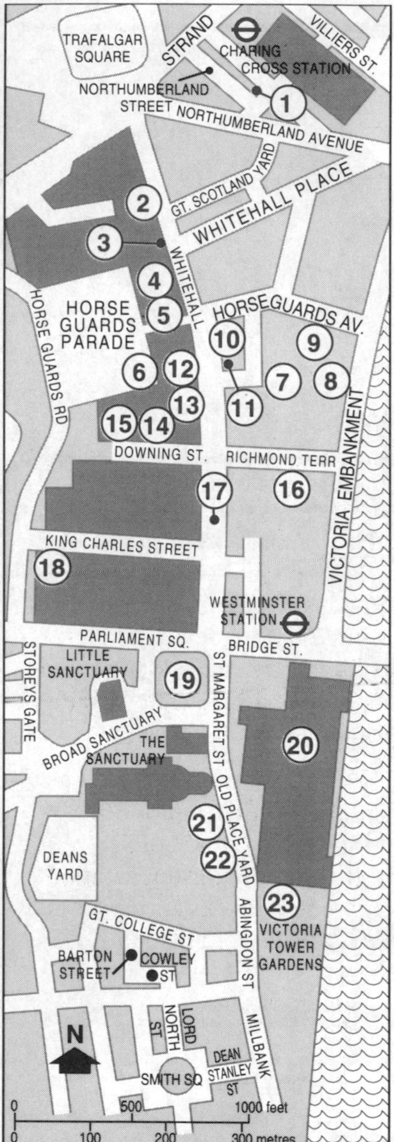

Locations

1 The Sherlock Holmes
2 Old Admiralty
3 Admiralty House
4 Parliamentary Council
5 Horse Guards
6 Treasury
7 Whitehall Palace
8 Queen Mary's Terrace
9 Henry VIII's Wine Cellar
10 Banqueting House
11 Welsh Office
12 Scottish Office
13 Cabinet Office
14 Whitehall Palace Tennis Courts
15 No 10 Downing Street
16 Richmond Terrace
17 The Cenotaph
18 Cabinet War Rooms
19 Parliament Square
20 Houses of Parliament
21 No 7 Old Palace Yard
22 Jewel Tower
23 Burghers of Calais Monument

Start *Charing Cross Station, Bakerloo, Jubilee and Northern lines. From the Bakerloo line leave by the Strand exit. Ahead Strand. First R Northumberland St. From the Jubilee and Northern lines leave by the Strand (south) exit ahead. L Strand. Third L Northumberland St. If viewing Mounting of the Guard at Horseguards (11.00 weekdays, 12.00 Sundays) return later to location 1.*

Location 1	**THE SHERLOCK HOLMES**
Northumberland Street	This was one of London's earliest theme pubs. Many souvenirs of Sherlock Holmes and the detective's creator, Conan Doyle, are displayed throughout. A re-creation of the 'study at No 221B Baker Street' is on the first floor beside the restaurant.

Leave by the Northumberland Street exit. Second L Northumberland Avenue. First R Great Scotland Yard. Second L Whitehall. Cross the road immediately.

Location 2

OLD ADMIRALTY *Ripley 1725*

Whitehall

Open by appointment and for groups only. Admission free.

Nelson took his orders in this building, much of which has changed little since his time.

Fronting Whitehall is the stone screen by *Adam* 1761.

Enter the courtyard and proceed to the central door. Await the guide.

The house replaced a building of 1695 on the same site and was primarily the residence of Lords of the Admiralty.

In the **vestibule** stands the original model for Nelson's statue in Trafalgar Square by *Baily*.

The first floor **Board Room** was used by the Lords, mainly as their office, but occasionally as a dining room, and the present Admiralty Board still holds its meetings here. Smoking has never been allowed –even Churchill obediently extinguished his cigar.

The room is much as Nelson knew it although the fireplace was moved from the south to the west wall in 1847. The carved surround to this by *Gibbons* (?), with the arms of Charles II, probably came from the earlier Admiralty building.

Above the fireplace is a wind dial by *Norden* (?) 1708.

The clock by *Bradley* 1697 was made for the Admiralty and has stood here since the room was built.

In a ground floor room Nelson's body lay before his funeral at St Paul's in 1805.

Exit from the courtyard R.

Location 3

ADMIRALTY HOUSE *S. P. Cockerell 1788*

Whitehall

This walled house was built to enlarge the First Lord of the Admiralty's accommodation and is entered, not directly from Whitehall, but from the Old Admiralty's courtyard, via its south wing.

Continue ahead.

Location 4

PARLIAMENTARY COUNCIL *Lane 1733*

36 Whitehall

The Council's ground floor has rusticated stonework. Its north bay was added in 1806.

Continue ahead.

Location 5

HORSE GUARDS *Kent* and *Vardy 1760*

Mounting the guard Monday–Saturday 11.00. Sunday 12.00. Guard inspection daily 16.00. Admission free. Mounted guardsmen are always on duty.

The Portland stone building was designed as headquarters for the General Staff and remained as such until 1876. It replaced the first mid 17C Horse Guards built for Charles II to protect Whitehall Palace. The palace has gone but its guard remains. Although *Kent* was the architect, work began after his death, and his successor *Vardy* may have made changes (?).

Proceed through the forecourt and arch to Horse Guards Parade.

The Trooping of the Colour takes place here annually on the second Saturday in June to honour the official birthday of the sovereign, who usually takes part.

Proceed to south side of Horse Guards Parade.

Location 6

TREASURY *Kent 1736*

Treasury Passage

The stone-faced building was originally planned to be almost twice its eventual size with turrets at either end. Some original interiors survive on the first floor.

Immediately west of the Treasury stands the brick house that now forms the rear of 10 Downing Street *Flitcroft* (?) 1735 (location 15).

•• *Return to Whitehall and cross the road. Proceed ahead along Horseguards Avenue. At the end follow the path R. Immediately R are the remains of Queen Mary's Terrace – a survivor from Whitehall Palace.*

Location 7

WHITEHALL PALACE

Cardinal Wolsey remodelled and enlarged York Place, the 13C London residence of the Archbishops of York, in 1514. It was confiscated by Henry VIII in 1529, and he then rebuilt and extended the house until what had become a royal palace stretched along the river to Westminster Hall. Although rather a jumble of medieval buildings, it eventually became the largest palace in Europe and incorporated a large banqueting hall; one of a type then known as 'white halls'. A fire in 1698 destroyed many of the buildings but, due to its dampness, the asthmatic William III had already left. After the fire the buildings were neglected, apart from the undamaged Banqueting House, and locations 8, 9, 10 and 14 are all that survive of this vast palace.

Location 8

QUEEN MARY'S TERRACE *Wren 1691*

Victoria Embankment

This riverside terrace, partly restored in 1939, was built for Mary II. The steps originally led directly to the river which then lapped the walls.

•• *Return to Horseguards Avenue. Immediately L is the Ministry of Defence Building. Assemble at the first door for the guide to view Henry VIII's Wine Cellar.*

Location 9

HENRY VIII'S WINE CELLAR *16C.*

Ministry of Defence, Horseguards Avenue

Closed at the time of writing.

This is the only part of Wolsey's York House to survive. The whole structure, weighing one thousand tons, was sunk and incorporated in the new building in 1949. The wine cellar was originally larger but not subterranean, as the existence of windows proves.

•• *Exit L. First L Whitehall.*

Location 10

BANQUETING HOUSE *Inigo Jones 1622*

Whitehall

Open Monday–Saturday 10.00–17.00. Admission charge.

This was the first building in England to be completed in the Classical style. Its saloon possesses a ceiling painted by *Rubens*. On a scaffold outside, Charles I was executed in 1649.

James I commissioned the Banqueting House to replace a short-lived structure, also possibly by Inigo Jones, that had burnt down in 1619. It functioned as a Chapel Royal from 1724 to 1890.

The north extension with the staircase by *J. Wyatt* 1798 replaced an earlier lean-to building from which Charles I approached the scaffold for his execution on 30 January 1649. A bust of the King marks the approximate position of the original window through which he is believed to have stepped (?).

The Banqueting House was originally built of golden Oxford and Northamptonshire stone which wore badly. It was entirely refaced in Portland stone, by *Soane*, 1830. The balustrade, however, was always of Portland stone and marked the earliest known use in London of this material.

Enter from the door in the north extension.

Vestibule. Displayed is a bust of James I by *Le Sueur*.

Stairway. The statuette of Rubens is by *Rysbrack*. There was never an integral staircase and the building is, therefore, believed to be part of a complex that was never completed.

Ascend the stairs to the first floor.

Saloon. This has been called the grandest room in England. Its proportions are exactly a double cube: 110 feet long, 55 feet high and 55 feet wide. Originally there was an apse at the south end but this was soon removed.

The famous ceiling by *Rubens* 1635 was added for Charles I and depicts the apotheosis of his late father, James I. Rubens received a knighthood and a pension for his work which was painted entirely in Belgium. Two mirrors facilitate viewing.

The throne is a replica.

Exit L and proceed to the next house but one.

Location 11

WELSH OFFICE *Marquand 1772*

Gwydyr House, Whitehall

The house was built as a private residence and named after an early Welsh owner.

Cross Whitehall.

Location 12

SCOTTISH OFFICE *Paine 1758*

Dover House, Whitehall

Open by appointment only. Admission free. The rotunda may be viewed from the entrance.

The original house is screened from Whitehall by a rotunda and colonnade by *Holland* 1787. This filled the forecourt and was commissioned by Frederick, Duke of York, when he owned the property.

Exit R. Remain on the west side.

In the centre of the road is the monument to First World War leader, Earl Haig by *Hardiman* 1937.

Continue to the next building.

Location 13

CABINET OFFICE *C. Barry 1845*

Whitehall

These offices originally housed the Treasury and replaced earlier buildings by *Kent* and *Soane* both of which soon proved to be too small.

Opposite, on the green, are 20C monuments to Raleigh by *Macmillan* 1929 and Field Marshal Montgomery by *Nemon* 1980.

First R Downing Street. (Since 1982 both entrances to Downing Street have been closed to the public for security reasons and the buildings may only be glimpsed.)

Location 14

WHITEHALL PALACE TENNIS COURTS *16C*

Downing Street

The red brick Tudor walls and the windows facing the quadrangle, just before No 10, are the remains of 'real' tennis courts belonging to Henry VIII's Whitehall Palace.

Location 15

No 10 DOWNING STREET

George II presented 'Number Ten' for the Prime Minister's residence in 1731 and Robert Walpole, England's first Prime Minister, became its occupant.

Originally, the house formed part of Sir George Downing's development of 1680 but it was rebuilt *c.*1723 and a new facade added in 1766.

The modest building is linked by a long corridor to the much larger house at the rear. The Prime Minister's offices and Cabinet Room are situated in the larger building. Although renovated in 1964 some interiors remain by *Soane* 1825. No 10 is linked internally with Nos 11 and 12, respectively the residences of the Chancellor of the Exchequer and the Government's Chief Whip.

Remain on the west side of Whitehall. Richmond Terrace is opposite.

Location 16

RICHMOND TERRACE *Chawner 1825*

This terrace, originally of eight houses, was built on the site of Richmond House that burnt down in 1791. It was rebuilt behind the façade as offices in 1988.

Continue ahead. In the centre of the road is the Cenotaph.

Location 17

THE CENOTAPH *Lutyens 1920*

Whitehall

This is the national memorial to those who fell in both World Wars. The Royal Family and prominent government members attend a remembrance service here every November and poppy wreaths are laid.

Continue ahead. First R King Charles St. L Horse Guards Rd. Proceed to the foot of Clive's Steps.

Location 18

CABINET WAR ROOMS

Clive's Steps, King Charles Street (930 6961)

Open daily 10.00–18.00. Admission charge.

Walkman tour provided free.

Established in 1938, Churchill and his War Cabinet governed from here during air raids throughout the Second World War. A suite of twenty rooms, redecorated in 1982, are exhibited. They include the Cabinet Room, Transatlantic Telephone Room, Map Room and Prime Minister's Room.

Return to Whitehall R. Proceed to Parliament Square. Cross the road towards the Churchill monument on the central pedestrian precinct.

Location 19

PARLIAMENT SQUARE

The square was laid out by *C. Barry* in the 19C when many narrow streets and houses were cleared.

Proceed anti-clockwise to view the statues.

Statues on the north side of the precinct are of Churchill by *Robert Jones* 1973, Smuts by *Epstein* 1958 and Palmerston by *Woolner* 1876.

On the west side is the monument to Canning by *Westmacott* 1832. This statue accidentally toppled in the sculptor's studio and killed a visitor. Other monuments are to Lord Derby by *Noble* 1874, Abraham Lincoln, a copy, (on the west side of the road), Lord Beaconsfield (Disraeli) by *Raggi* 1883 and Peel by *Noble* 1876.

From Churchill's statue, observe the exterior of the Houses of Parliament as described opposite.

Location 20

HOUSES OF PARLIAMENT
(Palace of Westminster)

(219 4272)

House of Commons in session. By appointment or queue on the day; the queue is generally short after 18.00. When Parliament is sitting, sessions are held Monday–Thursday 14.30 onwards, often until 22.00 and Friday 09.30 to 15.00. Prime Minister's Question Time takes place Tuesday and Thursday from 15.15.

House of Lords in session. Entry arrangements are as for the House of Commons. Sessions are held Tuesday, Wednesday and Thursday 14.30 onwards (occasionally Monday and Friday also).

General tours are now by appointment only.

Visitors to either Public Gallery are able to see the interior of Westminster Hall immediately L of the entrance.

The Palace of Westminster, 'mother of parliaments', was almost entirely rebuilt in the mid 19C. Although now occupied exclusively by Parliament, it remains officially a royal palace.

In the 11C the Court moved to Westminster alongside the already established abbey. Edward the Confessor carried out much rebuilding and his palace was soon to become the chief residence of the Norman kings. Westminster Hall was added by William Rufus slightly north of the Confessor's buildings. The Palace of Westminster remained the pre-eminent royal residence until a fire in 1532 persuaded Henry VIII to move to his recently acquired Whitehall Palace nearby. Parliament, however, continued to sit there until the disastrous fire of 1834. It was then decided to construct completely new Houses of Parliament in either Gothic or Elizabethan style and *Charles Barry,* with the help of *Augustus Pugin,* won the public competition.

The only ancient buildings retained were Westminster Hall and the undercroft and cloisters of St Stephen's Chapel. Foundations were laid in 1839 and the work completed in 1860. Practically every detail, including the furnishings and fittings, was personally designed by Pugin.

In spite of the romantic appearance of the Houses of Parliament, their layout is functional and basically symmetrical. The eleven-acre complex, incorporates more than 1,000 rooms and eleven courtyards. Its exterior is described from north to south.

St Stephen's Tower. Big Ben is the bell, not the clock, and was probably named after Sir Benjamin Hall, the overweight supervisor of its installation in 1859(?). The present bell was the second to be made, the first shattering on test. Big Ben still has a crack that was caused by its first hammer proving to be too heavy and it is believed that this crack gives the bell its unique tone(?). A light shines at night from the top of the tower when Parliament is sitting.

New Palace Yard. This courtyard, facing Bridge Street and Parliament Square, is named after the 'new' palace of William II 'Rufus', i.e. Westminster Hall. Edward the Confessor's earlier complex lay further south. A pillory once stood in the yard.

Westminster Hall. The north facade of the hall faces Bridge Street and the west facade, St Margaret Street. Westminster Hall was built by William II in 1099 as the focal point of the palace, for he considered the existing Great Hall of Edward the Confessor to be much too small and insignificant. When completed, the hall was a barn-like structure with all four walls visible and no extraneous buildings attached to it.

Westminster Hall was completely remodelled by Richard II's master mason *Yevele* in 1404. Its height was raised by two feet to accommodate a new roof, however, apart from this, the dimensions remained the same. Most of the thick side walls were kept, but as they were completely encased in new stonework

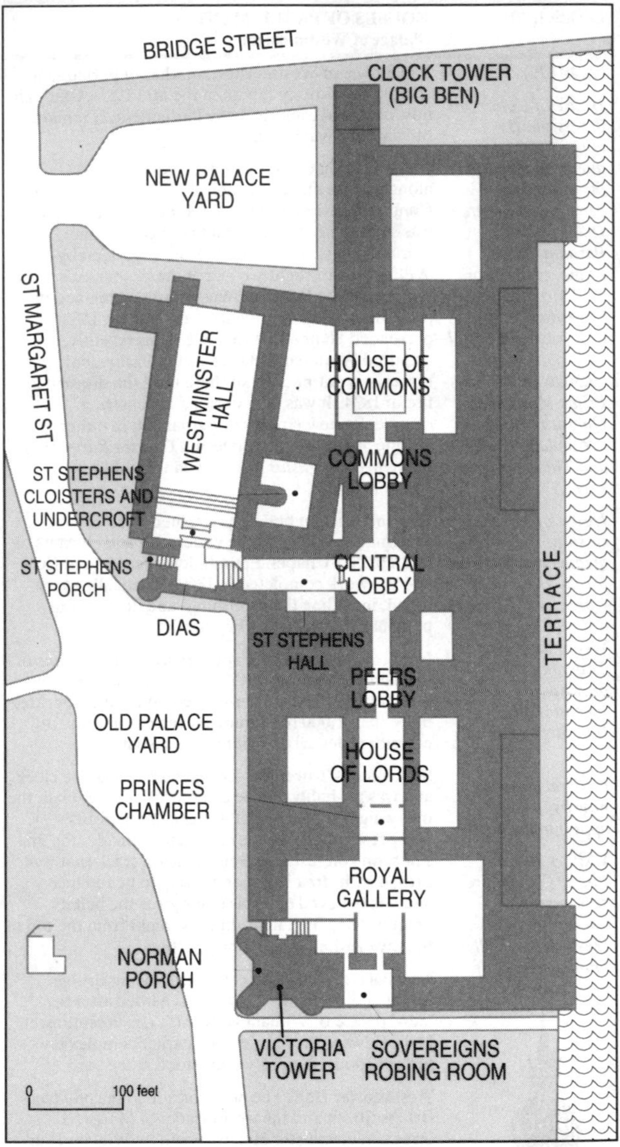

and the 11C windows enlarged, all Norman features disappeared. The north front was entirely rebuilt by *Yevele* and remains basically faithful to his design, although heavily restored in 1820.

Proceed R to the south-east corner of the pedestrian precinct.

The building that protrudes westward from the north end of Westminster Hall, together with the low structure that runs along the entire west facade, was added by *Pearson* in 1888.

The roof tiling and lantern were entirely renewed following Second World War bomb damage.

•• *Cross St Margaret Street R.*

On the green in front of Westminster Hall is a statue of Oliver Cromwell by *Thornycroft* 1899.

St Stephen's Porch. The porch is the public entrance to the Houses of Parliament and leads to the dais.

•• *Continue southward.*

Yevele's south wall of Westminster Hall was demolished when Barry's dais was built. However, its 14C window was incorporated in the new south wall. It was renewed following bomb damage.

Central Tower. This acts as a decorative ventilator to the Central Hall.

Old Palace Yard. This was originally the courtyard of Edward the Confessor's 'old' palace. Here, Guy Fawkes was hanged, drawn and quartered in 1606 and Sir Walter Raleigh beheaded in 1618.

The equestrian statue of Richard I 'Coeur de Lion' is by *Marrochetti* 1860.

Victoria Tower. At 336 feet this is still the world's highest square masonry tower. Its flagpole flies the Royal Standard when the sovereign is present and the Union Jack when Parliament is sitting. Around 1,500,000 documents are kept here, including all Acts of Parliament passed since 1497. Its porch, the 'Norman Porch', is the entrance used by the sovereign on State occasions.

•• *Return to St Stephen's Porch. Enter and ascend the stairs to the dais from where most of Westminster Hall's interior can be seen.*

Westminster Hall was, for over seven hundred years, the scene of lavish royal celebrations. These included coronation banquets, Christmas feasts and jousting.

Civil law courts were held in the hall from the mid 13C until 1882. Two kings were deposed here; Edward II in 1327 and Richard II in 1399. State trials also interrupted the courts from time to time. Those tried included Sir Thomas More 1535, Protector Somerset 1551, The Earl of Essex 1601, Guy Fawkes 1606, The Earl of Stafford 1641 and Charles I 1649.

Monarchs and great Prime Ministers are now laid in state within the hall. (Churchill in 1965.)

The original roof of the Norman hall was probably supported by two rows of inconvenient wooden pillars, and the ability of master carpenter *Hugh Herland* to provide a roof that would span the entire hall may have inspired Richard II to rebuild in 1394 (?). At the same time, *Yevele* was commissioned to remodel the hall in the Perpendicular style.

As with the exterior, no Norman work can be seen as it was either replaced or hidden. However, remains have been discovered of a Norman arcaded gallery at window level. A section of stonework in the east wall can be removed, to reveal a rounded arch.

Westminster Hall has been described as 'the finest timber-roofed building in Europe'. The hammerbeam structure spans sixty-seven feet, weighs six hundred tons and is the oldest known large scale example.

Carved on the hammerbeams are angels, with shields bearing the arms of England and France, carved by *Robert Grassington*.

The roof is supported by 14C stone corbels carved with the arms of England, France, Edward the Confessor and Richard II (white harts and lions).

Below the dais window is 'Moses' painted by *West* 1784, from George III's Chapel at Windsor.

•• *Descend the stairs, with guide only, to enter the hall and proceed clockwise. Alternatively, view the hall from the dais.*

On the 19C wall above the stairs are six 14C statues of early English kings.

The doorways and double stairs on the west wall were added by *Pearson* c. 1888. All the windows in this wall have been renewed.

The north window is basically Yevele's 14C work.

Beneath the sills of the east windows, also renewed, are five dilapidated statues of kings which originally stood outside the north and south fronts.

•• *Proceed to the Public Galleries or continue with the guided tour. Alternatively, exit to St Margaret Street L.*

Sovereign's Robing Room. The House of Lords sat here from 1941 and the bombed-out House of Commons occupied the Lords' undamaged chamber.

Frescoes of scenes from the life of King Arthur are by *Dyce*.

Royal Gallery. A model of the old Palace of Westminster and Charles I's death warrant are exhibited.

The two frescoes, 'The Death of Nelson' and 'The meeting of Wellington and Blucher', are by *Maclisse*.

Princes Chamber. This functions as an ante-room.

The House of Lords. The Lords first sat here in 1847. This House must still approve laws passed by the Commons, except financial, before they become statutory. The House of Lords is also the highest court in the land, where final appeals are heard each week (not in this chamber). The sovereign opens Parliament here, generally in November each year, and a ceremonial check is made in the cellars for explosives by Yeomen of the Guard. However, the site of the House of Lords has changed since Guy Fawkes plotted to blow it up, together with James I, during the opening ceremony in 1605. The gunpowder had been placed in a ground floor room beneath the Lords' chamber, not in a cellar. The detailing in this room, including the sovereign's throne, is judged to be *Pugin's* masterpiece.

The Lord Chancellor presides over the Lords from the Woolsack before the throne.

Peers Lobby. This is the Lords' voting lobby.

Central Lobby. The public can meet their respective Members of Parliament in this lobby. Here also, members of both houses talk informally.

Commons Lobby. House of Commons members discuss parliamentary matters here. The lobby leads directly to their chamber.

House of Commons Chamber. The entrance, known as the Churchill arch, was built of stones rescued from the earlier bombed chamber.

Above the doorway is the crest of Airey Neave who was assassinated in the members' car park by terrorists in 1979.

This chamber was rebuilt after the Second World War bombing, by *Giles Gilbert Scott*, 1951. The government and the opposition face each other two sword-lengths apart and are separated by two red lines on the floor. No member may cross them.

The House of Commons is supervised by the be-wigged Speaker who enters, preceded by the Sergeant-at-Arms bearing a mace, and followed by the train-bearer, chaplain and secretary.

No monarch has been allowed to enter the House of Commons since 1642 when Charles I burst in attempting to arrest five members, but found that 'the birds had flown'.

The Speaker's chair came from Australia, the table from Canada, the clerk's chair from South Africa and the despatch boxes from New Zealand. The two lobbies on either side of the House are the Division Lobbies. Members voting 'Aye' enter the lobby right of the Speaker. Those voting 'No' proceed to the lobby on his left.

St Stephen's Hall. The hall was built on the site of the mid-14C St Stephen's Chapel which had been presented to the Commons by Edward VI in 1547 and deconsecrated. Its cloistered undercroft survived the fire of 1834 and lies beneath this hall.

A brass plate marks the original position of the Speaker's chair.

St Stephen's Undercroft. This cannot at present be seen by the public. After the fire the undercroft was remodelled and dedicated as the Church of St Mary Undercroft. Members can marry in this chapel and their children may be christened here.

St Stephen's Cloisters 1529. These lie immediately east of Westminster Hall and also survived the fire. The two-storey cloisters are fan-vaulted but much restored. Again, they cannot generally be seen by the public.

Exit from the Houses of Parliament L. Continue to Old Palace Yard. Cross the road.

Location 21

NO 7 OLD PALACE YARD *Vardy* or *Ware (?) 18C*

This Palladian style, stone-faced building is the last remaining house in the yard.

Outside, stands the monument to George V by *Reid Dick* 1947.

Continue southward.

Location 22

JEWEL TOWER *Yevele 1366*

Abingdon Street

Open daily Easter–October 10.00–13.00 and 14.00–18.00. November–Easter 10.00–13.00 and 14.00–16.00.

Immediately to the east of the tower are remains of a recently excavated moat, filled in the 17C.

The tower occupied the south-west corner of the Palace of Westminster and was built by Edward III to house his personal treasures. It remained part of the Royal Wardrobe until 1547. Modifications were made early in the 17C to accommodate House of

Admission charge.

Lords records which were stored here from 1621–1862. After the Second World War, the tower was restored and opened to the public.

The doorway and all the windows of the Jewel Tower date from remodelling in 1719.

Enter the tower and turn immediately L.

Displayed in the vaulted chamber are 11C capitals, found buried in the fabric of Westminster Hall and the 8C Sword of the Palace of Westminster.

A marble support from Westminster Hall's 13C great high table is exhibited.

In the second, smaller chamber is a section of elm piling found beneath the Jewel Tower.

Ascend the stairs to the first floor.

A display, Parliament Past and Present, includes the Speaker's robes and the 8C Sword of the Palace of Westminster.

The iron, 17C strong-room door leads to the smaller chamber.

Ascend the stairs to the second floor.

Some of the measures for standards, which were kept here 1869–1938 for the Board of Trade, are on view in the second chamber.

A 30-minute video film relates the history of parliament.

Exit R Abingdon St. Cross the road and enter Victoria Gardens. Proceed ahead passing the Pankhurst monument.

Location 23

BURGHERS OF CALAIS MONUMENT *Rodin 1895*

Victoria Tower Gardens

The monument commemorates the burghers who surrendered the keys of Calais to Edward III in 1346.

Return to Abingdon St. R. First R Bridge St. and Westminster Station, Circle and District lines.

Alternatively, if continuing with itinerary 8, return to Abingdon St. R. Cross the road and continue ahead, passing Westminster Abbey and proceed to the east end of St Margaret's.

Alternatively, if continuing with itinerary 6, return to Abingdon St. R. Cross the road and continue ahead to the Henry VII Chapel which protrudes at the east end of Westminster Abbey.

Itinerary 8

8

Tate Gallery and the South Bank

This itinerary includes the Tate Gallery, where Britain's greatest collection of modern art is displayed, and the Archbishop of Canterbury's medieval palace at Lambeth.

Timing: Any afternoon is suitable, however, if an appointment has been made to see Lambeth Palace (well in advance) or a seat reserved at the South Bank Arts Centre, this will obviously affect the day chosen.

8

Locations

1 St Margaret Westminster
2 'Bridewell' Gate, Middlesex Guildhall
3 Barton Street
4 St John's Smith Square
5 Victoria Tower Gardens
6 Tate Gallery
7 Museum of Garden History
8 Lambeth Palace
9 Imperial War Museum
10 Westminster Bridge
11 South Bank Lion
12 County Hall
13 Hungerford Bridge
14 Royal Festival Hall
15 Queen Elizabeth Hall/ Purcell Room
16 Hayward Gallery
17 National Film Theatre
18 Museum of the Moving Image
19 National Theatre
20 Waterloo Bridge

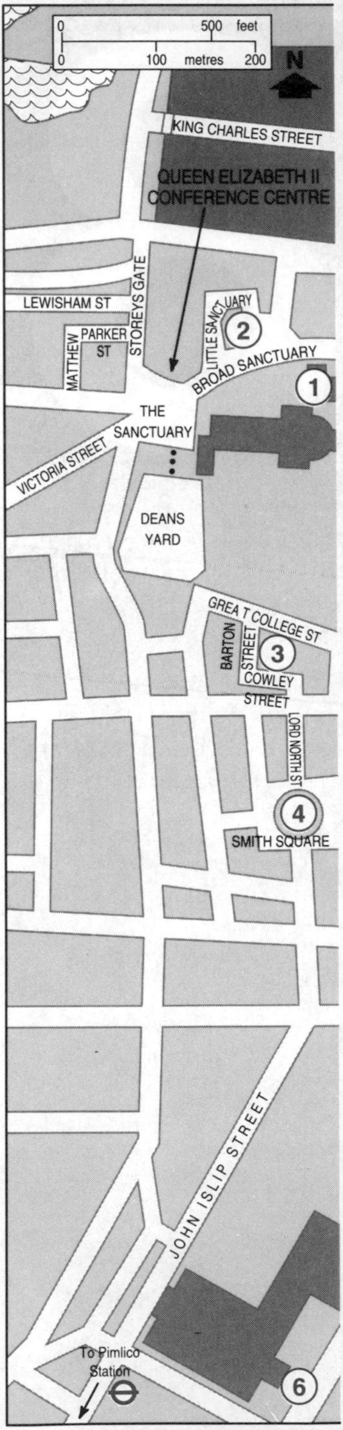

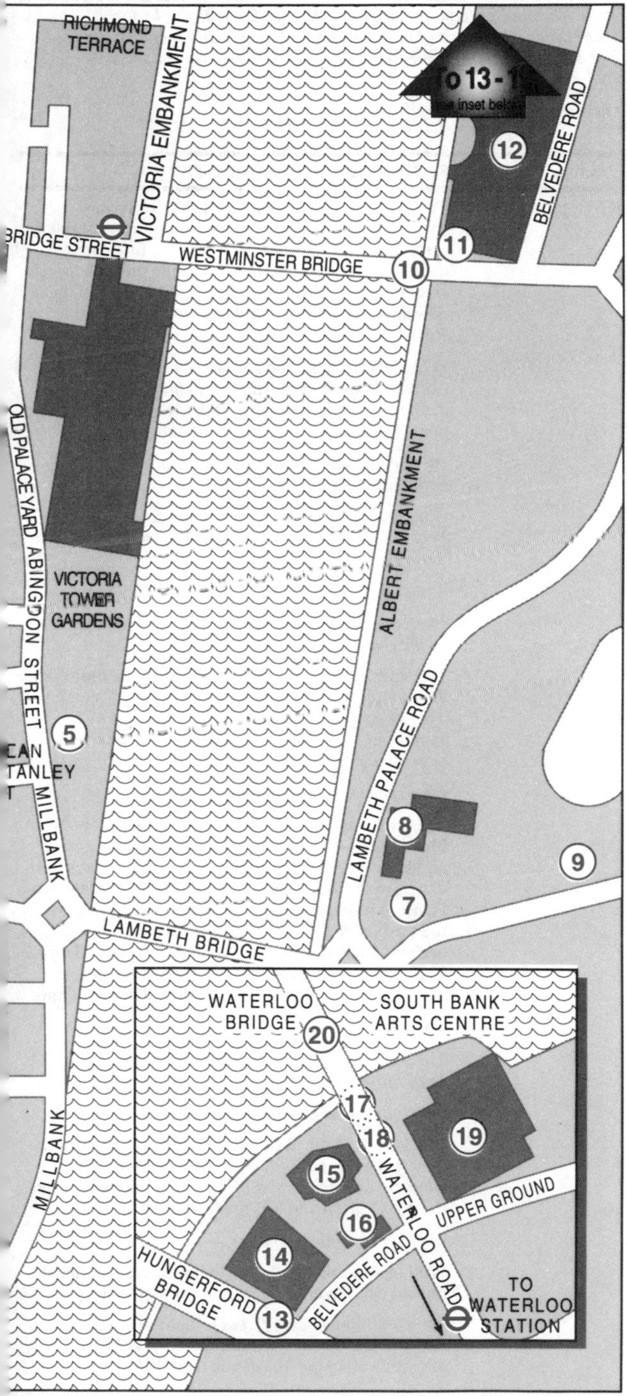
RICHMOND TERRACE
VICTORIA EMBANKMENT
BRIDGE STREET
WESTMINSTER BRIDGE
BELVEDERE ROAD
To 13 - 1
see inset below
12
11
10
OLD PALACE YARD
ABINGDON STREET
VICTORIA TOWER GARDENS
ALBERT EMBANKMENT
LAMBETH PALACE ROAD
5
CAN
TANLEY
MILLBANK
8
9
7
LAMBETH BRIDGE
MILLBANK
WATERLOO BRIDGE
SOUTH BANK ARTS CENTRE
20
17
18
19
15
16
14
13
WATERLOO ROAD
UPPER GROUND
BELVEDERE ROAD
HUNGERFORD BRIDGE
TO WATERLOO STATION

Start *Westminster Station, Circle and District lines. Leave by the Westminster Abbey exit. Ahead Bridge St. First L Parliament Square leads to St Margaret St. Cross the road and proceed to the east end of St Margaret's church.*

Alternatively, continue from itineraries 6 or 7.

Location 1	**ST MARGARET WESTMINSTER***

St Margaret Street

This is the House of Commons church. Its east window possesses London's most important stained glass. Edward the Confessor built the first parish church here in the 11C. Although the present church was built in 1523, due to 18C and 19C remodelling it now appears to be primarily a work of the Gothic Revival.

St Margaret's has been adopted by the House of Commons since 1614. Important marriages here include those of Pepys the diarist 1655, Milton the poet (his second) 1656 and Churchill 1908.

•➡ *To view the exterior, proceed clockwise returning to the east porch.*

Both the east and west porches are the 19C work of *Pearson.*

The walls were encased in Portland stone and the three upper stages of the tower rebuilt by *James* 1734.

•➡ *Return to St Margaret St and enter St Margaret's by the east door.*

The brass tablet, immediately R (push the button to illuminate it), commemorates Sir Walter Raleigh who was executed in Old Palace Yard nearby by James I in 1618. He is believed to have been buried beneath the altar (?).

•➡ *Proceed to the* **chancel.**

The most important feature of St Margaret's is its Flemish east window, commissioned by Ferdinand and Isabella of Spain in 1501. It commemorates the marriage of their daughter, Catherine of Aragon, to Prince Arthur, eldest son of Henry VII and heir to the throne. Arthur died and Catherine eventually became the first wife of his younger brother, Henry VIII. The window was fitted in three different buildings before finally being installed here in 1758.

•➡ *Proceed to the* **south aisle.**

The south windows, with abstract designs, are by *John Piper* 1967.

•➡ *Continue ahead to the west door.*

The font, L of the door, was made by *Stone* in 1641. Above the door are the arms of Charles II. The window, immediately R of the door, commemorates the poet Milton and was made in 1888.

•➡ *Exit from the west door.*

William Caxton, England's first printer, is buried in the old churchyard but his grave is unmarked.

•➡ *Turn immediately R and follow the path to Broad Sanctuary L. Second R Little Sanctuary. Proceed to the west wall of the Middlesex Guildhall.*

Location 2	**'BRIDEWELL' GATE, MIDDLESEX GUILDHALL**
Little Sanctuary	This gateway came from Westminster's 17C 'Bridewell' prison, named after Henry VIII's palace in the City which had been converted to a 'house of correction'. Its inscription is dated 1655. See the descriptive plaque. ●● *Return to Broad Sanctuary R. and continue ahead to the Sanctuary. Turn L and pass through the arch R to Deans Yard. Follow the yard first L and first R towards the arch in its south-east corner. Pass through the arch to Great College St L. First R Barton St.*

Location 3	**BARTON STREET** *c.1722*
	This is the first of three interconnecting 18C streets which are little changed. ●● *Proceed ahead to Cowley St, Lord North St and Smith Square.*

Location 4	**ST JOHN'S SMITH SQUARE** *Archer 1728*
Smith Square *Open for concerts only.*	This church, the second to be built under the 'Fifty New Churches Act', was gutted by bombs in the Second World War and restored as a concert hall. ●● *Proceed clockwise around the building to view the exterior. Alternatively proceed to location 6.* St John's is a rare London example of whole-hearted Baroque. The four corner turrets were designed to equalize the weight of the building which, it was feared, might sink in the marshy ground. Reputedly, St John's was described by Queen Anne as an 'upturned foot stool'. She did not live to see the church but may have been shown a drawing (?). ●● *Proceed to the east facade. First L Dean Stanley St. Cross Millbank and enter Victoria Tower Gardens. Proceed ahead.*

Location 5	**VICTORIA TOWER GARDENS**
	The Buxton memorial fountain by *Teulon* 1865 was transferred here from its original site in Parliament Square. From the gardens at this point are good views across the river to the medieval Lambeth Palace. ●● *Turn R and proceed southward through the gardens. Cross the approach road to Lambeth Bridge and again enter the gardens which continue. Where they end, cross Millbank, turn L and continue southward.*

Location 6	**TATE GALLERY** *S. Smith 1897 (main building)*
Millbank (887 8000) *Open Monday–Saturday 10.00–17.50. Sunday 14.00–17.50. Admission is free but a charge is generally made for special exhibitions.*	The Tate houses the largest collection of modern works of art in Britain. Here also, are displayed works by British artists from all periods, including the renowned Turner Bequest, accommodated, since 1987, in the new Clore Gallery. Sir Henry Tate, the inventor of sugar cubes, donated his own collection, together with £80,000, for a new building in 1891. The government provided the site which had previously been occupied by Millbank Prison. ●● *Enter the main building.*

Free guided tours daily at various times.

The basement restaurant (with outstanding wine list) is open for lunch only, Monday–Saturday 12.00–15.00. Reservations recommended (887 8877).

The permanent British Collection of paintings by artists working in Britain and born before 1860 is now combined chronologically with the modern collection of paintings and sculptures by all artists born after 1860. A printed up-to-date guide is available at the main entrance.

•● *Pass the shop and turn L to Room 15.*

Outstanding works include the following, which are frequently, although not always, on display:

'The Age of Innocence' *Reynolds*
Works by *Blake*
'Flatford Mill' *Constable*
'Boyhood of Raleigh' *Millais*
'The Kiss' *Rodin*
Impressionists and Post-Impressionists
'The Snail' *Matisse*

The Clore Gallery, which now houses the Turner Collection, was designed by *James Stirling*. It has its own entrance or may be approached via the main gallery.

•● *Exit L. Cross the road and proceed northward through the Embankment Gardens. First R Lambeth Bridge. First L Lambeth Palace Rd. Cross the road to the old church that adjoins the Lambeth Palace Gateway and now houses the Garden History Museum.*

Location 7

MUSEUM OF GARDEN HISTORY

St Mary at Lambeth, Lambeth Palace Road (261 1891)

Open from the first Sunday in March until the second Sunday in December, Monday–Friday 11.00–15.00 Sunday 10.30–17.00. Admission free.

The old parish church of St Mary has been deconsecrated and now accommodates a museum of garden history.

Externally, the tower is mostly 14C but the remainder is the work of *P. C. Hardwick* 1851.

This museum is operated by the Tradescant Trust. The John Tradescants, father and son, were 17C gardeners, and the museum illustrates their work.

In the chancel are two early 16C recessed tomb chests.

At the rear of the old churchyard, now the Tradescant Garden, are the tombs of the Tradescants and Captain Bligh of the *Bounty*.

•● *Exit R. Proceed to the gatehouse of Lambeth Palace and await the guide.*

Location 8

LAMBETH PALACE

Lambeth Palace Road

Open by appointment only. Admission free.

Lambeth Palace has been the residence of Archbishops of Canterbury since the 13C and many ancient buildings remain. Archbishop Langton acquired a manor house that stood on part of the present site *c.*1207 and this was later extended to become a palace. Its main entrance was originally from the river.

The Gatehouse (Morton's Tower). Built in 1486 for Archbishop Morton, it replaced an earlier structure. During the Commonwealth, much of the building accommodated royalist prisoners and a prison cell remains at the lower floor level. The tower now houses part of the library and the palace archives.

Visitors may not tour the palace unaccompanied and the route followed from here can vary.

Great Hall. This hall was built for Archbishop Juxon in 1663 and replaced an earlier building destroyed during the Commonwealth. Although there are some Renaissance details, it is basically an extremely late example of the Gothic style.

The restored hammerbeam roof is the last known genuine example to be built in London.

Lambeth Palace's library was established in 1610 and transferred here at the suggestion of architect *Blore* c.1830.

The oak tables were made in 1664.

Displayed in the hall is a bust by *Epstein* of Archbishop Fisher who crowned Elizabeth II in 1952.

Water (Lollard's) Tower. Built for Archbishop Chichele in 1435, this tower gained its name from the 'Lollards', who were reputedly imprisoned in its turret.

Post Room. This room, at the foot of Lollard's Tower, first acquired its 'post' in the 18C as a support to the roof. It was removed following the Second World War, but the timber roof, with its decorative bosses, remains.

Dividing this room is the screen that was made for the chapel in the 17C. It bears Archbishop Laud's arms.

Chapel. The original doorway of the 13C chapel also displays the arms of Archbishop Laud which were added in the 17C. The Lollard, John Wycliffe, was arraigned here for heresy.

Although mostly rebuilt after bombing, the chapel's 13C floor tiles, altar rail and bench heads survive.

A change in floor level denotes where the screen, now in the Post Room, originally stood.

Undercroft. This was constructed in the 13C and is the oldest remaining part of Lambeth Palace. There is a tradition that the marriage of Anne Boleyn and Henry VIII was annulled here in 1536 (?).

Cranmer's Tower. The tower was added in the mid-16C, reputedly for Archbishop Cranmer.

The **Guard Room,** remodelled in the 19C, housed the Archbishops' armour as well as their guards. Most of the roof timbers are original.

Exit R. Cross Lambeth Bridge Road. First R follow the river path (Albert Embankment).

Alternatively, to see the Imperial War Museum exit L. Proceed eastward through the old churchyard. First L Lambeth Palace Road. Seventh R enter the grounds of the museum (15 minutes walk).

Alternatively, take any eastbound bus to the museum.

Location 9

IMPERIAL WAR MUSEUM

Lambeth Road (416 5000)

Open daily 10.00-18.00. Admission charge but free after 16.30. Free film shows are given at weekends.

The museum, founded at the Crystal Palace in 1920, displays the history of Britain and the Commonwealth at war in the 20C.

Its building by *Lewis* 1815 originally housed the Bethlehem (Bedlam) lunatic asylum.

The dome and portico were added by *R. Smirke* 1840.

Exhibits include a German V1 'Doodlebug' and a Spitfire.

Many historic documents are displayed, including the Munich Agreement between Neville Chamberlain and Adolf Hitler, Hitler's last proclamation from the bunker, and Germany's 1945 surrender document.

•• *Exit L returning to Lambeth Palace and the riverside walk R.*

The famous riverside vista of the Houses of Parliament (itinerary 7) can now be seen.

Location 10

WESTMINSTER BRIDGE *Page 1862*

The bridge's immediate predecessor by *Labelye* 1748 was only the second to span the Thames in central London. Interested parties in the City, plus Westminster ferrymen, tried unsuccessfully to stop its construction and sabotage led to the collapse of a pillar. The view from the original bridge in 1802 was praised by Wordsworth in his poem 'On Westminster Bridge' and, although much changed, it is still one of London's finest.

•• *Continue ahead.*

Location 11

SOUTH BANK LION

The lion once stood above the entrance to the old Lion Brewery at the south end of Hungerford Bridge. It was cast in Coade stone in 1837 and is the best known work in that material. The lion has been adopted as the emblem of the South Bank Arts Centre.

•• *Cross the road and descend the steps ahead. Continue along the Albert Embankment.*

Location 12

COUNTY HALL *Knott 1912*

This was the headquarters of London's administrative body, the Greater London Council (GLC), dissolved in 1986. Its future use is uncertain.

•• *Continue ahead.*

Location 13

HUNGERFORD BRIDGE *Hawkshaw 1864*

A pedestrian suspension bridge was built by *Brunel* in 1836 to improve access to the new market which briefly occupied the site of the demolished Hungerford House. However, Charing Cross Station was built there in 1863 and the present structure also carries the railway line.

•• *Ascend the ramp R to the upper level walkway that links most of the buildings in the South Bank Arts complex.*

Location 14

ROYAL FESTIVAL HALL *Martin* and *Matthew 1951*

Belvedere Road (928 3191)

Guided tours daily 12.45 and 17.30 (charge).

This was the first building to be constructed in the South Bank Arts Complex and is the only survivor of the 1951 Festival of Britain. The hall seats 3,000 and was designed primarily for concerts as a replacement for the bombed Queens Hall. When completed, it was London's first public building in the 'Contemporary' style, now known as Modernism.

The hall was built in concrete but later clad in Portland Stone.

Continue ahead.

Location 15	**QUEEN ELIZABETH HALL/PURCELL ROOM** *1967*
Belvedere Road (928 3191)	These two halls each accommodate small concerts. The Queen Elizabeth Hall seats 1,100 and the Purcell Room 370. *Exit from the hall L and ascend the steps.*

Location 16	**HAYWARD GALLERY** *1968*
Belvedere Road (928 5708) *Open Thursday–Monday 10.00–18.00, Tuesday–Wednesday 10.00–20.00*	The gallery displays temporary exhibitions concentrating on 20C works. There are five galleries on two levels and three open-air sculpture courts. *Exit from the gallery R. Descend the steps L and proceed ahead to the National Film Theatre.*

Location 17	**NATIONAL FILM THEATRE** *1967*
South Bank (928 3232) *Only members of the British Film Institute are admitted but anyone can join here at any time and daily and monthly membership is available.*	The NFT screens over 2000 films a year, including the classics and foreign films. Like the Festival Hall it was created as part of the Festival of Britain in 1951 but has been rebuilt and enlarged to provide two cinemas seating 466 and 165. *The Museum of the Moving Image is approached from the same foyer as the National Film Theatre.*

Location 18	**MUSEUM OF THE MOVING IMAGE**
South Bank *Open daily 10.00–18.00. Admission Charge.*	Opened in 1988, within the same building as the National Film Theatre, this extensive museum tracks the history of cinema and television in chronological order. Exhibits from the formative years of the 'moving image' are a particular delight for children. Several hours should be allotted to explore the museum adequately. *Exit from the building. Ascend the steps and return to the upper level. Proceed ahead beneath Waterloo Bridge.*

Location 19	**NATIONAL THEATRE** *Lasdun 1976*
Upper Ground (928 2252) *Guided tours (charge) of 1¼ hours are given Monday–Saturday, 10.15, 12.30, 12.45, 17.30 and 18.00. When there is a matinée at the Olivier, times are 10.15, 12.45 and 17.45. Apply in person for these at the Lyttelton information desk or ring (633 0880).*	The National incorporates three separate theatres, the Olivier, the Lyttelton and the Cottesloe. The Olivier, the largest, seats 1,100. The theatre has become a social centre with its art exhibitions, restaurants and bars. *Return to the steps and ascend to Waterloo Bridge.*

Location 20 **WATERLOO BRIDGE** *Giles Gilbert Scott 1945*

The present structure replaced the elegant bridge designed by *Rennie* in 1817. It is well situated for night views of London's floodlit north bank. Somerset House lies next to the bridge and St Paul's Cathedral can be seen further east.

Return along Waterloo Rd to Waterloo Station, Bakerloo and Northern lines and British Rail.

Alternatively, cross the bridge and descend the steps R to the Victoria Embankment. Turn L and proceed to Temple Station, Circle and District lines.

Itinerary 9

9

Trafalgar Square and the Embankment

Trafalgar Square, dominated by Nelson's column, represents to many the centre of London. On its north side, within the National Gallery, can be seen some of the world's greatest paintings.

Timing: Mornings, Monday to Saturday, are preferable as the art galleries then open at 10.00. The Queen's Chapel of the Savoy is open Tuesday to Friday.

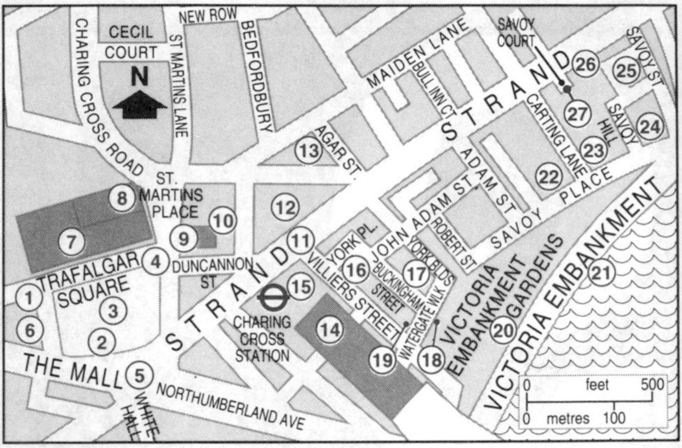

Locations
1 Trafalgar Square
2 Nelson Monument
3 Trafalgar Square Precinct
4 George IV Monument
5 Charles I Monument
6 Canada House
7 National Gallery
8 National Portrait Gallery
9 St Martin-in-the-Fields
10 St Martin's Parochial Buildings
11 Strand
12 West Strand Improvements
13 Old Charing Cross Hospital
14 Charing Cross Hotel
15 Charing Cross Monument
16 The Adelphi
17 Buckingham Street
18 York Water Gate
19 Gordon's Wine Cellar
20 Victoria Embankment Gardens
21 Cleopatra's Needle
22 Shell-Mex House
23 Savoy Hotel
24 Radio Station 2LO
25 The Queen's Chapel of the Savoy
26 Simpsons-in-the-Strand
27 Savoy Court

Start *Charing Cross Station, Bakerloo, Jubilee and Northern lines. From the Bakerloo line, after the ticket barrier, take the steps R (Trafalgar Square exit), then the first steps immediately R again. From the Jubilee and Northern lines, turn L at the barrier. Leave by the Trafalgar Square exit. Ahead Trafalgar Square.*

Location 1 — **TRAFALGAR SQUARE**

The square, traditionally named by William IV, was conceived by *Nash* in 1812 as the final stage in his Marylebone Park to Charing Cross scheme but he played no part in its final design. Its formation began in 1824 with the eastward extension of Pall Mall. The long-established Royal Mews stables, including a street evocatively named Dung Hill Mews, were then demolished. Public meetings and demonstrations have been held in the square since it was laid out and crowds gather here to celebrate New Year's Eve and Election Night. Since the Second World War, Norway has annually presented a tall conifer tree which is erected in the square. Carols are sung around it in the evenings at Christmastime.

Locations 2, 3, 4, 5, 6 and 7 are in Trafalgar Square.

Proceed to the base of Nelson's column.

Location 2 — **NELSON MONUMENT**

This 19C monument to England's greatest naval hero, is the best known in London. Its granite column and bronze capital by *Railton* are 170 feet high and the statue by *Baily*, in two pieces of Scottish stone

17 feet high. The statue was erected in 1843.

Proceed clockwise around the monument.

Bronze reliefs, on the podium, illustrate Nelson's major battles in the Napoleonic wars. The last was mounted in 1854 but none of them were cast from French cannon as is frequently alleged.

Proceed clockwise around the column to see the reliefs.

South side, Trafalgar 1805 *Carew*. West side, St Vincent 1797 *Watson*. North side, Nile 1798 *Woodington*.

East side, Copenhagen 1801 *Ternouth*.

The lions by *Landseer* were not completed until 1867.

Location 3

TRAFALGAR SQUARE PRECINCT *C. Barry 1840*

The sloping ground was levelled to create the precinct and a terrace was formed on the north side. Barry was forced against his will to provide for the Nelson column as he thought the square was too small.

Proceed to the south-east corner.

The monument to Havelock commemorates a brutal suppressor of the Indian Mutiny.

Proceed to the south-west corner.

The monument to General Napier, 1856, was the first in the square to commemorate an army leader.

Proceed northward.

The fountains by *Lutyens* 1936 commemorate Admirals Jellicoe and Beatty. Barry's originals now face Parliament in Ottawa, Canada.

Continue to the wall of the north terrace.

Busts against the wall commemorate Admirals Cunningham, Jellicoe and Beatty. Between them are bronze Standards of Imperial measurement.

Proceed R to the north-east corner of the precinct.

Location 4

GEORGE IV MONUMENT *Chantrey 1841*

This equestrian statue was commissioned by George IV in 1829 to surmount the Marble Arch, which originally stood in front of Buckingham Palace. However, the King died in 1830 and that site was considered inappropriate. It was another eleven years before the statue was completed and became the first monument to be erected in Trafalgar Square. 'King George IV' had to be added as by then few knew who the gentleman in the Roman toga represented.

Return to the south side of the precinct, and cross to the small traffic island with the Charles I monument.

Location 5

CHARLES I MONUMENT *Le Sueur 1633*

Charles I's equestrian statue, judged London's finest, looks towards the Banqueting House from where the King stepped to the scaffold for his execution on 30 January 1649. Every year on that day, wreaths are laid around the monument as a tribute.

Lord Weston commissioned this, the oldest equestrian statue in London, for his garden at Roehampton. When the Civil War broke out in 1642 the statue was transferred to the churchyard of St Paul, Covent Garden.

It disappeared but was rediscovered in 1660 in the possession of a brazier. Charles II purchased the work and ordered its erection here in 1675. The pedestal was carved by *Joshua Marshall* (?).

Traditionally, all distances from London are measured from this point.

Proceed to the west side of the square.

Location 6

CANADA HOUSE *R. Smirke 1827*

Trafalgar Square

This was built in Bath stone for the Union Club and is the only building, apart from the National Gallery, that survives from the square's initial development. The building was heightened and extended when it was converted to Canada House in 1924.

Continue ahead to the north side of the square R.

Location 7

NATIONAL GALLERY *Wilkins 1838*

Trafalgar Square (839 3321)

Open Monday–Saturday 10.00–18.00. Sunday 14.00–18.00. Admission free to the collection.

This is one of the world's major art galleries and European paintings from *c.* 1260–1920 are displayed.

On the lawn, to the west, is the statue of James II by *Gibbons* 1686, which originally stood in the privy garden of Whitehall Palace outside the Banqueting House. James had been Duke of York prior to his accession and the city of New York was named to commemorate him.

To the east, the bronze of George Washington is a copy of the marble statue by *Houdon* in Richmond, Virginia, USA.

The National Gallery was built to house the collection of Sir John Angerstein, purchased by the government in 1824. Its site had previously been occupied by the main building of the royal stables and, following the layout of Trafalgar Square, became one of the most important in London.

The bases and capitals of some of the columns came from the Prince Regent's Carlton House.

The building was extended to the north-east *c.* 1890 and the Sainsbury wing added to the west in 1991, to house the Early Renaissance works.

Ascend the steps beneath the central portico and enter the vestibule.

The interiors of the **vestibule** and, behind it, the **central hall**, were designed by *J. Taylor* in 1887 and those of most of the galleries by *E. M. Barry* in 1876. The Royal Academy of Arts moved here from Somerset House in 1837 and occupied much of the east side until 1868.

A printed guide to the whereabouts of the works, most of which are exhibited on one floor level, is provided at the information desk. The collection, rehung in 1991, is divided into four zones, defined by date; Sainsbury Wing 1260–1510; West Wing 1510–1600; North Wing 1600–1700; East Wing 1700–1920. A selection of the most popular works is as follows:

'The Wilton Diptych'
'The Battle of San Romano' *Uccello*
'Venus and Mars' *Botticelli*
Cartoon 'Virgin and Child' *Leonardo da Vinci*
'The Virgin of the Rocks' *Leonardo da Vinci*
'Bacchus and Ariadne' *Titian*
'Doge Loredan' *Bellini*

'Charles I on Horseback' *Van Dyck*
'Le Chapeau de Paille' *Rubens*
'The Ambassadors' *Holbein*
'Arnolfini and his Wife' *Van Eyck*
Self portrait *Rembrandt*
'The Fighting Temeraire' *Turner*
'The Haywain' *Constable*
'The Shrimp Girl' *Hogarth*
'The Toilet of Venus' *Velasquez*
'La Servante de Bocks' *Manet*
'La Première Sortie' *Renoir*
'The Bathers' *Seurat*
'Sunflowers' *Van Gogh*
'Water-lilies' *Monet*

Exit from the building. L St Martin's Place.

Location 8

NATIONAL PORTRAIT GALLERY
Christian and *Colling 1895*

St Martin's Place
(306 0055)

Open Monday–Saturday 10.00–18.00. Sunday 12.00–18.00. Admission is free but a charge is occasionally made for special exhibitions.

Eminent Britons are portrayed, mainly by paintings, but there are also some drawings, busts and photographs. The artistic quality is variable, as the aim of the gallery is primarily historical.

A selection of celebrated portraits is given with their gallery numbers.

At the top of the stairs ahead turn L and ascend by lift directly to level 5. Proceed clockwise.

1C *Elizabeth I.* 'Queen Elizabeth I' *Gheeraerts.* 'Shakespeare' *J. Taylor* (the Chandos portrait). Miniatures of 'Drake' and 'Raleigh' *Hilliard.*
2 *James I and Charles I* 'Thomas Howard, Earl of Arundel' *Rubens.*
9 *18C Art* Bust of 'Hogarth' *Roubiliac.* 'Dr Johnson', 'Laurence Stern' and 'Self-Portrait' all by *Reynolds.*
15 *Regency* Various portraits *Lawrence.*

Descend the stairs.

21 *Mid-Victorian Art* 'Ellen Terry' *Watts.*
25 *Edwardian* 'Self-Portrait' *Gwen John.* 'Henry James' and 'Frank Swettenham' *Sargent.*

A gallery on this floor houses special exhibitions.

Descend the stairs to the 20C Gallery.

Sketches of 'Somerset Maugham' and 'Churchill' *Sutherland.* Sutherland's finished painting was disliked by Churchill whose widow subsequently destroyed it.

Exit R. St Martin's Place. Cross the road.

Location 9

ST MARTIN-IN-THE-FIELDS* *Gibbs 1726*

St Martin's Place

Open daily 07.30–21.30. Brass-rubbing centre in the crypt, approached from Duncannon St, open Monday–Saturday 10.00–18.00. Sunday 12.00–18.00.

St Martin's is the best loved work of the Scottish architect James Gibbs.

The previous St Martin's, originally a 13C chapel, had been rebuilt in 1544. In that church, Charles II was baptized and Nell Gwyn, his favourite mistress, buried. When the present church was built it was surrounded by narrow streets, a clear view of its west facade only being revealed in 1824 when the formation of Trafalgar Square began with the eastward extension of Pall Mall. The position of St Martin's tower, rising centrally behind the huge portico of what is virtually a Classical temple, has always been controversial. This format was soon adopted for many churches, particularly in the USA.

Unlike the same architect's St Mary-le-Strand, St Martin's has few Baroque features.

The tower was rebuilt in 1824 as a replica.

St Martin's is the parish church of the sovereign and the coat of arms of George I is carved on the pediment.

Ascend the steps to the portico and enter the church.

Massive columns support the tunnel-vaulted ceiling which was plastered by the Italian craftsmen *Artari* and *Bagutti*.

The box pews (shortened) choir stalls and pulpit were made in 1799.

On the ceiling above the altar are the arms of George I.

North of the altar is the Royal Box. The Admiralty Box is on the south side.

At the east end of the north aisle is a portrait of Gibbs by *Soldi* 1740.

Leave the east end of the north aisle by the door L of Gibbs's portrait. Exit from the church by the next door L which leads to the old churchyard, now paved. Ahead, are St Martin's Parochial Buildings.

Location 10

ST MARTIN'S PAROCHIAL BUILDINGS

These three buildings, in late Regency style, formed part of Nash's West Strand Improvements scheme.

Situated on the St Martin's Lane corner, the **vicarage** was built three storeys high.

A roundel of St Martin by *Pitt* decorates the portico of **St Martin's Vestry Hall.**

St Martin's National School by *G. L. Taylor* 1830 had one huge room per floor, each accommodating 350.

Return to the church and exit to St Martin's Lane L. First L Duncannon St. Second L Strand. Immediately L are the West Strand Improvements.

Location 11

STRAND

The jollity of this thoroughfare, commemorated in the well-known music hall song 'Let's all go down the Strand', is a thing of the past. It is now dominated by commercial buildings. In the mid 13C the Savoy Palace became the first of many great houses to be built in Strand, originally called Stronde. Most of them were demolished in the late 17C and residential streets were laid out in their place.

In the late 19C more theatres lined Strand than any other street in London; they included the famous Gaiety and Tivoli. Shops, restaurants and pubs added to Strand's popularity and a rakish reputation was established. It's demise began when most of the south side was rebuilt for street widening *c.*1900.

Location 12

WEST STRAND IMPROVEMENTS *Herbert c.1830*

430–449 Strand

Like Trafalgar Square, the improvements were planned, although not executed, by *Nash*. The building is famous for its 'pepper-pot' domes.

Continue northward to the modern central section.

A fashionable shopping precinct, the Lowther Arcade, originally ran through the centre, but this was replaced in 1903 by a building for Coutts Bank designed in an unharmonious style. The present glass-faced structure took its place in 1981 when the rest of the building was restored externally. The interiors throughout have been rebuilt.

Continue ahead. Second L Agar St.

Location 13

OLD CHARING CROSS HOSPITAL *D. Burton 1834*

Agar Street

The stuccoed facade in Agar Street originally continued in the same style along William IV Street (first L) but was rebuilt and extended late in the 19C. It is no longer a hospital and is being redeveloped.

Return to Strand R. Cross the road to the Charing Cross Hotel facing the station's forecourt.

Location 14

CHARING CROSS HOTEL *E. M. Barry 1864*

Originally the site of the hotel and the station was occupied by Hungerford House. This was demolished and Hungerford Market took its place from 1830 until the station was built in 1863. The two upper storeys of the hotel are modern additions.

Proceed to the west side of the forecourt.

Location 15

CHARING CROSS MONUMENT
E. M. Barry and *T. Earp 1864*

Strand

This monument commemorates Charing's Eleanor Cross which stood further west, exactly where the Charles I monument now stands. It is not a replica. Queen Eleanor, consort of Edward I, died at Hanby, near Lincoln, in 1290 and the King erected a memorial where her body had rested on its journey to Westminster. The original cross at Charing was set up *c.*1293 but demolished by order of the Long Parliament in 1647. The Anglo-Saxon *cerr* meaning a bend (in the river) probably gave the ancient village of Charing its name (?). It did not derive from *chère reine* (dear queen) as many believe.

Exit from the forecourt R. First R Villiers St. Second L John Adam St.

Location 16

THE ADELPHI *c.1770*

The Adelphi was a speculative riverside development of houses by the Adam brothers (*adelphoi* is Greek for brothers) on the site of the early 14C Durham House. The development, initially unsuccessful, was only saved by a lottery – with the houses as prizes. Eventually, however, The Adelphi became a popular address for literary celebrities and Shaw, Hardy, Galsworthy and Barrie all lived here in the 19C.

The development consisted of Adelphi Terrace, which faced the river, and behind this, the central section of John Adam Street; two side streets, Robert Street and Adam Street completed the scheme. Most of the Adelphi was demolished in 1936.

Continue along John Adam Street. Second R York Buildings. First L Lower Robert St.

The archway ahead leads to Lower Robert Street, one of the underground tunnels that formed part of the sub-structure of the demolished Adelphi Terrace.

Return to John Adam St R. First R Robert St.

Nos 1, 2 and 3 on the south-west side are original.

Return to John Adam Street R. Cross the road.

Nos 8 (Royal Society of Arts), 6, 4 and 2 are original.

First L Adam Street.

On the corner is No 18 and opposite, on the east side, Nos 10, 9, 8 and 7. All these are original.

Return along John Adam St. Third L Buckingham St.

Location 17

BUCKINGHAM STREET *c.1676*

This is one of several streets developed on the site of York House. In 1626, George Villiers, first Duke of Buckingham, rebuilt or remodelled (?) York House, a 13C mansion that had been the residence of the Bishops of York. After Buckingham's assassination in 1628, the second Duke rarely lived at York House and, as he needed money, sold the estate to a developer in 1676. Buckingham stipulated, however, that the new thoroughfares should record his full name and title (the same as his father's), George Villiers, Duke of Buckingham. Five of them were, therefore, named George Court, Villiers and Duke Streets, Of Alley (now York Place) and Buckingham Street.
Many 17C and 18C houses remain in Buckingham Street. No 12, at the south-east end, was occupied by the diarist, Samuel Pepys from 1679–85. Its original staircase survives.

Descend the steps at the end of Buckingham Street to Watergate Walk. Immediately ahead is the York Water Gate.

Location 18

YORK WATER GATE *1626*

Watergate Walk

Once the watergate to York House, this is now the only survivor of the Strand's great riverside mansions, most of which had water gates to their gardens. The river was much wider before the embankment was built in 1870 and its water would have lapped against the steps which once led up to this gate. The York Water Gate was built by *Nicholas Stone* but there is no evidence that *Inigo Jones* was its designer as has been alleged. The arms of the Villiers family are carved on the stonework and there is a descriptive plaque on the south side.

Continue westward along Watergate Walk to Gordon's on the corner of Villiers St. Descend the steps to the bar.

Location 19

GORDON'S WINE CELLAR

47 Villiers Street

A Gordon's wine cellar has been established for many years in this basement, part of which runs beneath Villiers Street and pre-dates the remainder. Until recently, Gordon's had been owned by a Free Vintner who needed no licence and could open and close as he wished. The present owner, however, has a standard licence.

Some Victorian decor remains in the main cellar which, like the house above, is early 19C.

Leave by the Villiers St exit L. Second L proceed through Victoria Embankment Gardens.

Location 20 **VICTORIA EMBANKMENT GARDENS**

These gardens were created when the Victoria Embankment was constructed *c.*1870.

Leave the gardens by the second exit R. R Victoria Embankment. Cross the road.

Location 21 **CLEOPATRA'S NEEDLE**

Victoria Embankment

Cleopatra's Needle is London's oldest monument. It was first erected at On (Heliopolis) near Cairo by Pharaoh Thotmes III *c.*1500BC. The obelisk was relocated, together with its twin, at Alexandria, city of the Cleopatras, in 12BC. Mohammad Ali, Turkish Viceroy of Egypt, presented it to England in 1819 but due to technical difficulties, transportation did not begin until 1877. On the way to England, it was lost during a storm in the Bay of Biscay and six seamen were drowned. Fortunately, the needle was encased in a steel shell which remained afloat and was soon recovered.

The obelisk was erected on its present site in 1878 and commemorates Nelson and General Abercrombie. Its twin was presented to the United States and stands in Central Park, New York. Before the obelisk was erected, items in daily use in 1878 were buried below in a 'time capsule'. They included the morning paper, a photograph of Queen Victoria and a copy of Bradshaw's railway timetable.

The central hieroglyphics, inscribed for Thotmes III, record the erection of the obelisk and include prayers to the sun god. Ramses II added the inscriptions on the sides, describing his victorious battles.

The bronze sphinxes were cast for the pedestal by *Vulliamy* 1878.

Cross the road and turn R. First L re-enter the gardens. Follow the short path ahead to the Robert Raikes monument. Do not leave the gardens. Ahead, the building with the clock is Shell-Mex House.

Location 22 **SHELL-MEX HOUSE** *1886*

Savoy Place

This office block was built originally as the Cecil Hotel on the site of Cecil House. The hotel possessed 800 bedrooms and was Europe's largest. Its river facade was remodelled in 1931.

Remain in the gardens. The next building, R of Shell-Mex House, is the Savoy Hotel.

Location 23 **SAVOY HOTEL** *Collcutt 1889*

Savoy Place (836 4343)

Founded by Richard D'Oyly Carte, the hotel occupies the site of the Palace of Savoy built for Peter, Earl of Savoy, in 1245 and destroyed by Wat Tyler's rebels in 1381. The Savoy Hotel opened with seventy bathrooms – then an unheard of number for an hotel. Its original main entrance was in Savoy Hill. The riverside block was refaced in 1910.

Follow the path R and proceed eastward.

Facing the hotel is the monument to the composer of the Gilbert and Sullivan operas, Sir Arthur Sullivan, d.1900 by *Goscombe John* 1903.

Continue eastward to the end of the gardens.

Exit L Savoy Place. Proceed ahead. Just before Savoy Hill (first R) there is a wall plaque commemorating Radio Station 2LO.

Location 24

RADIO STATION 2LO

Institute of Electrical Engineers, Savoy Hill

The British Broadcasting Company (now Corporation) operated the world's first national radio station, 2LO, from this building in 1923.

First R Savoy Hill. Follow the bend in the road and cross to the Queen's Chapel of the Savoy.

Location 25

THE QUEEN'S CHAPEL OF THE SAVOY

Savoy Hill

Open Tuesday–Friday 11.30–15.30. Closed August and September.

The chapel was built *c.* 1516 and originally formed part of the Hospital of St John. It was adopted by the Royal Victorian Order in 1937.

All the walls are Tudor except for the south front which faces Savoy Hill and was rebuilt, together with the bell turret, by *R. Smirke c.* 1820.

Enter the single-storey extension. From the vestibule, the first door L leads to the **chapel.**

The building was gutted by fire and reconstructed internally by *S. Smirke* 1864.

Immediately ahead are the royal stalls.

The altar is unusually sited at the north end. Behind this is a small 14C Florentine painting.

Return to the vestibule. Turn L to the **vestry.**

The stained glass in the vestry window ahead that looks on to the vestibule is 13C and 14C and was presented in 1954.

Exit L. First L Savoy St. Second L Strand. Proceed to Simpsons facing the Strand Palace Hotel.

Location 26

SIMPSONS-IN-THE-STRAND

100 Strand (836 9112)

Lunch and dinner served daily, breakfast served Monday–Friday.

Simpsons is an old established restaurant and renowned for its traditional English roasts. It was founded on the same site in 1828 but the present building dates from 1904. The ground floor dining room still tends to be a male preserve at lunchtime Monday to Friday and reservations are then advisable.

Exit L. First L Savoy Court.

Location 27

SAVOY COURT

Savoy Court is the only highway in England where driving is on the right, a facility permitted by Act of Parliament so that carriages could pull up more easily outside the new Savoy Theatre. The theatre was built for Richard D'Oyly Carte in 1881 to house the new Gilbert & Sullivan operettas. It now adjoins the hotel's Strand block which was added in 1904.

Exit from Savoy Place L. If following with itinerary 10 cross Strand and proceed to the Vaudeville Theatre. Take the first alleyway R (with Nell Gwyn Tavern tiling). It is called Bull Inn Court but unnamed at this end. R Maiden Lane.

Alternatively, walk or take any bus westward along Strand to Charing Cross Station, Bakerloo, Jubilee and Northern lines.

Itinerary 10

10

Covent Garden and Lincoln's Inn

Covent Garden has recently been transformed from a fruit and vegetable market to one of London's liveliest sectors with shops, bars, restaurants and exhibitions. A hall, built in the year that Columbus discovered America, is the proudest possession of Lincoln's Inn.

Timing: A morning start, Tuesday to Friday, is recommended. The Soane Museum closes on Monday and throughout August. Telephone Lincoln's Inn and Gray's Inn first to ensure entry to their halls. Last admission to the Coram Foundation is 15.30 and the Dickens House Museum 16.30.

10

Locations

1 Rules
2 Covent Garden
3 St Paul, Covent Garden
4 No 43 King Street
5 The Market
6 Jubilee Market
7 London Transport Museum
8 Floral Hall
9 Theatre Museum
10 Royal Opera House, Covent Garden
11 Theatre Royal, Drury Lane
12 Somerset House
13 Courtauld Art Galleries
14 Roman Bath
15 The Watch House
16 St Mary-le-Strand
17 The Old Curiosity Shop
18 Lincoln's Inn Fields
19 Sir John Soane's Museum
20 Lincoln's Inn
21 Lincoln's Inn Library
22 Lincoln's Inn New Hall
23 New Square
24 Lincoln's Inn Old Hall
25 Lincoln's Inn Chapel
26 Old Square
27 Stone Buildings
28 Lincoln's Inn Gatehouse
29 Old Buildings
30 Carey Street Arch
31 The Seven Stars
32 Public Record Office
33 Gray's Inn Gateway
34 Gray's Inn
35 South Square
36 Gray's Inn Hall
37 Gray's Inn Chapel
38 Gray's Inn Square
39 Gray's Inn Walks
40 Thomas Coram Foundation
41 Dickens House Museum
42 The Lamb

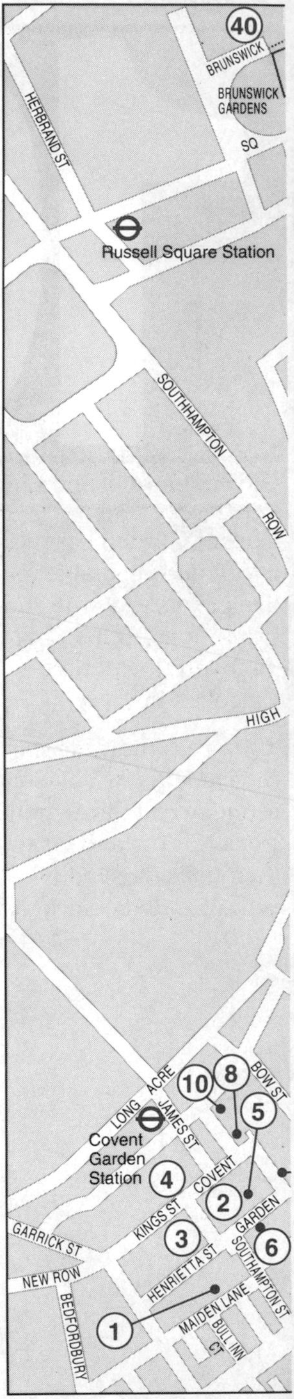

10

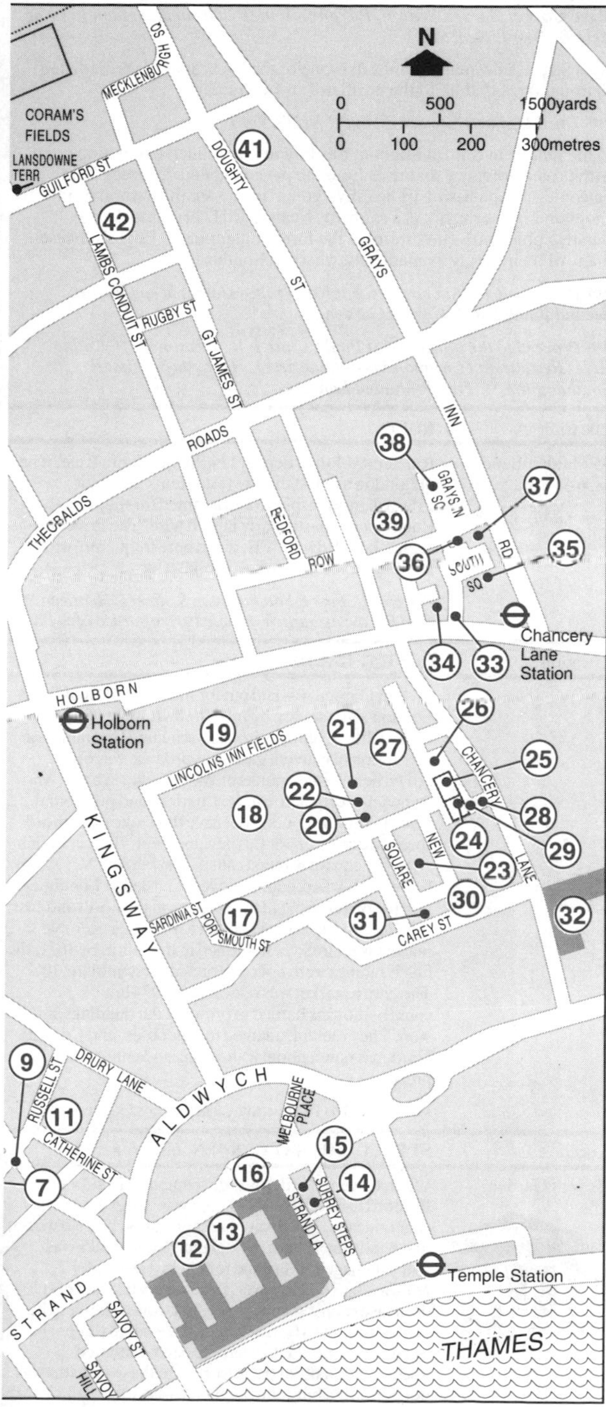
N
0
500
1500yards
0
100
200
300metres
MECKLENBURGH SQ
CORAM'S FIELDS
LANSDOWNE TERR
GUILFORD ST
DOUGHTY ST
LAMBS CONDUIT ST
RUGBY ST
GT JAMES ST
GRAYS INN RD
THEOBALDS ROADS
BEDFORD ROW
GRAYS INN SQ
SOUTH SQ
Chancery Lane Station
HOLBORN
Holborn Station
LINCOLNS INN FIELDS
KINGSWAY
CHANCERY LANE
NEW SQUARE
CAREY ST
SARDINIA ST
PORTSMOUTH ST
DRURY LANE
RUSSELL ST
CATHERINE ST
ALDWYCH
MELBOURNE PLACE
STRAND LA
SURREY STEPS
STRAND
SAVOY ST
SAVOY HILL
Temple Station
THAMES
7
9
11
12
13
14
15
16
17
18
19
20
21
22
23
24
25
26
27
28
29
30
31
32
33
34
35
36
37
38
39
41
42

Start *Covent Garden Station, Piccadilly line. Exit from the station to Long Acre R. First L Neal St.*

Neal Street, now pedestrianised, is one of the liveliest of the remodelled thoroughfares that lie to the north of Covent Garden.

Third L Shorts Gardens. First R Neal's Yard.

Quite unique in central London, this tiny square is filled to bursting point with potted greenery that rises from the pavement and descends from balconies. Emphasising its healthy, 'green' image are the natural food shops and restaurants. As a contrast, Neals Yard Dairy is stocked to bursting point with cholesterol in the form of hand-made English cheeses, many of them rarely available elsewhere in London.

Return to Covent Garden Station and follow James St southward. Second R and first L Covent Garden.

Proceed to the portico of St Paul's Church R (location 2). If visiting Rules Restaurant (Location 1) continue first L Henrietta St. First R Southampton St. First R Maiden Lane.

Location 1 — **RULES**

35 Maiden Lane
(836 5314)

Open daily 12.00–24.00.

Rules, established here in 1798 by Benjamin Rule, is one of London's oldest theatre restaurants. It has an Edwardian atmosphere and is famed for traditional English food, particularly jugged hare. The Prince of Wales, later Edward VII, dined here frequently with Lily Langtry, entering by a special door.

Exit L. First L Southampton St. First L Henrietta St. First R Covent Garden. Proceed to the portico of St Paul's.

Location 2 — **COVENT GARDEN**

Covent Garden was laid out for the Duke of Bedford as London's first square by *Inigo Jones c.* 1631. Only St Paul's Church remains from his scheme. The name is a corruption of convent garden as produce was once grown here for the monks of Westminster Abbey, who owned the forty-acre estate. Charles I had prohibited new building in London but gave the Duke of Bedford special permission for this development. Built in Italian style, the square was first called 'The Piazza'. Very soon, however, it was renamed Covent Garden as Londoners insisted on referring to the arcades on the north and east sides as 'the piazzas'. Although a fruit and vegetable market was already established in the centre by 1671, the first buildings were not constructed for it until the 19C. The entire market was relocated in 1974 but conservationists battled to preserve the buildings and won. They remain, adapted to other uses, and Covent Garden is now a popular shopping and entertainments precinct.

Locations 3 to 10 are situated in Covent Garden.

Location 3 — **ST PAUL, COVENT GARDEN** *Inigo Jones 1638*

Covent Garden

When Covent Garden was developed, the Duke of Bedford insisted that the church was designed economically. Allegedly, Jones promised him a barn but 'the handsomest barn in England' (?). St Paul's was badly damaged by fire and rebuilt as a replica by *T. Hardwick* 1793. However, its stone portico and east doorcase survived and are original. Jones planned the main entrance to be from the east, beneath this portico, but the altar would then have had to be situated unconventionally at the west end. In the event, this was not permitted but Jones kept his east portico – albeit with a false door. The portico originally stood on a plinth approached by steps. However, Covent Garden has since been raised to its floor level. It was here that Professor Higgins met Eliza Doolittle in Shaw's *Pygmalion* and later its musical version, *My Fair Lady*.

Proceed to the north side of Covent Garden. L King St. First L a passage leads to St Paul's churchyard.

The brickwork is Victorian and replaced Hardwick's stone walls; Inigo Jones's had been of stuccoed brick.

Enter the church from the west door and proceed through the screen.

The carved wreath L was presented by St. Paul's Cathedral. It is the work of *Grinling Gibbons* and commemorates his burial in the church.

Turner, the painter, was born nearby in Maiden Lane and baptized within the original building in 1775.

Wall tablets commemorate many actors.

The pulpit was made up from sections of an early 19C pulpit and lectern.

Two monuments by *Flaxman* face each other: on the north wall, L of the altar, Edward Hall, d.1798; on the south wall, John Bellamy, d.1794.

Return to King St R. Cross the road.

Location 4

NO 43 KING STREET *Archer (?) 1717*

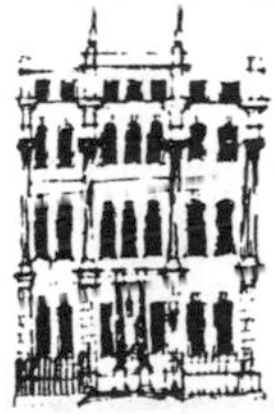

This is believed to be a rare domestic example of the work of Thomas Archer (?), the most Baroque of British architects. It was the first house to interrupt Inigo Jones's arcaded buildings on the north side of Covent Garden.

The top storey was added in the 19C and the doorway remodelled *c.* 1935.

Proceed to the large building in the centre of the square. It is still called the Market.

Location 5

THE MARKET *Fowler 1830*

This building originally housed the vegetable market and has been restored and subdivided into separate units. Five parallel thoroughfares divide the Market: North Row, North Avenue, Central Avenue, South Avenue and South Row.

A basement level is reached from South Avenue.

In North Avenue, the Apple Market is basically a crafts market, but antiques and bric-a-brac are sold here on Mondays.

After exploring the Market proceed to the Jubilee Hall on the south side.

Location 6

JUBILEE MARKET

Jubilee Hall, Covent Garden

Open daily 07.00–16.00. Tuesday to Friday, general market. Monday, flea market. Saturday and Sunday, arts and crafts market.

This is judged to be one of central London's best value street markets. The hall was redeveloped and extended in 1987. A sports centre now occupies its upper level.

Proceed to the east side of Covent Garden.

Location 7	**LONDON TRANSPORT MUSEUM**
The Flower Market, Covent Garden *Open daily 10.00–18.00. Admission charge.*	The museum occupies the ground floor of the hall which was built to house the flower market. Displayed is a collection of London Transport vehicles and posters. Included are the first steam-powered underground train and a replica of Shillibeer's 1824 horse-drawn bus – London's earliest public transport. *Exit R. Proceed ahead.*

Location 8	**FLORAL HALL** *E. M. Barry 1860*
Covent Garden	This hall adjoins the south side of the Royal Opera House and was built for spectators who wished to promenade during concerts. The east and west sections are constructed of intricate ironwork and glass. This building was once leased for the sale of fruit and vegetables, but never flowers, in spite of its name. Restoration is planned. *Turn R. Russell St. Proceed to the Tavistock St corner.*

Location 9	**THEATRE MUSEUM**
1e Tavistock Street (836 7891) *Open Tuesday–Sunday 11.00–19.00 Admission charge.*	Also part of the old flower market, the museum was opened in 1987 under the auspices of the V & A. Facing the Russell Street entrance are boxes from the Palace Theatre, Glasgow. The old Duke of York Theatre's box office is displayed R. *Descend the ramp.* The lower foyer displays 19C and 20C paintings. A permanent chronological display occupies the main gallery. The Gielgud and Irving galleries house temporary exhibitions. *Exit R. First L Bow Street.*

Location 10	**ROYAL OPERA HOUSE** *E. M. Barry 1858*
Bow Street (240 1911)	London's major venue for opera and ballet is the third building on the site. The original theatre, then known as the Theatre Royal, Covent Garden, opened here in 1732. The frieze behind the portico by *Flaxman* 1809 was saved from the previous building. A west extension to the Opera House was completed in 1982. *Return southward along Bow St. Second L Russell St. First R Catherine St.*

Location 11	**THEATRE ROYAL, DRURY LANE** *B. D. Wyatt 1812*
Catherine Street (836 8108) *Tours by appointment only. Admission free.*	'Drury Lane', as the Theatre Royal is generally called, possesses the only internal Georgian features to survive in a London theatre. This is the fourth building on the site; the main entrance is now in Catherine Street, not Drury Lane. Its immediate predecessor of 1794 was the first theatre in the world to fit a safety curtain, but it still burnt down fifteen years later. The then proprietor, Sheridan, watched the blaze from a café opposite. When begged to leave, he protested 'Cannot a man take a glass of wine by his own fireside'. Drury Lane was established in 1663 by Charles II's Royal Charter and it is said

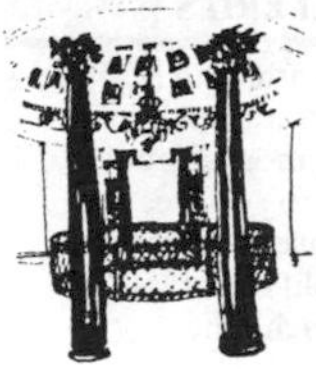

that the King first met Nell Gwyn in the original theatre c.1665 (?). There is reputed to be a Drury Lane ghost, 'The Man in Grey', but the tradition that a skeleton and dagger were discovered in the wall of the Circle is uncorroborated. For many years, Drury Lane has been the major London venue for musicals – mostly American since *Oklahoma* opened in 1946.

Drury Lane's portico was added by *Spiller* in 1820.

The columns forming the Russell Street colonnade by *Beazley* 1831 cannot have come from the old Regent Street Quadrant, as has been alleged, because these were not removed until 1848.

Internally, the vestibule, domed entrance hall, rotunda, staircases and first floor Grand Saloon remain by *Wyatt* but his auditorium was rebuilt in 1922.

Displayed in the vestibule is an 18C bronze statue of Shakespeare by *Cheere*.

Continue southward along Catherine St. Third R Aldwych. First L Strand. Just before St Mary's, the church ahead in the middle of the road, view the facade of the entrance to Somerset House which stands on the south side of Strand.

Location 12 **SOMERSET HOUSE** *Chambers c.1790*

Strand

Courtyard open Monday to Friday 10.00–17.00. Admission free.

Somerset House was the first building to be planned specifically for government offices. It was built on the site of Protector Somerset's mid-16C palace, demolished in 1777. Although designed in the severe Palladian style, much of the building's exterior was embellished with carvings by eminent 18C sculptors including *Bacon the Elder*, *Nollekens* and *Wilton*.

Cross Strand to the Somerset House entrance.

The design of this facade 1776–80 is believed to reproduce some features added by *Inigo Jones* to the old palace in the 17C. (?). First floor rooms, 'The Fine Rooms', were built to accommodate, R the Royal Academy of Arts and L the Royal Society and Antiquaries Society. The Courtauld Institute's collection of paintings is now displayed in these rooms.

Enter the courtyard.

The statue immediately ahead depicts George III in a toga, with Father Thames at his feet by *Bacon the Elder*.

Return northward and turn R. Proceed to the locked gate ahead.

Through the gate can be seen the east wing, added by *R. Smirke* in 1829. Kings College occupies this block.

Return westward and proceed ahead to the west wing.

This was added by *Pennethorne* in 1856 in imitation of Chambers's style and thus completed the original plan. It can be seen that the less important facades here were not clad in stone.

The riverside facade, which is entirely in harmony with the design of Chambers, is best seen from Waterloo Bridge (itinerary 8).

Return towards Strand and enter the block from the archway.

Location 13 — **COURTAULD INSTITUTE GALLERIES**

Somerset House, Strand

Open Monday–Saturday 10.00–18.00. Sunday 14.00–18.00. Admission charge includes gallery guide.

Special exhibitions are held from time to time.

In 1972, the Registry of Births, Deaths and Marriages vacated the Strand block of Somerset House, which incorporated the Fine Rooms, the most splendid interiors of Sir William Chambers to survive. Eventually, it was decided to restore them for the Courtauld Institute, at the time split over two buildings widely separated from each other.

Paintings are exhibited in the rooms designed originally for the Royal Academy and comprise several donated collections. Although they include outstanding old masters and more modern works, particularly British, the highlights are undoubtedly the exceptional French Impressionist and Post-Impressionist paintings, most of which are extremely well known from reproductions.

Ascend by lift to the second floor (descending later by the great west staircase).

Surviving on this floor is the famous Great Room of the Royal Academy, where members' paintings were hung 'above the line' (the cornice) as part of the summer exhibitions held in the room 1780–1836. It was here that many of the great works of Constable, Gainsborough, Lawrence, Reynolds and Turner were first shown in public.

The French Impressionist and Post-Impressionist paintings, which attract most visitors include: 'The Card Players', 'Mont St Victoire' and 'Le Lac d'Annecy', *Cézanne*; 'A Bar at the Folies Bergère', *Manet*; 'La Loge', *Renoir*; 'Self-Portrait with Bandaged Ear', *Van Gogh*; 'Nevermore', *Gauguin* and 'Jane Avril', *Toulouse Lautrec*.

Exit to Strand R. First R Surrey St. Proceed through the arch first R to Surrey Steps and continue to Strand Lane.

Location 14 — **ROMAN BATH**

Strand Lane

Although not open, the bath is lit and may be viewed through a window. It is now believed that this is not Roman and does not even pre-date the 15C. However, the lead pipework may be earlier. This bath is referred to by Dickens in *David Copperfield*. See the descriptive panel.

Continue ahead.

Location 15 — **THE WATCH HOUSE**

Strand Lane

This Regency house, with its canopied balcony, overlooks the lane. From here could be observed the landing of goods from the river, which were subject to a tithe payable to St Mary-le-Strand Church.

Return to Strand L. Cross to St Mary's in the centre of the road.

Location 16 — **ST MARY-LE-STRAND*** *Gibbs 1717*

Strand

St Mary-le-Strand escaped the Second World War and has been judged London's best example of a small church in the Italian Baroque style. The earliest records of St Mary's date from 1143 but the first building, sited nearer the river, was demolished in 1549 for the construction of Protector Somerset's palace.

The famous Strand Maypole is known to have been standing on the site of the present church by 1619 but this was removed during the Commonwealth. However, a new 134 foot high maypole, erected in 1661, remained here until 1714. The first rank for the Hackney Carriage, predecessor of the taxi, was established beside it in 1634.

St Mary's, commissioned in 1714, was the first church to be built under the 'Fifty New Churches' Act. Initially, Gibbs planned a short bell tower for its west end, instead of a steeple. In addition, possibly influenced by the old maypole (?), he designed a 250-foot column to stand outside the west front. This would have been 80 feet taller than Nelson's column in Trafalgar Square and the highest structure to be erected in Europe since Roman times. A massive statue of Queen Anne was made in Italy for its top, but the Queen died in 1714 and both the projected column and its statue were abandoned. The fate of the statue, which was paid for, is unknown.

St Mary's was Gibbs's first commission, and, unlike St Clement Danes further east, it was specifically designed from the outset for its 'island' site.

•• *Enter from the west porch.*

It is not known how much of the interior is Gibbs's work as his contract was terminated in 1715. There are surprisingly few decorative features apart from the coved, coffered ceiling which, although in the Italian style, is the work of English craftsmen.

•• *Proceed to the* **chancel.**

Original furnishings include the two doorcases in the chancel, the communion rail, the font and the pulpit. The pulpit, however, lost its canopy in the 19C and was reduced in height.

Above the chancel arch are the arms of George I.

The two paintings in the chancel, above the doorcases, are by the American *Mather Brown* 1784.

The blue east windows are a recent discordant addition.

•• *Exit R and cross to the north side of Strand R. First L Melbourne Place. L Aldwych. Second R Kingsway. Second R Sardinia St. First R Portsmouth St. Cross the road.*

Location 17

THE OLD CURIOSITY SHOP *c.1567 (?)*

13–14 Portsmouth Street

The shop, allegedly London's oldest (?), was named after the Dickens book. It now sells souvenirs but is believed to have once been a dairy, obtaining milk from cows which grazed nearby in Lincoln's Inn Fields.

•• *Exit R to Lincoln's Inn Fields.*

Location 18

LINCOLN'S INN FIELDS

Houses were built around the fields in the mid-17C against the wishes of members of the adjacent Lincoln's Inn.

•• *Proceed northward along the west side.*

Nos 57–58 by *Jaynes* 1730.
Nos 59–60 Lindsay House by *Inigo Jones* (?) 1640.
No 65 by *Leverton* 1772.

No 66, architect unknown, *c.*1641. This was built in the Dutch style.

Proceed R along the north side to the Soane Museum in the centre.

Location 19

SIR JOHN SOANE'S MUSEUM

12–14 Lincoln's Inn Fields (405 2107)

Open Tuesday–Saturday 10.00–17.00. Closed August. Admission free.

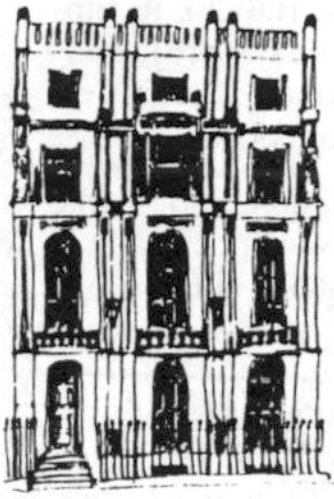

This museum displays, uniquely, the skills of a great architect together with his private collection of works of art. From 1812 until his death in 1837, Soane owned all or part of these three houses in a complicated way. He designed the facade of No 13, the central house, in his characteristic style but, for No 14, simply matched the plain front of No 12 which he had designed earlier.

Enter No 13.

Soane made internal amendments as he added to his collection, which is still spread across parts of all three properties. The subtlety of his room division is masterly. Little has been altered since the architect's death. Rooms with major exhibits are seen as follows:

Dining Room. Astronomical clock. Portrait 'Sir John Soane' by *Lawrence.*

Picture Room. Two famous series of paintings, 'The Rake's Progress' and 'The Election' by *Hogarth.* Hogarth based his later etchings on these.

Descend the stairs R.

Sepulchral Chamber. Sarcophagus of Pharaoh Seti I.

Ascend the stairs.

New Picture Room. Paintings by *Canaletto* and cartoons by *Raphael.*

Breakfast Room. The domed ceiling is typical of Soane.

Ascend the stairs to the **Drawing Room.**

Exit from the house L and proceed to the east side of the square. Turn R and follow the wall of Lincoln's Inn. At the end L is the main entrance.

Location 20

LINCOLN'S INN

Lincoln's Inn Fields

Open daily 08.00–19.00.

To ensure seeing the chapel and old hall, telephone the porter's lodge in advance (405 6360). Admission free.

Alone of the four Inns of Court, Lincoln's Inn survived the Second World War relatively unscathed. Its hall was built in 1492.

Records of the Honourable Society of Lincoln's Inn date from 1422 and, although it is not certain when the lawyers moved here, they were, by then, already occupying buildings on the east side that had previously formed the London residence of the Bishops of Chichester. The derivation of 'Lincoln' is unclear but there is believed to be a connection with Henry Lacey, Earl of Lincoln and the Society has adopted. his arms.

Enter the main gates and proceed ahead. First L ascend the steps. First R cross the terrace. Ascend more steps ahead to the library. Request permission from the librarian to view the library and New Hall.

Location 21

LINCOLN'S INN LIBRARY *Philip Hardwick c.1843*

This was built, together with New Hall, in Neo-

Tudor style. It was extended eastward and the interior remodelled by *George Gilbert Scott* 1873.

Exit and proceed directly ahead to New Hall.

Location 22

LINCOLN'S INN NEW HALL
Philip Hardwick c.1845

Much of the interior is the work of P. C. Hardwick. There is a hammberbeam roof and a screen. The large fresco, 'Justice', was painted by *Watts* in 1859.

Return to the porter's lodge on the south side of the main entrance to Lincoln's Inn and request permission to view Old Hall and the Chapel. Proceed along the north side of New Square.

Location 23

NEW SQUARE *Serle 1697*

Henry Serle, a member of Lincoln's Inn, built the houses as a private development which he named Serle's Court. 'Brewsters' Gate was erected in the 19C.

Charles Dickens worked in one of the chambers in this square as an office boy.

Continue ahead.

Location 24

LINCOLN'S INN OLD HALL

Open when not in use, or by arrangement with the porter.

This brick building was originally erected in 1492 and replaced the earlier hall of the Bishops of Chichester. An extension was built in 1624 at the south end and incorporated two further bay windows. Due to structural problems, the hall had to be rebuilt as a replica in 1924, however, most of the original material was re-used. At the same time, the brick entranceway, with its room above, was added at the north end between the hall and the chapel. Before New Hall was built, members of Lincoln's Inn used this building as their dining hall but it also periodically served as a law court from 1717 until 1882. Dickens set the court scene at the beginning of *Bleak House* in this hall.

Proceed through the arch in the entranceway L to the door R.

Set in the wall L of this door is an arch that may have come from the previous 13C hall (?).

Enter the door R. The narrow door immediately ahead leads directly to the hall.

The collar-beam roof is original and much of the linenfold panelling is 16C.

Numbers on stones around the windows denote positional guides for the reconstruction work.

The arms of distinguished members, featured in the stained glass windows, include those of Sir Thomas More, immediately L, in the bay at the north end. More declined the Treasurership in 1511.

It seems unlikely that any part of the screen was designed by *Inigo Jones* as has been alleged. This is believed to be part 16C with 17C additions (?).

The large painting on the north wall, 'St Paul before Felix', is by *Hogarth* 1748.

Exit L. Turn R to view the west facade of the chapel.

Location 25

LINCOLN'S INN CHAPEL* *Inigo Jones (?) 1623*

Open Monday to Friday 12.00–14.30, or by arrangement with the porter.

The architect of Lincoln's Inn's stone-clad chapel is uncertain but it is recorded that a model for it was made by *Inigo Jones* and approved in 1618.

This chapel, in late Perpendicular style, replaced a smaller 13C Early English building that lay further to the south. It was extended westward by one bay, pinnacles were added and the low forebuilding constructed by *Salter* in 1882. Much restoration took place following bomb damage in the First World War.

Proceed ahead through the arch in the forebuilding to the undercroft.

Eminent members of Lincoln's Inn are buried beneath the floor of the undercroft which was designed, unusually, to be open. Here also, it was once customary for mothers to leave unwanted babies to be cared for by the Society. These infants were generally given the surname Lincoln.

Ascend either stairway at the west end to view the interior.

The roof was renewed by *Salter* in 1882.

On the south side, restored early 17C stained glass by *Van Linge* (?) depicts the Apostles.

Treasurers' Coats of Arms are illustrated in many of the other windows.

The pew ends are original.

The Communion Table was made *c.*1700 and the altar rail in the late 17C.

The canopied pulpit is early 18C.

Exit from the chapel. Return to the arch. Turn R and proceed to Old Square on the north side of the chapel.

Location 26

OLD SQUARE *George Gilbert Scott 1876*

Built in Neo-Elizabethan style, this square was originally the part of Old Buildings that formed the courtyard of the Bishops of Chichester's residence.

Continue ahead.

Location 27

STONE BUILDINGS *R. Taylor 1780*

Most of this three-sided range is stone-faced, hence the name. Immediately L, at the south end, No 7, with the pediment and pilasters, was added by *Philip Hardwick* in 1845.

Return to Old Square first L. Pass the east end of the chapel and proceed to Old Buildings and the Gatehouse L.

Location 28

LINCOLN'S INN GATEHOUSE *1958*

Chancery Lane

This is a replica of the original gatehouse of 1521. The oak door made in 1564 was re-installed. Above the arch, facing Old Buildings, are the arms of three Treasurers, Lord Upjohn, John Hawles and Princess Margaret.

Proceed through the gate to Chancery Lane.

Above the arch on this side are the arms of Henry Lacey, Henry VIII and Sir Thomas Lovell.

Return to Old Buildings L.

Location 29	**OLD BUILDINGS**
	Old Buildings forms a quadrangle on the east side of Old Hall. The houses south of the gateway were built in the 16C but most have been rebuilt using some of the original materials.
	Continue ahead to No 21 in the south-west corner. Follow the passage L (signposted to Hale Court). Proceed to the room ahead.
	Within this room is a piece of wood from the old gatehouse carved 'Anno Domini 1518'. Surviving in this room are *in situ* 16C wall paintings.
	Return to Old Buildings and follow the vaulted passage (1583) first L. This leads to the western continuation of Old Buildings.
	The houses here were built on the south side L in 1524 and on the west side ahead in 1534. Most are original and with their polygonal stair turrets provide a rare London example of Tudor brickwork.
	Proceed ahead. First L New Square. Continue to the arch in the south-east corner.

Location 30	**CAREY STREET ARCH** *1697*
Carey Street	The gateway is known as Wildy's Arch as this legal bookseller has been established here since 1832. Arms of Henry Lacey and Henry Serle are displayed above.
	Exit to Carey St R.

Location 31	**THE SEVEN STARS** *1664*
Carey Street	This low-ceilinged pub retains much of its Victorian interior.
	Exit L Carey St. Second R Chancery Lane. Cross the road. First L enter the courtyard of the Public Record Office.

Location 32	**PUBLIC RECORD OFFICE**
Chancery Lane (405 0741)	The Public Record Office houses government archives and legal documents.
Museum open Monday to Friday 09.30–17.00. Admission free. Gatekeepers will provide a pass to the courtyard and the museum.	*Proceed to the courtyard. Turn R.*
	Built in the wall is a section of an arch from the 13C Rolls Chapel that once stood on part of the site.
	Return to the gate and enter the museum R.
	A new display illustrates England's history from the Domesday Book to the present. Treaties and military despatches are included.
	Exit from the museum and request to view the hall opposite.
	Three monuments from the old Rolls Chapel are ranged L along the wall of the room:
	Richard Alington, d.1561, and his wife.
	Lord Bruce of Kinloss, d.1611.
	Dr Yong, Master of the Rolls, by *Torrigiani* c.1516.
	Exit from the Public Record Office R and proceed to the end of Chancery Lane. R High Holborn. Cross the road and proceed to the Gray's Inn gateway immediately past The Cittie of Yorke.

Location 33	**GRAY'S INN GATEWAY**
High Holborn	The gateway is a modern reproduction of the 1688 original which was destroyed by Second World War bombs.

Location 34	**GRAY'S INN**
Open 08.00–19.00. Admission free. *The hall and chapel are open by appointment only.*	Gray's Inn has been recorded since the early 14C. Its name derives from the Lords Grey of Wilton whose inn (residence) stood on the site. The Society's emblem of a griffin is seen throughout. *Proceed ahead through the next arch to South Square R.*

Location 35	**SOUTH SQUARE**
	Although laid out in 1685, the only house in this square to survive the bombing was No 1 where Charles Dickens was apprenticed for one year in 1827. It is dated 1759. In the centre is a statue of Sir Francis Bacon, a 17C Treasurer, by *Pomeroy* 1912. *Proceed ahead to the library in the south-east corner and await the guide to the hall and chapel.*

Location 36	**GRAY'S INN HALL**
Open by appointment only. Admission free.	Although built in the 16C, the hall had to be almost completely rebuilt after Second World War bombing and little of the original structure remains. Its screen, however, is London's finest example of Elizabethan carving. Shakespeare's *Comedy of Errors* reputedly had its opening performance in Gray's Inn Hall in 1594 (?). Winston Churchill first met Franklin Roosevelt at a function here before the Second World War. *Enter the hall.* The late 16C wooden screen at the west end survived as it had been stored elsewhere for safety. It was reputedly made from a wrecked ship of the Spanish Armada (?). Treasurers' arms are illustrated both in the stained glass and on the panelling. Paintings portray Elizabeth I and various Elizabethan statesmen. The Parliament Clock was made in 1797.

Location 37	**GRAY'S INN CHAPEL**
Open by appointment only. Admission free.	The chapel adjoins the east end of the hall and was originally built in 1698 to replace the Inn's 14C chapel. Its interior had been remodelled in 1840 but, like the hall, was almost completely rebuilt after bomb damage. *Exit R. The passage, first R, leads to Gray's Inn Square on the north side of the hall.*

Location 38	**GRAY'S INN SQUARE** *1676*
	The houses in this square suffered less Second World War bomb damage than those in South Square. *Pass through the archway immediately L in the south-west corner and proceed to Field Court passing Gray's Inn Walks R.*

Location 39

GRAY'S INN WALKS

These private gardens were reputedly laid out early in the 17C by *Bacon* (?). The gate was made in 1723.

Continue ahead. Take the passage first R. Ascend the steps first L and leave Gray's Inn. Proceed ahead. First R Bedford Row. Continue ahead to Gt James St. First L Rugby St. R Lamb's Conduit St. Second L Guilford St. First R Lansdowne Terrace. Enter Brunswick Gardens R. Follow the path ahead. Exit from the north side and proceed to the Coram Foundation in the north-east corner of Brunswick Square.

Location 40

THOMAS CORAM FOUNDATION

40 Brunswick Square (278 2424)

Generally open Monday-Friday 10.00–16.00. Admission charge. As the hall is sometimes closed for functions, telephone first to ensure that it may be viewed.

Thomas Coram, a sea captain born in 1668, was moved by the plight of abandoned (foundling) infants and eventually obtained funds to build the Foundling Hospital in nearby Coram's Fields, where unwanted children could be reared and cared for. Benefactors included Handel the composer and Hogarth the painter. The hospital was built by *Jacobsen* in 1742 but demolished in 1926 when new premises were acquired.

The Foundation's present interiors incorporate the gallery, staircase and Court Room from the 18C hospital.

Hallway. A model of the old hospital is displayed.

Ascend the stairs to the first floor.

Landing. Handel's bust is by *Roubiliac*.

The painting of Coram is by *Hogarth*.

Proceed ahead.

Court Room. The panelling and ceiling were removed from the old Court Room and re-assembled here as a replica.

Royal signatures are displayed.

Examples of tokens left by mothers to identify their children are also exhibited.

The painting, 'Moses before Pharaoh's daughter' by *Hogarth* was donated by the painter.

Anteroom. The painting, 'March of the Guards to Finchley' by *Hogarth* was also donated by the painter.

Gallery. The cartoon, 'Massacre of the Innocents', is by *Raphael.*

An early manuscript of Handel's *Messiah* (not in the composer's hand) was presented by the composer.

Hogarth's punch bowl is exhibited.

Exit ahead and take the path L between the car park and the sports ground to Mecklenburgh Square. Proceed ahead to the east side which becomes Doughty St. Cross Guilford St and continue to the Dickens House Museum.

Location 41	**DICKENS HOUSE MUSEUM**
48 Doughty Street (405 2127) *Open Monday–Saturday 10.00–17.00. Admission charge.*	Charles Dickens lived in this early 19C house from 1837–9. Here, in what is the only London survivor of his family residences, he wrote most of *Oliver Twist*, *Nicholas Nickleby*, completed *The Pickwick Papers* and began *Barnaby Rudge*. Dickens mementoes are displayed throughout. The first floor drawing room was restored in 1984. The Dotheboys Hall display case, in the second floor bedroom, proves that Dickens did not exaggerate the horrific boys' schools in *Nicholas Nickleby*. Smike's prototype was a boy called George Taylor whose 'happy' letter home to his mother is followed by a bill for his tombstone. *Exit R. First L Guilford St.* On the north side are Corams Fields, site of the original Foundling Hospital; only its colonnade survives. *Third L Guilford Place leads to Lambs Conduit St.*

Location 42	**THE LAMB**
Lambs Conduit Street	This Victorian pub retains cut glass, snob screens and weatherboarding. Edwardian stage photographs decorate the walls. *Exit R. First L Guilford St. Third L Herbrand St and Russell Square Station, Piccadilly Line.*

Itinerary 11

11

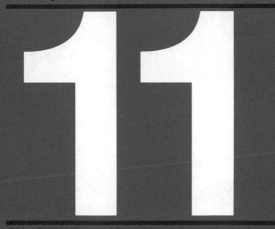

City Churches and Taverns

England's most beautiful synagogue and fourteen of the City's finest churches are included. Three of them pre-date the Great Fire and most of them escaped major Second World War bomb damage. It is not possible, or even desirable, to see all their interiors on the same day.

Timing: The churches of greatest interest are open from Tuesday to Thursday. Check current opening times of the Spanish and Portuguese Synagogue in advance.

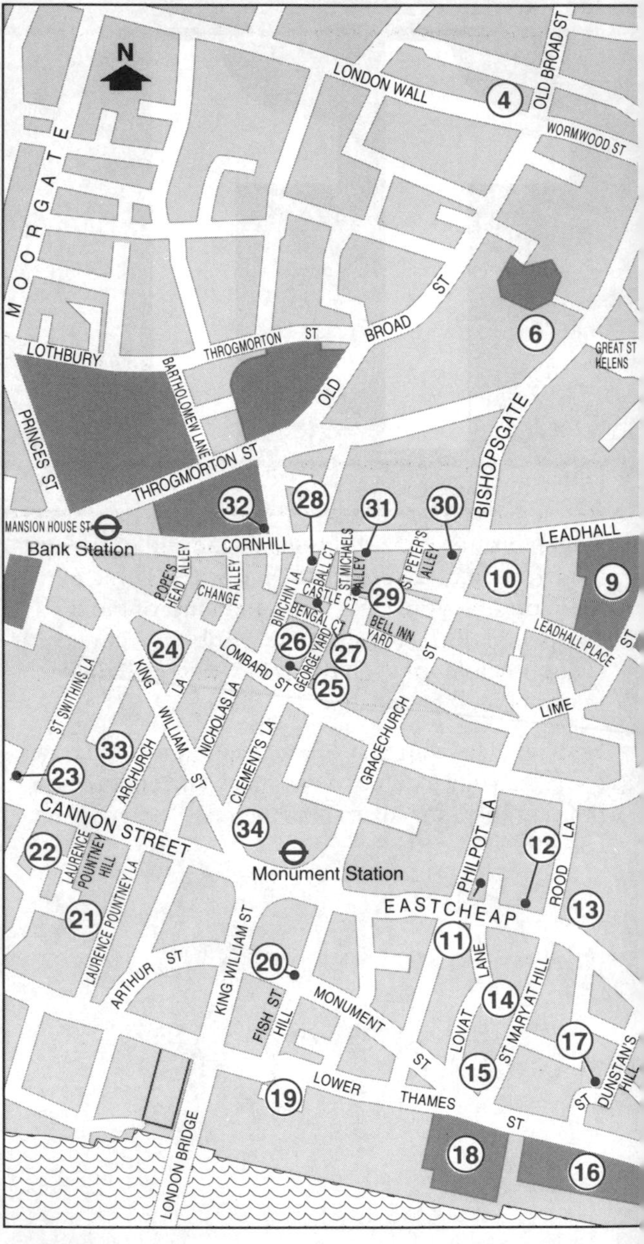
N
LONDON WALL
OLD BROAD ST
WORMWOOD ST
MOORGATE
LOTHBURY
THROGMORTON ST
BROAD ST
OLD
BARTHOLOMEW LANE
PRINCES ST
THROGMORTON ST
BISHOPSGATE
GREAT ST HELENS
MANSION HOUSE ST
Bank Station
CORNHILL
LEADHALL
POPE'S HEAD ALLEY
CHANGE ALLEY
BIRCHIN LA
BALL CT
CASTLE CT
ST MICHAELS ALLEY
ST PETER'S ALLEY
BENGAL CT
BELL INN YARD
GEORGE YARD
LOMBARD ST
LEADHALL PLACE
ST
KING WILLIAM ST
LA
NICHOLAS LA
ST SWITHINS LA
CLEMENT'S LA
GRACECHURCH ST
LIME
ARCHURCH
CANNON STREET
LAURENCE POUNTNEY HILL
LAURENCE POUNTNEY LA
Monument Station
PHILPOT LA
ROOD LA
EASTCHEAP
KING WILLIAM ST
ARTHUR ST
FISH ST HILL
MONUMENT ST
LOVAT LANE
ST MARY AT HILL
ST DUNSTAN'S HILL
LOWER THAMES ST
LONDON BRIDGE
4
6
9
10
11
12
13
14
15
16
17
18
19
20
21
22
23
24
25
26
27
28
29
30
31
32
33
34

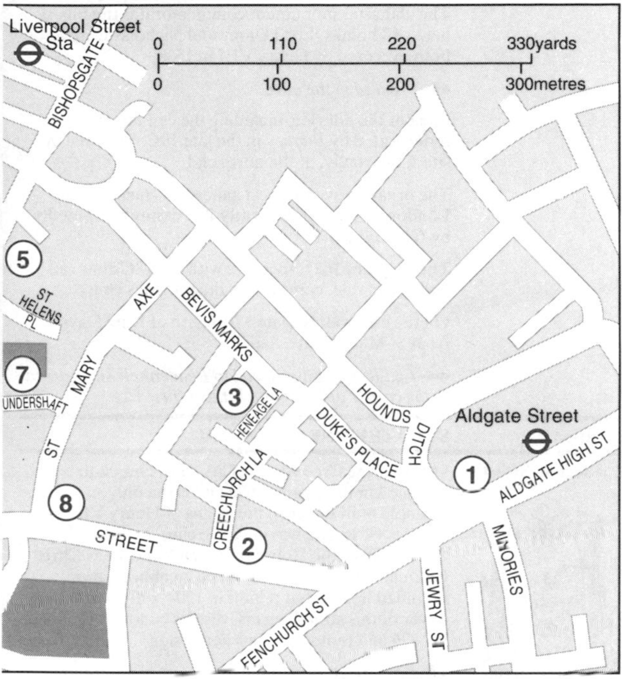

Locations
1 St Botolph-without-Aldgate
2 St Katherine Cree
3 Spanish and Portuguese Synagogue
4 All Hallows-on-the-Wall
5 Nat West Tower
6 St Helen Bishopsgate
7 St Andrew Undershaft
8 Lloyds
9 Leadenhall Market
10 Philpot Lane Mice
11 Nos 33–35 Eastcheap
12 St Margaret Pattens
13 St Mary-at-Hill
14 Watermens Hall
15 Custom House
16 St Dunstan-in-the-East (tower)
17 Old Billingsgate Market
18 St Magnus-the-Martyr
19 The Monument
20 Nos 7 and 7a Laurence Pountney Lane
21 Nos 1 and 2 Laurence Pountney Hill
22 The London Stone
23 St Mary Woolnoth
24 St Edmund-the-King
25 Bengal Court
26 The George and Vulture
27 Simpsons of Cornhill
28 Jamaica Wine House
29 St Peter-upon-Cornhill
30 St Michael Cornhill
31 Royal Exchange Pump
32 St Mary Abchurch
33 St Clement Eastcheap

Start *Aldgate Station, Circle and Metropolitan lines. Exit R Aldgate High St.*

Location 1 — **ST BOTOLPH-WITHOUT-ALDGATE**
Dance the Elder 1744

Aldgate High Street

The present St Botolph's replaced a 16C church but, prior to this, there had been an enlarged Saxon building on the site. It is dedicated to England's patron saint of travellers.

Enter directly to the **baptistry** *which was formed in 1965.*

The Renaissance style cover of the font is 18C.

Flanking the door are busts of Robert Dow, d.1612, and Sir John Cass, d.1718, by *Winter* 1966.

The alabaster monument commemorates the burial here of Thomas, Lord Darcy and Nicholas Carew, both executed by Henry VIII in 1538.

•● *Proceed to the* **nave**.

Most of the interior, including the ceiling, was redecorated by *Bentley* in the late 19C. The altar is sited, unusually, at the north end.

The organ above the west gallery by *Harris* 1676 is London's oldest and its early 18C casing is reputedly by *Gibbons* (?).

The pulpit of 1621, together with the 18C altar rail and sword rest, comes from the previous church.

On the east wall is a late 17C figure of King David from St Mary Whitechapel.

•● *Exit R. Continue ahead to Leadenhall St. Proceed to the corner of Creechurch Lane (first L).*

Location 2

ST KATHERINE CREE* *1631*

Leadenhall Street

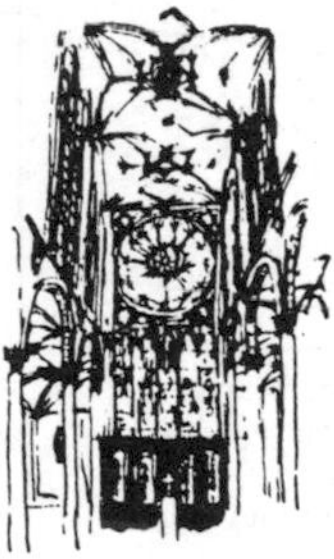

St Katherine Cree was the City's last church to be designed in the Gothic style and is the only surviving example built between the reigns of Henry VIII and Charles II. Its site was once the churchyard of the 11C Priory of the Holy Trinity, also known as Christ Church. 'Cree' is believed to be an abbreviation. Founded in 1280 but rebuilt in 1504, only part of the tower of this structure survives. Its cupola was added in 1776 and replaced an earlier design.

•● *Enter from Leadenhall St.*

Unfortunately, 'temporary' offices in the aisles disfigure St Katherine's interior. The organ gallery and Corinthian capitals of the columns are, surprisingly, the only Classical feature of the church.

The organ was made by *Schmidt* in 1686 but renewed. Allegedly, this was played by Purcell, Wesley and Handel (?). Its decorative 17C case is outstanding.

The 17C stained glass in the north aisle's west window, R of the organ, came from St James Dukes Place.

On the north wall are the arms of Charles II.

Decorated bosses in the vaulted roofs of the nave and aisles bear the arms of City Livery Companies.

A rare Carolean font of alabaster stands L of the altar. It was presented by Lord Mayor John Gayer *c.*1640. The pulpit and reredos are 18C.

St James Duke Place provided the 18C reredos.

The lectern was assembled from 17C joinery.

At the east end, the rose window allegedly represents the toothed wheel on which St Katherine was tortured during the persecution of Christians by Emperor Maxentius in 307 (?). The tracery design is reputedly modelled on the great rose window of Old St Paul's Cathedral. Its 17C stained glass is original.

At the east end of the south aisle is the monument to Sir Nicholas Throkmorton, d.1570, Chief Butler of England and father-in-law of Raleigh. Throgmorton Street was named after him.

A cartouche of 17C glass survives in the central of the south aisle.

Return to the east end of the north aisle. A door leads to the churchyard, now a public garden.

On the wall ahead is the Avenon doorway dated 1631. This originally formed the Lombard St entrance to the churchyard.

Return to the church and exit R. First R Creechurch Lane. Third L Bevis Marks. Second L enter this courtyard Duke Place via the archway.

Location 3

SPANISH AND PORTUGUESE SYNAGOGUE*
Avis 1701

Bevis Marks
(626 1274)

Usually open Friday and Sunday Telephone for entry times. Admission charge.

This, England's oldest synagogue, was built by a Quaker who returned his fee; Queen Anne provided a beam. Most of the fittings are original and the candles of the early 18C Dutch chandeliers are lit on special occasions.

Return to Bevis Marks L. Cross Bishopsgate (fourth L). Continue ahead. Wormwood St becomes London Wall. Cross the road to All Hallows, just past the Old Broad St junction (first R).

Location 4

ALL HALLOWS-ON-THE-WALL
Dance the Younger 1767

London Wall

Open daily but closes 13.00–14.00.

This is London's only surviving building of importance by *George Dance the Younger,* who called it 'my first child'. The first recorded All Hallows was built on a bastion of the Roman wall in the early 12C and rebuilt in the 13C. Although this escaped the Great Fire, it deteriorated and was replaced by the present church.

Remnants of London Wall lie immediately to the west.

Return eastward and apply at the first door L (83 London Wall) to enter the church.

The simplicity and spatial balance of the interior had an important influence on Dance's pupil, John Soane. All Hallows is now the headquarters of the Council for the Care of Churches which is why most of the floor space is occupied by bookcases. Its most important feature is the coffered ceiling which, although damaged by Second World War bombing, has been restored as an exact reproduction.

When constructed, the church was surrounded by buildings and it is lit, therefore, by high-level lunette windows.

Unusually, the pulpit can only be reached from the vestry. It was built as a 'three-decker' but the lower sections have been removed.

The chandelier was presented in 1763 by a parishioner who almost immediately went bankrupt.

Behind the altar is a copy of the painting by *Pietro da Cortona* in the Church of Conception, Rome.

Exit L. Second R Bishopsgate. Until destroyed by a terrorist bomb, St Ethelburga, a small 14C church, stood on the east side of the road. Reconstruction appears unlikely.

Pass through the arch R and proceed to the National Westminster Bank piazza.

Location 5

25 Old Broad Street

Access to the top floor viewing area is no longer permitted.

NAT WEST TOWER *1980*

At 600 feet, this was, until the Canary Wharf Tower (800 feet) was built in 1990, Britain's highest and Europe's second highest, solid structure. The tower can accommodate 2,500.

Return to Bishopsgate. Cross the road and proceed through the archway to Great St Helen's.

Location 6

Great St Helen's (283 2231)

Badly damaged by a terrorist bomb in April 1993, the church is due to reopen late 1995.

ST HELEN BISHOPSGATE* *13C*

This medieval building possesses the finest Carolean woodwork in central London, together with more monuments than any London church apart from Westminster Abbey and St Paul's Cathedral.

St Helen's is dedicated to the mother of Constantine, the first Christian Emperor of Rome, who ruled in the 4C. By tradition, it was she who discovered the true cross (?). The present St Helen's parish church was created at the Reformation by linking two churches that had existed side by side since the 13C. Although sharing one wall, they were originally separated internally and provided R the parish church and L a nunnery's church.

St Helen's parish church, first recorded in 1150, was rebuilt in the 13C. A nunnery became established within its grounds *c.*1210 and it is believed that the nuns erected their church shortly after St Helen's had been rebuilt (?). The nun's church, London's only surviving example, was originally slightly longer but the parish church was soon extended westward, thereby lining up the two buildings and providing the existing double frontage.

Both windows in the 13C west wall were formed in the 15C. The bell tower is 17C.

The doorway L was formed *c.*1500 and the entrance doorway R *c.*1300.

To see the south facade, proceed R of the church following Undershaft.

The south doorway is dated 1633.

Blocked 13C lancet windows were revealed when adjoining houses were demolished in 1966.

The east extension to the 13C south transept was built in 1374.

Return to the west front and enter the church. Proceed L towards the nuns' church (or nuns' choir).

The floor was raised by 3ft to its original level in 1995.

All except one of the existing arches in the dividing wall were formed *c.*1480 but they probably replaced even earlier openings, as the chancel's east arch is 14C. Wooden screens between them were removed in 1538 when the nunnery was dissolved.

Some timbers in the tie-beam roof, built *c.*1480 to span both churches, are original.

Nuns' church nave. The structure in the corner that appears to be of rusticated stone is in fact of timber and forms part of the bell turret.

Turn R and follow the north wall.

The small 13C lancet window in the corner is the only example that was not filled or replaced.

Eighteen monuments were brought to St Helen's from St Martin Outwich in 1874. Outstanding, is the canopied altar tomb of Hugh Pemberton, d.1500, and his wife Katherine. Bronze figures on the small plaque represent ten of his sons, others are lost.

The font was made in 1632.

Continue eastward.

The doorway *c.*1500 leads to steps, once 'the night staircase' to the nuns' dormitory.

Nuns' chancel. The blocked doorway *c.*1500 was the processional entrance from the nuns' vestry, but the function of the side recesses is uncertain.

On the wall, below the penultimate window, is the monument to Martin Bond, d.1643. He is shown in his military tent.

Nuns were able to view the altar through the angled slots of the squint at the east end of the wall, which was combined with the 'Easter Sepulchre' above in 1525 to form a memorial to Johane Alfrey.

In front of the squint is the tomb chest of the founder of the Royal Exchange, Sir Thomas Gresham, d.1579.

The first rows of the choir stalls are mid-17C but the back rows on each side are 15C.

Turn R.

All the east windows of St Helen's were renewed *c.*1893.

Beneath the east arch lies the tomb chest of Elizabeth I's ambassador to Spain, Sir William Pickering, by *Cure* (?) 1574.

Proceed past this monument to the parish church.

Parish church chancel. This was remodelled by *Pearson* *c.*1893 when the reredos and the wooden screens were completed.

The Communion table is 17C.

Right of this table, against the second pier, the rare wooden sword rest, made in 1665, is the oldest in London. In front of this is the tomb chest of Sir John Crosby, d.1475, and his wife.

Proceed immediately L to the **south transept.**

Immediately R is a 13C lancet window that was opened up in 1966.

Much damaged by the bomb, the tomb chest of Julius Caesar (Adelmare) by *Stone* (?) 1636 commemorates a Master of the Rolls and Privy Councillor of James I.

The south window R was formed in the 17C.

The transept's doorway was created in 1995. Its case, brought from the south door, was made *c.* 1633 from old church furnishings. The Stuart coat of arms probably came from a reredos (?)

Continue ahead to the north section of the subdivided east chapel.

Chapel of the Holy Ghost. The tomb chest of John de Oteswich and his wife *c.*1500 is the oldest monument in the church.

Patterned, 15C floor tiles may be viewed, below the floor hatch.

Proceed to the south-east **Lady Chapel** *R.*

The piscina and niches in the east wall are 14C. The seated female alabaster figure in the south-west corner was possibly carved by *Colt* (?) *c.*1600.

Return to the chancel and proceed L to the **parish church nave**.

Immediately R is an 18C sword rest.

The pulpit L is a rare Carolean example and probably made *c.*1633 (?).

Proceed ahead.

Against the south wall, before the doorcase, is the large monument to Richard Staper, 1608.

The south doorcase *c.*1635, although practically contemporary with that of the south transept, has fluted Corinthian columns, denoting a greater Renaissance influence.

Immediately past this doorway is the badly damaged monument to a clothmaker, Sir John Spencer, d.1609.

The organ gallery was constructed in 1995 to accommodate the instrument which, with its case, was made in 1744, and originally stood in a west gallery.

Just before the west door is a late 18C poor box supported by a 17C carved beggar.

Exit from the church L. First L Undershaft. R St Mary Axe. Cross the road and proceed to St Andrew Undershaft. Enter by the door in the north side at the end of the path. On Monday and Thursday mornings continue to the south porch.

Location 7

ST ANDREW UNDERSHAFT *1532*

St Mary Axe
(283 7382)

This is another church that escaped both the Great Fire and Second World War bombing. It contains ironwork by *Tijou* and an unusual monument.

St Andrew Undershaft gained its name from the Cornhill Maypole or 'shaft' which stood outside the church throughout the Middle Ages until destroyed by Protestants in 1549.

The top section of the 15C tower was rebuilt in 1883.

Enter the church and proceed to the north aisle.

Most of the woodwork is late 17C or early 18C.

At the east end of the north wall is the monument to John Stow, d.1605, by *Stone.* His 'Survey of London' valuably described the city before the Great Fire demolished so much of it. At a special ceremony, held every April, the Lord Mayor of London replaces the quill pen.

Proceed to the **chancel.**

The altar rail of 1704 is a rare example in a Lond church of the work of the French ironsmith *Tijou.*

The organ by *Harris* and its case are late 17C.

In the spandrels (corners) of the arcade arches are monochrome paintings executed in 1726.

The pulpit is late 17C. A tablet on the west wall of the south aisle commemorates the painter Holbein, d.1543.

Five monarchs are depicted in the late 17C west window: Edward VI, Elizabeth I, James I, Charles I and William III. Originally the last section featured another king, probably Charles II or James II (?). The feet were kept but they don't fit the new figure.

Below this window is the font by *Stone* 1634.

Exit from the church L. R Leadenhall St (or from the south porch R Leadenhall St). Cross the road. First L Lime St. Approached directly from the street is the lift to Lloyds' public viewing gallery.

Location 8

LLOYDS *Rogers 1986*

Lime Street (623 7100)

Public viewing and exhibition gallery open Monday–Friday 10.00–14.30. Admission free.

Lloyds is the world's largest international insurance market and has no connection with the bank of that name. It began as a 17C coffee house and has occupied many different premises in the City. The new Lime Street building, its largest ever, was designed by *Richard Rogers*, architect of the Pompidou Centre in Paris. Lloyds is a society of insurance underwriters who work together in separate syndicates.

A traditional feature of The Underwriting Room, the Lutine Bell, has been retained. This was recovered from a frigate which sank in 1799 loaded with gold worth one and a half million pounds. The bell now rings only on ceremonial occasions.

Exit R. First R Leadenhall Place leads to Leadenhall Market.

Location 9

LEADENHALL MARKET *H. Jones 1881*

Open Monday–Friday

This is a general market but meat and poultry predominate. It was founded in the 14C and named after Leaden Hall, a manor house on the site.

The foundations of London's bascilica, the largest Roman building outside Italy, lie 30 feet below ground level. They were surveyed in 1886 and sections remain in the basements of some of the shops.

Proceed ahead. Third L follow the central avenue. R Lime St. Continue ahead to Philpot Lane. Proceed to the end and cross the road.

Location 10

PHILPOT LANE MICE

Alfred Marks Bureau Philpot ane (23–25 stcheap)

Between the ground and first floors is a cornice. Where the two buildings join, black mice are depicted eating cheese. They were added by the late Victorian builders who reputedly discovered mice nibbling at their lunch of bread and cheese (?).

L Eastcheap.

n 11

NOS 33–35 EASTCHEAP *1868*

These two adjoining buildings, are the City's best example of 'horror movie' Victorian Gothic.

Continue to the Rood Lane corner (first L).

...ation 12	**ST MARGARET PATTENS*** *Wren 1687*

...astcheap

Much of the woodwork is original and by *Cleer*.

On either side of the door are the only examples of canopied church wardens pews in London. The ceiling of one is inscribed 'CW 1686'.

The choir stalls were made from the original congregation pews.

By tradition, the name of the church derives from Pattens, iron-soled shoes, examples of which are displayed on the south wall. However, it is more likely that the true source was a Mr Pattin, benefactor of an earlier St Margaret's (?).

The reredos and pulpit are original.

At the east end of the south wall is the monument to Sir Peter Delme, d.1728, by *Rysbrack*.

A second reredos in the north aisle was assembled from a 17C door case.

Above the west door is the coat of arms of James II.

Exit L.

The former rectory, next to the church L, has a rare, early 19C shop front.

Cross Eastcheap. Proceed immediately ahead, St Mary-at-Hill. Enter the churchyard of St Mary-at-Hill via the path between Nos 6 and 7.

Location 13	**ST MARY-AT-HILL*** *Wren 1676*

St Mary at Hill

Open Monday–Friday 10.00–13.00

St Mary's, probably founded in the 12C, was formerly renowned for its dark woodwork which, although partly original, had been sensitively remodelled and supplemented in the 19C. It is not yet clear how much can be restored following a disastrous fire in 1990.

Proceed through the churchyard.

The east end, together with the interior of St Mary's, was rebuilt by *Wren* after the Great Fire but all of the north wall and the south wall were renewed externally in 1826.

The interior was restored by *Savage* 1849. Its original woodwork included the reredos and pulpit, and was by *Cleer* but the mid-19C work by *W. G. Rogers* proved virtually indistinguishable.

Following a fire, in which 50% of the woodwork was lost, the major furnishings are no longer on view.

Although the west front of the church survived the Great Fire, it was eventually rebuilt by *Gwilt* 1788.

First L a passage returns to St Mary at Hill.

At the end of the passage, the pediment of the arch facing the road is decorated with a skull and crossbones.

R St Mary at Hill. Proceed to the stone-faced building.

Location 14

WATERMENS HALL *Blackburn 1780*

St Mary at Hill
Open by appointment only. Admission free.

The original stone-faced building was designed in the Adam style and accommodates the Court Room and Parlour. The adjoining houses R, Nos 17 and 16, were acquired in 1890. Following slight bomb damage, the hall was restored in 1950.

Enter and await the guide.

The Company of Watermen and Lightermen of the River Thames was founded in 1555, and is closely associated with the Livery Companies. It still examines apprentices on behalf of the Port of London Authority.

Parlour. This was remodelled in 1961 when its ceiling was decorated in the Adam style.

Court Room. Both the furnishings and the room itself are little changed. Some of the paintings came from the earlier hall.

Displayed are members' silver badges and the Master's chair, made *c.*1800.

Freeman's Room. This was created in 1984 by combining two rooms. The matching chandeliers, recently acquired, were made in 1830. Members' coats and badges displayed include a 'Doggetts Coat and Badge' which is presented to the apprentice who wins this annual rowing contest between London Bridge and Chelsea.

Exit R. First L Lower Thames St. Cross the road.

Location 15

CUSTOM HOUSE

Lower Thames Street
Open by appointment only.

Built by *D. Laing* in 1817, his central section had to be reconstructed in 1825 following subsidence and was re-designed by *R. Smirke.*

The east wing was rebuilt after Second World War bombing.

Cross the road. Ahead St Dunstan's Hill.

Location 16

ST DUNSTAN-IN-THE-EAST *Wren 1697*

St Dunstan's Hill

All that remains, after the Second World War are the walls and tower with its distinctive Gothic steeple, copied by Wren from the pre-Great Fire church of St Mary-le-Bow.

Return to Lower Thames St R. Cross the road. Old Billingsgate Market faces (first R) St Mary at Hill (the street).

Location 17

OLD BILLINGSGATE MARKET *H. Jones 1875*

Lower Thames Street

The building's function as a fish market ended when this was transferred to the Isle of Dogs in 1981. Converted to an international banking centre, which never opened; its eventual use is now uncertain.

Continue ahead.

Location 18

ST MAGNUS-THE-MARTYR* *Wren 1676*

Lower Thames Street

When the buildings were removed from old London Bridge to widen the roadway *c.*1760, two west bays of St Magnus were demolished and the east pavement of the bridge was re-aligned to pass through the tower. Because of this, the north doorway is no longer positioned centrally. London Bridge has been re-sited.

The only original round window is the example above the north door, the others were formed in 1782.

Although dated 1709, the clock, projecting from the tower, is believed to be 17C (?).

Enter beneath the tower.

Much 17C work remains but the interior has frequently been remodelled and restored. The canopied pulpit and reredos are original.

Surmounting the reredos is a Crucifixion scene carved by *Martin Travers* in 1924.

L of the early 18C altar rail is a highly decorative sword rest made in 1708.

The font at the west end of the south aisle, was presented in 1683.

Exit to the old churchyard R.

The timber post, immediately L, came from a Roman wharf and was discovered nearby in Fish Street Hill.

L Lower Thames St. First R Fish St Hill leads to Monument St.

Location 19

THE MONUMENT *Hooke (?) 1677*

Monument Street

Open May–September, Monday–Saturday 09.00–17.40. Sunday 14.00–17.40. October–April, Monday–Saturday 09.00–15.40. Admission charge.

The Monument commemorates the Great Fire. Its height of 202 feet, still the greatest of any isolated stone column in the world, is also the distance to the bakers premises in nearby Pudding Lane where the fire started. The fire burned for four days from 2 September 1666 and four-fifths of the City was destroyed. Only seven people, however, are known to have been killed.

The architect of the Monument is uncertain. *Wren*'s column would have been surmounted by a statue of Charles II but the final design was probably the work of Wren's assistant, *Hooke*.

The relief on the west side of the pedestal by *Cibber* depicts Charles II surveying the City.

On the other three sides are Latin inscriptions with translations. An addition to the north side in 1681 accused Papists of causing the fire and this was not finally removed until 1830.

There is no lift and 311 steps lead to a viewing area. This was enclosed in 1842 after a total of six people had committed suicide by jumping from it.

Return to Lower Thames St R. Second R Laurence Pountney Lane. First L follow the path through the old churchyard.

Location 20

7 and 7a LAURENCE POUNTNEY LANE

These late-17C houses, best viewed from the churchyard L, are rare in the City.

Continue ahead through the old churchyard. First R Laurence Pountney Hill.

Location 21

1 and 2 LAURENCE POUNTNEY HILL *1703*

Now converted to offices, these adjoining houses have been judged to possess London's finest early 18C domestic exteriors.

Continue ahead. Second L Cannon St. Cross the road and pass the St Swithins Lane junction (first R).

Location 22

THE LONDON STONE

Oversea-Chinese Banking Corporation
111 Cannon Street

The London Stone has been built into the south wall of the bank and lies behind a grille. It was originally sited on the opposite side of Cannon Street, approximately in the present centre of the road, which was later widened. The gateway of the Roman Government House stood immediately behind and the stone may have been a distance measuring point.

Return eastward. First L St Swithins Lane. Proceed to the end. Cross King William St immediately to St Mary Woolnoth's on the corner.

Location 23

ST MARY WOOLNOTH* *Hawksmoor 1727*

Lombard Street

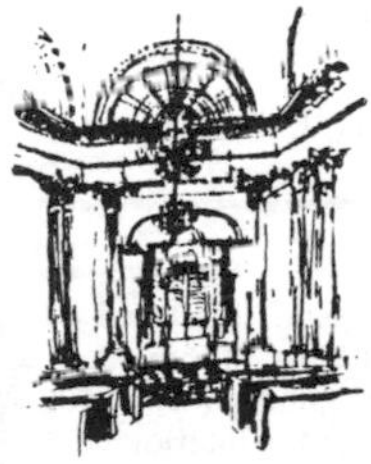

An early Saxon church on the site was built by Wulfnoth, hence, presumably, the name (?). The exterior, with its flat-topped turrets and rusticated stone, is judged to be the most original of all the City's churches.

On either side, the entrances to Bank Station once led to the burial crypt and carved cherubs heads still surmount the arches.

Enter the church beneath the tower.

Hawksmoor amazingly achieves spaciousness from the small triangular site with his favourite cube-within-a-cube layout.

The organ by *Schmidt*, with its casing, was made in 1681.

The reredos and canopied pulpit are original but the galleries were removed in the 19C.

Exit R. First R Lombard St. Cross the road and proceed to St Edmund's on the George Yard corner (fifth L).

Location 24

ST EDMUND-THE-KING *Wren* or *Hooke (?) 1679*

Lombard Street

Founded *c.* 1000, this church is dedicated to Edmund, King of the East Anglians. He was captured by the invading Danes in 870 and, refusing to renounce Christianity, was allegedly tied to a tree and shot with arrows (?) in the manner of St Sebastian.

First L George Yard. Proceed to the rear of the church.

The 17C iron gates and railings L originally enclosed the old churchyard.

Return to the south front and enter the church.

The original font, L of the entrance, has an exceptional cover decorated with gilded figures of the apostles. Unfortunately, this is now rarely displayed.

As in the earlier church, the altar is unusually sited at the north end. Although the interior was remodelled in 1864 and 1880 much original woodwork remains, including the wall panelling, font rail, organ case, reredos, Communion rail and table.

The paintings of Moses and Aaron on the reredos are by *Etty* 1833.

The lectern was made up from 17C panelling.

An 18C sword rest is displayed.

Exit R. First R Birchin Lane. First R Bengal Court.

Location 25

BENGAL COURT

Open at all times but restaurants and most pubs operate Monday–Friday 11.00–15.00 only.

This is one of many entranceways to the maze of alleys that run south of Cornhill and still follow their medieval pattern.

Bengal Court leads to George Yard. First L follow the passage to The George and Vulture.

Location 26

THE GEORGE AND VULTURE

3 Castle Court (626 9710)

Redevelopment is threatened, therefore it is advisable to telephone.

The restaurant was once a coaching inn with its coach yard, George Yard, behind. Its part-17C building, which replaced a medieval inn, was featured by Dickens in *The Pickwick Papers*. Chops and steaks are grilled on an early 19C range in the dining room. The George and Vulture is no longer an inn and there is, therefore, no separate bar; however, this may change.

Exit from the main door L. First L Castle Court. First R Ball Court.

Location 27

SIMPSONS OF CORNHILL

38½ Cornhill (626 9985)

In spite of its strange address, Simpsons is entered from Ball Court. Don't confuse this establishment with Simpsons-in-the-Strand, the restaurant famed for its roasts. It was built in 1757 but the interior, together with its fittings, is a modern reproduction. Unlike the George and Vulture, Simpsons does have a separate bar.

Return to Castle Court. L St Michael's Alley.

Location 28

JAMAICA WINE HOUSE

St Michael's Alley

This late-19C pub was built on the site of Pasqua Rosa's which opened in 1652 as London's first coffee house. The ground floor is still subdivided by original mahogany screens.

Exit L St Michael's Alley.

Immediately L is the tower (*Hawksmoor* 1722), and south wall of St Michael's (location 31).

Follow the alley to Bell Inn Yard. First L Gracechurch St. First L St Peter's Alley.

Location 29

ST PETER-UPON-CORNHILL* *Wren 1682*

Cornhill

St Peter's was allegedly founded by Lucius in 179 as the first Christian church in London (?). Several buildings on the site, the highest point in the City, preceded St Peter's but no traces of them remain.

Continue to Cornhill R. Enter the vestibule.

Ahead, on the wall R, is a 17C shelf from which bread was dispensed to the poor. Beneath is a German (?) 17C chest.

•• *Turn L and enter the nave.*

Much original woodwork remains, including the doorcases, reredos, part of the canopied pulpit and the organ case. The organ is by *Schmidt.*

Most of the chancel screen was reputedly designed by Wren's daughter (?) and is one of only two contemporary screens in a Wren church.

Ask to see the vestry at the west end where there is a Cromwellian Communion table and a 14C plaque which came from the pre-fire church. This plaque was re-engraved after the Great Fire and refers to the Roman foundation of the church. Also displayed is a letter from the composer Mendelssohn who played the church's organ in 1842.

•• *Exit L Cornhill.*

Location 30 — **ST MICHAEL CORNHILL** *Wren 1672*

Cornhill

Although much of the exterior of this church remains Classical, its interior was remorselessly Gothicized by *George Gilbert Scott c.*1860.

The tower of the earlier church survived the Great Fire but later became unsafe and was replaced by the present Neo-Gothic design by *Hawksmoor* 1722 (a strange prophesy of Scott's work; best viewed from St Michael's Alley as previously indicated).

All the windows were remodelled by *Scott.*

•• *Enter the church from Cornhill.*

The pelican in the vestibule R was made as an altarpiece in 1775. In the centre of the vestibule is the original font. Its stem is 19C.

•• *Proceed to the nave L.*

The reredos by *Scott* incorporates 17C paintings of Moses and Aaron by *Streater*.

The organ L is by *Harris*. Its rebuilt casing incorporates gilt cherubs' heads from the original.

•• *Exit L. Cross Cornhill. Proceed to the blue water pump on the edge of the pavement.*

Location 31 — **ROYAL EXCHANGE PUMP**

Cornhill

This water pump is dated 1799. A relief illustrates the 17C Royal Exchange.

•• *Continue westward. First L Change Alley. Second R Lombard St. First L Abchurch Lane. Continue ahead past the King William St intersection towards the end of the lane. Cross to the paved area R, once the graveyard of St Mary Abchurch.*

Location 32 — **ST MARY ABCHURCH*** *Wren 1686*

Abchurch Lane
(626 0306)

Open Tuesday and Thursday 12.00–14.30.
Also Monday, Wednesday and Friday 10.00–16.00 (dependent on staff).

In spite of its small size, this is judged to be one of Wren's most attractive churches. St Mary's was first recorded in the 12C.

•• *Enter St Mary's from the paved area.*

The dome was painted by *William Snow c.*1710.

The marble font L of the entrance is by *Kempster* and its cover by *W. Emmett* 1686.

The gilded pelican above the north doorcase originally served as the weathervane, but was removed from the spire in 1764.

The reredos was painstakingly re-assembled after Second World War bombs had shattered it into two thousand fragments. It is the only authenticated work by *Gibbons* in a City parish church.

The canopied pulpit is by *Gray* 1685.

Exit to Abchurch Lane R. L Cannon St. Second L King William St. First R Clement's Lane.

Location 33

ST CLEMENT EASTCHEAP *Wren 1687*

Clements Lane

St Clement's, like its Strand namesake, also claims to be the 'Oranges and Lemons' church of the nursery song (?). It has more justification, as Spanish oranges were once sold nearby alongside old London Bridge.

Enter from Clements Lane.

The interior was remodelled in the 19C.

Original 17C fittings, many carved by *Maine,* include the font with its cover, the canopied pulpit and, on the south wall, the coat of arms of Charles II.

Below the arms is a small breadshelf.

The organ, once played by Purcell, was moved from the south to the west wall in 1935 and the reredos was unfortunately remodelled at the same time.

Exit L. L King William St and Monument Station, Circle and District lines.

Alternatively, if continuing with itinerary 12, exit L. L King William St. R Cannon St. First L Martin Lane.

Itinerary 12

12

Southwark and City Livery Companies

Southwark, with its ancient cathedral and inns lies south of the river and is approached via London Bridge. Many of the City's oldest Livery Companies are also seen.

Timing: The day chosen depends on any arrangements that have been made to visit one of the City Livery Companies.

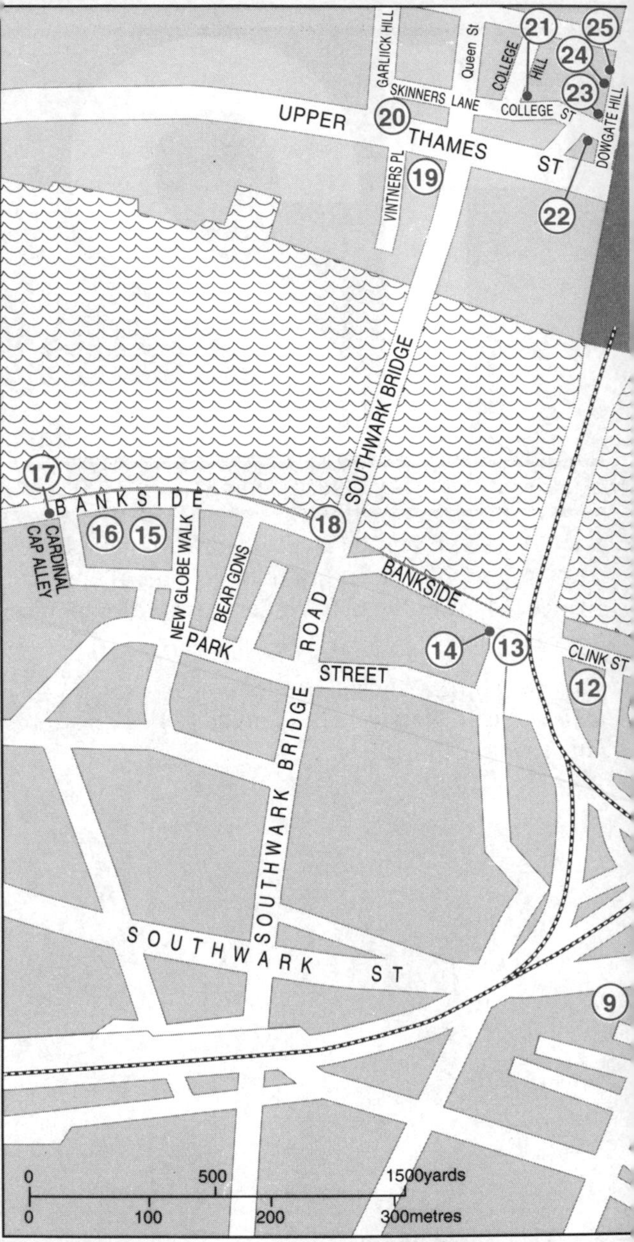

Locations
1 Olde Wine Shades (El Vino's)
2 Fishmongers Hall
3 London Bridge
4 London Dungeon
5 Winston Churchill's Britain at War Experience
6 Guys Hospital
7 Old Operating Theatre Museum
8 The George
9 No 50 Borough High Street
10 Southwark Cathedral
11 Winchester House
12 Clink Prison Museum
13 Bankside
14 The Anchor

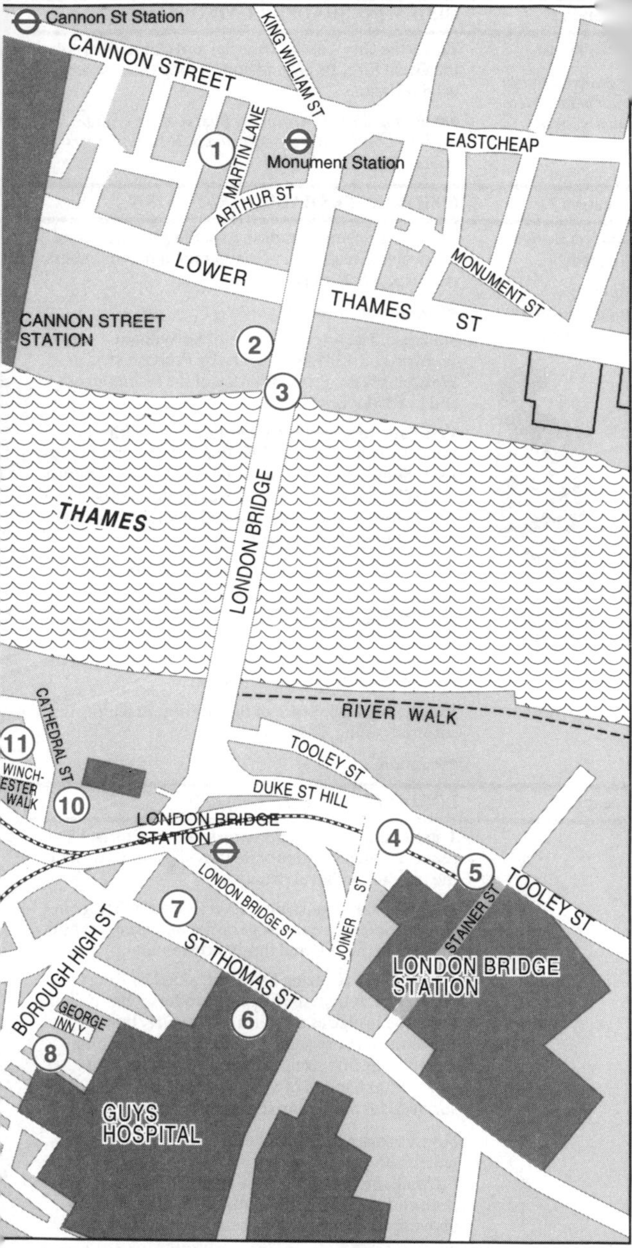

15 Shakespeare International Globe Centre
16 Cardinal's Wharf
17 Provost's Lodging
18 Southwark Bridge
Vintners Hall
20 St James Garlickhythe
21 St Michael Paternoster Royal
22 Innholders Hall
23 Dyers Hall
24 Skinners Hall
25 Tallow Chandlers Hall

t *Monument Station, Circle and District lines. Leave by the London*
e exit to Cannon Street ahead. First L Martin Lane.
atively, continue from itinerary 11.

ation 1

OLDE WINE SHADES (EL VINO'S) *1663 (?)*

rtin Lane

atrons must not wear jeans. Men must wear ties.

This is the City's oldest wine bar and claims to pre-date the Great Fire. Its ground floor ceiling retains some original beams.

●● *Exit R. First L Arthur St. First R King William St leads to London Bridge Approach. R Fishmongers Hall R overlooks the river.*

Location 2

FISHMONGERS HALL *H. Roberts 1834*

London Bridge Approach

Open by appointment only. Admission free.

The Fishmongers, established in the 13C, are one of the twelve Great Livery Companies and its members still inspect fish sold in the City.

●● *Enter and await the guide.*

Staircase. The wooden statue of Sir William Walworth, d.1385, was carved by *Pearce* c.1685. Walworth was a Prime Warden of the Fishmongers and Lord Mayor of London.

Vestibule. In a display case is the dagger with which Walworth allegedly stabbed Wat Tyler at Smithfield in 1381. Some claim that this is also the 'dagger' featured in the City's coat of arms. However, this was designed long before Walworth's time and incorporated not a dagger but St Paul's sword.

Above, is the 'Duke of Edinburgh' by *Annigoni.*

Drawing Room. In this room, remodelled in 1951, hangs the best known portrait of Elizabeth II – by *Annigoni.* The painting was commissioned by the Fishmongers in 1952 together with the painting of the Duke of Edinburgh, already seen.

Banqueting Hall. Much of the interior, including the coffered ceiling, is original.

●● *Exit R.*

Location 3

LONDON BRIDGE *H. King 1973*

The present bridge of pre-stressed concrete, is, like its predecessor, sited approximately sixty yards west of the famous medieval structure.

Although there must have been a London Bridge in Roman times the earliest to be documented was built of wood in the 10C and frequently rebuilt.

Early in the 11C, King Ethelred, aided by King Olav of Norway, fought the Danish invaders. Olav pulled down the bridge as a defensive measure, thus giving rise to the nursery song 'London Bridge is Falling Down'. The first stone bridge was completed in 1209 by *Peter,* a chaplain of St Mary Cole Church, and survived for more than six hundred years.

Houses began to appear before the end of the 13C, and the bridge was almost entirely covered by buildings including shops, a chapel and gateways at both ends. At night the south gate was closed and above this, the heads of executed criminals were fixed.

All of the buildings were removed from London Bridge in 1757 to help the traffic flow and permit the passage of heavy goods. The piers were refaced and given hooded alcoves in 1759. The old bridge itself was demolished in 1831 and a new bridge of granite built slightly further west, on the present site, by *Rennie.* In 1973 it was dismantled and re-erected at Lake Havasu City, Arizona.

•▬ Cross the bridge. First L Duke St Hill leads to Tooley St. Proceed to the Joiner St corner (first R).

Location 4

LONDON DUNGEON

34 Tooley Street

Open daily April–September 10.00–18.30, October–March 10.00–17.30. Admission charge.

This waxwork display, in a 19C. warehouse, depicts London's horror history. Some actual instruments of torture and execution are also exhibited. Groups are guided for the 'Jack the Ripper Experience'.

•▬ Exit R. and continue to the Stainer Street corner (first right).

Location 5

WINSTON CHURCHILL'S BRITAIN AT WAR EXPERIENCE

64/5 Tooley Street

Open daily 10.00–17.30 (closes October–March 16.30). Admission charge.

With particular appeal to the over-sixties, this museum describes the everyday life of Londoners throughout the Second World War, 1939–45. A contemporary lift descends to a replica of an air raid shelter set up in a London Underground station, where many Londoners slept, in uncomfortable, cramped conditions, for weeks on end. Air raid sounds, the smell of burning wood and the flash of exploding bombs add realism to a London street during the Blitz. A wartime pub, shops and an Anderson Shelter are recreated and there is a wealth of evocative ephemera: Vera Lynn songs, memorable editions of newspapers, posters and packs of the products available (from time to time) in the shops.

Location 6

GUYS HOSPITAL

St Thomas Street

The courtyard and chapel are generally open. Admission free.

In the middle of the yard is a statue of the founder, Thomas Guy, d.1724, by *Scheemakers*.

The central block of the hospital was built by *T. Dance* c.1728, but its stone facade was remodelled by *Jupp* 1774. Both statues are by *Bacon*.

The east wing by *Steere* 1741 was rebuilt after bomb damage; its facade is a replica. Opposite is the west wing by *Jupp* 1777.

•▬ Proceed R to the chapel (with a cross above).

Within stands the monument to Guy by *Bacon* 1779.

•▬ Exit from the chapel R and pass through the colonnade, approached through the central block. Proceed to the green L.

On the green is one of the alcoves *c.*1760 from Old London Bridge.

•▬ Return to St Thomas St L. Cross the road and proceed to the houses just before old St Thomas's parish church (now Southwark Cathedral's office).

Location 7

OLD OPERATING THEATRE MUSEUM

9A St Thomas Street

Open daily 10.00–16.00. Closed mid December–early January. Admission charge.

This old operating theatre of St Thomas's Hospital, Britain's only surviving 19C example, was opened up in 1956 and restored.

The houses, seen just before the old church, were built in 1819 as the residences of St Thomas's Hospital's superintendent, apothecary, secretary and gatekeeper. The hospital's courtyard formerly stood behind.

St Thomas's Hospital, London's oldest, was founded at Southwark *c.*1106 as part of an Augustinian monastery. Much rebuilding took place, particularly in the early 18C, when St Thomas's parish church, now Southwark Cathedral's office, was also rebuilt by *Thomas Cartwright* 1703.

The hospital left Southwark in 1865, only the 18C women's surgical block remains, now accommodating a post office. The hospital's chapel ceased to be the parish church in 1898.

➡ *Enter the tower of the old church and ascend the spiral stairs to the reception area. Steps lead to the* **Herb Garret**.

Herbs for the hospital's apothecary were once hung from the beams to dry. Displays illustrate the history of medicine including its early, terrifying aspects.

➡ *Ascend more stairs to the operating theatre itself.*

The women's surgical ward adjoined the chapel and this room was converted to form its operating theatre in 1821.

The operating table is contemporary and came from University College. Sawdust was scattered from a box kept below, by the surgeon, wherever blood flowed. The present box is a reproduction.

The 'standings' for onlookers, mostly students, have been restored. The door R leads to what was the women's surgical block (not open).

➡ *Exit R. L Borough High St. Third L (at the George Inn sign) George Yard.*

Location 8

THE GEORGE *1677*

71 Borough High Street (703 2917)

Although galleried coaching inns were once common, the 17C George is London's only survivor. A George Inn, patronized by Canterbury pilgrims, is known to have stood on the site since the Middle Ages, but this burnt down in 1676. Charles Dickens refers to its replacement, the present building, in *Little Dorritt*. Two adjoining blocks, forming the north and east sides, were demolished by the railway company in 1889 and what remains is, therefore, only the south range. There are bars and restaurants but accommodation is no longer provided.

➡ *Enter the first door to the bar R.*

This bar retains much of its original interior with beams and an inglenook fireplace. A Parliament Clock of 1797 stands in the corner.

➡ *Exit to Borough High St L. Cross the road at the war memorial. Proceed through the gate to the yard adjoining No 50 (G. C. Hocking).*

Location 9

NO 50 BOROUGH HIGH STREET *c.1542*

In the yard is a rare, timber-framed building with a protruding first floor. Built as the Goat Inn, its interior is entirely modern.

➡ *Exit L. Return northward along Borough High St.*

Standing before the railway bridge, on the east side, is the 18C building, now a post office, built as the women's surgical block of old St Thomas's Hospital.

➡ *Pass beneath the railway bridge. Turn immediately L to the steps and descend the flight R.*

Location 10

SOUTHWARK CATHEDRAL*

Borough High Street

Southwark Cathedral was London's first com Gothic building and, apart from Westminster it is London's largest survivor in that style. The church on the site formed part of St Mary Overie, nunnery established in 606. By tradition, 'Overie' meant 'over the river' referring to a ferry service operated for the nuns' financial benefit between the City and Southwark.

Augustinian canons acquired the property in 1106 and immediately rebuilt the church. A fire *c.* 1212 necessitated further rebuilding and this continued throughout most of the 13C. Although the Early English style was adopted, much of the 12C masonry in the transepts and nave was retained, and some Norman features may still be seen. Following the dissolution of the priory in 1540 this became the parish church of St Saviour. Much restoration took place in the 19C and the nave was twice rebuilt. St Saviour's became the Cathedral and Collegiate Church of St Saviour and St Marie Overie in 1905.

Proceed westward following the south facade.

Most external features, including all the flint facing, date from the 19C restoration. An exception is the tower, its top stage is 15C and the stage below 14C, possibly by *Yevele* (?).

The nave, west of the tower, was completely rebuilt by *A. Blomfield* 1890–97.

At the east end, ascend the steps. R Cathedral St leads to the newly-formed riverside terrace and the north facade of the cathedral.

Traces of 12C work survive in the north and east walls of the north transept. Church offices in flint and stone were built in 1987.

Return to the south porch. Enter the cathedral. Turn L and proceed clockwise.

Nave south aisle. The late-13C nave became ruinous and was demolished in 1838. This was replaced by *Henry Rose* in 1840 but his work met with derision and was entirely rebuilt by *A. Blomfield* in Early English style to complement the 13C chancel.

Immediately L, built into the south wall, is a section of early Gothic arcading, possibly late 12C (?).

Nave west end. The font and its cover, by *Bodley*, are late 19C.

Three figures from the organ case of 1703 stand on the sill of the west window.

Nave north aisle. Wooden bosses, displayed against the west wall, were saved from the 15C roof.

The round-arched recess in the north wall, which probably accommodated a tomb (?), and the round-arched doorway R are from the 12C Norman church which apparently stood two feet lower.

Just before the north transept is the canopied tomb chest L of John Gower, d.1408. He was the Poet Laureate of both Richard II and Henry IV and a friend of fellow poet Geoffrey Chaucer.

Behind the next door, which was once the prior's but

now leads to the vestry, are Norman door jambs. Within, R is a Holy Water stoup.

North transept. The genuine 13C section of the cathedral has now been reached. The vaulting and north window were rebuilt by *Wallace* 1830.

On the west wall L is the monument to Joyce Austin by *Stone* 1633. Below this is a Jacobean Communion table.

On the north wall, the monument to Lionel Lockyer, d.1672, commemorates a famous quack doctor. Its inscription praises 'His virtues and his PILLS'.

The rare 1674 wooden sword rest is from St Olave's.

The two rounded arches R are Norman but much restored. They originally connected the transept with an apse, since demolished.

Crossing. The piers may pre-date the 13C fire (?).

Above the arches runs a late-14C gallery.

The ceiling bosses are 15C. From the centre hangs a rare chandelier, made in 1680.

The 19C stone pulpit was designed by *Blomfield.*

•● *Proceed eastward to the* **Harvard Chapel.**

This chapel, originally dedicated to St John the Evangelist, was almost entirely rebuilt by *Blomfield* in 1907 to commemorate John Harvard, founder of Harvard University, USA. He was baptized in the cathedral in 1608 and emigrated to America in 1638. His memorial window was made in the USA in 1907.

Much of the north wall is Norman, including the pier R in the north-east corner.

The spired tabernacle by *Pugin* 1851 was brought from Ramsgate in 1971.

The small 16C Italian 'pieta' was painted by *Garofalo.*

On the south wall, immediately L of the entrance, is a plaque commemorating Oscar Hammerstein, the American lyricist, d.1960.

•● *Exit L to the north aisle of the chancel and proceed R through the wooden screen to the choir, which occupies the west end of the chancel.*

The choir was restored by *Gwilt Jnr* in 1823.

Its stalls were designed by *Blomfield.*

A floor slab in front of the central stalls R commemorates the burial of Edmond Shakespeare, d.1607, younger brother of William Shakespeare. The position of his grave is unknown.

Sanctuary. A blind arcade runs above the aisles at triforium level but there is no passageway.

Above this, the clerestory was rebuilt by *Gwilt* in 1823.

Design changes in the north and south walls probably denote the work of separate architects (?).

The stone reredos was presented by Bishop Fox in 1520. Its carved niches would originally have been occupied by figures of saints, probably destroyed the Reformation (?). It was restored by *Wallace* 1833 who added the canopies, demi-angels and frieze. The present statues were made by Nich 1905. The lower section was gilded in 1929; the central gilding is recent.

Return to the north aisle of the chancel which forms part of the ambulatory. Turn R.

Chancel north aisle. Immediately L is the brightly-coloured monument to John Trehearne, d.1618, 'Gentleman Portar to James I'.

Just before the gate, an early effigy, against the wall L, of a knight *c.*1279 is possibly a member of the Warrenne family (?).

Opposite R is the canopied tomb chest of Richard Humble and his two wives *c.*1618.

Pass through the gate ahead.

Retrochoir. This once served as the Courtroom of the Bishops of Winchester. It became dilapidated and the 13C building was restored, gratuitously, by *Gwilt* in 1833. Immediately L, the Elizabethan inlaid chest, presented *c.*1588, is a 'Nonsuch' chest. These are so-named because they depict Nonsuch Palace.

On the west wall R, the 14C decorated blind tracery is original.

The screens and furnishings of the chapels were made by *Comper c.*1935.

Chancel south aisle. Immediately past the gate R is the canopied tomb chest of Lancelot Andrewes, Bishop of Westminster, d.1626. The canopy was replaced by *Comper c.*1935. Just before the steps to the south transept, a section of tesselated (mosaic) pavement has been laid. This came from a 7C Roman villa and was found in the churchyard.

South transept. This was mostly rebuilt for Cardinal Beaufort *c.*1420. His 15C. coat of arms is on the east wall R of the organ.

The vaulting and south window were rebuilt and the tracery of the other windows restored by *Blomfield* in 1907.

Nave south aisle. Immediately L is the alabaster monument to William Shakespeare by *McCarthy* 1912 which commemorates the poet's connection with Southwark, where he almost certainly lived, and its Elizabethan playhouses. The Shakespeare memorial window above was installed in 1954.

Exit from the south porch R. Ascend the steps to Cathedral St R. First L continue to St Mary Overie Dock.

Moored at the dock is the last remaining topsail schooner *Kathleen and May*. This trading vessel, built in 1900, belongs to the Maritime Trust; it may be boarded every day.

Exit from the ship. Ahead Pickford's Wharf.

Location 11

WINCHESTER HOUSE

ckford's Wharf

Behind the railings can be seen all that remains of the London residence of the Bishops of Winchester who lived here until the 17C.

The gable of the 14C Great Hall retains its original rose window tracery restored in 1972. The blocked first floor doorway once formed the main entrance.

Proceed ahead to Clink St.

.ion 12

CLINK PRISON MUSEUM

.ink Street

pen daily 10.00–.8.00. Admission charge.

One of London's four horror/imprisonment museums, the Clink occupies the basement of warehouses built after Clink Street had been reduced to rubble by fire in 1814.

From the 12C until its demolition in 1780, the Clink Prison occupied most of Clink Street, part of it stretching beneath the Great Hall of Winchester House. The expression 'in the clink' is still used as a reference to imprisonment. The name probably derives from the clinching iron with which fetters and chains were riveted to miscreant's hands and feet. Outside the entrance hung the prison's sign, depicting a fiddle, which seems to have been the origin of 'on the fiddle' (cheating).

Initially, the prison, which was under the control of the bishops of Winchester, was used to incarcerate prostitutes and their clients that had broken the house rules of the Bankside stews but, on the return of troops from the First Crusade, political prisoners were held in the Clink, many being subjected to physical torture. During the religious turmoil of the 16C, 'heretics', both Catholic and Protestant, almost exclusively made up the inmates. From the 17C, the complex served as a debtor's prison.

Instruments of torture are displayed and there are some tableaux, but most of the exhibits comprise panels describing the appalling inhumanity of the times.

Location 13

BANKSIDE

Unbelievably, in the Tudor period, Southwark was the equivalent of London's present West End. It lay outside the City Council's puritanical jurisdiction and Bankside became the site of pleasure gardens, inns and the famous Elizabethan playhouses in which Shakespeare acted – the Rose, Swan, Globe and Hope. Many of them were destroyed by fire and no traces remain. For alternative recreation, numerous brothels or 'stews', some owned by the Bishops of Winchester, lined the river.

Location 14

THE ANCHOR *c.1775*

Bankside

The Anchor's original Georgian interior was unfortunately remodelled by the brewery to provide a more 'Ye Olde' appearance in the 1960s. The rambling 18C exterior, however, remains little changed. Earlier inns stood on the site and much of the surrounding area was occupied in the 18C by the brewery that belonged to the Thrales, close friends of Dr Johnson who almost certainly drank here. The great high tide of 1928 is recorded on the wall of the ale bar by a brass plaque.

Exit L. Pass beneath Southwark Bridge and continue ahead to New Globe Walk (second L).

Location 15	SHAKESPEARE INTERNATIONAL GLOBE CE

New Globe Walk

Museum open daily 10.00–17.00. Admission charge. Globe Theatre open for perfomances from summer 1995.

When completed, the complex, brainchild of American actor and director, the late Sam Wanamaker, is planned to incorporate two theat a museum, an education centre and an audio-visua archive and library. Its riverside site formed part of the grounds of Winchester House (location 11), and traces of the bishop's fish ponds were discovered during excavations.

Of greatest interest is the circular Globe Theatre, a recreation of Southwark's Elizabethan Globe Theatre, where Shakespeare himself acted and all his great tragedies were first performed. This stood approximately 200m to the south-east of the present building, and is commemmorated by a wall plaque on the south side of Park Street, just east of Southwark Bridge Road.

Construction methods and building materials have closely matched those of the Elizabethan period; they include red brickwork, English oak, lime plaster and thatch. The audience capacity of the theatre is 1500; most will be seated under cover, but one third will stand in the uncovered 'yard' around the stage. As the intention is to faithfully reproduce a contemporary Shakespearean performance, neither electric lighting nor amplification will be employed.

The museum describes the construction of the new theatre and the evidence for its appearance and detailing. Among the exhibits is the contract record of a carpenter who worked on the original Globe of 1599. That theatre burnt down 29 June 1613, during the first performance of Shakespeare's final play, *Henry VIII*. All visitors to the museum are shown around the new theatre.

Location 16	**CARDINAL'S WHARF** *c.1710*

49 Bankside

Occupies the site of a famous Elizabethan brothel, 'The Cardinal's Hat'. It is unlikely that Wren lived in the present building while St Paul's was under construction, as alleged, because the cathedral was completed by 1710. Information on the plaque refers to an earlier building.

Proceed to the next house.

Location 17	**PROVOST'S LODGING** *1712*

51–52 Bankside

This remodelled house is now the residence of the Provost of Southwark Cathedral and was built slightly later than No 49.

Return along Bankside to the steps that lead to Southwark Bridge.

Location 18	**SOUTHWARK BRIDGE** *George 1921*

The steps on the west side of Southwark Bridge once led down to the ferries and predate the bridge itself. The first Southwark Bridge, the work of *Rennie*, was completed in 1819. It was then the largest bridge ever to have been built of cast iron.

Ascend the steps R and cross Southwark Bridge to the north bank. First L Upper Thames St. First L Vintners Place.

19

VINTNERS HALL *1671*

Thames

n by
ointment only.
dmission free.

Much of the present building dates from 1671 and its interior is the finest of all the 17C Livery Company halls to survive. The Vintners Company, still active in the wine trade, is one of the twelve Great Livery Companies. Its Charter was granted in 1364 and the present site acquired in 1446. Only the Vintners, together with the sovereign and the Dyers Company, have the right to own swans on the Thames.

The statue of a Vintry Ward schoolboy, on the west wall, was made *c.* 1840.

To view the interior, return to Upper Thames Street R. Enter the first door R and await the guide.

Court Room. This is one of London's oldest rooms and contains much original 17C woodwork, including most of the coats of arms on the cornice. The Master's chair is 18C.

Staircase. The sumptuously carved balustrade by *Woodroffe* 1673 is one of the finest in London.

The **hall** is decorated with carved festoons and heads. Its ceiling was renewed in 1932. The screen was made in 1822. There is an early 18C sword rest.

Exit and cross Upper Thames St R. First L the passage (Doby Court) leads behind St James's to Skinners Lane L. L Garlick Hill. Enter the church.

Location 20

ST JAMES GARLICKHYTHE* *Wren 1683*

Garlick Hill
(248 7546)

St James's was first recorded in 1170. The present church has been described as a miniature St Stephen Walbrook without the dome.

Due to the extent of clear glass, the church became known as 'Wren's Lantern'.

Although there was some Second World War bomb damage much 17C woodwork was saved including the canopied pulpit, reredos, stalls and west gallery.

The scallop shell emblem of St James of Compostela, to whom the church is dedicated, is seen throughout.

Exit R. First R Skinners Lane. Cross Queens St and proceed to College St ahead.

Location 21

ST MICHAEL PATERNOSTER ROYAL *Wren 1694*

College Street

St Michael's, the 'Dick Whittington church', was first recorded in 1229. 'Royal' in the name, is a corruption of La Riole near Bordeaux, from where local vintners imported their wines. St Michael's was rebuilt after being gutted by bombs in the Second World War, and is now the headquarters of the Mission to Seamen.

Enter from College Street.

Dick Whittington, four times Lord Mayor, lived in a house in College Hill, next to the earlier church destroyed in the Great Fire, and was buried in the churchyard in 1423. The modern south window R depicts him with his cat. The helpful cat legend is believed to originate from an early 17C engraving of Whittington which at first showed him with his hand on a skull. This was later altered to a small cat, as it fitted the same area and was considered preferable

The canopied pulpit, reredos, lectern and font cover are original.

Exit L.

Next to the church, behind a screen wall, is the south facade of Skinners' Hall *c.* 1670 (location 23).

Continue past Little College Lane (first R) to Innholders Hall R.

Location 22

INNHOLDERS HALL

College Street

Open by appointment only. Admission free.

The Innholders Charter was granted in 1514. Their present hall was built in 1671 but partly rebuilt, including the present facade, in 1886. It was damaged by bombs and has been much restored.

The doorcase is 18C.

Enter from College Hill and await the guide.

Vestibule. Displayed are examples of rare 17C stained glass and the licence granted to the Company by Henry VIII.

Court Room. Most of this room dates from 1670 including the panelling and fireplace surround. The ceiling was partly restored following bomb damage in the Second World War.

Hall: The chimney-piece, much of the panelling and the minstrels gallery are original.

Exit R. L Dowgate Hill. Proceed ahead, first gate L.

Location 23

DYERS HALL *Dyer 1840*

10 Dowgate Hill

Open by appointment only. Admission free.

The Dyers, and Vintners, share the ownership of swans on the Thames with the sovereign.

Enter and await the guide.

A glass-vaulted corridor leads to the Court Room.

Exit L and proceed to the next gate L.

Location 24

SKINNERS HALL

8½ Dowgate Hill

Open by appointment only. Admission free.

The Skinners is one of the twelve Great Livery Companies and alternates sixth and seventh position of priority with the Merchant Taylors. The south facade of the hall has already been seen. The building facing the street was remodelled by *Jupp* in 1790. From within the courtyard can be seen the east facade of the livery hall, 1670.

Enter the door ahead and await the guide.

Livery Hall. The building was remodelled in 1850. Allegorical 19C paintings by *Frank Brangwyn* may be illuminated.

The **staircase** was constructed *c.* 1670. Its surrounding plasterwork dates from 1737.

Court Room. Much of the decor, including the Virginia cedar panelling, was completed in 1670.

Exit L and proceed to the next gate L.

Location 25

TALLOW CHANDLERS HALL

4 Dowgate Hill

Open by appointment only. Admission free.

The Company's Royal Charter was granted in 1462 and the site for the hall acquired in 1476. The present hall by *Caines* (?) 1672 was partly rebuilt in the 19C and again following the Second World War but much 17C work remains.

•• *Enter and await the guide.*

Parlour. The panelling and ceiling are original.

Staircase. The walls are lined with 17C leather panels.

Hall. Most of the 17C woodwork, including the reredos, is original. Displayed within is the oldest operative Grant of Arms in London, dated 1456.

•• *Exit L. Cross the road to Cannon St Station, Circle and District lines.*

Itinerary 13

13

Knightsbridge, Belgravia and Mayfair

Knightsbridge and Mayfair constitute 'luxury London', and some of the world's most exclusive shops and hotels are established in these two elegant districts. Equally elegant, Belgravia houses many foreign embassies.

Timing: Mornings, Tuesday to Thursday are preferable. The Wellington Museum closes Monday and Friday.

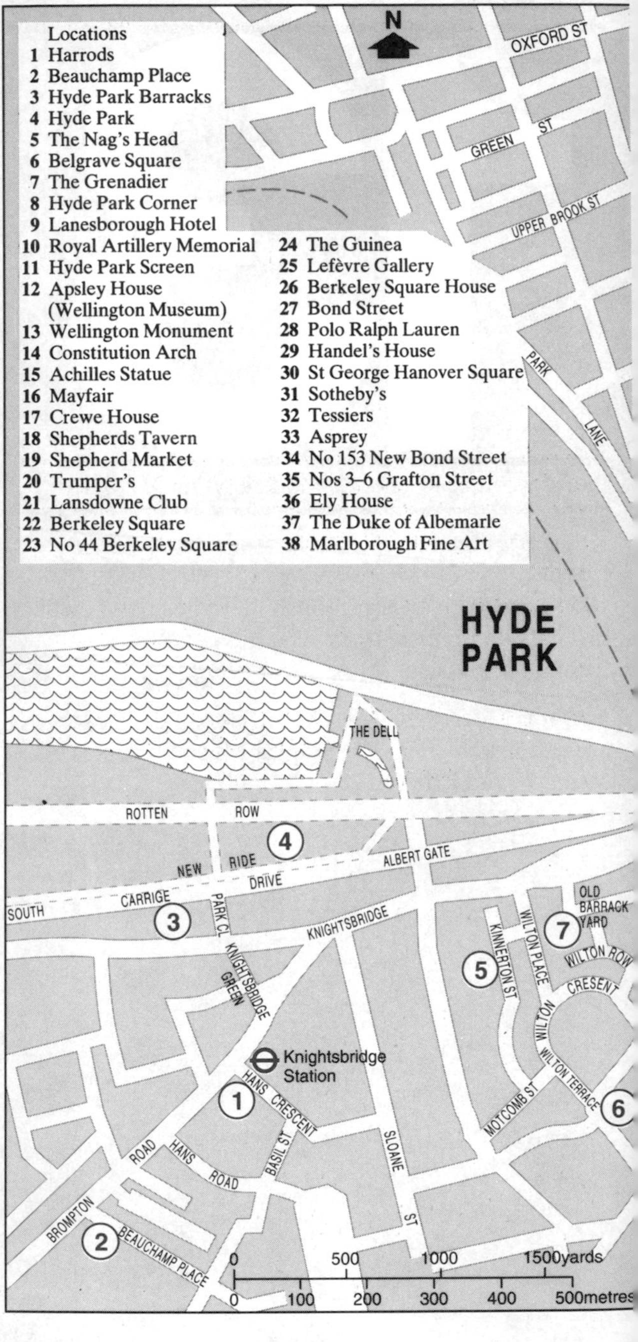
Locations
1 Harrods
2 Beauchamp Place
3 Hyde Park Barracks
4 Hyde Park
5 The Nag's Head
6 Belgrave Square
7 The Grenadier
8 Hyde Park Corner
9 Lanesborough Hotel
10 Royal Artillery Memorial
11 Hyde Park Screen
12 Apsley House (Wellington Museum)
13 Wellington Monument
14 Constitution Arch
15 Achilles Statue
16 Mayfair
17 Crewe House
18 Shepherds Tavern
19 Shepherd Market
20 Trumper's
21 Lansdowne Club
22 Berkeley Square
23 No 44 Berkeley Square
24 The Guinea
25 Lefèvre Gallery
26 Berkeley Square House
27 Bond Street
28 Polo Ralph Lauren
29 Handel's House
30 St George Hanover Square
31 Sotheby's
32 Tessiers
33 Asprey
34 No 153 New Bond Street
35 Nos 3–6 Grafton Street
36 Ely House
37 The Duke of Albemarle
38 Marlborough Fine Art
N
OXFORD ST
GREEN ST
UPPER BROOK ST
PARK LANE
HYDE PARK
THE DELL
ROTTEN ROW
NEW RIDE
ALBERT GATE
DRIVE
SOUTH CARRIGE
PARK CL
KNIGHTSBRIDGE
OLD BARRACK YARD
WILTON ROW
KINNERTON ST
WILTON PLACE
WILTON CRESENT
KNIGHTSBRIDGE GREEN
Knightsbridge Station
HANS CRESCENT
WILTON TERRACE
MOTCOMB ST
SLOANE ST
BASIL ST
HANS ROAD
BROMPTON ROAD
BEAUCHAMP PLACE
0 500 1000 1500yards
0 100 200 300 400 500metres

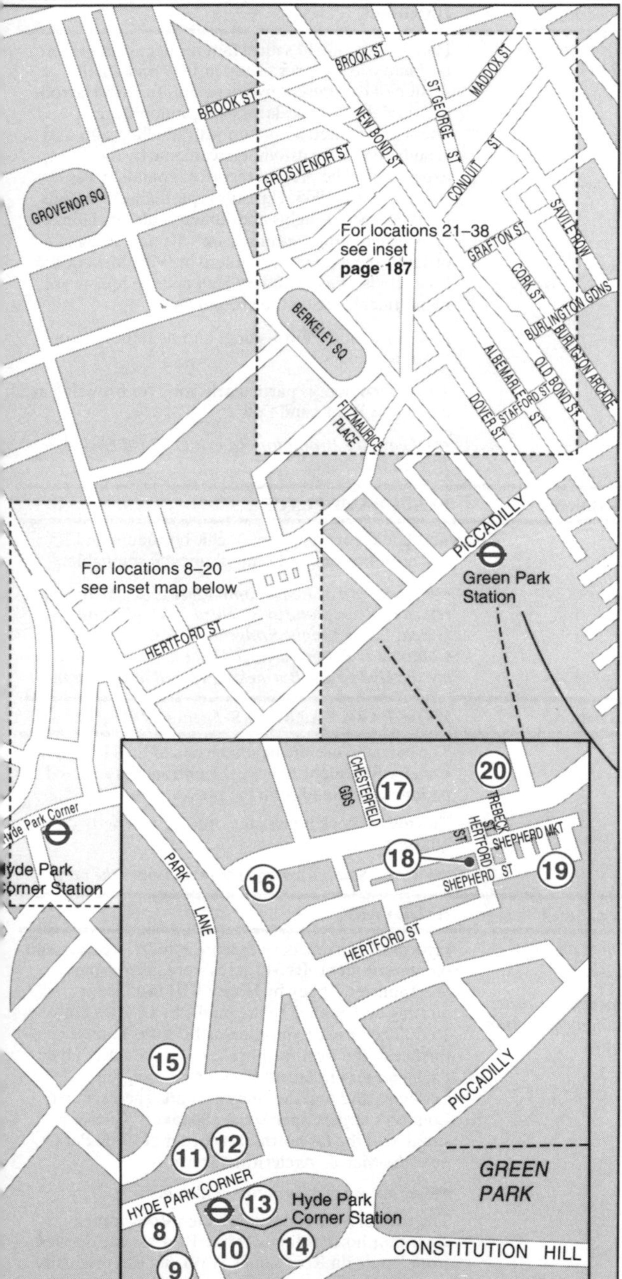

Start *Knightsbridge Station, Piccadilly line. Leave by the Brompton Rd (Harrods) exit. Cross Hans Crescent ahead and proceed to Harrods.*

Six people died at the east end of Hans Crescent, outside Harrods, when a terrorist car bomb exploded just before Christmas 1983.

Location 1	**HARRODS**
Brompton Road (730 1234)	Harrods, the world's most famous department store, originated as a grocer's shop in 1849 on a small section of the present five-acre site. In 1895 Harrods installed the first escalator in a London store; attendants waited at the top with smelling salts and brandy to revive customers overcome by the experience. The present terracotta building was constructed in 1905. Harrods is particularly famous for its Christmas lights and January sale. It claims to provide anything within reason – Ronald Reagan ordered an elephant from them in 1975. Most of the Food Halls, the Perfumery Hall and the Menswear Department, are on the ground floor. Ladies Fashions, Furnishings and Antiques are on the upper floors. The second floor is particularly good for browsing as it includes Books and Pets. *Leave the Brompton Rd exit L. Third L Beauchamp Place.*

Location 2	**BEAUCHAMP PLACE** *c.1800*
	This late Georgian street of chic boutiques and restaurants is one of London's most fashionable. *At the end of Beauchamp Place cross the road and return to Brompton Rd R. Third L Knightsbridge Green. Cross Knightsbridge to Park Close ahead. Continue to South Carriage Drive L. Immediately L are the Hyde Park Barracks. Proceed to the entrance.*

Location 3	**HYDE PARK BARRACKS** *Spence 1970*
	The barracks are the headquarters of the Household Cavalry Regiment. Above the entrance is a carved pediment retained from the previous building. The tower block houses the officers' married quarters. *Cross South Carriage Drive and enter the park.*

Location 4	**HYDE PARK**
Open dawn to dusk. *Speakers' Corner Sunday afternoon only.*	Hyde Park's name derives from a 'hide', a Saxon unit of measurement. Its 340 acres were taken from Westminster Abbey by Henry VIII in 1536 for hunting and opened to the public by Charles I in 1637. The Great Exhibition of 1851 was housed further to the west, within the Crystal Palace. Hyde Park merges imperceptibly with Kensington Gardens, and together they cover 630 acres, inner London's largest open space. Speakers' Corner is situated in the far north-east corner of Hyde Park near the Marble Arch (itinerary 16). *Cross the two earth tracks ahead.* The tracks, New Ride and Rotten Row, form a circuit for horse riding. Rotten Row's name derives from Route du Roi (King's Way) and was originally part of a straight road between Kensington Palace and Hyde Park Corner laid out for William III in the late 17C. It was the first thoroughfare in England to be lit at night – from lamps in the trees. *Proceed ahead to the Serpentine lake.* The Serpentine was formed in 1730 by damming the

Westbourne Stream which now runs underground. A summer bathing lido lies at the south-west end of the lake and here the water is purified for swimmers.

Rowing and motor boats may be hired in summer from the lake's north bank.

Follow the lakeside path R. Turn L at the first path and proceed to the north side of the lake. Turn R at the first path. The Dell lies immediately R.

The Dell is a nook with flowers, a waterfall and a rockery. The black Cornish stone weighs seven tons.

Continue ahead and leave the park at Albert Gate. L Knightsbridge. First R Wilton Place. First R and L Kinnerton Street.

Location 5

THE NAG'S HEAD

53 Kinnerton Street

The pub, in this quiet mews, once possessed London's smallest bar but has recently been remodelled. Many Victorian fittings remain.

Exit R. L Motcomb St. Second R Wilton Terrace. R Belgrave Square.

Location 6

BELGRAVE SQUARE

Most of Belgravia was laid out by Thomas Cubitt for the Grosvenor family who still own the freeholds. To permit construction work, the swampy land was filled with gravel from St Katharine's Dock.

The terraces were designed by *Basevi* in 1827 but the corner mansions are the work of various architects. Many of the properties now accommodate embassies.

To see the whole square turn R and proceed anti-clockwise. Alternatively, turn L and proceed to location 7 as indicated.

No 12 in the north-west corner is by *R. Smirke* c.1830.

The Spanish Embassy has for long been the leaseholder of No 24 in the south-west corner by *Kendall* (?) c.1827.

In the east corner, No 37 Seaford House by *P. Hardwick* 1842 originally possessed a portico.

Leave the square at Wilton Crescent in the north corner. First R Wilton Row. Proceed to the end.

Location 7

THE GRENADIER

Wilton Row

The pretty mews creates a country-in-town setting and it is popular to drink outside this 18C pub in summer beneath the vine, which occasionally fruits. Once used as a mess by the Duke of Wellington's officers, the Duke himself and even George IV were allegedly customers.

The ceiling is covered with bank notes and labels.

Exit from the pub L. First L the wooden door leads to Old Barrack Yard.

The stone at the top of the steps R is by tradition the Duke of Wellington's mounting stone.

Pass through the arch ahead. Turn L and R and continue to Knightsbridge. Cross the road immediately and proceed R to Hyde Park Corner.

Location 8

HYDE PARK CORNER

The 'Corner' now refers to a large roundabout that can only safely be traversed by inconvenient pedestrian subways.

A toll gate stood here until the early 19C when Hyde Park Corner was still the western entrance to London. Knightsbridge was then a country village.

Remain on the north side to view locations 9 to 14. On the south side of Knightsbridge is the Lanchester Hotel.

Location 9

LANESBOROUGH HOTEL *Wilkins 1827*

Hyde Park Corner

This Classical, stuccoed building was originally St George's Hospital but its function ended in the 1980s. Restoration to a luxury hotel has been sympathetic.

On the traffic island, facing the hotel, is the **Royal Artillery Memorial**.

Remain on the north side.

Location 10

ROYAL ARTILLERY MEMORIAL *Jagger 1925*

Hyde Park Corner

The howitzer of the memorial points in the direction of the Somme, where many of the regiment died in the First World War.

Continue ahead. The Hyde Park Screen is immediately L.

Location 11

HYDE PARK SCREEN *D. Burton c.1825*

Hyde Park Corner

Planned as a grand entrance to Hyde Park, the screen was commissioned as part of Burton's overall design which included the Constitution Arch and various park lodges.

Continue ahead to Apsley House.

Location 12

APSLEY HOUSE (WELLINGTON MUSEUM)

Hyde Park Corner (499 5676)

Open Tuesday–Sunday 11.00–17.00. Admission charge.

This museum is accommodated in the home of the first Duke of Wellington. Outstanding paintings are exhibited. Apsley House, known as 'Number One, London', was built of brick for Baron Apsley by *R. Adam* in 1778. It was purchased by Wellington from his brother in 1817 and 'The Iron Duke' lived here until his death in 1852. Wellington commissioned *B. D. Wyatt* in 1829 to reface the house in Bath stone, add a portico and build a west extension. It became the Wellington Museum in 1947. Internally, some *Adam* interiors remain (as indicated) but most are by *Wyatt*.

Enter Apsley House.

Entrance Hall. First C BC bust of Cicero. Bust of Wellington by *Pistrucci*.

Turn L.

Plate and China Room. There is a fine display of porcelain and plate, including the Empress Josephine's Egyptian service and the Prussian service. Wellington's and Napoleon's swords are also exhibited.

Return to the hall and proceed ahead.

Inner Hall. This was the original entrance hall. Exhibited here are busts of Wellington and a dramatic portrayal of Waterloo.

Stairwell. The nude statue of Napoleon by *Canova* 1806 was presented to the Duke by George IV.

The staircase is by *Adam*.

Ascend the stairs to the first floor (or take the lift).

Piccadilly Room. *Adam.* Displayed are 17C Dutch paintings and 'Chelsea Pensioners Reading the Waterloo Despatch' by *Wilkie*.

Portico Room. *Adam.* This has been judged one of the finest rooms in the house.

Waterloo Gallery. The gallery was added for Wellington so that more guests might be accommodated at the annual Waterloo reunion banquet. It was decorated in the 18C French style that set a fashion in London. This room now houses the most important paintings in the collection. They include: 'Wellington on Horseback' *Goya,* 'St Francis Receiving The Stigmata' and 'Unknown Man' *Murillo,* 'Spanish Gentlemen', 'Young Men Eating', 'Pope Innocent X' and 'The Water Seller of Seville' *Velasquez,* 'Agony in the Garden' *Correggio*.

Yellow Drawing Room. Painting of William IV by *Wilkie*; 'Isaac blessing Jacob' by *Murillo*.

Striped Drawing Room. Painting of Wellington by *Lawrence*. Busts are exhibited of Spencer Perceval, Britain's only Prime Minister to be assassinated (in the House of Commons), and Pitt the Younger by *Nollekens*.

Dining Room. Waterloo Banquets were held in this room before the Waterloo Gallery was built. The silver Portuguese centrepiece dominates the room. Painting of George IV by *Wilkie*.

Corridor. More porcelain is displayed.

At the end of the corridor descend by lift to the basement.

Basement. Caricatures of Wellington and uniforms are exhibited and temporary exhibitions held.

Exit and remain on the north side of the road. On the traffic island facing Apsley House is the Wellington monument.

Location 13

WELLINGTON MONUMENT *Boehm 1888*

Hyde Park Corner

The Duke is depicted riding his favourite horse, Copenhagen.

Remain on the north side to view the Constitution Arch, also on the traffic island,

Location 14

CONSTITUTION ARCH *D. Burton 1846*

Hyde Park Corner

The arch originally stood further west, in line with the Hyde Park Screen, and was then called the Pimlico Arch. Burton intended that there should be a relatively small quadrega (horse-drawn chariot) on the top and trophies carved on the panels. Instead, against Burton's wishes, a huge equestrian statue of Wellington was immediately erected surmounting the structure, which then became known as the Wellington Arch. The trophies were never carved. When the roundabout was made in 1883, the arch was transferred to its present position and Wellington's statue moved to Aldershot. The present 'Victory' by *A. Jones* replaced this in 1912.

Return to and pass through the Hyde Park Screen. Cross Carriage Rd. Turn R towards Park Lane L.

Location 15 — **ACHILLES STATUE** *Westmacott 1822*

Hyde Park

'Achilles' was erected by George IV to commemorate Wellington's victories.It was cast from the bronze of captured French cannons and actually depicts a Roman horse tamer, not Achilles. The statue was commissioned and paid for by grateful British ladies who were, however, shocked by its nudity in spite of the fig leaf.

Cross Park Lane by the underpass facing the Hilton Hotel. Proceed northward along Park Lane. Second R Curzon St. Cross the road and continue ahead. Crewe House (location 17) is on the Chesterfield Gardens corner (second L).

Location 16 — **MAYFAIR**

Mayfair, now entered, is the area bordered by Oxford Street, Regent Street, Piccadilly and Park Lane. It was laid out in the 18C as a fashionable residential quarter but most of the houses now accommodate offices or have been replaced by hotels.

Location 17 — **CREWE HOUSE** *Shepherd 1730*

15 Curzon Street

Crewe House, a rare, central London example of a detached Georgian mansion set within its own grounds, was named after the Marquess of Crewe, a former occupant.

Continue eastward. First R Hertford St. Continue to Shepherds Tavern R.

Location 18 — **SHEPHERDS TAVERN**

50 Hertford Street

On the pub's first floor landing is an 18C sedan chair, converted to form a public telephone booth.

Exit R Hertford St. First L Shepherd St.

Location 19 — **SHEPHERD MARKET**

Shepherd Market is Mayfair's most village-like sector with small shops, cafés and pubs. It has long been known for its friendly, albeit acquisitive, ladies.

In 1688 James II decreed that a fair, then held in Haymarket, should be transferred to wasteland, now Shepherd Market. This May fair, although terminated in 1708, eventually gave its name to the whole district. Edward Shepherd then opened a food market in what was still an open square but its centre has been built over.

Continue ahead. Fourth L and first L Shepherd Market. Second L Trebeck St.

The plaque at the corner of Trebeck Street and Shepherd Market commemorates the fair.

Proceed north to Curzon St R. Cross the road.

Location 20 — **TRUMPER'S**

9 Curzon Street

Established since 1875 as Court hairdressers, George F. Trumper at one time cut the hair of every male member of the Royal Family.

Exit L. Second L Fitzmaurice Place.

Location 21	**LANSDOWNE CLUB** *R. Adam 1768 (part)*

9 Fitzmaurice Place

The residence, first Shelburne, then Lansdowne House, was rebuilt in 1936 using the original stones. However, the reconstructed building is much narrower and sited further back. Although little original work survives *in situ* internally, two outstanding Adam interiors from the house are exhibited in the USA. The Drawing Room is in the Philadelphia Museum and the Dining Room in the Metropolitan Museum, New York.

Exit L and proceed ahead to Berkeley Square. Remain on the west side.

Location 22	**BERKELEY SQUARE**

The square was named to commemorate Berkeley House that stood on the south side from 1664 to 1733

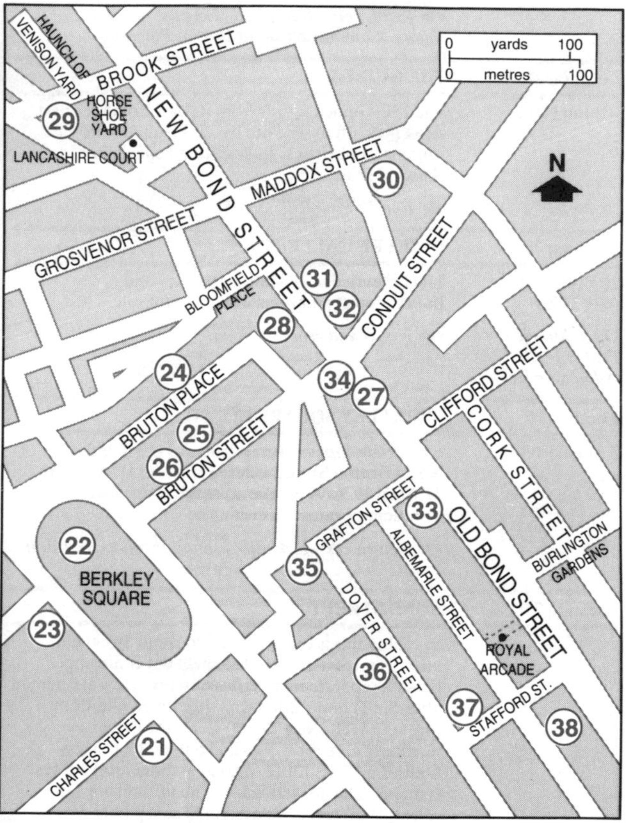

21 Lansdowne Club
22 Berkeley Square
3 Clermont Club
The Guinea
Lefevre Gallery
Berkeley Square
ouse
nd Street
28 Polo Ralph Lauren
29 Handel's House
30 St George Hanover Square
31 Sotheby's
32 Tessiers
33 Asprey
34 No 153 New Bond Street
35 3–6 Grafton Street
36 Ely House
37 Duke of Albemarle
38 Marlborough Fine Art

when it was replaced by Devonshire House. Few nightingales are now reported!

Nos 45–46 were probably built by *Ware* (?) *c.*1750. At No 45 Clive of India committed suicide by cutting his own throat in 1774.

The early 19C Pump House in the centre of the square replaced an equestrian statue of George III.

Proceed ahead to No 44 in the centre of the west side.

Location 23	**NO 44 BERKELEY SQUARE (CLERMONT CLUB)** *Kent 1744*
Open by appointment only. Admission free.	This residence, built for Lady Isabella French, has been judged 'the finest terrace house in London' (Pevsner). Its staircase and Baroque drawing room (now a gaming room) are exceptional. *Exit L. First R proceed along the north side of the square. Continue ahead to Bruton Place.*

Location 24	**THE GUINEA**
Bruton Place	The 18C Guinea serves from its bar, London's best steak pies, often sold out by 13.30, and award-winning sandwiches. Its restaurant specializes in charcoal grills. *Exit L. First R Bruton St.*

Location 25	**LEFEVRE GALLERY**
20 Bruton Street (629 2250) *Open Monday–Friday 10.00–17.00. Admission free.*	The Lefèvre displays contemporary and Impressionist paintings which are for sale. *Exit R and cross the road.*

Location 26	**BERKELEY SQUARE HOUSE**
Bruton Street	Part of this great concrete pile was built on the site of No 27 Bruton Street, where Elizabeth II, was born, 21 April 1926. A plaque, L of the main entrance, commemmorates the event. *Return eastward and continue ahead to New Bond Street.*

Location 27	**BOND STREET**

In reality this is two streets, Old Bond Street and New Bond Street, which connect but confusingly possess separate numbering systems. They are named after Sir Thomas Bond who developed Old Bond Street in 1680. New Bond Street, the longer, northerly extension, was laid out by the Earl of Oxford in 1721. Little of great architectural interest remains. The attraction is the luxurious shops, a selection of which are described as separate locations.

Proceed northward.

Passed L are 148 Fine Art Society and 144–146 Partridge Fine Arts.

Location 28	**POLO RALPH LAUREN**
143 New Bond Street (629 3249)	The shop, with its outstanding 19C front, belonged for many years to the chemists Savory & Moore.
	•■ *Continue northward.*
	Passed L is No 113, Yves St Laurent.
	•■ *First L Brook St.*

Location 29	**HANDEL'S HOUSE** *c.1730*
25 Brook Street	G. F. Handel, the German-born composer, lived in this house for thirty-five years, until his death in 1759. The *Messiah* was written here. This building and its neighbour, No 27, are the only survivors of the street's original properties.
	•■ *Return to New Bond Street R. First L Maddox St. First R St George St.*

Location 30	**ST GEORGE HANOVER SQUARE*** *James 1724*
St George Street 	St George's, judged the West End's most impressive church, was built under the 'Fifty New Churches Act' and dedicated to honour George I. Important weddings in the church have included those of writers Shelley 1814, George Eliot (Mary Evans Lewis) 1880 and John Buchan 1907, and politicians Disraeli 1839, Asquith 1877 and a 'ranchman' destined to become President of the United States, Theodore Roosevelt 1886. Handel, St George's most famous parishioner, had his own pew.
	On either side of the entrance are early 20C cast iron dogs by *A. Jones* (?) brought here in 1940.
	•■ *Enter beneath the portico.*
	The interior of the church resembles St James Piccadilly. The gallery, organ case (part), pulpit, altar rails, coat of arms of George I and reredos are original. The reredos incorporates a painting of 'The Last Supper' by *Kent.*
	Flemish stained glass *c.*1525 in the east window was installed in 1840.
	In the chapel, at the east end of the north aisle, are two angels from a German altarpiece *c.*1500.
	•■ *Return to New Bond St L and proceed southward.*

Location 31	**SOTHEBY'S**
34–35 New Bond St (493 8080)	Sotheby's, the world's largest auctioneers, were established in 1744 and moved here in 1917.
Open for previews and auctions Monday–Friday 09.00–16.30. Admission free.	Above the kiosk, R of the entrance, is an Egyptian statue of the god Sekhmet *c.*1320 BC.

Location 32	**TESSIERS**
26 New Bond Street (629 6405)	These long-established jewellers possess Bond Street's finest 18C shop front.
	•■ *Continue southward.*
	Passed L is No 8 Bentley & Co, long-established jewellers, with an elegant Classical façade.

At the junction with Piccadilly cross Old Bond St to the west side and return northward.

Passed are Nos 43 Agnews (arts), 28 Charbonnel et Walker (chocolatiers), 27 Gucci, 26 Chanel, 180 Boucheron (jewellers), 175 New Bond St, Cartier.

Location 33	**ASPREY**
166–169 New Bond Street (493 6767)	Asprey, founded in 1781, moved to Bond Street in 1847. They possess the Royal Warrant and are goldsmiths, silversmiths, bookbinders and manufacturers of leather goods. China, glass and antiques are also sold on the premises. *Continue northward.*

Location 34	**NO 153 NEW BOND STREET**
	The two-storey section of the building is surmounted by a carved stone screen by *Henry Moore*. *Return southward. First R Grafton St. Proceed ahead to the bend in the road.*

Location 35	**NOS 3–6 GRAFTON STREET** *R. Taylor* (?) *c.1760*
	These wide-fronted houses, with unusually large door-cases, form a terrace on the west side. *Continue ahead to Dover Street.*

Location 36	**ELY HOUSE** *R. Taylor 1772*
37 Dover Street	The stone-faced, Palladian house was built for the Bishops of Ely. A bishop's mitre is carved above the central, first floor window. Seated on the railings outside are cast-iron lions by *Stevens* 1852. *Cross the road and continue southward to the Stafford St corner.*

Location 37	**THE DUKE OF ALBEMARLE** *1696*
Dover Street	Within this pub, the only original building remaining in Dover Street, is displayed the Stafford Street sign, dated 1772. *Exit L Stafford St. First R Albemarle St. Cross the road.*

Location 38	**MARLBOROUGH FINE ART**
6 Albemarle Street (629 5161) *Open Monday–Friday 10.00–17.30. Saturday 10.00–12.30. Admission free.*	The gallery specializes in important 19C and 20C paintings. *Exit L. R Piccadilly and Green Park Station, Piccadilly and Victoria lines.* *Alternatively, if continuing with itinerary 14, exit R. Second R Royal Arcade. Cross Old Bond St and continue ahead to Burlington Gardens.*

Itinerary 14

14

Piccadilly and St James's

The area covered is very much 'gentleman's London', with elegant menswear shops in Jermyn Street and exclusive clubs in St James's Street. The clubs are open only to members and their guests.

Timing: Mornings, Monday to Friday are recommended.

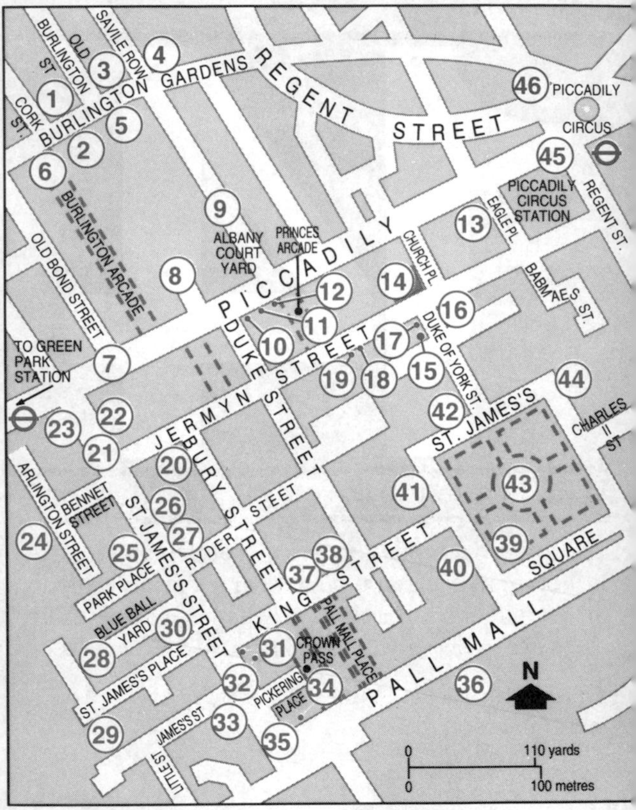

Locations

1 Cork Street
2 Museum of Mankind
3 Royal Bank of Scotland
4 Savile Row
5 Albany (north entrance)
6 Burlington Arcade
7 Piccadilly
8 Burlington House (Royal Academy of Arts)
9 Albany
10 Fortnum and Mason
11 Swaine, Adeney, Brigg
12 Hatchards
13 Simpsons
14 St James Piccadilly
15 The Red Lion
16 Jermyn Street
17 Harvie & Hudson
18 Paxton and Whitfield
19 Floris Perfumes
20 Turnbull and Asser
21 St James's Street
22 White's
23 50 St James's Street
24 No 21 Arlington Street
25 Brooks's
26 Boodles
27 The Economist Plaza
28 Blue Ball Yard
29 Spencer House
30 Carlton Club
31 Lobb
32 Lock & Co
33 No 74 St James's Street
34 Pickering Place
35 Berry Bros and Rudd
36 Schomberg House
37 Christie's Fine Art
38 Spink & Son
39 St James's Square
40 No 20 St James's Square
41 No 15 St James's Square
42 Chatham House
43 William III Monument
44 No 4 St James's Square
45 Piccadilly Circus
46 'Eros' Fountain

Start *Green Park Station, Piccadilly and Victoria lines. Leave by the Piccadilly north side exit. L Piccadilly. Fourth L Old Bond St. First R Burlington Gardens. First L Cork St. Alternatively, continue from itinerary 13.*

Location 1	**CORK STREET**
	Many of London's private art galleries are located in Cork Street. Works exhibited are for sale. Well established on the west side are No 16 Piccadilly and No 2 Waddington. On the east side are No 20 Redfern and No 19 Browse and Darby. •• *Return to Burlington Gardens L. Cross the road.*
Location 2	**MUSEUM OF MANKIND** *Pennethorne 1869*
6 Burlington Gardens (437 2224) *Open Monday–Saturday 10.00–17.00. Sunday 14.30–18.00. Admission free.*	Particularly suitable for children, this imaginatively displayed museum, the British Museum's Department of Ethnography, exhibits on two floors the skills of non-industrialized people. •• *Exit and cross the road R. Pass the Old Burlington St corner (first L).*
Location 3	**ROYAL BANK OF SCOTLAND**
7 Burlington Gardens	Built as Queensberry House by *Leoni*, 1723, the exterior was rebuilt by *Vardy junior* and *Bonomi*, 1789. The ground floor was remodelled and the porch added for the bank by *Philip Hardwick* in 1855. •• *Continue to Savile Row L. Cross the road.*
Location 4	**SAVILE ROW**
	The street is world famous for high quality – and high priced – gentlemen's bespoke tailoring. No 3, was the headquarters of The Beatles' company, Apple. Here, John, Paul, George and Ringo conducted their business. On the roof of this building, at lunchtime on 30 January 1969, the group gave their final public performance. It was stopped by the police following complaints about the noise! •• *Return to Burlington Gardens and cross the road immediately. Ahead lies the entrance to Albany.*
Location 5	**ALBANY (NORTH ENTRANCE)**
	The two single-storey lodges, now shops, on either side of the entrance, together with the brick houses that flank them, were designed by *Holland* in 1803. •• *Proceed westward. First L Burlington Arcade.*
Location 6	**BURLINGTON ARCADE** *Ware 1819*
	The arcade was devised by Lord George Cavendish to form a west screen for his adjacent Burlington House. It is London's most exclusive shopping precinct. Running and whistling are forbidden and the arcade is patrolled by two uniformed beadles who lock it at night. The original Piccadilly frontage was rebuilt in Baroque style by *Pite* in 1931. •• *L Piccadilly. Proceed to Burlington House.*

Location 7

PICCADILLY

Piccadilly, laid out in the 17C, runs for almost a mile from Hyde Park Corner to Piccadilly Circus. Its name derived from a 16C mansion known locally as 'Pickadill Hall' as its owner, Robert Baker, manufactured pickadills (lace frills). The Dutch word for scraps of cloth 'Pikedillekens' is probably the origin (?).

•• *Enter the courtyard of Burlington House.*

Location 8

BURLINGTON HOUSE (ROYAL ACADEMY)

Piccadilly
(734 3471)
Open daily 10.00–18.00. Admission is free but there is a charge for major exhibitions. Free guided tours of the private rooms Tuesday–Friday at 13.00 (but telephone first).

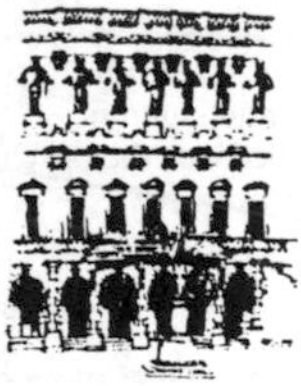

Burlington House was begun by *Sir John Denham* for himself in 1664, but completed as a two-storey residence, for the first Lord Burlington by *May* 1668. This was remodelled early in the 18C by *Campbell* for the third Lord Burlington who had visited Italy and been converted to Palladianism. The Royal Academy of Arts, founded in 1768, moved from Somerset House in 1868.

The three-sided range, fronting Piccadilly, was built by *Banks and Barry* in 1873. A ground floor arcade and upper storey with statues of artists, were added to the house by *S. Smirke* in 1874.

In the courtyard is a statue of the Academy's first president, Sir Joshua Reynolds by *Drury* in 1931.

•• *Enter through the arcade.*

The **entrance hall** was formed in 1873 by combining three rooms. The central panels of the ceiling, brought from Somerset House, were painted by *West* and the remainder by *Angelica Kauffman.*

The **staircase** originally stood further east but was repositioned in 1818. The two wall paintings by *Ricci* had flanked the earlier staircase. The roundel ceiling above the stairwell is by *Kent.*

•• *Ascend to the Sackler galleries on the second floor. Outside, at the end of the landing, is the Michelangelo tondo.*

The unfinished 'Mother and Child' tondo by *Michelangelo* is the only example of his sculpture in England.

•• *Exit L. First L Albany Court Yard.*

•• *Tours of the private rooms include the following:*

Saloon. This is judged to be the finest room in Burlington House and is probably the one surviving example designed by *Campbell* (?). The ceiling was painted by *Kent* and the wall panelling carved by *Guelfi.*

Council Room. This adjoins the Saloon and occupies the area that previously housed the stairwell. It was remodelled by *Ware* in 1818. The ceiling by *Ricci* was retained and the fireplace, carved by *Wilton* in 1780, was brought from Somerset House.

Reynolds Room. This former ballroom is sometimes used as a cinema and may be inaccessible. The room is entirely the early 19C work of *Ware* although in the style of *Campbell.*

Location 9	**ALBANY**
Albany Court Yard	Albany, London's most exclusive address, is divided into very private apartments, one of which was formerly occupied by Prime Minister Edward Heath. The main building, Albany House by *Chambers* 1770, was constructed as Melbourne House for Lord Melbourne who then exchanged the property for Dover House, Whitehall, with Frederick, Duke of York and Albany. It was sold later for conversion into apartments and two blocks were built in the garden by *Holland* in 1804. *Exit and return to Piccadilly R. Cross the road to Fortnum and Mason.*

Location 10	**FORTNUM AND MASON**
191 Piccadilly (734 8040)	Although a department store, Fortnum's is renowned for its ground floor food hall. The shop was established in 1707 by Mr Mason, an experienced grocer, and Mr Fortnum, one of Queen Anne's footmen. The external clock, with Mr Fortnum and Mr Mason becoming mobile on the hour, attracts onlookers. This was added when the store was rebuilt in 1927. Fortnum's remains London's most fashionable food shop and the assistants retain morning dress. At the rear is the Soda Fountain restaurant, *the* place for afternoon tea. *Leave by the Piccadilly exit R and proceed to the next shop.*

Location 11	**SWAINE, ADENEY, BRIGG**
185 Piccadilly (734 4277)	Founded in 1750, this is London's most fashionable stockist of umbrellas, hunting gear and luggage. *Continue eastward.*

Location 12	**HATCHARDS**
197 Piccadilly (437 3924)	Hatchards was established on its present site with a capital of £5 by John Hatchard in 1797. The shop was rebuilt in 1908 and its front is a reproduction. Allegedly, Fred Astaire danced on Hatchard's staircase in a pre-war musical film (?). However, that staircase would have been the predecessor of the existing structure. Most new, non-technical books are available in this shop which was extended in 1984. Luxury bindings and rare editions are on the second floor. *Exit R and pass Church Place (first R).*

Location 13	**SIMPSONS** *Emberson 1935*
Piccadilly (734 2002)	Ladies' and gentlemen's ready-made clothing are stocked by Simpsons who own the well-known 'Daks' trademark. The functionally designed store was one of London's first to be built in a modern style. *Return westward and proceed to St James's.*

Location 14	**ST JAMES PICCADILLY*** *Wren 1684*
Piccadilly	This church, renowned for society weddings, was rebuilt following Second World War bomb damage, and a new spire added by *Richardson* in 1968. Authenticated carvings by *Grinling Gibbons* were saved. St James's was considered by Wren to be his most practical church.

Enter the church and proceed L to the north aisle.

Immediately L is the marble 'Adam and Eve' font, in which Pitt the Elder and the painter William Blake were baptized. This, together with the reredos and organ case, was carved by *Gibbons* in 1684.

The pulpit dates from 1862.

The organ by *Harris* came from the Whitehall Banqueting House which served for a period as the Chapel Royal.

Exit R. First R Church Place. R Jermyn St. First L Duke of York St.

Location 15

THE RED LION

Duke of York Street

This small Victorian 'gin palace' pub possesses exceptional cut glass. Its lunchtime buffet is varied and reasonably priced. Fish and chips, served every Friday and Saturday, are an unusual bar speciality.

Exit L. Proceed to Harvie and Hudson on the Jermyn St corner L.

Location 16

JERMYN STREET

Jermyn Street was laid out in the late 17C. but nothing remains from this period. It possesses many fashionable shops with gentlemen's shirtmakers predominating. The following selection are all on the south side.

Proceed westward.

Location 17

HARVIE & HUDSON

97 Jermyn Street (839 3578)

These well known shirtmakers possess one of London's best mid-Victorian shop fronts.

Location 18

PAXTON AND WHITFIELD

93 Jermyn Street (930 9892)

Paxton and Whitfield are England's most famous cheesemongers. Their shop front is Victorian but the firm was established elsewhere in London in the 18C. Sampling of selected cheeses takes place daily.

Location 19

FLORIS PERFUMES

89 Jermyn Street (930 2885)

Floris, Court perfumers, were established in 1730.

Location 20

TURNBULL AND ASSER

71 Jermyn Street (930 0502)

This, one of the longest established of Jermyn Street's shirtmakers, provided actor Robert Redford's vast collection for the film *The Great Gatsby*.

Proceed to the end of Jermyn St. R St James's St.

Location 21

ST JAMES'S STREET

St James's Street was laid out early in the 17C but little was built until St James's Square was completed nearby in 1675. Like Pall Mall, which joins it at the south end, St James's Street is renowned for gentlemen's clubs. These clubs evolved from coffee houses which had become fashionable in the City in the mid-17C. Gentlemen with similar interests would gather at their favourite coffee house to discuss business, collect messages and peruse the news sheets which preceded daily papers. During the 18C, many of the customers formed clubs, acquired premises and devoted themselves to political, social and gambling, rather than business, activities. Overnight accommodation was provided and famous chefs were employed. Just before the First World War approximately 150 clubs provided some members with what was virtually their London residence. Now, less than thirty remain and few provide the gastronomic delights of earlier years.

Proceed northward.

Location 22

WHITE'S CLUB *J. Wyatt (?) 1788*

37–38 St James's Street

White's was founded in a coffee house of the same name in 1693. Originally favoured by Tories, it is now London's longest established club.

The bow window was added in 1811 and the facade remodelled in 1852.

Cross the road.

Location 23

NO 50 ST JAMES'S STREET *B. D. Wyatt and P. Wyatt 1827*

50 St James's Street

This building was originally Crockford's Club and later the Devonshire Club. Its facade was altered in 1875 and the building completely restored in 1991.

Return southward remaining on the west side. First R Bennett St. Proceed to the end. Immediately ahead is No 21 Arlington St.

Location 24

NO 21 ARLINGTON STREET *Chambers 1769*

Built for Viscount Weymouth, this is one of the West End's finest remaining houses. Windows on the ground and attic floors have been remodelled.

Return to St James's St R. Between Nos 60 and 61 is Brooks's.

Location 25

BROOKS'S *Holland 1778*

St James's Street (no number)

The club was founded in 1762 by William Almack. Charles Fox was a member and Brooks's became a Whig counterpart to the Tory White's. Its building is little altered.

Remain on the west side. Seen opposite on the east side is Boodles.

Location 26

BOODLES *Crunden 1775*

28 St James's Street

Boodles club was founded in a coffee house in 1762. The facade was inspired by Adam's Royal Society of Arts building at the Adelphi.

The bay window was added in 1824.

Continue southward. Just past Boodles is the modern Economist *complex. Again, remain on the west side.*

Location 27

THE ECONOMIST PLAZA *A. & P. Smithson 1964*

25–27 St James's Street

This group of office blocks spaced around a small plaza has been judged one of London's most sensitive modern developments

Continue southward. Second R Blue Ball Yard.

Location 28	**BLUE BALL YARD** *1742*
	The Stafford Hotel's suites L were originally built as stables and the grooms lived above. *Return to St James's St R. First R St James's Place. Proceed to Spencer House at the end L.*

Location 29	**SPENCER HOUSE** *Vardy/Stuart 1766*
St James's Place (499 8620) *Open Sundays (not January or August) 11.30–17.30 for one hour guided tour.* *Advance bookings may be made by telephone Tuesday–Friday 10.00–13.00. Admission charge.*	The Palladian style mansion was built, allegedly, to designs by *General Gray* (?), as the London residence of the first Earl Spencer. The Spencers have not lived here since 1927 and its extensive restoration was completed recently. A member of the family, the Princess of Wales, reopened Spencer House in 1990. The main rooms overlook Green Park and some retain 18C interiors by *J. Stuart* and *Holland*. Eight state rooms are open to the public. *Return to St James's St R.*

Location 30	**CARLTON CLUB** *Hopper 1827*
69 St James's Street	The Carlton was originally known as 'Arthurs' as the club was founded by Arthur Wellesley, Duke of Wellington in 1832. Restoration took place following the terrorist bombing in 1990. *Cross the road to the east side and continue southward.*

Location 31	**LOBB**
7–9 St James's Street (930 3664)	Lobb are England's most famous bespoke shoemakers. The firm, founded in the 18C by John Lobb, possess many Royal Warrants. Lobb's original building in the street was demolished for redevelopment in the 1960s. *Continue southward.*

Location 32	**LOCK & CO.**
6 St James's Street (930 8874)	Established in 1700, Lock moved to the present building in 1764. Lock were the first hatters to make the bowler hat and still call this style a 'Coke', as it was first specified by William Coke for his gamekeepers in 1850. Messrs Bowler supplied the material. *Remain on the east side. Opposite Lock, on the west side, is No 74.*

Location 33	**NO 74 ST JAMES'S STREET** *Basevi* and *S. Smirke 1845*
	Built originally as the Conservative Club, the building is an extremely late example of the Palladian style. *Continue southward. First L Pickering Place.*

Location 34	**PICKERING PLACE** *1731*
	This alleyway retains its 18C timber wainscotting on which a plaque 'The Republic of Texas Legation 1842–5', commemorates the American state's diplomatic office, once situated in the building. *Continue to the small square ahead.* By tradition, the last duel in England was fought here. The marble bust is of Lord Palmerston. *Return to St James's St and proceed to the first shop L.*

Location 35	**BERRY BROS AND RUDD**

3 St James's Street
(930 1888)

These wine merchants were founded in 1680. Although their premises date from 1730 the shop front and interior were remodelled in the early 19C.

Continue southward. First L Pall Mall. Pass Pall Mall Place (second L). Cross the road and continue ahead to Schomberg House.

Location 36	**SCHOMBERG HOUSE** *1698*

80–82 Pall Mall

Schomberg House was designed for a Dutchman, the third Duke of Schomberg, in the Dutch style, which is unique in central London. It was subdivided in 1769. Thomas Gainsborough, the painter, had an apartment in the house and died here in 1788. The interior of Schomberg House was completely rebuilt as offices in 1958 and the exterior of the east wing, which had been demolished in 1850, was rebuilt as a replica; the match is perfect.

Return westward. First R Pall Mall Place. Cross immediately to the north side of King St.

Location 37	**CHRISTIE'S FINE ART**

8 King Street
(839 9060)

Open Monday–Friday 09.00–16.45. Admission free.

These renowned auctioneers were founded in 1766.

Exit L and proceed to Spink & Son.

Location 38	**SPINK & SON**

7 King Street
(930 7888)

Open Monday–Friday 09.30–17.30.

Spink, founded in 1666, are the largest art dealers in the world. They specialize in coins and medals and English and Oriental works.

Exit L. Second R St James's Square.

Location 39	**ST JAMES'S SQUARE**

This was laid out in 1673, as the West End's first square, by Henry Jermyn on land presented to him by Charles II. Jermyn, later Duke of St Albans, was also responsible for many of the surrounding streets and has been called 'the founder of the West End'. Only one of the square's original houses remains. When completed, there was a small boating pond in the centre which was replaced by the present garden with its wooden shelter by *Nash* in 1822 and the William III monument (location 43).

Continue southward to No 20 in the south-west corner.

Location 40	**NO 20 ST JAMES'S SQUARE** *R. Adam 1789*

The house, built as a residence for Sir Watkin Williams Wynn, is now offices but some Adam interiors remain. The facade of its neighbour, No 21, is surprisingly not by Adam but was remodelled as a replica in 1936.

Return northward and continue along the west side of the square.

Location 41	**NO 15 ST JAMES'S SQUARE** *J. Stuart 1766*

'Athenian' Stuart designed this stone-faced residence as Lichfield House and it was the first London example of the Greek revival. The first floor windows were lowered and a balcony added by *S. Wyatt* in 1794.

•● *Continue eastward along the square's north side.*

Location 42

CHATHAM HOUSE *Flitcroft 1736*

10 St James's Square

Chatham House was the residence of three Prime Ministers, Pitt the Elder, Lord Derby and Gladstone.

•● *Enter the central gardens and proceed to the William III monument.*

Location 43

WILLIAM III MONUMENT
Bacon the Younger 1807

Gardens open Monday–Friday 10.00–16.30.

This equestrian statue has a macabre touch as it includes the molehill over which the King's horse stumbled at Hampton Court in 1702 before throwing him. William broke his collar bone and died soon afterwards of pneumonia.

•● *Return to the north side of the square R. Proceed to No 4 in the north-east corner.*

Location 44

NO 4 ST JAMES'S SQUARE *1676*

This is the only original house in the square but it was remodelled following a fire in 1725, probably by *Leoni* or possibly *Hawksmoor* (?). Internally, the stairway and Court Room are outstanding. The top floor, above the original eaves cornice, was added later.

The most violent episode in St James's Square occurred in April 1984 when Yvonne Fletcher, a policewoman, was shot dead from the adjoining house, No 5, then occupied by the 'Libyan Peoples' Bureau'. She is commemmorated by a plaque in the pavement.

•● *Proceed southward. First L Charles II St. First L Lower Regent St. Proceed ahead to Piccadilly Circus.*

Location 45

PICCADILLY CIRCUS

Piccadilly Circus was planned by Nash, early in the 19C, as part of his Regent Street scheme. Originally named Regent's Circus (South), none of Nash's buildings remain and the circus is no longer circular but triangular. Piccadilly Circus became established in the late 19C as the 'hub of the Empire' and, like Trafalgar Square, is a focal point for national rejoicing.

Location 46

'EROS' FOUNTAIN *Gilbert 1892*

Piccadilly Circus

Known throughout the world as 'Eros', the fountain's statue actually represents the Angel of Christian Charity and is a memorial to Lord Shaftesbury. This was the first statue to be cast in aluminium.

Rock Circus open daily 11.00–21.00. Admission charge.

To the north the **London Pavilion** has been redeveloped to provide a shopping and entertainment complex. Opened in 1990, **Rock Circus** is a Madame Tussaud's waxworks exhibition of pop music.

•● *Descend via the subway to Piccadilly Circus Station, Bakerloo and Piccadilly lines.*

•● *Alternatively, if continuing with itinerary 15, leave the subway at the Shaftesbury Avenue exit. Turn R and proceed eastward along Coventry St.*

Itinerary 15

15

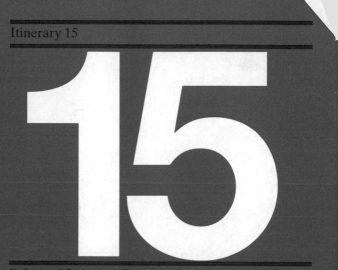

Soho and Leicester Square

Soho is London's most Continental sector and now also accommodates 'Chinatown'. Drinking clubs, sex shows and beckoning ladies have created its 'naughty' image which can still be found, in spite of puritanical legislation.

Timing: Monday to Saturday are recommended but the House of St Barnabas (location 20) is open only Wednesday afternoons and Thursday mornings.

15

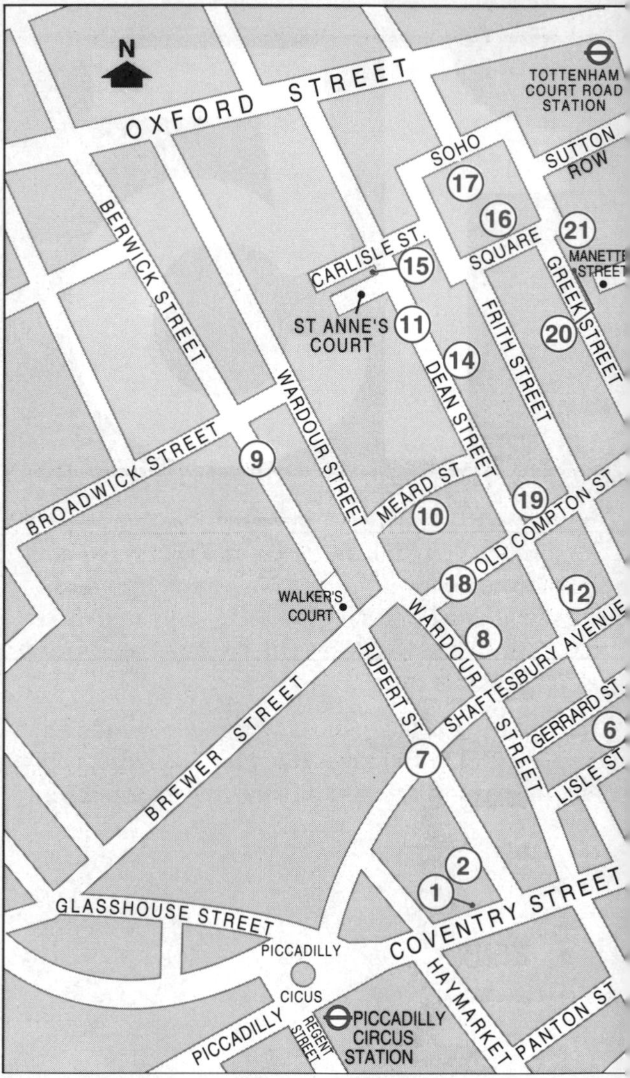

Locations

1 The Trocadero
2 Guinness World of Records
3 Leicester Square
4 Soho
5 Notre Dame de France
6 'Chinatown'
7 Shaftesbury Avenue
8 St Anne Soho
9 Berwick Street
10 Meard Street
11 Dean Street
12 The French House
13 Coach and Horses
14 Leoni's Quo Vadis
15 Rippon
16 Soho Square
17 Charles II Statue
18 Old Compton Street
19 Patisserie Valerie
20 Milroy's
21 House of St Barnabas
22 Charing Cross Road
23 St Giles-in-the-Fields
24 Foyles
25 Zwemmer
26 Cecil Court
27 The Salisbury
28 Goodwins Court
29 The Lamb and Flag

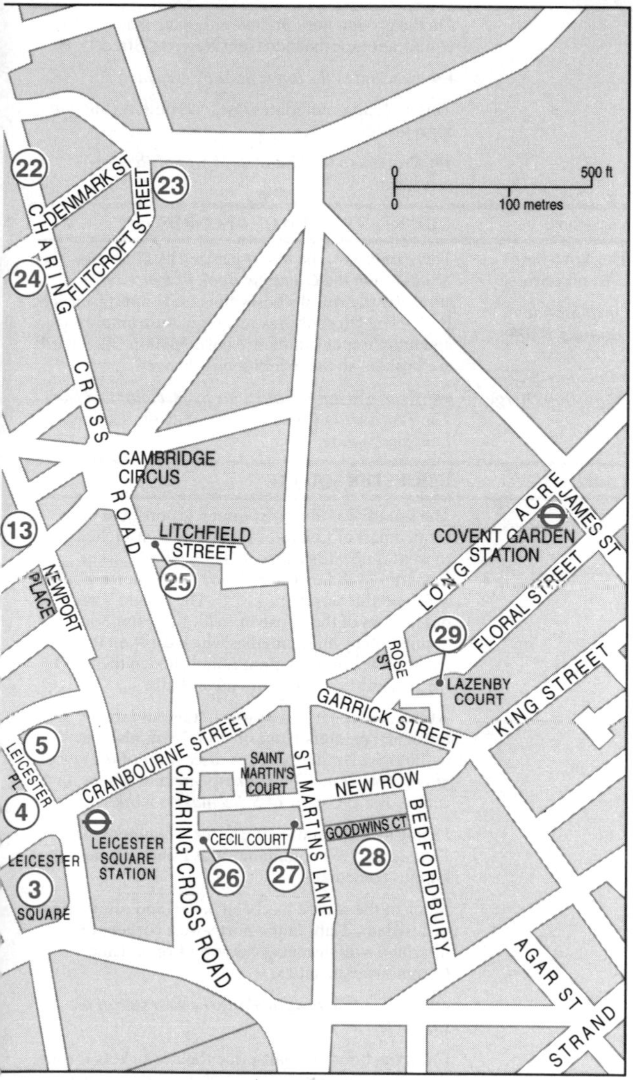

Start *Piccadilly Circus Station, Bakerloo and Piccadilly lines. Leave by the Shaftesbury Avenue exit. Turn R and proceed eastward along Coventry Street. Alternatively, continue from itinerary 14.*

Location 1	**THE TROCADERO**
Coventry Street *Open daily 10.00–22.00*	Opened in 1984, the site of the Trocadero's two-acre shopping and entertainment complex was formerly occupied by three long-established restaurants, The Trocadero ('The Troc'), Scotts and Lyons Corner House. Most of the facades of these have been retained but the interior of the centre is entirely new and features an air-conditioned central atrium. There are three levels.

On the ground floor are two shopping malls and a restaurant (approached from Newport Street).

Descend to the lower floor by escalator.

This level accommodates fast food outlets (but due for revision).

Proceed to the Guinness World of Records exhibition.

Location 2

GUINNESS WORLD OF RECORDS

The Trocadero, Coventry Street

Open Monday–Saturday 10.00–22.00. Last admission 20.00. Admission charge.

This exhibition, the first organized by Guinness, brings to life the *Guinness Book of Records*, currently the world's bestselling book apart from The Bible. The latest display techniques are employed and there is much audience participation. As records are broken, so the exhibition is changed.

Return to the ground floor by escalator and leave The Trocadero by the Coventry St exit L. Continue to Leicester Square.

Location 3

LEICESTER SQUARE

The square was always common ground and once formed part of Leicester Fields which stretched north to what is now Lisle Street. The second Earl of Leicester built Leicester House on the north side in 1631 and this stood until 1683. The square was laid out in front of the house in 1670. Leicester Square is dominated by huge cinemas which carry on the tradition of entertainment established in the 19C by the Alhambra and Empire music halls.

At the corner gates are busts of famous local residents: painters Hogarth and Reynolds, the pathologist Hunter, and the discoverer of the law of gravity, Newton. The Shakespeare monument, in the centre, is a 19C copy of *Scheemakers* work.

Facing this, the statue of Charlie Chaplin by *Doubleday* 1981 commemorates London's most famous comedian.

Much of the square has been paved and reserved for pedestrians. Slabs in the north-west corner are inscribed with distances between London and Commonwealth cities.

Proceed southward along the west side of the square R.

From the booth L, half-price theatre tickets for the day's performances are sold after 12.00 for matinees and 14.30–18.30 for evening performances (cash only). Be early to queue for the most popular shows.

Return to the north side of the square R. First L Leicester Place. Cross the road and proceed to the church. Soho has now been entered.

Location 4

SOHO

Soho is the area which lies immediately east of Mayfair and is bounded by Oxford Street, Charing Cross Road, Leicester Square and Regent Street. Once the local fox-hunters cry was 'So-ho' and they gathered for refreshment at an establishment known as the So-Ho which possibly gaves it name to the area (?). Great mansions, built for the nobility early in the

17C, are now only commemorated by street names, eg Newport, Monmouth and Leicester.

Since French Huguenots arrived in 1685, Soho has been an enclave for European immigrants, and Continental restaurants abound. However, the south section is now London's 'Chinatown'. Soho remains popular with criminals and vice-racketeers but is not dangerous to those outside their fraternity. Sex shops and shows, now reduced by legislation, together with ladies who solicit illegally, are mostly to be found in the centre. Scattered around are a diminishing number of rather seedy afternoon drinking clubs where members and their friends overcame England's once strange drinking laws. Visitors must be invited, and signed-in, by a member.

Location 5 — **NOTRE DAME DE FRANCE**

Leicester Place

The Chapel of the Blessed Sacrament within this church was decorated by *Jean Cocteau* in 1965.

Exit R. R Lisle St.

Location 6 — **'CHINATOWN'**

London's small 'Chinatown' comprises Lisle Street, Gerrard Street, Newport Place and parts of Wardour Street and Shaftesbury Avewnue. The many Chinese shops and restaurants are crowded on Sunday afternoons when families traditionally lunch together. A Dragon Dance is held in the streets at Chinese New Year (late January or early February).

L Newport Place. First L Gerrard St. R Wardour St. Proceed ahead to Shaftesbury Avenue (second R).

Location 7 — **SHAFTESBURY AVENUE**

Named after the reforming seventh Lord Shaftesbury, the avenue, now synonymous with 'theatreland', was constructed in 1886.

Cross Shaftesbury Avenue immediately and continue along Wardour St. Ascend the steps R to the old churchyard of St Anne's.

Location 8 — **ST ANNE SOHO**

Wardour Street

St Anne's was dedicated to honour Queen Anne by its benefactor Henry Compton who had been her tutor. The church by *Wren* or *Talman* (?) 1675 was gutted by bombs in the Second World War and only its replacement tower and steeple by *S. P. Cockerell* 1806 remain. George II had worshipped in the church whilst Prince of Wales.

The old churchyard, raised to accommodate 10,000 burials, has been a public garden since 1891. A wall plaque beside the tower, commemorates Theodore, King of Corsica, d.1756, who became a Soho resident. He was eventually imprisoned for insolvency and optimistically registered his kingdom, which he had already lost, for the benefit of his creditors. His epitaph was written by Hugh Walpole.

The ashes of writer Dorothy L. Sayers, creator of Lord Peter Wimsey, were scattered beneath the tower in 1957.

Redevelopment around the tower took place in 1991.

Return to Wardour St R. Third L Brewer St. Proceed to No 11, Richards Fish.

Location 9	**BERWICK STREET**
Market open Monday–Saturday 09.00–17.30.	Apart from the sex shops, Berwick Street provides the venue for one of London's best value fruit and vegetable markets. It was established in the 18C. Prices are reduced rapidly around 17.00.

First R Broadwick St. Second R Wardour St. Second L Meard St.

Location 10	**MEARD STREET**

Soho's earliest buildings make up most of the south side. The street was laid out in 1692 and some original houses remain. Many friendly ladies operate. There is a tradition that the street was named by French Huguenots who lived here in the 17C. Evidently an open sewer ran through the middle and the French word *merde* for excrement eventually became corrupted to 'Meard'. Sadly, this is untrue. The thoroughfare was originally named Meard's Street and commemorates the carpenter, John Meard, who built it.

R Dean St.

Location 11	**DEAN STREET**

Dean Street was laid out *c.*1685 and honours Henry Compton, Dean of the Chapel Royal. Much rebuilding took place *c.*1730. On the corner of Meard Street R Nos 68 and 67 are early examples.

Cross the road. Continue southward passing Old Compton St (first L).

Location 12	**THE FRENCH HOUSE**
49 Dean Street	Until recently, the pub was called the York Minster, but it had been known unofficially for many years as the French Pub due to the nationality of its consecutive hosts, father and son. Although the famous Gaston Berlemont retired in 1989, the pub still possesses Soho's most Bohemian atmosphere and good wine is sold by the glass.

Exit L. First L Romilly St.

Location 13	**THE COACH AND HORSES**
29 Romilly Street	This Soho landmark, better known as 'Norman's', achieved even wider fame in 1989, through the West End hit *Jeffrey Bernard is Unwell* by Keith Waterhouse. Both the play's subject and author are habitués and the entire performance is set in the pub, which has been run by members of Norman's family for fifty years.

Exit R. First R Dean Street.

Location 14	**LEONI'S QUO VADIS**
26 Dean Street	Karl Marx lived in a room above this long-established Italian restaurant from 1851 to 1856.

Cross the road and continue northward.

No 78 is Dean Street's best-preserved early 18C house.

Continue ahead passing St Anne's Court (first L).

Location 15	**RIPPON**
88 Dean Street	The late 18C shop front is a rare London example of the Rococo style.
	•● *Continue ahead. First R Carlisle St. Proceed to Soho Square.*

Location 16	**SOHO SQUARE**
	Soho Square was laid out by Geoffrey King in 1681 and first known as King Square. It soon became a fashionable address. The Duke of Monmouth's residence, Monmouth House, stood on the south side where Bateman's Buildings are now; it was demolished in 1773.
	Although no original houses remain, No 38, Warwick House by *Sanger* 1735, on the Carlisle Street corner L, possesses an outstanding mid-19C shop front.
	•● *Continue ahead to the storehouse in the centre of the square and proceed immediately L to the Charles II statue.*

Location 17	**CHARLES II STATUE** *Cibber late-17C*
	The statue, now in poor condition, was removed by W. S. Gilbert, the librettist, to the garden of his house at Harrow Weald in 1876 but re-erected in the square in 1938. Four figures originally stood against the pedestal representing English rivers but they remain at Harrow Weald.
	•● *Return to the west side of the square L. First R Frith St. Second R Old Compton St.*

Location 18	**OLD COMPTON STREET**
	This, Soho's most important shopping street, was begun in 1677 and, like Dean Street, named after Henry Compton.
	•● *Continue ahead.*

Location 19	**PATISSERIE VALERIE**
44 Old Compton Street	Tea, coffee and rich gateaux are served in atmospheric, albeit utilitarian, surroundings.
	•● *Exit L. Second L Greek St. Continue towards Soho Square.*

Location 20	**MILROY'S**
3 Greek Street	Milroy's, the mecca of malt whiskies, is the first port of call for many wealthy Japanese and American visitors to London. A vast range, usually hovering around 350, is kept in stock and, for rarities, prices can reach several thousand pounds – per bottle. Customers are frequently offered a tasting before purchase. Advice from the exuberant Mr Milroy is treated with as much reverence as his whiskies.

Location 21	**HOUSE OF ST BARNABAS** *Pearce 1746*
1 Greek Street *Open Wednesday 14.30–16.15. Thursday 11.00–12.30. Admission free.*	The house is one of London's few domestic buildings that may be visited. It is believed to be the prototype of Dr Manette's house described by Charles Dickens in *A Tale of Two Cities* (?). Temporary accommodation is now provided for homeless women.

The interior is famous for its decorative plasterwork – particularly around the **main staircase** and first floor **Council Room**.

A rare **'crinoline' staircase**, with its banister rails bowed to accommodate crinolines, leads to the bedrooms.

In the garden is a mulberry tree, the last survivor of the many planted by the Hugeunots to establish the Soho silk industry in the 17C.

The chapel, in 13C style, was built in 1862.

●■ *Exit R to Soho Square R. First R Sutton Row. R Charing Cross Road.*

Location 22

CHARING CROSS ROAD

The road was laid out in 1887 and replaced an area of mean houses and streets. It is undistinguished architecturally and much of the south end has been redeveloped. Charing Cross Road is famed for its bookshops (some close on Saturday).

●■ *Second L Denmark St.*

The street houses several music publishers and has long been known as 'Tin Pan Alley'.

●■ *First R Flitcroft St. Cross the road and proceed to the west facade of St Giles's.*

Location 23

ST GILES-IN-THE-FIELDS *Flitcroft 1733*

St Giles High Street

St Giles's was established in 1101 as the chapel of a monastic leper hospital, founded by Queen Matilda, consort of Henry I. It is dedicated to the patron saint of outcasts. A village soon grew up around the hospital and by 1200 its chapel was also being used by the villagers. Following the Reformation, the chapel became the parish church. St Giles's was rebuilt in 1630, but London's Great Plague broke out nearby in November 1664 and so many were buried in its churchyard that the building was structurally damaged. The present church was commissioned under the Fifty New Churches Act of 1711 and Flitcroft won the architectural competition against Gibbs and Hawksmoor.

Prisoners on their way from Newgate to Tyburn for execution were charitably offered a soporific drink from 'St Giles's Bowl' as they passed by. The bodies of many were soon returned to the churchyard for burial. Famous men buried in St Giles's churchyard include Oliver Plunket the Bishop of Armagh who was murdered in 1661, painter Godfrey Kneller 1723, and architect Sir John Soane 1823. Actor David Garrick was married in the church in 1749.

The tower rises immediately above the west front, as at St Martin-in-the-Fields. Flitcroft, the architect's name, is prominently carved below the pediment.

Facing the west door is the 'Resurrection Arch' made in 1800, and so-called because it originally incorporated a wooden 'Day of Judgement' lunette made for St Giles's lychgate in 1687. Now inside the church, it has been replaced here with a facsimile.

●■ *Enter the north door from Denmark St.*

In the **vestibule** L, the cast of the Baring monument by *Flaxman* was placed here as a memorial to the sculptor.

●■ *Continue ahead to the* **rotunda.**

Flitcroft's original model of St Giles is displayed R.

The iron chest, in the **south porch**, is believed to be 17C and Continental (?).

Following its restoration the original wooden 'Day of Judgement' lunette is displayed above the doorcase.

•• *Proceed L to the* **nave.**

St Giles's interior, although modified in the 19C, is little changed and evokes that of St Martin-in-the-Fields. The four brass chandeliers are believed to be 18C. (?).

•• *Turn L to the* **north aisle.**

At the west end, the monument to George Chapman, d.1634, was reputedly designed by the poet's friend *Inigo Jones* (?). Chapman translated Homer into English.

The white pulpit, at the east end of the aisle, came from the West Street Chapel. It was originally the top section of a three-decker pulpit from which both John and Charles Wesley preached 1743–91.

The pulpit in the **nave** was made for the previous church in 1676

Paintings of Moses and Aaron, on either side of the original reredos, are by *Francisco Vieira the Younger* c.1800.

The organ casing above the west gallery was made for the church in 1734.

At the west end of the **south aisle** is a rare Greek-style font made in 1810.

•• *Exit from the church L. First L Charing Cross Road. Cross the road and proceed to the Manette St corner (first R).*

Location 24

FOYLES

113–119 Charing Cross Road (437 5660)

Two brothers, William and Gilbert Foyle, failed the Civil Service entry examination in 1904 and sold their unwanted textbooks via a small advertisement. The response was so great that they decided to become booksellers. In 1906 W. & G. Foyle opened at Nos 121/123 Charing Cross Road on the north side of Manette Street.

They expanded across the road ten years later, but these premises were demolished in 1966 and the present five-storey building was constructed. Foyles vacated Nos 121/123 in 1983. Their Antiquarian Book Department is housed in Beeleigh Abbey, the 12C family home of the Foyles.

Foyles claim to stock around six million books of all types at any one time and are, therefore, the world's largest booksellers. Their famous literary luncheons at the Dorchester Hotel, to honour successful authors, were inaugurated in 1930 by Christina Foyle, daughter of William, one of the founders.

•• *Exit R. Continue southward passing Cambridge Circus. First L Litchfield St.*

Location 25

ZWEMMER

24 Litchfield Street
(836 4710)

Larger new premises, acquired in 1983, facilitate the display of books specializing in the arts. Many are unobtainable elsewhere in England.

Exit R. L Charing Cross Road. Pass Leicester Square Station. Second L Cecil Court.

Location 26

CECIL COURT

Although laid out in 1670, the existing buildings are Victorian. Most are occupied by speciality book and print shops.

L St Martin's Lane.

Location 27

THE SALISBURY

St Martin's Lane

This pub, popular with theatregoers, has outstanding cut glass and brass statuettes typical of a late Victorian gin palace. Its buffet is popular for lunchtime and pre-theatre snacks. The letters 'SS', cut in the windows, represent 'Salisbury Stores', as the pub was evidently built as a grocer's shop.

Exit to St Martin's Lane. Cross the road to the alleyway, between Nos 55 and 56 St Martin's Lane.

Location 28

GOODWINS COURT

This discreet alleyway immediately widens to reveal identical, perfectly preserved 'Regency' bow-windowed shops fronts on the south side. It has been alleged that they were made *c.*1900.

L Bedfordbury. R New Row. First L Garrick St. First R Rose St. Ahead Lazenby Court.

Location 29

THE LAMB AND FLAG

Rose Street

In Lazenby Court, which runs beside the Lamb and Flag, the poet Dryden was attacked in 1673 and the Coopers Arms, as the pub was then called, became known as the 'Bucket of Blood'. See the plaque above. The building is late 17C but its facade has been remodelled.

Enter from Lazenby Court.

There are now three bars but the most atmospheric is the one entered on the ground floor at the rear. Many early Victorian fixtures remain.

Exit R Lazenby Court. Ahead Rose St. R Garrick St. Ahead Cranbourne St and Leicester Square Station, Northern and Piccadilly lines.

Itinerary 16

16

Oxford Street and Regent Street

Mayfair's 'Little America' and England's most valuable art bequest, the Wallace Collection, are visited, together with Selfridge's, one of London's major stores.

Timing: To complete the itinerary allow a whole day. Monday to Saturday is preferable but Speakers' Corner in Hyde Park only operates on Sunday afternoons.

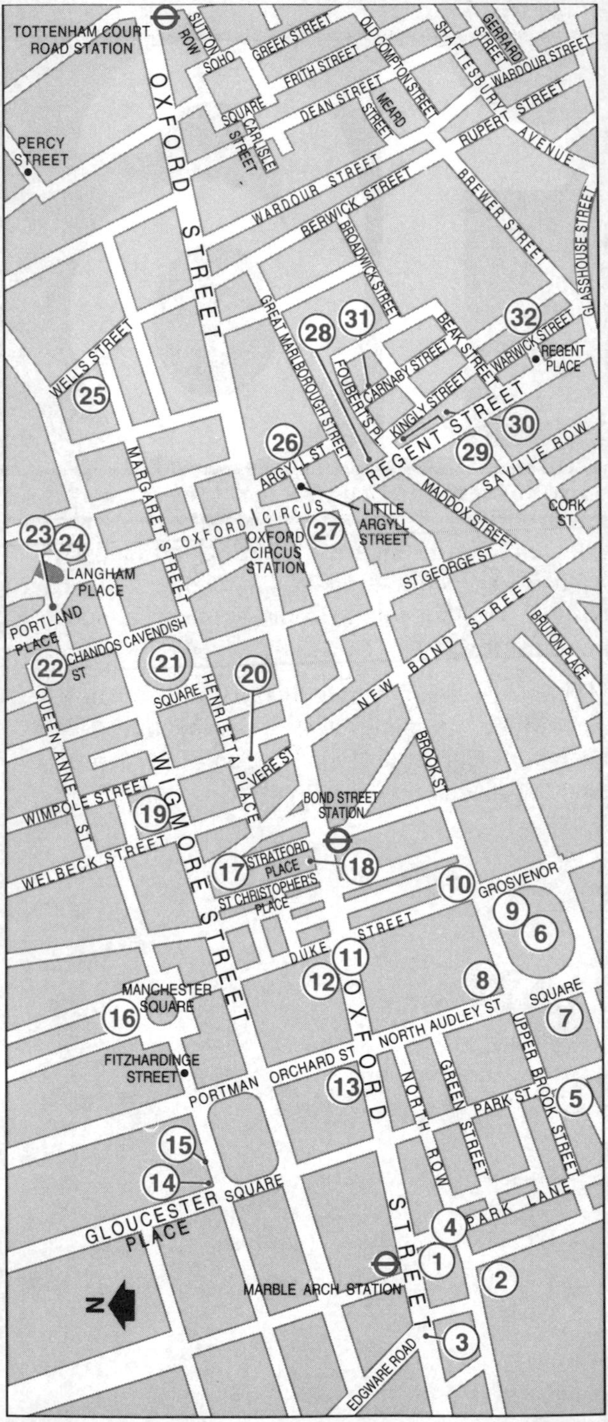
TOTTENHAM COURT ROAD STATION
SUTTON ROW
SOHO
GREEK STREET
FRITH STREET
OLD COMPTON STREET
SHAFTESBURY
GERRARD STREET
WARDOUR STREET
DEAN STREET
MEARD STREET
SQUARE
CARLISLE STREET
RUPERT STREET
AVENUE
PERCY STREET
OXFORD STREET
WARDOUR STREET
BERWICK STREET
BREWER STREET
BROADWICK STREET
GLASSHOUSE STREET
GREAT MARLBOROUGH STREET
28
31
32
BEAK STREET
WARWICK STREET
REGENT PLACE
CARNABY STREET
FOUBERT'S PL
KINGLY STREET
REGENT STREET
30
29
SAVILLE ROW
WELLS STREET
25
26
ARGYLL ST
MARGARET STREET
MADDOX STREET
CORK ST.
LITTLE ARGYLL STREET
OXFORD CIRCUS
OXFORD CIRCUS STATION
27
23
24
LANGHAM PLACE
ST GEORGE ST
PORTLAND PLACE
CHANDOS ST
CAVENDISH SQUARE
21
22
20
HENRIETTA PLACE
BRUTON PLACE
NEW BOND STREET
QUEEN ANNE ST
BROOK ST
VERE ST
WIGMORE STREET
WIMPOLE STREET
19
BOND STREET STATION
WELBECK STREET
17
STRATFORD PLACE
18
ST CHRISTOPHER'S PLACE
10
GROSVENOR SQUARE
9
6
DUKE STREET
11
12
8
MANCHESTER SQUARE
16
NORTH AUDLEY ST
7
UPPER BROOK STREET
FITZHARDINGE STREET
ORCHARD ST
PORTMAN SQUARE
13
NORTH ROW
GREEN STREET
PARK ST
5
15
14
GLOUCESTER PLACE
PARK LANE
4
1
2
MARBLE ARCH STATION
N
EDGWARE ROAD
3

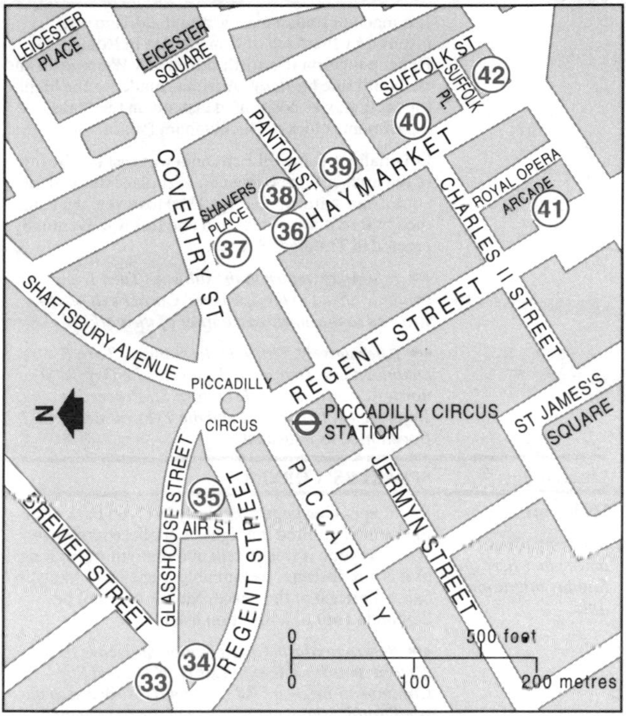

Locations
1 Marble Arch
2 Speakers' Corner
3 Tyburn Memorial
4 Park Lane
5 Le Gavroche
6 Grosvenor Square
7 United States Embassy
8 Eisenhower's Headquarters
9 Roosevelt Memorial
10 John Adam's House
11 Oxford Street
12 Selfridges
13 Marks and Spencer
14 RIBA Heinz Gallery
15 Home House
16 The Wallace Collection
17 Stratford House
18 St Christopher's Place
19 Wigmore Hall
20 St Peter Vere Street
21 Cavendish Square
22 Chandos House
23 Portland Place
24 All Souls Langham Place
25 All Saints Margaret Street
26 London Palladium
27 Regent Street
28 Liberty
29 Jaeger
30 Hamleys
31 Carnaby Street
32 The 'Bavarian Chapel'
33 Garrard
34 Aquascutum
35 Café Royal
36 Haymarket
37 Paperchase
38 Design Centre
39 Burberry
40 Theatre Royal Haymarket
41 Royal Opera Arcade
42 Suffolk Place/Suffolk Street

Start *Marble Arch Station, Central line. Leave the station by the Hyde Park exit and ascend the first steps L (Exit 3) to the Marble Arch traffic island.*

Location 1 — **MARBLE ARCH** *Nash*

Oxford Street

The Marble Arch was designed to provide the triumphal entrance to Buckingham Palace where it stood from 1833–47. Re-sited here in 1851, as the north-east entrance to Hyde Park, it eventually proved to be a hindrance to traffic and became isolated when the roundabout was enlarged in 1908. Now, only senior members of the Royal Family and the Royal Horse Artillery may pass through the arch.

It is made of Italian marble and the design was inspired by the Arch of Constantine in Rome. Relief panels on the north side are by *Westmacott* and the south side by *Baily*. A frieze, made for the blank top section, was positioned instead on the State Apartments block at Buckingham Palace.

Originally, a statue of Britannia was cast for the top of the arch but it was decided to replace this with an equestrian statue of George IV. However, the King died before it was completed and this was eventually erected in Trafalgar Square.

If Sunday, return to the subway. Turn L and continue ahead to the Speakers' Corner exit (exit 4). Proceed to the north-east corner of the park.

Alternatively, return to the subway. Turn R, continue to the station, and leave by the Oxford St north side exit (exit 1). R Oxford St. Proceed to Edgware Rd (second R) and the Tyburn Memorial (location 3) as indicated.

Location 2

SPEAKERS' CORNER

Hyde Park

Speaking usually takes place here on Sunday afternoons only.

Public speaking began regularly in Hyde Park after Parliament granted the right of public assembly in 1872. Anyone is free to talk about anything, as long as it is not obscene, treasonable, racialist or likely to cause a breach of the peace. Money may not be demanded nor amplification used.

Return to Marble Arch Station and leave by the Oxford St north side exit (exit 1). R Oxford St. Continue to Edgware Rd (second R). Proceed to the small traffic island in the centre of the road at the junction of Oxford St and Edgware Rd.

Location 3

TYBURN MEMORIAL

Oxford Street/
Edgware Road

A memorial stone in the traffic island records one of London's major horror spots, as here, from 1195 until 1783, those condemned to death in London and Middlesex were publicly executed. Tyburn's first permanent gallows were built in 1579 in the form of a triangle that could deal with three at a time. Many victims were brought here in an open cart from Newgate Prison in the City, hence the expression 'gone west', meaning finished. Executions took place every six weeks and up to fifteen men, women and children were hanged at each session. A perk for the hangman was that he was allowed to keep the victims' clothes.

Flogging, torturing and hanging, drawing and quartering were additional delights for the public who watched, often from specially erected galleries. It is recorded that almost 20,000 saw highwayman Jack Sheppard hanged in 1724. The nobility and ladies were amongst those who attended these fashionable performances at Tyburn until they were transferred to a new public site outside Newgate Prison in 1783.

Return to Marble Arch Station and walk through the subway to the Park Lane exit (exit 2). Proceed ahead southward and pass the North Row junction (first L). Nos 93 to 99 Park Lane are immediately L.

Location 4

PARK LANE

In the 15C this thoroughfare was called Westminster Lane and later Tyburn Lane but all semblance of a lane disappeared when land was claimed from Hyde Park *c.*1960 and a dual carriageway formed. Park Lane is now renowned for its luxury hotels which include, from north to south, Grosvenor House, the Dorchester (recently converted by the Sultan of Brunei to one of the world's most luxurious hotels), the London Hilton, the Londoner, the Inn on the Park and the Intercontinental.

The best surviving Regency houses in Park Lane are Nos 93 to 99 at the north end between the North Row and Green Street junctions. They were built *c.*1820 and have been much altered, although their canopied bow windows are still reminiscent of Brighton's Regency sea front.

Continue ahead from the Green St junction. Second L Upper Brook St. Cross the road and proceed to the Park St junction (first R). On the corner is Le Gavroche Restaurant.

Location 5

LE GAVROCHE

43 Upper Brook Street (730 2820)

Le Gavroche became, in 1982, the first restaurant in Britain to be awarded the world's highest food accolade – three Michelin stars. French cuisine, decor and prices are the tops.

Continue ahead to Grosvenor Square. Turn R and proceed to the United States Embassy.

Location 6

GROSVENOR SQUARE

Although first laid out by Richard Grosvenor as recently as 1725, few of the remaining houses now pre-date the 19C. Occupying six acres, this is Mayfair's largest square and has for long been known as 'Little America'.

Location 7

UNITED STATES EMBASSY *Saarinen 1961*

Grosvenor Square (499 9000)

The building occupies all the west side and dominates the square. Surmounting its roof, the eagle by *Roszak* has a wing span of 35 feet.

Return to the north side of the square. Turn R.

Location 8

EISENHOWER'S HEADQUARTERS

20 Grosvenor Square

A wall plaque, L of the first door, commemorates General Eisenhower's European Headquarters which were situated in this building during the Second World War.

Continue ahead. At the north-east corner enter the central garden.

Location 9

ROOSEVELT MEMORIAL *Reid Dick 1948*

This was unveiled by the wife of FDR in 1948.

Return to the north-east corner of the square.

Location 10

JOHN ADAM'S HOUSE *c.1750*

9 Grosvenor Square

John Adam, later to become the second US President, was the first American Minister to Great Britain and lived in this house from 1785–88.

First L Duke St (immediately L of No 9). Fourth L Oxford St. Cross the road.

Location 11	**OXFORD STREET**
	This, London's longest shopping thoroughfare, runs eastward from Marble Arch in a straight line to Tottenham Court Road, where it changes character and becomes New Oxford Street. The road was certainly laid out in Roman times and possibly earlier. It shed its earlier name of Tyburn Road in the 18C and was renamed to commemorate the De Vere family who had been 16C Earls of Oxford and Lords of the Manor of Tyburn. Much of the street was developed by Edward Harley who also became Earl of Oxford (unrelated to the De Veres). Only buses and taxis are allowed along most of its length. Mainly non-luxury items are sold by the huge department stores which proliferate. Oxford Street has little of architectural value and is tiring to both the feet and the eye. It is best taken in small doses.

Location 12	**SELFRIDGES** *Burnham and Atkinson 1908*
Oxford Street	This enormous, Neo-Classical department store, was founded by the American, Gordon Selfridge, in 1908 and remains London's most imposing example. Its decorations that celebrate Christmas and other national events are lavish. Selfridges is representative of its type and sells a wide variety of items. Baird gave the world's first public television demonstration from this building. *Leave by the Orchard St exit at the west end of the store. Cross the road to Marks and Spencer.*

Location 13	**MARKS AND SPENCER**
Orchard Street	Marks and Spencer is probably England's best known chain store. Continental visitors have long been attracted to these shops due to the relatively low prices of the clothing. This is the group's largest branch. *Leave by the Orchard St exit L. Second L Portman Square. First R follow the west side of the square and proceed ahead to Gloucester Place. Cross the road immediately and proceed to the entrance, in Gloucester Place, of 21 Portman Square.*

Location 14	**RIBA HEINZ GALLERY** *J. Adam 1776*
21 Portman Square (580 5533) *Open for special RIBA exhibitions. Admission free.*	The house was built, with fraternal devotion, to match the exterior of the adjoining No 20 Portman Square, designed by the architect's more famous brother, Robert. *Exit L. First L Portman Square.*

Location 15	**HOME HOUSE** *R. Adam 1776*
Home House, 20 Portman Square *The staircase may be viewed at most times.*	The house was built and furnished by Robert Adam for the Countess of Home. *Exit L. Continue along the north side of Portman Square and proceed ahead following Fitzhardinge St. Third L Manchester Square. Proceed R to the north side. Enter Hertford House L.*

Location 16 **THE WALLACE COLLECTION**

Hertford House, Manchester Square (935 0687)

Open Monday–Saturday 10.00–17.00. Sunday 14.00–17.00. Admission free.

The Wallace Collection is renowned for its 18C French paintings and furniture. The building was constructed as Manchester House by the fourth Duke of Manchester in 1776. It was leased, for a short time, to the Spanish Embassy but remodelled and renamed by Sir Richard Wallace in 1872. Wallace was the natural son of the fourth Marquess of Hertford and inherited his collection of works of art. This was added to and eventually brought here from France.

The Wallace Collection, the most valuable of the nation's art bequests, was opened to the public in 1900. In 1983 the galleries were air-conditioned and many of the paintings cleaned. Furniture, porcelain and armour are displayed in addition to the paintings. Every item is identified throughout and there are two floors. The furniture includes work by the master 17C and 18C French cabinet makers *Boulle* and *Riesener*.

Ascend the stairs.

Stairway. The balustrade, *c.*1735, was brought to Hertford House from Palais Mazarin, now the Bibliothèque Nationale, Paris.

Following restoration of the entrance hall and a major gallery in 1995, many of the exhibits will be relocated. These include paintings by *Boucher*, *Fragonard* and *Watteau*, and examples of the English and Dutch schools. The best known paintings include:

Venetian scenes by *Canaletto* and *Guardi*.

'Titus' *Rembrandt,* 'The Laughing Cavalier' *Hals,* 'George IV' *Lawrence*, 'Lady with a Fan' *Velasquez* and 'The Rainbow Landscape', *Rubens*.

Exit from Hertford House L. Third L Duke St. Fifth L Oxford St. Fourth L Stratford Place.

Location 17 **STRATFORD HOUSE (THE ORIENTAL CLUB)**
Edwin 1773

11 Stratford Place

Open to members only.

The grounds of the house once stretched to Oxford Street and on the R, surmounted by a lion, is one of the original gate posts.

This mansion was built as Derby House, for Lord Derby, on land leased by Edward Stratford. Its site had previously been occupied by the Lord Mayor of London's Banqueting House. The east wing, which includes the ballroom, was added in 1909.

Internally, the decor is mostly in the Adam style and some of the ceilings and fireplaces are original. The staircase is 19C.

The Tyburn stream crosses Oxford Street at this point, now in an underground conduit. 'Ty' meant boundary and for many years the Tyburn marked the boundary of the City of Westminster.

Return to Oxford St R. First R Gees Court leads to St Christopher's Place.

Location 18 **ST CHRISTOPHER'S PLACE**

The houses in this Victorian street were remodelled and the roadway pedestrianized in 1982. It now comprises fashionable boutiques and restaurants.

R Wigmore St. Cross the road and continue eastward. Pass the Welbeck St junction (third L).

Location 19	**WIGMORE HALL**
Wigmore Street (935 2141)	This long-established concert hall specializes in chamber music and recitals.

Continue eastward along Wigmore St. First R Wimpole St.

No 50, the house occupied by 'The Barretts of Wimpole Street', stood much further north but no longer exists.

First R Henrietta Place. First L Vere St.

Location 20	**ST PETER VERE STREET** *Gibbs 1724*
Vere Street	St Peter's was built as a private chapel for Edward Harley, third Earl of Oxford. It was first known as the Mary-le-bone Chapel and later the Oxford Chapel. The church is now administered by the London Institute for Contemporary Christianity and its aisles have unfortunately been partitioned as offices. Good plasterwork, however, remains. The 19C stained glass windows were designed by *Burne-Jones*.

Exit R. First R Henrietta Place. First L and R Cavendish Square. Proceed ahead on the north side to Nos 11 and 14.

Location 21	**CAVENDISH SQUARE**

Cavendish Square was first laid out in 1717 for Robert Harley, later second Earl of Oxford. It formed part of the earliest development of the fields north of Oxford Street.

The only houses of architectural interest that remain are the two identical Portland stone buildings, Nos 11 and 14, which were built as a speculative development *c.*1770 in the centre of the north side. Above the arch is a bronze 'Madonna and Child' by *Epstein*.

Continue eastward. First L Chandos St. Proceed to the end.

Location 22	**CHANDOS HOUSE** *R. Adam 1771*
Royal Society of Medicine 2 Queen Anne Street	Chandos House, built of stone, is judged to be one of the best surviving houses designed by Adam in central London. The iron lamp standards and railings are original and are also the architect's work. Chandos House was the Austro-Hungarian embassy from 1815–71.

Return along Chandos St. First L and L Portland Place.

Location 23	**PORTLAND PLACE**

Portland Place was a fashionable close of houses, mostly designed by *James Adam* in 1774. Originally there were gates at the north end. The owner of Foley House, which closed the south end, insisted on maintaining his unrestricted views of the park, hence the street's unusual width. The best remaining houses are Nos 46 and 48.

Cross the road and proceed northward to Nos 46 and 48. Return southward and continue to the end of Portland Place. Ahead Langham Place.

Nash began New Street (now Langham Place and Regent Street) at the south end of Portland Place, originally intending that it should continue ahead in a straight line. He purchased Foley House, which stood in the way, and immediately demolished it. Just south of the house, however, the residents of Cavendish Square would not allow the new street to interfere with their properties. The frustrated Nash then built Langham House on the site and his new street had to curve around it. Langham House was demolished in 1864 and the present building constructed as the Langham Hotel. It now provides accommodation for the BBC.

Proceed to All Souls Church on the east side.

Location 24

ALL SOULS LANGHAM PLACE *Nash 1824*

Langham Place

Nash designed All Souls with a curved portico and tower which helped to disguise the bend in the road. His combination of a spire and a Classical building earned Nash some ridicule. All Souls was clad, unusually for Nash, with Bath stone rather than stuccoed brick.

Enter the church.

Restored after Second World War bombing, the original galleries have been retained but the furnishings are ultra-modern.

The altarpiece by *Richard Westall* was presented by George IV.

Exit L. Fourth L Margaret St.

Location 25

ALL SAINTS MARGARET STREET* *Butterfield 1850*

Margaret Street

This church is regarded as the epitome of High Victorian Gothic. Its rather forbidding exterior of red and black brick contrasts with the interior, where a multiplicity of materials has been used.

Exit L. Second R Wells St. Third R Oxford St. Fourth L Argyll St.

Location 26

LONDON PALLADIUM

Argyll Street (437 7373)

Once famed as a venue for leading American entertainers, the theatre now concentrates on musicals.

Exit R. First L Little Argyll St. L Regent St.

Location 27

REGENT STREET

Regent Street is one of London's most popular shopping streets. Clothing shops predominate, with quality and prices fitting neatly between Oxford Street and Bond Street. The best known are on the east side whilst tourist and airline offices favour the west side.

Nash chose the line of Regent Street, first called New Street, to divide the fashionable West End from the less salubrious Soho on its way to the Prince Regent's Carlton House in Pall Mall. The curve of The Quadrant at the Piccadilly end was designed to disguise the directional change necessitated by the prohibitive expense of acquiring Golden Square. Originally, The Quadrant was the only section of Regent Street where shops were permitted and it w fronted on both sides of the road with colonnades. These were removed in 1848, partly to increase natural light to the shops, but also because they attracted ladies of easy virtue. Regent Street was a success, but businesses could not expand and the palatial but relatively small buildings which had created the 'finest street in Europe' were doomed. Now only the route is unaltered, all the original architecture, by Nash, and others, being replaced between 1905 and 1930.

Proceed ahead to Gt Marlborough St (first L).

Location 28

LIBERTY

260–278 Regent Street (734 1234)

Opened by Arthur Liberty at 218a Regent Street in 1875, Liberty are famous for their printed fabrics and household goods. An early supplier was William Morris, and some of his 19C designs are still current. Many items sold here in the 1920s and 1930s are now sought after as collectors pieces.

To the rear, fronting Great Marlborough Street, is the Tudor-style extension built in 1924. On the hour, above its clock, St George and the Dragon continue their fight. The timbered interior of this part of the store was made up from two men-o'-war, HMS *Hindustan* and *Impregnable*.

Proceed southward along Regent St to the Foubert's Place corner (first L).

Location 29

JAEGER

204 Regent Street (734 8211)

Jaeger, established to promote the health of woollen clothing, still specialize in woollen goods for both sexes and make few concessions to the avant-garde.

Location 30

HAMLEYS

188–196 Regent Street (734 3161)

Hamleys was founded in the 18C at High Holborn and is the world's largest toy shop; an excellent place in which to calm a fractious child.

Return northward to Foubert's Place R. Second R Carnaby St.

Location 31

CARNABY STREET

This pedestrian precinct became famous in 'The Swinging Sixties' for its outrageous fashion. Souvenirs now dominate and the street has lost its glamour. Refurbishment is planned.

Second R Beak Street. Second L Warwick St. Proceed to the Church of the Assumption facing Regent Place (first R).

Location 32

THE 'BAVARIAN CHAPEL' *c.1785*

Church of the Assumption and St Gregory Warwick Street

This is a unique survivor of the embassy chapels which were for long the only venues where British subjects could legally attend Catholic Mass before emancipation in 1829. Its predecessor was built early in the 18C for the Portuguese Embassy in what were then the back gardens of Nos 23 and 24 Golden Square. This was destroyed in the Gordon Riots of 1780 and rebuilt. In 1847 the Bavarian Embassy acquired the present building which is still referred to as the Bavarian Chapel. Bavaria joined the German federation in 1871.

Enter by the first door L.

Most of the interior was remodelled in the 19C.

Above the main door R the motto of the Wittelsbach family, rulers of Bavaria, remains 'In Treu Fest' (steadfast in loyalty).

Exit L. First R Glasshouse St. Proceed to Garrard on the Regent St corner.

Location 33	**GARRARD**
112 Regent Street (734 7020)	Garrard are the jewellers responsible for the maintenance of the royal regalia. In February each year it is their duty to clean and polish the Crown Jewels in the Tower of London.

Proceed to Aquascutum on the opposite corner of Glasshouse Street.

Location 34	**AQUASCUTUM**
100 Regent Street (734 6090)	The company manufactures and sells clothing in the upper price range for men and women. Aquascutum raincoats are particularly famous.

Continue southward just past the Café Royal on the Air Street corner (second L).

Location 35	**CAFE ROYAL**
68 Regent Street (437 9090)	The restaurant was founded in 1865 but rebuilt in 1923. However, the original gilt caryatids and mirrors were refitted in the new Grill Room which has a plush, late Victorian atmosphere. Before their accession to the throne, Edward VIII and George VI were regular diners at the present Café Royal, as were Edward VII, Whistler, Shaw and Oscar Wilde at its predecessor.

Cross Piccadilly Circus (itinerary 14) by subway and proceed clockwise. Leave by the Haymarket exit (subway 4). At the top of the stairs proceed ahead, and follow the signs to Haymarket. Cross the road immediately to No 34.

Location 36	**HAYMARKET**
	Haymarket, much older than Regent Street, was first recorded in 1657. A market for hay was held in the street three times a week until 1830.

Location 37	**PAPERCHASE**
34 Haymarket	This 18C shop was, from 1720 until 1982, the premises of Fribourg and Treyer, tobacco and snuff merchants. Its unaltered survival in this position is astonishing.

Proceed southward remaining on the east side. Pass the Shavers Place junction (first L).

Location 38	**DESIGN CENTRE**
28 Haymarket (839 8000)	Well-designed British goods are displayed; staff will advise where items may be purchased.

Exit L. Pass the Panton St junction (first L).

Location 39	**BURBERRY**
18 Haymarket (930 3343)	This ladies' and gentlemen's clothing store is world-famed for its trench raincoats.

Exit L. Continue southward.

Location 40 | **THEATRE ROYAL** *Nash 1821*

Haymarket
(930 9832)

Although the theatre's exterior was designed by Nash, its interior was completely remodelled in 1904.

Cross Haymarket immediately and proceed ahead following Charles II St. First L Royal Opera Arcade.

Location 41 | **ROYAL OPERA ARCADE** *Nash 1817*

When built, this shopping arcade, which retains its original lamps, ran directly behind the Opera House in Haymarket, since replaced by Her Majesty's Theatre. There were never shops on the east side as access to the Opera House was needed.

Exit L Pall Mall. First L Haymarket. First R Suffolk Place.

Location 42 | **SUFFOLK PLACE/SUFFOLK STREET** *Nash c.1825*

Although merely side streets, the north section of Suffolk Place and most of Suffolk Street possess the only houses that remain from Nash's Regent Street scheme.

Nos 18 and 19 appear to be houses but are, in fact, the rear of the Theatre Royal and their 'windows' are false.

Return to Haymarket R. Cross the road and continue northward to Piccadilly Circus Station, Bakerloo and Piccadilly lines.

17

British Museum and Bloomsbury

One of the world's greatest museums of antiquities is visited, together with Hawksmoor's only London church to be built west of the City. This itinerary is suitable for a rainy day as much of it is indoors.

Timing: Monday to Saturday is preferable, allowing a whole day. The Percival David Foundation of Chinese Art is open Monday to Friday. The Petrie Museum of Egyptology at University College is open Monday to Friday but closes from 12.00–13.15.

17

Locations
1 Holy Trinity
2 Fitzroy Square
3 British Telecom Tower
4 Charlotte Street
5 Pollock's Toy Museum
6 Bedford Square
7 British Museum and British Library
8 St George Bloomsbury
9 Sicilian Avenue
10 Bloomsbury Square
11 No 17 Bloomsbury Square
12 Woburn Square
13 Percival David Foundation of Chinese Art
14 Woburn Walk
15 St Pancras
16 St Pancras Chambers
17 Gower Street
18 University College

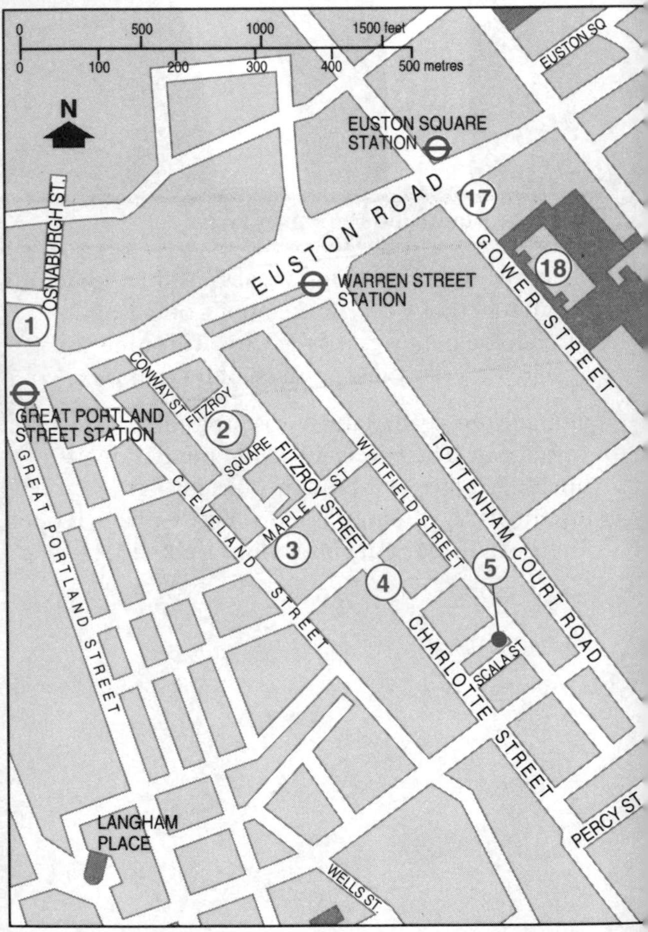

Start *Great Portland Street Station, Circle and Metropolitan lines. Leave by the Marylebone Road exit R. Remain on the south side. Opposite, on the north side, is Holy Trinity. It is unnecessary to cross the road.*

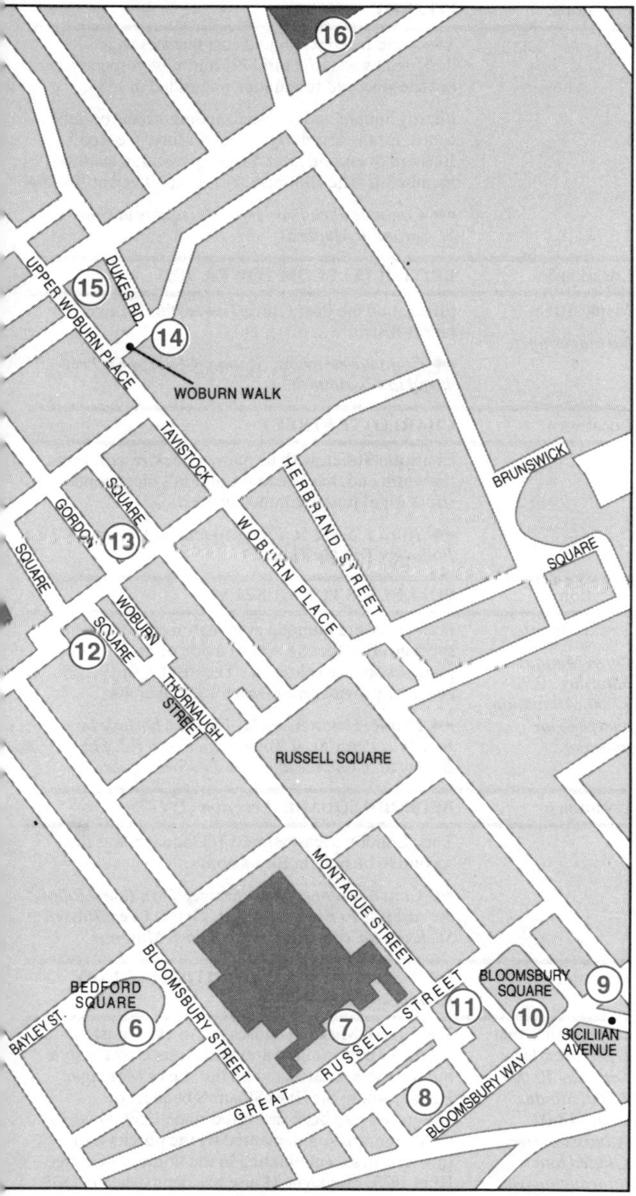

Location 1	**HOLY TRINITY** *Soane 1828*
Marylebone Road	Outside, L of the entrance, is an external pulpit. The church was designed, unusually, with its altar at the north end and the interior, partly remodelled in 1878, now accommodates the SPCK bookshop. *Continue eastward along Marylebone Road. Third R Conway St. Proceed to Fitzroy Square and continue ahead to the south-west corner of the square.*

Location 2

FITZROY SQUARE

The stone-faced south and east terraces were designed by *R. Adam* in 1794 and 1798 respectively, but the stuccoed remainder was added in 1835.

Fitzroy Square and the surrounding streets became a centre for the arts early in this century. George Bernard Shaw and later Virginia Woolf, a leading member of 'The Bloomsbury Group', lived at No 29.

Continue ahead and leave the square at Conway St. Second L Maple St.

Location 3

BRITISH TELECOM TOWER *1965*

Maple Street

No longer open

First called the Post Office Tower, this is London's tallest structure at 620 feet.

Continue eastward. Second R Fitzroy St. Proceed ahead to Charlotte St.

Location 4

CHARLOTTE STREET

Charlotte Street, with its many Greek restaurants at the south end, has become London's most popular street for al fresco summertime eating.

Third L Scala St. First L Whitfield St. Enter Pollock's Toy Museum.

Location 5

POLLOCK'S TOY MUSEUM

1 Scala Street

Open Monday–Saturday 10.00–17.00. Admission charge to the museum.

Pollock's were founded at Islington *c.*1810. They specialized in theatre scenes made of card; 'penny plain, twopence coloured'. The display of 19C and 20C toys provides nostalgia for the over 40s.

Exit R. First R Scala St. First L Charlotte St. Fourth L Percy St. R Tottenham Court Rd. First L Bayley St. Continue ahead to Bedford Square.

Location 6

BEDFORD SQUARE *Leverton* (?) *1775*

This, London's least altered 18C square, was the second to be built in Bloomsbury.

Continue along the north side. Turn R and follow the east side to Bloomsbury St. First L Great Russell St. Enter the courtyard of the British Museum.

Location 7

BRITISH MUSEUM AND BRITISH LIBRARY
R. Smirke 1823–47

Gt Russell Street
Open Monday–Saturday 10.00–17.00. Sunday 14.30–18.00. Admission free. Guided tour information 636 1555.

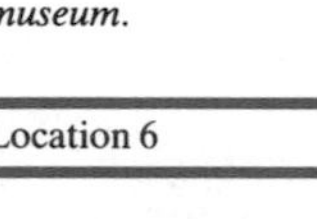

The British Museum houses the world's most extensive collection of antiquities. Its Grecian style building was constructed on the site of Montague House, where Sir Hans Sloane's bequest of antiquities had been displayed since 1759. Sloane's collection was supplemented by the purchase of further works, culminating in the library of George III in 1823. Montague House was demolished in 1838.

Enter beneath the central portico and proceed directly ahead to the information desk for a gallery plan.

Primary exhibits are on the ground floor (large sculptures) and the upper floor. A suggested order for viewing galleries with outstanding exhibits is given.

Return towards the entrance and turn R. Continue through the bookshop. Turn first R and proceed through ***26*** *to* ***25***.

25 Large Egyptian sculptures. Immediately L is the Rosetta stone.
20 and **19** Nimrud.
21 Ninevah.
6 Bassae Temple frieze.
8 The Duveen Gallery was built in 1938 to house the Elgin Marbles.
7 Nereid Monument from Xanthos.
9 Caryatid from the Erectheum, Athens.
12 Sculptures from the Tomb of Mausolus, one of the seven wonders of the ancient world.
14 Portland Vase.
25 Large Egyptian sculptures (continuation).

•• *At the end of the gallery ascend the stairs L. or return to the entrance hall for the lift which ascends to face gallery* **40**. *From the stairs turn L and proceed ahead to* **61**.

61 and **60** Egyptian mummies.
90 The only known large scale cartoon by *Michelangelo* 'Virgin and Child'.
56 Treasures from the tombs at Ur.
51 Facing the entrance to this gallery is the Persian royal guard from the palace of Darius.
41 Sutton Hoo Treasures.
40 Mildenhall Treasures.
35 Lindow Man

•• *Proceed to the main stairway. Descend to the entrance hall. Turn L and continue ahead to the British Library Reading Room.*

The British Library.
One copy of every UK publication must by law be sent to this library. In 1995 its collection totalled over eighteen million books occupying 430 miles of shelving. Most are kept elsewhere.

The library is due to move to St Pancras in 1996.

Open for viewing (accompanied by an attendant) precisely on the hour Monday–Saturday 11.00–16.00. Admission free.

The **Reading Room** occupies the site of the former courtyard and was built by *S. Smirke* in 1857. Marx studied and wrote much of *Das Kapital* in this room which seats 400 readers and contains 30,000 books.

•• *Leave the Reading Room. Proceed towards the museum's exit. Turn L to the other British Library rooms.*

Displays include the following:

30 Magna Carta, Lindisfarne Gospels, Death Warrant of the Earl of Essex, literary autographs.
32 (The King's Library). Displays of historic books include the Gutenberg Bible. Shakespeare's signature is displayed.

33C This former British Library room opened in 1994 as the Mexican Gallery. It houses the finest display of Pre-Columbian Mexican art outside its country of origin.

•• *Return to the main hall and exit from the museum R Great Russell St. First L Museum St. Third L Bloomsbury Way.*

Location 8

ST GEORGE BLOOMSBURY *Hawksmoor 1731*

Bloomsbury Way

St George's was one of the twelve churches to be built for expanding outer London parishes under the Fifty New Churches Act of 1711. Six were designed by Hawksmoor.

The obelisk-shaped spire is based on Pliny's description of the tomb of Mausolus. Originally, lions and unicorns decorated its base but these were removed in the 19C. Surmounting the church is a statue of the unpopular George I representing St George. This led to some ridicule. Reproductions of the spire as it originally appeared are on the two lamp standards flanking the steps.

Before entering the church, pass through the gate in the west corner and proceed along the passage adjacent to St George's. R Little Russell Street.

The **north facade** is designed in Renaissance style.

Return to the south facade and enter the church.

Originally, the altar was placed conventionally at the east end, however, this was moved in the 19C to its present position in the north baptistry.

Proceed to the **east apse**.

The east apse, where the altar had been, was blocked in and a new gallery constructed across it to increase the seating. This was later removed. The ceiling relief in this apse and the gilded flower in the ceiling of the nave are both by *Isaac Mansfield*.

Exit to Bloomsbury Way L. Ahead Bloomsbury Square. Fourth R Sicilian Avenue.

Location 9

SICILIAN AVENUE *Wortley 1905*

This colonnaded avenue was planned as a pedestrianized shopping street in the Italian style.

Return to Bloomsbury Square L and proceed ahead to Nos 4–6 in the south-west corner.

Location 10

BLOOMSBURY SQUARE

The fourth Earl of Southampton developed the square, as Southampton Square, in 1661 and built his mansion on the north side. No original houses remain.

In the south-west corner Nos 4–6 by *Flitcroft* (?) are mid-18C.

Proceed to the north-west corner of the square.

Location 11

NO 17 BLOOMSBURY SQUARE

This early 18C building, remodelled by *Nash* in 1773, was the young architect's first use of stucco in London.

L Russell St. First R Montague St. Proceed to Russell Square. Continue ahead and pass the road barrier to Thornhaugh St which leads to Woburn Square.

Location 12

WOBURN SQUARE

Formed in 1822, by James Sim, the name of the square commemorates Woburn Abbey, family seat of its landowner, the Duke of Bedford. All the original Georgian buildings were demolished in one of Londons great post-war acts of vandalism, primarily to make way for undistinguished extensions to London University.

First R Gordon Square. Proceed ahead to No 53 in the south-east corner.

Location 13

PERCIVAL DAVID FOUNDATION OF CHINESE ART

53 Gordon Square (387 3909)

Open Monday–Friday 10.30–17.00. Admission free.

A comprehensive collection of ancient Chinese porcelain is displayed on three floors.

Exit L. First L Tavistock Square. Proceed R to the north-east corner of the square.

Location 14

WOBURN WALK *Cubitt 1822*

This thoroughfare, originally called Woburn Buildings, possesses some of London's best late Georgian shop fronts. They continue along the west side of Dukes Road.

First L Dukes Rd. Proceed ahead to the east end of St Pancras L.

Location 15

ST PANCRAS* *W. and H. Inwood 1822*

Euston Road

Closed Monday afternoon and Tuesday.

Both east wings of St Pancras, London's first Neo-Grecian church, feature copies of the caryatids from the Erechtheum in Athens. Unfortunately, the ladies were made too tall and the removal of their middle sections gives them a dumpy appearance.

First L Euston Rd. First L Upper Woburn Place.

The design of the tower of St Pancras was inspired by the Tower of the Winds, Athens, and its portico, like the east wings, was influenced by the Erechtheum.

Enter the church from the portico.

The High Altar was made in 1914 when the church was remodelled. In the Chapel of the Blessed Sacrament, at the east end of the south aisle, the original High Altar may still be seen.

The pulpit and lectern are original.

Exit R. First R Euston Rd. Proceed ahead. Pass Midland Rd (fourth L). Cross the road to St Pancras Chambers.

Location 16

ST PANCRAS CHAMBERS *George Gilbert Scott 1869*

Euston Road

Fronting St Pancras Station this was originally built as the Midland Grand Hotel. Scott based his design on drawings, rejected by Palmerston, for the Foreign Office in Whitehall. A variety of medieval elements has produced a Victorian Gothic fantasy.

After a lengthy period as offices, this building has been restored externally; its future use is uncertain.

Exit from St Pancras Chambers and cross the road. Take any bus from the south side of Euston Rd to Euston Square. First L Gower St.

Location 17

GOWER STREET *c.1790*

The west side of Gower Street, from University College southward, provides one of London's longest unbroken stretches of late Georgian houses.

Continue ahead to London University L.

Location 18

UNIVERSITY COLLEGE *Wilkins 1829 (part)*

Gower Street
(387 7050)

The central range is open Monday–Friday, 09.30–17.00. Jeremy Bentham's 'auto icon' is displayed in term time, or by appointment.

The Petrie Museum is open Monday–Friday, 10.00–12.00 and 13.15–17.00. Admission to everything is free.

The central range fronting Gower Street was built in 1985 to complete the original design.

•■ *Proceed through the courtyard.*

The domed central range by *Wilkins*, completed in 1829, is reminiscent of the same architect's National Gallery. The wings were added later.

•■ *Enter this building by the side door L of the steps. Ascend to the first floor.*

The **Flaxman Gallery** displays early 19C plaster casts of sculptures by *John Flaxman*.

Ask here for directions to view the mummified body of Jeremy Bentham and printed instructions to reach the Petrie Museum. (It is complicated.)

•■ *Proceed to Jeremy Bentham's 'auto icon' at the building's south junction.*

Jeremy Bentham (1748–1832) arranged that his body should be preserved after his death and displayed in a glass case. It was bequeathed to his physician who presented it to University College in 1850. The mummified head exists, in poor condition, but was almost immediately replaced by the present wax effigy. Bentham's walking stick, 'Dapple' and clothing, apart from the vest, are original.

•■ *Proceed to the* **Petrie Museum**.

The accommodation for the exhibits is cramped and new premises are being sought. Rare fragments from El Amarna, the most naturalistic period of ancient Egyptian art, are displayed.

•■ *Return to Euston Rd R. Euston Square Station, Circle and Metropolitan lines. Alternatively, return to Euston Rd L. Warren Street Station, Northern and Victoria lines.*

Itinerary 18

18

South Kensington

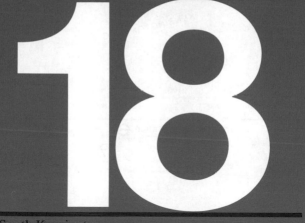

South Kensington accommodates four large museums which, together with Kensington Gardens, are particularly suitable for children.

Timing: Monday to Saturday are preferable, the museums all close on Sunday morning and are very crowded on Sunday afternoon. They are large and should be visited selectively. A morning start is recommended as the itinerary includes much to see. The weather is, of course, irrelevant for the museums but it should be fine to enjoy Kensington Gardens. If convenient, Kensington Palace (itinerary 21) may be added.

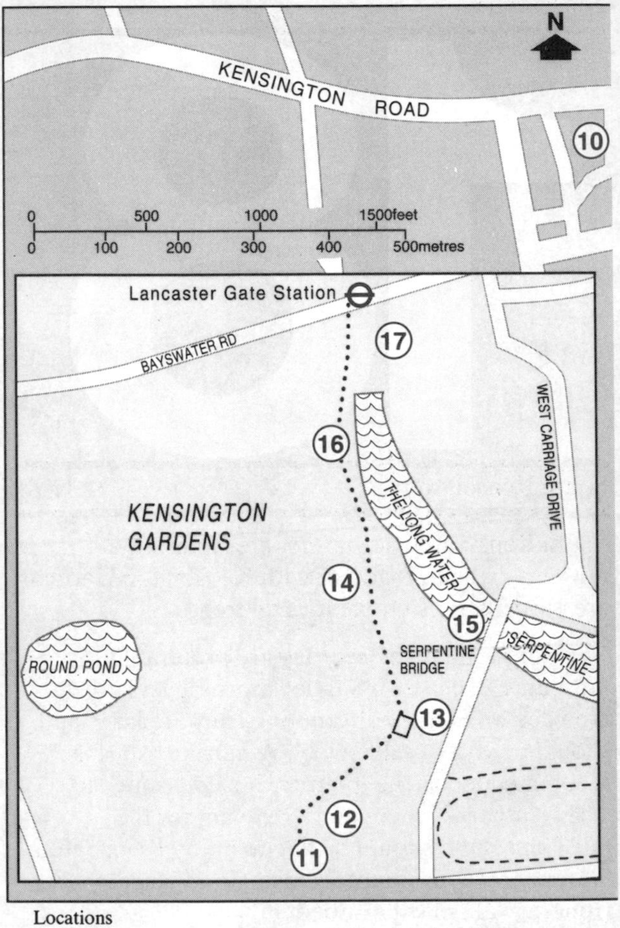

Locations

1 Pelham Place
2 Michelin House
3 Natural History Museum
4 Science Museum
5 Victoria and Albert Museum
6 Brompton Oratory
7 Holy Trinity Brompton
8 The Queen's Tower
9 Royal Albert Hall
10 Royal College of Organists
11 Albert Memorial
12 Kensington Gardens
13 Serpentine Gallery
14 Kensington Gardens Temple
15 Serpentine Bridge
16 Peter Pan Statue
17 Queen Anne's Alcove

Start *South Kensington Station, Circle, District and Piccadilly lines. Leave by the exit L of the stairs. L Pelham St. First R Pelham Place.*

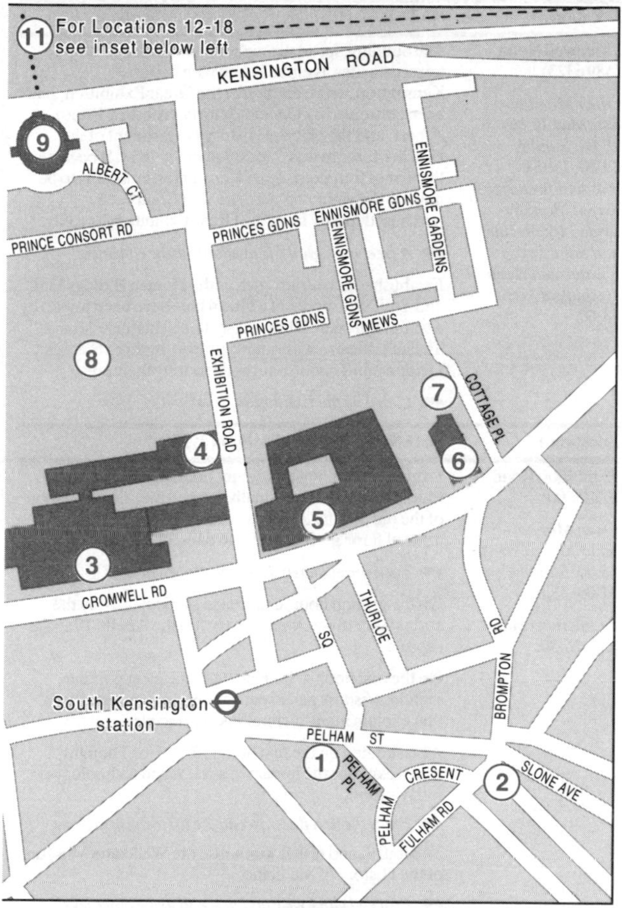

Location 1	**PELHAM PLACE** *Basevi (?) c.1830*

Pelham Place is one of London's most attractive streets and when the fruit trees blossom in May, it is reminiscent of a scene from *Mary Poppins.*

L Pelham Crescent. L Fulham Rd. Cross the road and proceed to the Sloane Avenue junction (first R). Michelin House is on the corner.

Location 2	**MICHELIN HOUSE** *Epinasse 1910*

81 Fulham Road

This was, until 1985, the English headquarters of the French tyre manufacturers. The building is one of London's best examples of the Art-Nouveau style. Ceramic panels illustrate early motoring rallies. It has been developed by Conran to provide a shop, a restaurant and a bar.

First L Pelham St. First R Thurloe Square. Third L Cromwell Road. Continue past the Exhibition Rd junction (second R). Cross the road to the Natural History Museum and enter the central gates.

Location 3

NATURAL HISTORY MUSEUM *Waterhouse 1880*

Cromwell Road (589 6323)

Open Monday–Saturday 10.00–18.00. Sunday 13.00–18.00. Admission charge except Monday–Friday 16.30–1800 and Saturday, Sunday and Bank Holidays 17.00–18.00.

The building, faced throughout with pink and blue terracotta tiles, is embellished with beasts. A Kensington Arts Centre, like the Great Exhibition, had been conceived by Queen Victoria's consort, Prince Albert, and the Natural History Department of the British Museum was relocated here in 1880. It became the first of four permanent Kensington museums to be built on the eighty-six acre site which had been purchased, partly from the Great Exhibition's profits.

A free 'mini guide' is available at the entrance.

Established favourites such as the Human Biology Hall and a full-size model of a blue whale have been joined by a completely new Dinosaur section. This includes a lifelike tableau – with sound effects – of three Deinonychi Tenontosaurus devouring their prey.

Leave by the Exhibition Road exit L.

Location 4

SCIENCE MUSEUM *Allison 1913*

Exhibition Road (938 8000)

Open Monday–Saturday, 10.00–18.00. Sunday 11.00–18.00.

Admission charge until 16.30.

Exhibits in this huge museum, one of London's major tourist attractions, originally formed the science section of the old South Kensington Museum. More than seven acres of floor space are spread over five levels.

Turn immediately R into the East Hall.

On the ground floor, children in particular enjoy the early steam trains, vintage cars and the Apollo 10 space capsule.

On the first floor is 'Launch Pad', the most popular section. Visitors participate in simple demonstrations that explain many technological principles.

Also situated on the first floor is 'Food for Thought' which explains the impact of science and technology on today's food.

From the first floor ascend the lift to the fifth floor.

The fourth and fifth floors house the Wellcome Museum of the History of Medicine.

Proceed clockwise and descend to the other levels.

The third floor displays early aeroplanes, including the 'Vickers Vimy' in which Alcock and Brown first flew the Atlantic. *Science in the 18th century* includes George III's collection of scientific instruments. Developments in modern medicine are explained in *Health Matters*; an iron lung and Watson and Crick's DNA model are exhibited. Much of the second floor is devoted to shipping.

Exit from the museum and cross the road to the Victoria and Albert Museum (location 5).

Location 5

VICTORIA AND ALBERT MUSEUM

Exhibition Road (938 8500)

Open Tuesday–Sunday, 10.00–17.50. Monday 12.00–17.50. Admission by voluntary contribution.

The 'V&A' specializes in the fine and applied arts and houses the world's greatest collection of English furniture. Most countries and periods, apart from antiquities, are represented in its vast collection but only a limited number of paintings and drawings are included.

The building immediately L of the Exhibition Road entrance is the recently remodelled Henry Cole Wing, one of several buildings added in Italian Renaissance style by *Fowke c.* 1866.

Enter the museum from Exhibition Road.

When the Great Exhibition of 1851 ended, many of the exhibits were displayed at the Museum of Manufacturers in Marlborough House. This was transferred to South Kensington in 1857 to establish the South Kensington Museum. Its first director was Henry Cole who had organized the Great Exhibition for Prince Albert. The iron and glass 'Brompton Boilers', was replaced by the present east range and the museum renamed the Victoria and Albert in 1899. The entrance hall forms the Rodin Gallery, where bronzes by the French sculptor are displayed.

Obtain a free map from the information desk.

Proceed L through the bookshop in the Henry Cole Wing. Ascend by lift to level 6.

Paintings and sketches by *Constable.* The bequest includes some of Constable's best known paintings and is the largest collection of his works in England.

Descend to level 4.

Tudor portrait miniatures by *Hilliard.*

Descend to level 1.

The main section of the museum has four floor levels and exhibits are divided into Art and Design and Materials and Techniques galleries. Antique furniture, the chief glory of the museum, is displayed on three floor levels, each directly above the other. A suggested order for viewing galleries with outstanding exhibits is given. Follow the map.

Proceed ahead through the entrance hall. Ascend the steps to Lower Level B and the **British Art and Design 1600–1715** galleries.

54 Great Bed of Ware. At least six at a time could sleep in this Tudor bed.
58 Interior of the Music Room from Norfolk House.

Ascend the stairs L to Level C.

British Art and Design 1750–1900 continues the English furniture display.

125 Part of the Glass Drawing Room from Norfolk House by *R. Adam.*

At gallery **118** *descend the stairs to Level A. Turn R and descend the steps to gallery* **21**. *Turn immediately R and descend more steps to Lower Level A.*

European furniture from the 17C and 18C in galleries **1a** to **7**, includes the **Jones Collection**.

At gallery **7** *ascend the stairs to Level A. Turn L.*

48 Facade of Sir Paul Pindar's house *c.*1600.
Museum shop The huge cartoons by *Raphael* 1519 illustrate scenes from the lives of St Peter and St Paul. They were designs for tapestries in the Vatican's Sistine Chapel. Charles I purchased the cartoons for Hampton Court in 1623.
41 Tippoo's Tiger, *c.*1790.
21 Samson slaying a Philistine by *Giambologna.*
The **William Morris Room** was decorated as a restaurant by the famous Victorian designer in 1866. Its stained glass is by *Burne-Jones.*
14 Terracottas by *A. and P. Della Robbia.*
16 Virgin and Child roundel by *Donatello* 1456.

43 Eltenburg Reliquary 12C.
50 Neptune and Triton statue by *Bernini c.*1622.

Continue ahead to the Cromwell Rd exit and leave the building.

The museum's Cromwell Road block was built by *A. Webb* 1909 in Renaissance style. Its foundation stone was laid by Queen Victoria in 1899. See the inscription by the entrance.

Turn L and continue to Brompton Rd.

Location 6 — Brompton Road

BROMPTON ORATORY *Gribble 1878*

Apart from Westminster Cathedral this is London's most important Roman Catholic church. Its official name is the Church of the Oratory of St Philip Neri and The Immaculate Heart of Mary. The church was built in Italian Baroque style with a dome by *Sherrin* above the crossing. It is famed for choral music.

Enter the church and proceed along the **nave**.

The statues of the Apostles between the pilasters by *Mazzuoli* 1685 came from Siena Cathedral in Italy.

In the south transept's **Lady Chapel** is an altar from Brescia, Italy, made in 1693.

Exit L. First L Cottage Place.

Location 7 — Cottage Place

HOLY TRINITY *Donaldson 1829*

Holy Trinity, built in contrasting style to the Oratory, was one of London's earliest Gothic Revival churches.

Continue northward along Cottage Place. L and R Ennismore Garden Mews. L Ennismore Gardens. Continue to Princes Gardens. L Exhibition Rd. First R Imperial College Rd. Proceed to the forecourt R of the Imperial College of Science and Technology.

Location 8 — Imperial College Road

THE QUEEN'S TOWER *Collcutt 1893*

The Queen's Tower originally formed the central focal point of the Imperial Institute, built, in Renaissance Revival style, to mark the 1887 Golden Jubilee of Queen Victoria. The remainder of the complex, which accommodated a library, laboratories, a conference room and exhibition galleries, was demolished between 1957–67 to permit the expansion of the Imperial College. In 1962 the Commonwealth Institute, as the Imperial Institute had been renamed, was relocated at Holland Park (see page 259).

Conservationsists gained a reprieve for the Queen's Tower, which, at great expense, was converted to become a free-standing campanile.

Two stone lions sleepily guard the tower, originally, with two others, they flanked the entrance to the Imperial Institute.

The 287ft high tower is clad with Portland Stone. Much of the lower level, together with the foundations, has been rebuilt as part of the conversion work.

Retained in the belfry are the ten bells presented to the Institute by the Prince of Wales (later Edward VII), who had received them as a gift from Melbourne, Australia.

•• Return to Imperial College Road, L. First L Prince Consort Road. First R Albert Court. Second R proceed towards the north side of the Royal Albert Hall (facing Kensington Gardens).

Location 9 — **ROYAL ALBERT HALL** *Fowke Scott 1871*

Kensington Gore (589 8212)

Princec Albert suggested the erection of this hall, which was named to commemmorate him. It is now one of London's leading venues for a variety of events, chiefly concerts, and 5,200 spectators can be seated. Popular promenade concerts are given every day between mid-July and mid-September culminating in the famous 'Last Night of the Proms'.

The external terracotta frieze illustrates the triumph of the arts.

•• Proceed to the west side of the hall. Cross to the Royal College of Organists (the highly decorative building).

Location 10 — **ROYAL COLLEGE OF ORGANISTS** *Cole 1875*

Kensington Gore

This building is renowned for its exuberant Renaissance style decoration by *Moody*.

•• Return northward. Cross Kensington Gore Rd and proceed to Kensington Gardens and the Albert Memorial.

Location 11 — **ALBERT MEMORIAL** *George Gilbert Scott 1872*

Kensington Gardens

Due to extensive restoration, much of the exterior will be hidden from view for some years.

A plethora of materials, including marble, bronze and mosaic are incorporated in this 175 foot high monument to Prince Albert. Many sculptors were commissioned for its two hundred figures. The bronze statue of Albert reading the Great Exhibition catalogue is by *Foley*.

•• Proceed to the gardens behind the monument.

Location 12 — **KENSINGTON GARDENS**

These gardens, originally the private grounds of Kensington Palace, were laid out in a formal style by *Henry Wise* for Queen Anne early in the 18C. The Long Water, Round Pond and Broad Walk were added later for George II's consort, Queen Caroline.

Kensington Gardens merge imperceptibly with Hyde Park further east. They were opened to the public for the first time by George II in 1754, initially on Saturdays only, and it was not until the 19C that William IV permitted daily access.

A tour is suggested as follows:

•• Follow the northbound path behind the Albert Memorial. Take the third path R and proceed to the Serpentine Gallery. Enter from the north side facing the lake.

Location 13 — **SERPENTINE GALLERY** *Tanner 1908*

Open Monday–Saturday 9.00–17.30, Sunday 14.30–17.30. Admission free.

Built originally as a tea house, the gallery holds exhibitions of contemporary works of art.

•• Exit L. Take the path first R and proceed ahead. Overlooking the path L is the temple.

Location 14 **KENSINGTON GARDENS TEMPLE** *Kent c.1735*

This Greek-style temple was added to the gardens for Queen Caroline as part of the development of the Long Water and Serpentine.

Continue ahead.

In the middle distance L is the equestrian statue 'Physical Energy' by *Watts*. On the opposite side of the lake R is 'The Arch' by *Moore* 1979.

Continue to the Long Water. The bridge can be seen R.

Location 15 **SERPENTINE BRIDGE** *Rennie 1826*

This small but elegant road bridge is the only example of the great engineer's work to survive in London.

Proceed ahead following the lake. Overlooking the path L is the Peter Pan statue.

Location 16 **PETER PAN STATUE** *Frampton 1912*

The statue of J. M. Barrie's hero was erected overnight as a surprise for the local children. Peter may, or may not, be holding his pipes which regularly disappear. The statue was modelled by a young lady; in pantomime, it is still usual for Peter Pan to be played by a female.

Continue to the head of the lake where there are fountains and an Italianate pavilion. Proceed behind this to the path ahead R.

Location 17 **QUEEN ANNE'S ALCOVE** *Wren 18C.*

Designed for Queen Anne as a summer house, this stone alcove was first erected south of Kensington Palace.

Return westward through the gardens. First R Marlborough Gate. Exit and cross Bayswater Rd immediately to Lancaster Gate Station, Central line.

Alternatively, if viewing Kensington Palace (itinerary 20), return to the southwest section of the gardens following the diagonal path which is signposted to the Round Pond. At the pond turn immediately R and cross the grass to Kensington Palace.

Itinerary 19

19

Madame Tussaud's and London Zoo

This itinerary is particularly appreciated by children. Fine weather is essential to enjoy Regent's Park and London Zoo to the full.

Timing: The Jewish Museum is open Sunday–Thursday; all other locations are open every day including Sunday mornings.

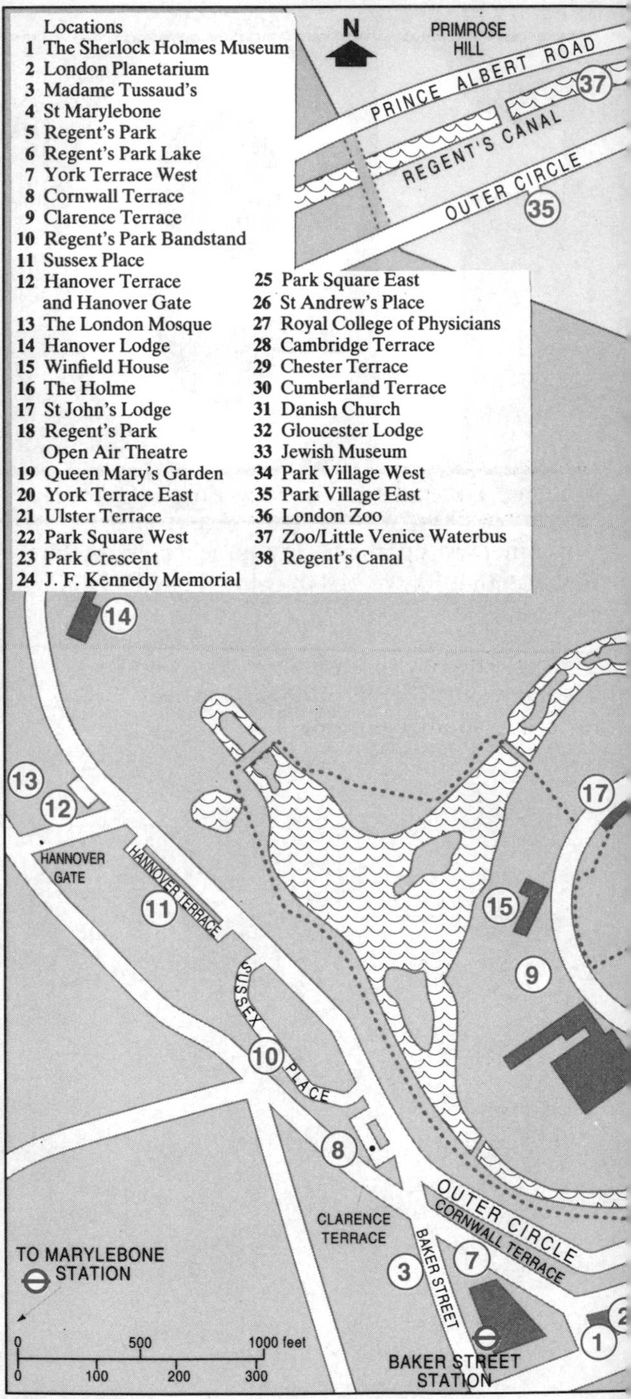
Locations
1 The Sherlock Holmes Museum
2 London Planetarium
3 Madame Tussaud's
4 St Marylebone
5 Regent's Park
6 Regent's Park Lake
7 York Terrace West
8 Cornwall Terrace
9 Clarence Terrace
10 Regent's Park Bandstand
11 Sussex Place
12 Hanover Terrace and Hanover Gate
13 The London Mosque
14 Hanover Lodge
15 Winfield House
16 The Holme
17 St John's Lodge
18 Regent's Park Open Air Theatre
19 Queen Mary's Garden
20 York Terrace East
21 Ulster Terrace
22 Park Square West
23 Park Crescent
24 J. F. Kennedy Memorial
25 Park Square East
26 St Andrew's Place
27 Royal College of Physicians
28 Cambridge Terrace
29 Chester Terrace
30 Cumberland Terrace
31 Danish Church
32 Gloucester Lodge
33 Jewish Museum
34 Park Village West
35 Park Village East
36 London Zoo
37 Zoo/Little Venice Waterbus
38 Regent's Canal
N
PRIMROSE HILL
PRINCE ALBERT ROAD
REGENT'S CANAL
OUTER CIRCLE
HANNOVER GATE
HANNOVER TERRACE
SUSSEX PLACE
OUTER CIRCLE
CORNWALL TERRACE
CLARENCE TERRACE
BAKER STREET
TO MARYLEBONE STATION
BAKER STREET STATION
0 500 1000 feet
0 100 200 300

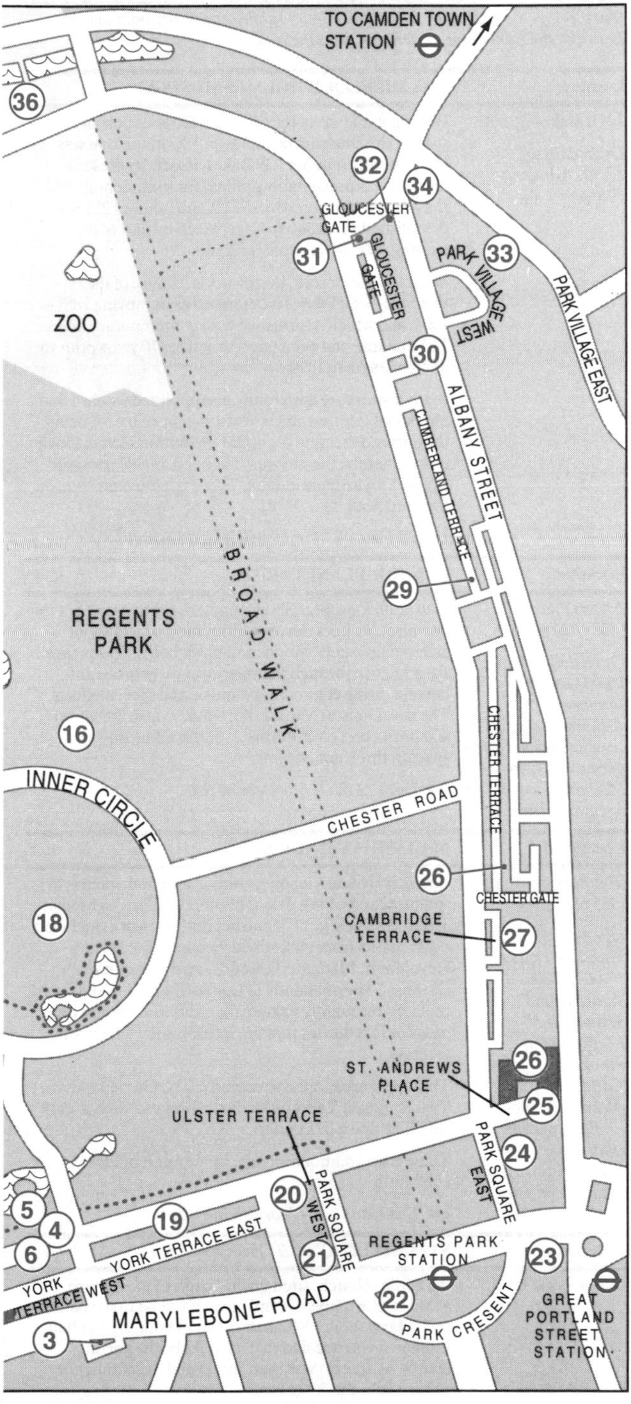
TO CAMDEN TOWN STATION
ZOO
REGENTS PARK
BROAD WALK
GLOUCESTER GATE
GLOUCESTER GATE
PARK VILLAGE WEST
PARK VILLAGE EAST
ALBANY STREET
CUMBERLAND TERRACE
CHESTER TERRACE
CHESTER ROAD
INNER CIRCLE
CHESTER GATE
CAMBRIDGE TERRACE
ST. ANDREWS PLACE
ULSTER TERRACE
PARK SQUARE EAST
PARK SQUARE WEST
YORK TERRACE EAST
YORK TERRACE WEST
MARYLEBONE ROAD
REGENTS PARK STATION
PARK CRESENT
GREAT PORTLAND STREET STATION
36
32
34
31
33
30
29
16
26
18
27
26
25
24
20
5
4
19
6
21
23
22
3

Start *Baker Street Station, Bakerloo, Circle, Jubilee and Metropolitan lines. Leave by the Baker Street exit R and cross the road.*

Location 1	THE SHERLOCK HOLMES MUSEUM
221B Baker Street *Open daily 10.00–17.30. Admission charge.*	Popular with fans of the Sherlock Holmes detective stories, this museum occupies an 18C house that was until recently number 239 Baker Street. Its present number was presumably granted for sentimental reasons: there never was a 221B and number 221 was demolished years ago to be replaced by part of the existing Abbey National Building. What the visitor sees, therefore, is a house of the type that Sherlock Holmes is described as occupying 1881–1904, and which is furnished with contemporary items. The building had been unoccupied for 70 years prior to its conversion in 1990. Many visitors are apparently disappointed to learn that Sherlock Holmes and Dr Watson never existed, being the inspired creations of writer Sir Arthur Conan Doyle; unfortunately, the museum has been unable to obtain Conan Doyle memorabilia. There is a souvenir shop on the third floor. *Exit R. First left Marylebone Road. Cross the road.*

Location 2	LONDON PLANETARIUM
Allsop Place (486 1121) *Open daily 12.20–16.00 (later in summer). Admission charge. A combined ticket also permits entry to Madame Tussaud's at a reduced price.*	Half hour-long 'Star Shows' explore the mysteries of the universe. Visitors discover little-known facts about asteroids, planets, moons and black holes. Shows take the audience through the solar system, galaxies and beyond, using commentary, music and special effects. The new Digistar Mark 2, the world's most advanced star projector, gives the effect of travelling through space in three dimensions. *Exit L. First L Marylebone Rd.*

Location 3	MADAME TUSSAUD'S
Marylebone Road (935 6861) *Open daily: Monday–Friday 10.00–17.30. Saturday and Sunday 09.30–17.30 (later in summer). Admission charge. A combined ticket similarly permits entry to the Planetarium, again at a reduced price.*	As this is Britain's leading visitor attraction, queues in summer can be long. It was founded in Paris by Madame Tussaud's uncle in 1770 and her first waxworks included death masks from guillotined victims of the French Revolution. Madame Tussaud's own museum was established permanently in London in 1835. Exhibits are replaced frequently to keep the exhibition topical but many old favourites remain, including the Chamber of Horrors. Three new areas opened recently: The Garden Party, Two Hundred Years of Madame Tussaud's and a 'dark ride' The Spirit of London. There is no additional charge for any part of the exhibition. *Exit L and cross Marylebone Rd.*

Location 4	ST MARYLEBONE *T. Hardwick 1817*
Marylebone Road	An earlier church, sited on the banks of the Tyburn, St Mary-le-Burn (the stream), gave its name to the parish of St Marylebone. When the present building was half finished it was decided that it would be the parish church. A steeple was then added and the number of portico columns increased. *Enter the church.*

The high altar is at the south end. An apse was added to the church and the choir completely remodelled in 1884.

In the small chapel L of the altar is a nativity painting by *West*.

Apply to an attendant to see the 'Browning Room'.

The poets Robert Browning and Elizabeth Barrett were married clandestinely at St Marylebone in 1841. The 'Browning Room', R of the exit, contains souvenirs of the poet. An 18C bread shelf is also displayed.

Exit ahead. Cross the road to York Gate and enter Regent's Park. Proceed ahead.

Location 5

REGENT'S PARK

Regent's Park is one of the world's most successful fusions of nature and buildings. It occupies most of the old Marylebone Park which was taken by Henry VIII for hunting from Barking Abbey at the Reformation. After the Civil War, Cromwell divided the park into a number of farms. The estate reverted to the Crown in 1811 and the Prince Regent ordered redevelopment. His architect *Nash* planned a garden city with trees, a lake, villas, a royal summer house and an inner circus ringed with houses. Palatial style terraces were to surround the park.

In the event, only eight of the twenty-six villas were built, no terraces appeared around the circus and no royal summer house graced the development. Nevertheless, the park with its trees and lake was laid out and terraces were built around its perimeter. As planned, new thoroughfares linked the park with George IV's soon-to-be-abandoned Carlton House and the whole scheme was completed in 1825. Regent's Park now accommodates London Zoo and is bounded on the north side by the Regent's Canal.

Although the terraces have been restored externally, most of their interiors have been remodelled. They stretch clockwise around Outer Circle from the north-east to the south-west of the park. Some were designed by *Decimus Burton,* the young architect son of James Burton who financed and built much of the scheme, but Nash had to approve all the work. Every terrace was completed in the 1820s and named after the sons of George III. Only three of the original detached villas remain – Hanover Lodge, The Holme and St John's Lodge.

Just before the bridge, follow the footpath L by the side of the lake.

Location 6

REGENT'S PARK LAKE

The lake is fed by the Tyburn stream which now flows in a conduit below the ground. Forty skaters died here in 1867 when the ice broke.

Proceed in a clockwise direction almost to the end of the lake.

The terraces are described in the order passed.

Location 7

YORK TERRACE WEST

Nash originally designed this, together with York Terrace East, as one unbroken block, but in the event divided it to retain a view of St Marylebone Church.

Location 8	**CORNWALL TERRACE** *Burton*
	This was the first terrace to be built, although it was preceded by Nash's Park Crescent.
Location 9	**CLARENCE TERRACE** *Burton*
	The facade of this rebuilt terrace is a facsimile of the original. From here can be seen the bandstand on the opposite side of the lake.
Location 10	**REGENT'S PARK BANDSTAND**
	A terrorist bomb exploded just outside this bandstand in 1982 killing five people.
Location 11	**SUSSEX PLACE**
	With its cupolas, this is the most distinctive of all the terraces. Nash incorporated features from his own unused designs for rebuilding the Prince Regent's Carlton House.
Location 12	**HANOVER TERRACE AND HANOVER GATE**
	The terrace is visible from the park; Hanover Gate is a small lodge that can only be seen from Park Road.
Location 13	**THE LONDON MOSQUE** *Gibberd 1977*
	The mosque, with its dome and minaret, was built on the site of North Villa.
Location 14	**HANOVER LODGE**
	This villa, now part of Bedford College, lies next to the mosque. It can only be seen from the road and even then is completely hidden by trees in summer. •● *At the children's pond cross the lake by the bridge R.* From the bridge there is a view L, when the trees are bare, of Winfield House.
Location 15	**WINFIELD HOUSE**
	The house was built in 1936 for the Woolworth heiress Barbara Hutton (Winfield was the second name of the founder, F. W. Woolworth) but is now the official residence of US ambassadors. It occupies the site of Hertford Villa. The clock from the old church of St Dunstan-in-the-West, Fleet Street, was acquired in 1830 for Hertford Villa which was then renamed St Dunstan's Villa. In 1917 the building became a home for the sightless and gave its name to St Dunstan's Institute for the Blind. The clock was returned to the church in 1930 and the villa was demolished a few years later. •● *Cross the bridge.* The point is now reached from where boats may be hired on the lake in summer. From here there is a view R, if the trees are bare, of The Holme which overlooks the lake.
Location 16	**THE HOLME** *Burton 1818*
	This villa, the second to be built, was designed by the eighteen-year-old architect as a residence for his father. The Holme became a private house once more in 1984. Its east facade is seen later.

Continue ahead following the north side of the lake. Cross the lake again by the next bridge.

Ahead L can be seen St John's Lodge.

Location 17	**ST JOHN'S LODGE** *Raffield 1818*
	This was the first villa to be constructed and, surprisingly, neither Nash nor Burton was the architect.
	First R Inner Circle. Pass the entrance to The Holme (location 15) and cross the road. Enter Queen Mary's Gardens (location 18). Turn R. Pass the south (Jubilee) gate and proceed to the small lake.
	Alternatively, if visiting the Open Air Theatre, take the first path L after entering the gardens and proceed northward.
Location 18	**REGENT'S PARK OPEN AIR THEATRE**
(935 1537)	Plays have been performed here since 1932.
Open summer evenings only (dependent on weather).	*Return southward. Pass the south (Jubilee) gate and proceed to the small lake.*
Location 19	**QUEEN MARY'S GARDEN**
	Until disbanded in 1932, the Royal Botanic Society leased this section of the park. Queen Mary, consort of George V, then instigated its conversion to the garden which is named to commemorate her.
	Follow the path anti-clockwise around the small lake.
	The fossil wood is passed on the north side.
	In summer the display of roses is famous.
	Return to the south (Jubilee) gate and exit from the garden. Cross the road and proceed ahead following the road to York Bridge. Cross the bridge. Follow the first path L and continue through the park.
Location 20	**YORK TERRACE EAST**
	This, the first terrace R, is the twin of York Terrace West passed earlier.
Location 21	**ULSTER TERRACE**
	Ulster Terrace is the smallest in the Regent's Park development.
	Exit from the park first R. Continue ahead to Park Square West (the street).
Location 22	**PARK SQUARE WEST**
	Park Square replaced the north section of the circus that was planned by Nash but never built.
	Proceed ahead and cross Marylebone Rd to Park Crescent.
Location 23	**PARK CRESCENT**
	This crescent, which marked the beginning of the entire scheme, represents the south section of the planned circus. A new parish church was originally to have stood in the centre. However, it was eventually decided that St Marylebone, under construction further west, would be improved to provide this. The crescent has been completely rebuilt as a replica but the gates, which once closed both ends, have not been replaced.

Follow the crescent to the end. First R Marylebone Rd. Proceed to the wall, facing Marylebone Road at the east side of Park Crescent.

Location 24

J. F. KENNEDY MEMORIAL *Lipchitz 1965*

The monument was unveiled by the President's brothers Robert and Edward.

Cross Marylebone Road and turn L. First R Park Square East.

Location 25

PARK SQUARE EAST

The three central properties originally housed the Diorama, a 19C entertainment that opened here in 1823. Dioramas were in vogue until the invention of the cinema.

First R St Andrew's Place.

Location 26

ST ANDREW'S PLACE

The south and east sides were designed by *Nash*.

Return to the corner building R.

Location 27

ROYAL COLLEGE OF PHYSICIANS *Lasdun 1964*

11 St Andrew's Place

This modern building includes the Censor's room which incorporates 17C panelling, brought here from the college's earlier premises in the City.

Cross Outer Circle and re-enter the park at the south-east corner. Follow the path R. Take the first exit R. Cross the road. Cambridge Terrace lies R of Chester Gate (the street) immediately ahead.

Location 28

CAMBRIDGE TERRACE

Following restoration this terrace again stretches to Chester Gate.

Proceed ahead along Chester Gate (the street). First L Chester Terrace (the street). Pass through the arch.

Location 29

CHESTER TERRACE

This is the longest unbroken facade of all the terraces. Its builder, Burton, originally embellished the facade with statues. However, he and Nash were not by then on the best of terms and the architect insisted that they were removed. He did, however, permit them at Cumberland Terrace which follows.

Proceed ahead and pass through the second arch. R Cumberland Place. L Chester Place. L and first R Cumberland Terrace (the street). Enter the garden and continue to the end.

Location 30

CUMBERLAND TERRACE

With its decorative reliefs and statues, this has been judged the most impressive example of all Nash's work. The terrace is pre-eminent because it was intended to provide a vista for the Prince Regent's proposed summer palace.

Leave the garden at the north end. First R Outer Circle. First R St Katherine's Precinct.

Location 31	**DANISH CHURCH** *Poynter 1829*
St Katherine's Precinct	This Gothic Revival church was originally the chapel of St Katherine's Hospital which had been founded near the Tower of London by Queen Matilda in 1147. The hospital moved to Regent's Park as its buildings were demolished for the construction of St Katherine's Dock in 1825. Some of the fittings from the old chapel were installed in the present building. St Katherine's Church was taken over by London's Danish community in 1958. In the garden R is a replica of Denmark's Jelling runic stone. The private houses flanking the church were built as residential blocks for hospital staff. The hospital was destroyed in the Second World War. *Return to Outer Circle R. First R Gloucester Gate. On the south corner R is Gloucester Lodge.*

Location 32	**GLOUCESTER LODGE**
	Gloucester Lodge, together with Gloucester Gate Lodge opposite, represents the northern limit of Nash's buildings surrounding the park. *Ahead Parkway. Second R Albert St.*

Location 33	**JEWISH MUSEUM**
129/31 Albert Street *Open Sunday–Thursday 10.00–16.00. Admission charge.*	Transferred here from Bloomsbury in 1994, the new museum is greatly expanded. Of particular interest are the many Jewish ceremonial items exhibited. These include a 16C Venetian ark and antique circumcision equipment. *Return to Parkway L. Third L. Albany St. First L Park Village West.*

Location 34	**PARK VILLAGE WEST**
	This curving street, judged one of London's prettiest, was commenced by *Nash* 1824 but completed by *Pennethorne*. It begins with detached villas and ends with a terrace which is entirely the work of James Pennethorne. He was the adopted son of Mrs Nash and eventually took over much of Nash's practice. *Return to Albany St R. First R Park Village East.*

Location 35	**PARK VILLAGE EAST**
	Although built at the same time as Park Village West, its houses are semi-detached; some of London's earliest examples. The east side was demolished in 1906 for the railway. *Return to Gloucester Gate and re-enter the park. Follow the path ahead towards London Zoo. Proceed R along Broad Walk. First L Outer Circle. Continue ahead to the main entrance to London Zoo L.*

Location 36	**LONDON ZOO (ZOOLOGICAL SOCIETY OF LONDON)**
Regent's Park (722 3333) *Open daily March–October. Monday–Saturday 10.00–17.30 (or dusk, whichever is earlier).*	Sir Stamford Raffles, the founder of Singapore, conceived the Zoological Society and became its first president in 1826. The gardens were opened to members, on a five-acre site within Regent's Park, shortly after his death in 1827. The layout and buildings were by *Burton*. All that remains of his work are the Tunnel, Terrace Walk, Giraffe House (remodelled), old Ravens' Cage and the Clock Tower from the old

November–February daily 10.00–16.00. Admission charge. Visitors are advised of the timing of daily events on arrival.

Elephant bathing April–September, daily.

Feeding daily April–September.

Rides in the Riding Square Easter to September, daily, 13.30–15.45, llama cart, pony and trap and camels.

Camel House. This, the world's oldest zoo, was opened to the public in 1847 on Mondays and Tuesdays only. The entrance fee of 1/- (5p) was kept until 1942. London Zoo now covers 36 acres. Major sights include: elephant bathing, lion terraces, the Children's Zoo, where animals may be stroked and nocturnal animals in the Clore Pavilion's 'Moonlight World'.

●● *From the main entrance proceed clockwise.*

Passed in the following order are:

North-west side: Apes.

South-east corner: Lions, tigers.

South-west side: Children's Zoo, penguins, elephants/rhinos, storks, reptiles.

North-west side: Aquarium.

●● *Proceed through the tunnel.*

Camels/llamas, giraffes/zebras, cattle, oryx.

●● *Cross the bridge R.*

Snowdon Aviary, owls, cranes/geese.

●● *Cross the bridge R.*

Insects, otters, mammals, 'Moonlight World'.

●● *Proceed to the boat landing-stage R, opposite the Snowdon Aviary, for the Waterbus to Little Venice and the Zoo's boat* Invicta (Summer only).

●● *Alternatively, cross the bridge R to the Prince Albert Road exit. Take bus 274 westward to Baker Street Station, Bakerloo, Circle, Jubilee and Metropolitan lines.*

Location 37

ZOO/LITTLE VENICE WATERBUS

(286 6101)

Operates from Easter to late summer. The last boat leaves at 17.25 (Sunday and Bank Holidays 18.30).

The boat travels south-westward along the Regent's Canal to Little Venice.

Location 38

REGENT'S CANAL *Morgan 1820*

At Little Venice, the canal links with the main Grand Union Canal that runs northward to the Midlands. Eastward it joins the Thames at Limehouse. Beneath Macclesfield Bridge, the second bridge passed westward, the *Tilbury*, a barge loaded with gunpowder, exploded in 1874, killing its crew of three and destroying the bridge.

●● *Leave the Waterbus R and proceed to Warwick Avenue Station, Bakerloo line.*

Itinerary 20

20

Chelsea

This comprehensive tour includes the Royal Hospital, Chelsea's 'village' and the fashionable King's Road.

Timing: Mornings are preferable. King's Road is at its liveliest on Saturday. The Royal Hospital's hall and chapel close 12.00–14.00. Chelsea Old Church closes on Saturday at 13.00 and all day Monday. Carlyle's House is closed Monday and Tuesday and all winter. Chelsea Physic Garden is open Sunday and Wednesday afternoons from mid-April to mid-October.

20

Locations

1 Sloane Square Station
2 Peter Jones
3 Duke of York's Headquarters
4 Royal Avenue
5 Burton's Court
6 St Leonard's Terrace
7 Royal Hospital
8 National Army Museum
9 Oscar Wilde's House
10 Chelsea Physic Garden
11 Cheyne Walk (east section)
12 Cadogan Pier
13 Crosby Hall
14 Cheyne Walk (west section)
15 Chelsea Old Church
16 Chelsea Village
17 Lawrence Street
18 No 51 Glebe Place
19 Carlyle's House
20 King's Road
21 Argyll House
22 Nos 213 and 215 King's Road
23 Nos 229 and 231 King's Road
24 Nos 119–123 Sydney Street
25 St Luke
26 The Pheasantry
27 Holy Trinity

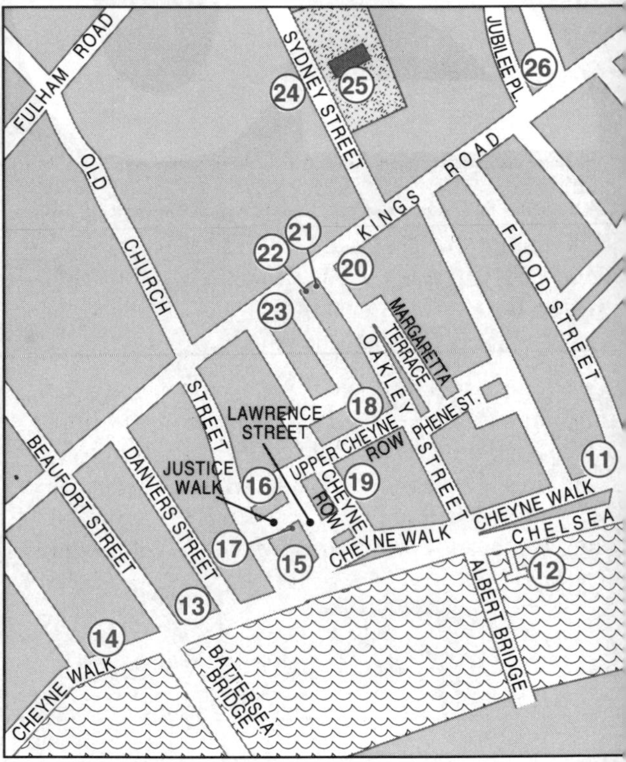

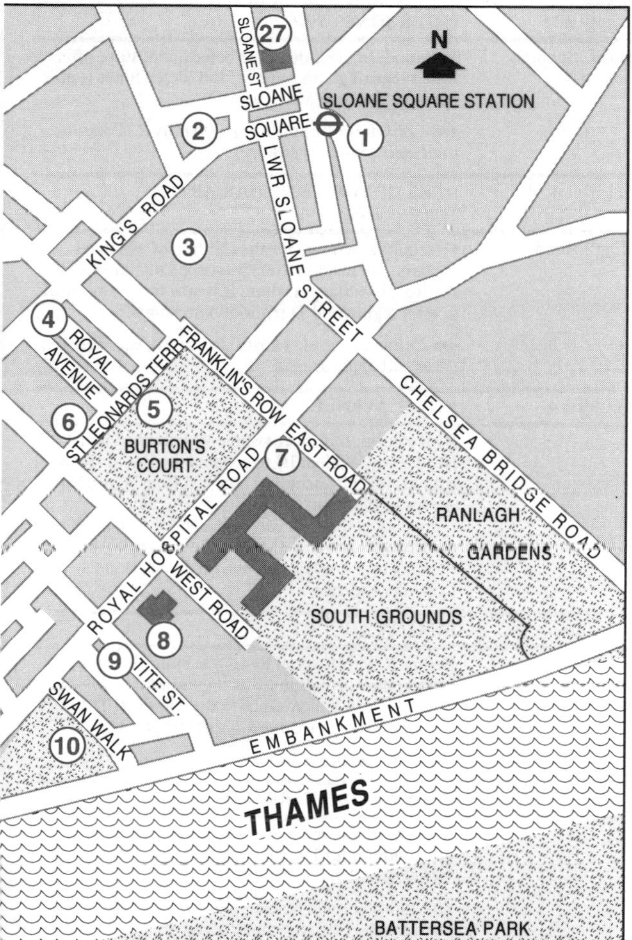

Start *Sloane Square Station, Circle and District lines. Remain on the platform. No other underground station serves Chelsea, but frequent buses run along the King's Road to Sloane Square and the West End.*

Location 1

SLOANE SQUARE STATION

This Underground station is remarkable for the cast-iron conduit, running above the lines at high level, which carries the Westbourne, one of London's streams that now flow below ground.

Exit to Sloane Square and proceed ahead to King's Road (location 20). Cross the road.

Location 2

PETER JONES *1936*

Sloane Square

This modern, well-designed department store offers a wide range of goods but not food. Peter Jones is now open on Saturday afternoons.

Leave by any of the King's Rd exits R. Cross the road and continue westward.

Location 3

DUKE OF YORK'S HEADQUARTERS *Saunders 1801*

King's Road

First built as a home for the children of widowed soldiers, the headquarters was originally known as the Royal Military Asylum. It is now the premises of several regimental Territorial Army units.

Continue ahead. Third L Royal Avenue. Proceed to the end of the avenue.

Location 4

ROYAL AVENUE

By tradition, this short avenue was planned in the late 17C by William III to connect the Royal Hospital with his recently acquired house at Kensington (?). It got no further than King's Road. The oldest remaining houses are early 19C. and the first half of the east side L is a modern reproduction. Writer Ian Fleming chose Royal Avenue for James Bond's London residence.

Location 5

BURTON'S COURT

Before Royal Hospital Road was built, this green formed the north grounds of the hospital and its 18C gate was the main entrance to the complex. The posts are surmounted by carved martial trophies.

R St Leonard's Terrace.

Location 6

ST LEONARD'S TERRACE

St Leonard's Terrace provided surprisingly tranquil surroundings for Dracula's Irish creator, Bram Stoker, who lived at No 29.

The mid-Georgian houses, Nos 31–39 *c.*1765, are judged to be Chelsea's finest terrace.

At No 39 return eastward and proceed to the end of the terrace.

The portico of The Duke of York's Headquarters lies ahead.

R Franklin's Row. Enter the Royal Hospital grounds through the gate ahead (London Gate).

Location 7

ROYAL HOSPITAL *Wren 1692*

Royal Hospital Road
(730 0161)

The grounds and courtyards are open Monday–Saturday 10.00 until dusk. Sunday 14.00 until dusk.

The Royal Hospital, founded by Charles II, is a residence and infirmary for army pensioners. Infirm soldiers, once cared for in monastic hostels, had been neglected since these were disbanded at the Reformation. Stephen Fox, the first Paymaster General of the Army, together with the diarist John Evelyn, proposed that a military hospital should be built in London. Charles II was the first English monarch to establish a regular army and he, inspired by Louis XIV's Hotel des Invalides in Paris, and

Ranelagh Gardens close 12.45–14.00.

The Great Hall, museum and chapel are open Monday–Saturday, 10.00–12.00 and 14.00–16.00. Sunday 14.00–16.00.

The Council Chamber is also open at the above times but not Saturday or Sunday or when in use. Telephone for confirmation.

The public may attend Parade Service held in the chapel every Sunday at 11.00.

Admission throughout is free (apart from the Chelsea Flower Show).

allegedly encouraged by Nell Gwyn (?), presented the site for that purpose. Wren was appointed architect in 1682; the complex took ten years to build and when completed provided accommodation for 476 men.

Over four hundred pensioners still live here and wear blue or scarlet 18C uniforms. The Founder's Day Parade is held every June to celebrate Charles II's return to London on his birthday, 29 May 1660. It is known as Oak Apple Day to commemorate Charles's escape from Cromwell's troops by hiding in an oak apple tree in 1651. The parade is usually attended by a member of the Royal Family and may be seen by invitation only.

•➡ *Continue along East Road and cross the road to the* **museum** *(fourth door L).*

This forms part of the hospital's administrative east range added by *Soane* in 1819.

In the entrance hall is the table on which the Duke of Wellington's body lay in state in the Great Hall in 1852.

Photographs and pensioners' medals are displayed within the museum.

•➡ *Exit L. Proceed to the gate (Garden Gate) and enter South Grounds. Enter Ranelagh Gardens first L. Proceed to the central summer house.*

Ranelagh Gardens. Here, and in South Grounds, the Chelsea Flower Show has been held every May since 1913. These gardens were public pleasure grounds from 1724–1805. The summer house stands on the site of the 18C rotunda, where fashionable entertainments were held. See the descriptive panels.

•➡ *Return to Garden Gate and East Road. First L* **Light Horse Court.**

The north wing R was destroyed by bombs in 1918, rebuilt and again destroyed in 1945, this time by a rocket. It has once more been rebuilt as a replica.

The lamp standard in the centre of the court covers a well.

•➡ *Proceed ahead to the south-west corner of the court. Enter the building and continue to the* **Council Chamber** *(second door L).*

The Council Chamber can only be seen accompanied by a pensioner on official duty (always in scarlet).

The panelling and fireplace are original.

Charles II's chair and foot stool are displayed.

•➡ *Exit L and proceed ahead to* **Figure Court.** *Turn R and proceed northward.*

The construction of the Royal Hospital began here. In the centre is the bronze 'figure' of Charles II by *Gibbons,* which gave this court its name.

•➡ *Continue to the portico and enter the north range. Ascend the stairs R to the* **chapel.**

The woodwork throughout is original and the altar rail was carved by *W. Emmet.*

The painting on the coved section of the ceiling, 'The Resurrection', is by *Ricci.*

Exit, descend the stairs and ascend the stairs immediately ahead to the **Great Hall.**

Wellington was laid in state here in 1852. Too many were admitted to pay their respects and some were killed in the crush.

Leather five-gallon bombards (flagons for water or ale) are generally displayed. The dining tables are original but have all been divided in two.

The mural depicting Charles II was painted by *Verrio* and *Cooke*.

Exit and descend the stairs. Turn R and proceed R through the colonnade to **College Court** *ahead.*

The central lamp standard is identical to that in Light Horse Court.

Continue ahead and exit from the north-west corner of the court towards West Road R. Before the gate L are the old **stables.**

These were designed by *Soane* in 1814; they now serve as a storehouse.

Exit through the gates. L Royal Hospital Road.

Location 8

NATIONAL ARMY MUSEUM

Royal Hospital Road

Open daily 10.00–17.00. Admission free.

This modern building houses an exhibition of the British Army's history from 1485 to the present day – including the Gulf War.

Exit L Royal Hospital Road. First L Tite Street. Cross the road.

Location 9

OSCAR WILDE'S HOUSE

34 Tite Street

Oscar Wilde, the wit and dramatist, lived here with his wife from 1884 until his trial in 1895.

Return to Royal Hospital Road L. Second L Swan Walk. Cross the road and enter the Physic Garden.

Location 10

CHELSEA PHYSIC GARDEN

Royal Hospital Road (352 5646)

Open mid-April to mid-October. Wednesday and Sunday 14.00–17.00. Also during the Chelsea Flower Show 12.00–17.00. Admission charge.

Founded in 1673 by the Apothecaries Society, this was the second botanical garden to be established in England (Oxford's was first). The land eventually became the property of Sir Hans Sloane, who was himself a botanist and president of the Royal Society.

Approximately 7,000 varieties of plant are grown within the four-acre garden. They are now used mainly for teaching purposes. Cotton seeds from here probably helped to create the cotton industry in the southern USA.

The tall olive tree often bears fruit, due to Chelsea's warm micro-climate.

In the garden is a faded 18C statue of Sloane by *Rysbrack*. The rock garden is the oldest in Britain.

Return to Royal Hospital Road L. Third R Cheyne Walk.

Location 11

CHEYNE WALK (EAST SECTION)

Many houses were built early in the 18C and some of their cast iron gates and railings are outstanding; Nos

5 and 14–16 possess the finest examples. Rosetti occupied No 16, Tudor House, in 1862 and this then became a meeting place for the Pre-Raphaelites.

Henry VIII's Manor House, built in 1537, occupied the site of Nos 19–26 and survived until it was demolished following the death of its owner, Sir Hans Sloane, in 1753. The present houses were built *c.*1760.

At No 24 cross the road to Cadogan Pier.

Location 12

CADOGAN PIER

Chelsea Embankment

The apprentice Watermen's race, rowed from London Bridge to this pier in late July, is probably England's oldest annually contested event (?). It originated in 1715 to celebrate the accession to the throne of George I, and was sponsored by Thomas Doggett, joint manager of Drury Lane Theatre. The King was a Whig supporter and Doggett made a bequest for a coat of orange (the Whig colour) and a silver arm badge depicting the white horse of Hanover, to be presented annually to the winner. The race, organized by the Fishmongers Company, has been known as 'Doggett's coat and badge' ever since. Many followers still wear 18C. dress.

From this pier, also in July, Roman Catholics re-enact Sir Thomas More's last journey from his Chelsea house to the Tower of London and eventual execution. More's private landing stage was, however, slightly further west, approximately where Battersea Bridge now stands.

Return to Cheyne Walk L. Cross Oakley St and continue ahead to Chelsea Old Church.

The large monument in the churchyard R commemorates Sir Hans Sloane, d.1753, by *Wilton.* Return to view the church later (location 15).

Continue ahead to the Danvers St junction (second R). Crosby Hall is on the west corner ahead. Enter its garden.

Location 13

CROSBY HALL *1466*

Chelsea Embankment

The stone-built Crosby Hall formed part of wool merchant Sir John Crosby's 15C City residence, Crosby Place. It was carefully dismantled at its original Bishopsgate site in 1910 and rebuilt here on what was once part of the gardens of Sir Thomas More's house. Until recently Crosby Hall was a training school, but is now a private residence and no longer open to the public

When Crosby died in 1475, Crosby Place had become the tallest private residence in London. It was then occupied by Richard III and later, Thomas More. Crosby Hall escaped the Great Fire but was last used domestically in 1672. After a fire in 1674 had destroyed the rest of the house, the hall was converted to a chapel. In 1769 it became a warehouse and later a restaurant.

Most of the external stonework has been renewed and the original material is obvious from its worn appearance. The stairway is an addition.

Continue westward to the Beaufort St junction (first R). No 91 is on the west corner ahead.

Location 14

CHEYNE WALK (WEST SECTION)

On the Beaufort Street corner Nos 91–92, 1771, possess large Venetian windows. No 91 has been attributed to *Adam* (?).

Proceed along Cheyne Walk.

Lindsey House, Nos 96–101, is the oldest residence in Chelsea. It was built in 1674 on the site of Thomas More's farm, as a mansion for the third Earl of Lindsey, but is now subdivided. The stuccoed facade was originally of undecorated brickwork.

No 96 was one of many Chelsea residences occupied by the American painter, Whistler.

Continue ahead.

Turner, the painter, spent his last years anonymously as 'Puggy Booth' at No 119 and died there in 1851. The house has been much remodelled.

Return eastward to the Old Church St junction (third L).

Immediately ahead, facing the river, is one of London's most ornate lamp standards. It depicts two climbing boys and was cast to commemorate the opening of the Chelsea Embankment in 1874.

Proceed to the church.

Location 15

CHELSEA OLD CHURCH*

Old Church Street

Open Sunday, and Tuesday–Friday 11.00–13.00 and 14.00–17.00. Saturday 11.00–13.00.

Most of the church was destroyed by bombs and the nave and tower have been completely rebuilt. However, sections of the walls of the 13C chancel and the 14C Lawrence Chapel, together with practically all of the 14C More Chapel, were saved and it was also possible to restore most of the monuments. There is a tradition that Henry VIII secretly married Jane Seymour here in 1536, immediately after Anne Boleyn had been beheaded (?). This was Chelsea's parish church until 1820.

Enter and turn L.

Nave (north side). The font was made in 1673, but its cover is a reproduction.

Stained glass in the west window of the north wall is 17C Flemish.

The monument to Lady Jane Cheyne 1699, in the niche just before the chancel, was carved by *P. Bernini,* the son, or nephew (?), of the great Italian sculptor. The figure is by *Raggi.*

The 17C Jervoise memorial R is designed as a Roman arch.

Proceed ahead to the **Lawrence Chapel.**

Stained glass L in the west window is 16C German or Flemish (?).

Facing the window, the monument to Sarah Colville, d.1631, depicts her shrouded figure.

Turn L and proceed to the east wall.

The Stanley monument 1632, with its realistically carved children's busts, provides an early English example of Renaissance sculpture.

Above R, the small monument to Thomas Lawrence 1593 includes an alabaster group of the goldsmith's family.

Proceed to the **chancel.**

On the north wall L of the altar is the monument to Thomas Hungerford, d.1581, and his wife.

Against the south wall, R of the altar, is the Sir Thomas More monument 1532. His two wives are buried in the tomb. More wrote the epitaph himself, intending to lie here also, but his headless body was almost certainly buried in the Chapel of St Peter ad Vincula within the Tower of London following his execution on Tower Green in 1535. More's head, which was kept by his daughter, Margaret Roper, at her home in Eltham, is buried at St Dunstan, Canterbury.

Proceed R to the pulpit.

The pulpit *c.*1690 is judged to be one of London's finest.

Proceed south-eastward to the **More Chapel.**

This chapel almost entirely escaped Second World War bomb damage. Although built in 1325, it was remodelled in 1528 for More, who worshipped here

The columns that support the arch from the chancel have Renaissance capitals, made in the French style. They were part of the 1528 remodelling and represent some of England's earliest Renaissance work. It has been alleged that *Holbein* designed them (?).

In the south-east corner L, is the tomb of Jane Guildford, Duchess of Northumberland, made in 1555; she was the mother-in-law of Lady Jane Grey.

A wall tablet commemorates the American-born writer Henry James. He became a British citizen and died at Chelsea in 1916.

Proceed westward along the nave.

Nave (south side). The huge wall monument commemorates Gregory, Lord Dacre, d.1594.

The west window on the south wall incorporates 17C Flemish stained glass.

In front of this window are chained 17C and early 18C volumes, the only examples in a London church. They were presented by Sir Hans Sloane.

The window on the west wall incorporates a 17C German stained glass cartouche.

Exit R.

Location 16

CHELSEA VILLAGE

Due to its many grand houses, Chelsea in the early 18C was called 'a village of palaces'. The only buildings that remain from this period are the Royal Hospital, fragments of Chelsea Old Church and Lindsey House. However, many Georgian and early Victorian streets still give parts of Chelsea a 'village' character. Some of the most attractive are seen between locations 16–20. Plaques on the houses indicate Chelsea's popularity with writers and artists.

First R Justice Walk. Proceed ahead to Lawrence Street.

Location 17

LAWRENCE STREET

Much of this street occupies the site of Chelsea's original Manor House which was demolished in 1704 when Lawrence Street was laid out. The street's name commemorates Thomas Lawrence, a 16C owner of the manor.

Immediately ahead, facing Justice Walk, are Nos 23 and 24. They are early 18C and their doors unusually share one pediment.

Proceed R towards the river.

At the end of the street is the **Cross Keys**, one of Chelsea's few pubs that retain a partly Victorian interior. There is a rear patio for summer drinking and snacks.

Return northward to No 16 in the north-west corner.

A plaque outside No 16 records the **Chelsea Porcelain Works** 1745–84.

R Upper Cheyne Row. First L Glebe Place. Follow the bend and continue ahead to No 51.

Location 18

NO 51 GLEBE PLACE

The cottage, with its pantiled mansard roof, is one of Chelsea's most picturesque, but claims that this was once Henry VIII's hunting lodge are unsupported. It was probably built *c.*1715, as the entrance to old Cheyne House, constructed at that time, once stood nearby.

Return to Upper Cheyne Row. Continue ahead to Cheyne Row. Carlyle's House, No 24, is on the east side L.

Location 19

CARLYLE'S HOUSE *1708*

24 Cheyne Row (352 7087)

Open April–October, Wednesday to Saturday 11.00–17.00. Sunday 14.00–17.00. Admission charge.

Thomas Carlyle, a once fashionable writer of historical books, lived here from 1834 until his death in 1881. His wife Jane was responsible for the decor, much of which remains. She lived here with him until her earlier death in 1866, but their marriage was renowned for its turbulence.

Carlyle's house, including many of his possessions, was opened as a museum in 1895. The painting, 'A Chelsea Interior', which illustrates the ground floor parlour as it appeared in 1857 and now hangs there, shows how little the appearance of the room has changed.

Exit R. First R Upper Cheyne Row. R Oakley St. First L Phene St. First L Margaretta Terrace. R Oakley St. L. King's Rd.

Location 20

KING'S ROAD

King's Road was laid out shortly after the Restoration as a private royal path for Charles II. Officially, its function was to enable the King to reach Hampton Court more easily from Whitehall Palace. By tradition, however, a more important aim was to provide a direct route to Nell Gwyn's house at Fulham (?). Local tenants were given access in the 18C but the general public were not allowed to use the road until George IV opened it in 1830. Although undistinguished architecturally, King's Road is famed for the advanced fashions adopted by some of its youthful devotees, best exhibited on Saturday afternoons. There are many boutiques and pubs.

Continue westward to the second house.

Location 21

ARGYLL HOUSE *Leoni 1723*

311 King's Road

Argyll House was designed in Palladian style by *Leoni,* a Venetian protégé of Lord Burlington. It was named by the Duke of Argyll who lived here from 1769 to 1770. Initials on the gate 'JP' were those of the first owner John Perrin. The house is little altered either externally or internally.

Proceed to the two adjoining houses.

Location 22

NOS 213 AND 215 KING'S ROAD *1720*

Arne, the composer of 'Rule Britannia', and Ellen Terry, the actress, lived at No 215.

Continue westward.

Location 23

NOS 229 AND 231 KING'S ROAD *1620* (?)

These adjacent shops are reputed, but without evidence, to date from 1620 (?). If so, they have been much altered. It is said that the buildings once faced south rather than the King's Road which they would have pre-dated.

Return eastward along King's Road. Third L Sydney St.

Location 24

NOS 119–123 SYDNEY STREET

All the windows of this early 19C terrace have been renewed but No 119, now a restaurant, possesses one of London's most delicate Regency doorways.

Cross the road L.

Location 25

ST LUKE *Savage 1820*

Sydney Street

St Luke's was London's first church to be designed in the Gothic Revival style. It was built as Chelsea's new parish church because Chelsea Old Church was no longer big enough. Charles Dickens married here in 1836.

Exit L. Second L King's Rd. Proceed ahead to the Pheasantry just past the Jubilee Place corner (third L).

Location 26

THE PHEASANTRY

152 King's Road

The original house was built in 1765 and therefore could have had no connection with Charles II, as has often been alleged. Pheasants were bred here from 1865 to 1878 and the building has retained the name 'Pheasantry' for much of its life.

It was acquired in the late 19C by the French Joubert family, furniture manufacturers and interior designers, who extended and remodelled the premises to resemble a 17C French mansion. From 1917 to 1932 Princess Astafieva leased part of the house for a Russian ballet school; her pupils included Markova, Fonteyn and Anna Neagle. Diaghilev used the school's premises for rehearsals. The Joubert family sold the property in 1932 and it then became the Pheasantry Club, a dining venue for 'intelligent bohemians' who included Augustus John and Dylan Thomas. This closed in 1968. Following resistance by conservationists, the threatened exterior of the Pheasantry was saved and it re-opened in 1983 housing a restaurant, café and cocktail bar.

The gateway, modelled on the Arc du Carrousel in Paris, was reputedly added in the mid-19C (?). Its bronze quadrega (horses and charioteer) and the two bronze caryatids (painted in error) have recently been restored.

The eagles on either side of the forecourt are probably those which stood at the entrance to the adjacent Box Farm, demolished in 1900 (?).

The present facade of the Pheasantry dates from the remodelling by the Jouberts in 1881, which included the ironwork in Louis XV style, and the three white trade plaques.

Continue eastward to Sloane Square. Second L Sloane Street.

Location 27	**HOLY TRINITY** *Sedding 1888*
Sloane Street	The harmonious style, both externally and internally, was influenced by the Pre-Raphaelites.

Stained glass for the east window was made by *William Morris* to a design suggested by *Burne-Jones*.

Exit L. Proceed to Sloane Square and Sloane Square Station, Circle and District lines.

Itinerary 21

21

Kensington Palace and Holland Park

In addition to Kensington Palace, the remains of the Jacobean Holland House are seen and the itinerary begins with the Portobello Road 'flea' market.

Timing: The Portobello Road market is held every Saturday, but Linley Sambourne House is open only on Wednesday and Sunday afternoons.

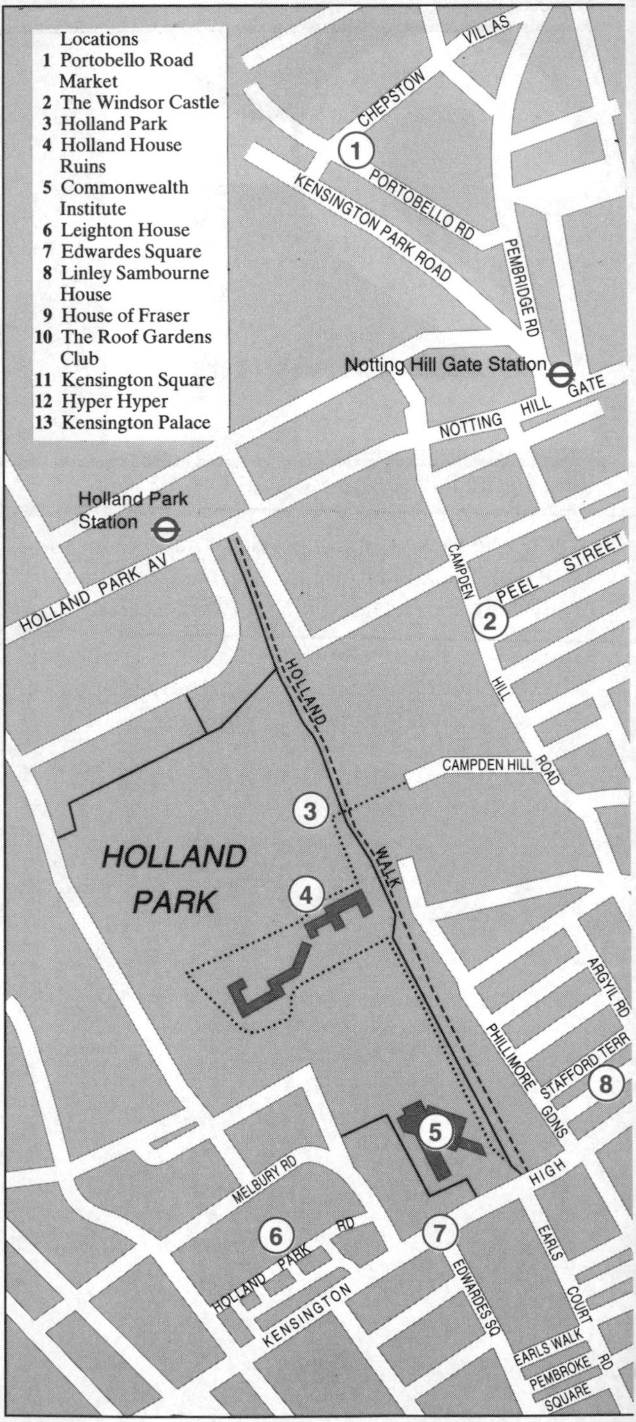
Locations
1 Portobello Road Market
2 The Windsor Castle
3 Holland Park
4 Holland House Ruins
5 Commonwealth Institute
6 Leighton House
7 Edwardes Square
8 Linley Sambourne House
9 House of Fraser
10 The Roof Gardens Club
11 Kensington Square
12 Hyper Hyper
13 Kensington Palace
CHEPSTOW VILLAS
PORTOBELLO RD
KENSINGTON PARK ROAD
PEMBRIDGE RD
Notting Hill Gate Station
NOTTING HILL GATE
Holland Park Station
HOLLAND PARK AV
CAMPDEN HILL
PEEL STREET
HOLLAND WALK
CAMPDEN HILL ROAD
HOLLAND PARK
ARGYLL RD
PHILLIMORE GDNS
STAFFORD TERR
HIGH
MELBURY RD
HOLLAND PARK RD
KENSINGTON
EDWARDES SQ
EARLS COURT RD
EARLS WALK
PEMBROKE SQUARE

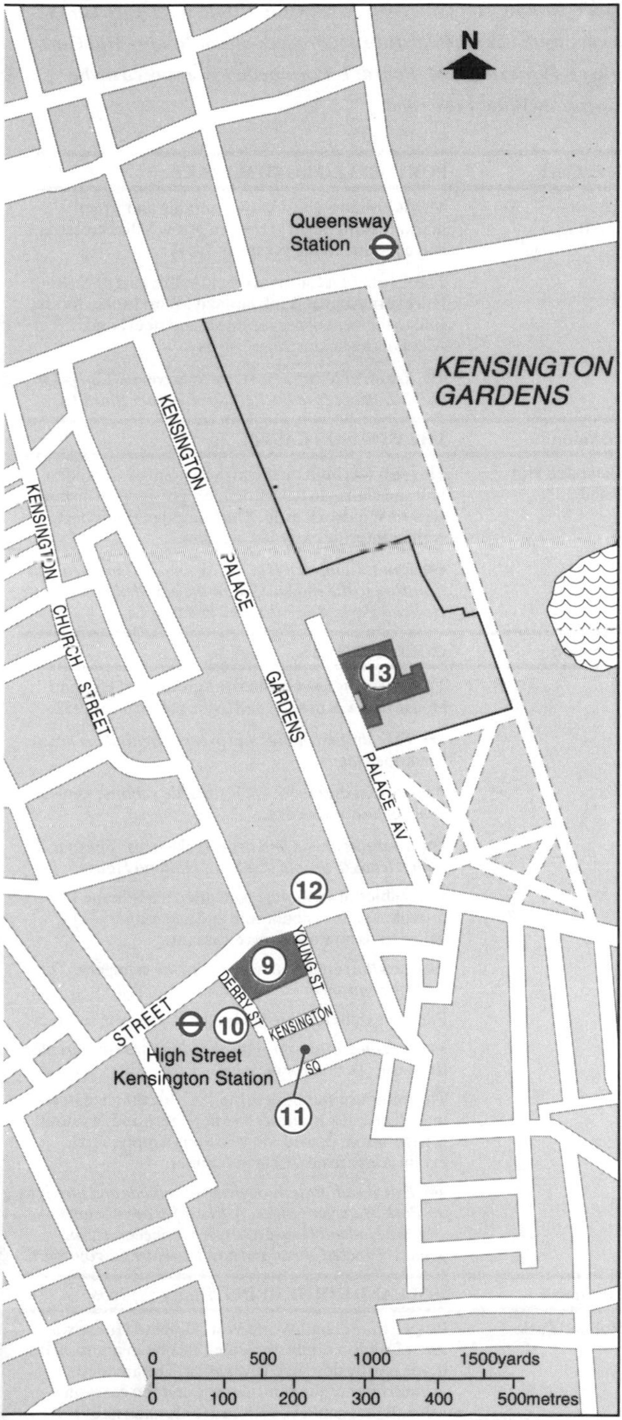
N
Queensway
Station
KENSINGTON
GARDENS
KENSINGTON
PALACE
GARDENS
KENSINGTON
CHURCH
STREET
PALACE
AV
13
12
9
YOUNG ST
DERRY ST
KENSINGTON
SQ
STREET
10
High Street
Kensington Station
11
0
500
1000
1500yards
0
100
200
300
400
500metres

Start *Notting Hill Gate Station, Central, Circle and District lines. Leave by the Pembridge Rd exit. Proceed ahead Notting Hill Gate. First R Pembridge Rd. Fourth L Portobello Rd. Proceed to the Chepstow Villas crossroad.*

Location 1	**PORTOBELLO ROAD MARKET**
Saturday 08.30–16.30	This is London's best known antique and street market. Stalls begin at the Chepstow Villas crossroad and continue to the Westway flyover.

The Caribbean Carnival is held in this part of Notting Hill every August Bank Holiday. West Indian food is sold to the beat of reggae music and steel bands. Alcohol can be purchased all day.

Return to Notting Hill Gate R. Second L Campden Hill Rd. Proceed to the Peel Street corner (third L).

Location 2	**THE WINDSOR CASTLE** *1835*
Campden Hill Road	This pub was built on the highest point of Campden Hill and claims to have originally possessed a distant view of Windsor Castle. The Campden Bar is best, with its internal early 19C window.

Exit L Campden Hill Rd. Second R Campden Hill. Continue to the end and follow the paved alley ahead to Holland Park. Enter the park and turn L.

Location 3	**HOLLAND PARK**

The park originally formed the grounds of Holland House and was not opened to the public until 1952.

Take the first path R and proceed behind the house (described later).

Animals, in the enclosure R, include rabbits, emus, peacocks and chickens.

Continue ahead and descend the steps. The first path L leads to the old **stables** *of Holland House.*

The stables of 1640 were converted early in the 19C to provide a summer ballroom and an orangery. The ballroom is now a luxury restaurant.

Pass the restaurant which joins the **orangery**. *Turn L for the entrance.*

Free art exhibitions are held in the orangery in summer.

Exit and follow the path ahead towards the circular **ice house**. *Turn L for the entrance.*

The ice house was built in the 18C. Ice that had been made naturally in winter was kept here and, without refrigeration, provided a year-long supply. Art exhibitions are now held in summer.

Exit ahead. Pass through the colonnade and turn R to the Park Manager's office. Ask here for permission to view the Holland House courtyard (unnecessary in winter). Proceed ahead and turn L to enter the courtyard.

Location 4	**HOLLAND HOUSE RUINS** *Thorpe* (?) *1605*
Holland Park	Before the Second World War, Holland House was inner London's only remaining Jacobean mansion but it was mostly destroyed by bombs. The arcaded ground floor of the central range and the east wing were all that could be restored (only externally).

The courtyard is open during the winter. Other times by arrangement (602 6016).

Plays are acted here on summer evènings. Telephone for details (633 1706).

Built for a City merchant, Sir Walter Cope, the house became known as 'Cope Castle'. Two wings were added later for his daughter and the residence was renamed Holland House in 1624 when her husband became the first Earl of Holland. Following the Civil War, the house was acquired by General Fairfax as his headquarters. It is alleged that Oliver Cromwell held meetings with the deaf General Ireton in its vast grounds, where his shouted instructions could not be overheard (?). The statesman, Charles James Fox, lived here as a child in the late 18C. Under the 19C ownership of the third Earl of Holland, Holland House became a fashionable social and political centre.

The east wing now forms part of the King George VI Memorial Youth Hostel.

Facing the south facade are the original gate piers by *Inigo Jones,* 1629.

Continue to the east end of the park and take the path R. Proceed to the Commonwealth Institute. Enter the building R.

Location 5

COMMONWEALTH INSTITUTE

Kensington High Street (603 4535)

Open Monday–Saturday 10.00–16.30. Sunday 14.30–17.00. Admission free. There is occasionally an admission charge to special exhibitions.

The Commonwealth Institute evolved from the 19C Imperial Institute, founded at South Kensington. The building, with its distinctive hyperbolic paraboloid roof, was opened in 1962. The institute's aim is to provide information about countries within the British Commonwealth. There are displays for each member, together with an arts centre and a library.

Exit R Kensington High St. First R Melbury Road. First L Holland Park Rd.

Location 6

LEIGHTON HOUSE *Aitchison 1866*

12 Holland Park Road

Open Monday–Saturday 11.00–17.00. Admission free.

The house was built for Lord Leighton. Of greatest interest is the Arab Hall which was added later and tiled with ancient ceramics. Apart from this, Leighton House provides a typical mid-Victorian domestic interior. Free exhibitions are held.

Exit L. Second R Melbury Rd. First L Kensington High St. Second R Edwardes Square. Proceed ahead following the east side of the square.

Location 7

EDWARDES SQUARE *1820*

The east side of the square is little changed. At the far end, the Scarsdale pub, a mid-Victorian addition, has a popular terrace for summer drinking.

Exit L. Second L Pembroke Square. L Earls Court Rd. Fourth R Kensington High St. Second L Phillimore Gardens. Second right Stafford Terrace.

Alternatively, if not viewing Linley Sambourne House (open Wednesday and Sunday only), continue along Kensington High St to Barkers store (location 9).

Location 8	**LINLEY SAMBOURNE HOUSE**
18 Stafford Terrace *Open March–October, Wednesday 10.00–16.00, Sunday 14.00–17.00. Admission charge.*	This mid-Victorian house was the home of Linley Sambourne, *Punch* cartoonist from 1874 to 1911. Its interior possesses London's best example of late Victorian domestic decor. After Sambourne's death, the house was lived in successively from 1911 to 1946 by his son Roy, followed by his niece; miraculously, little was changed. The house, acquired in 1978, is now operated by the Victorian Society. *Exit R. R Argyll Rd. Second L Kensington High Street. Cross the road and proceed ahead, passing High Street Kensington Station, to Barkers store.*

Location 9	**HOUSE OF FRASER**
Kensington High Street	Until recently known as Barkers, this is the last survivor of the thoroughfare's many department stores. It virtually functions as a local version of Selfridges but there is no food store. *Exit to Kensington High St L. First L Derry St. Cross the road to No 99, The Gardens Club. Take the lift to the top floor.*

Location 10	**THE ROOF GARDENS**
99 Derry Street (937 7994) *The restaurant is open to the public but the bar is members only.*	For many years, this was the roof garden of Derry and Toms store. Later it belonged to Biba's and then became Regine's Club. Members of the public are welcome to view these unique London roof gardens. Drinks are served midday, plus lunch and dinner. *Exit R. First L Kensington Square. Continue ahead and turn R following the east side of the square to Nos 11–12 in the south-east corner.*

Location 11	**KENSINGTON SQUARE** *1685*
	This, the first of the Kensington squares, was built, surprisingly, before William III moved into Kensington House nearby. Originally called King's Square, in honour of James II, it was surrounded by fields until 1840. Many of the houses on the south and west sides are original. Nos 11–12 are the least altered. *Return northward and leave the square at Young St ahead. R Kensington High St. Cross the road just before the Royal Gardens Hotel.*

Location 12	**HYPER HYPER**
Kensington High Street	Six caryatids provide an unusual frontage to what is now a collection of boutiques. The ground floor café at the rear occupies a Pullman railway carriage c.1900. *Exit L. Second L Palace Avenue. Proceed through the gates and continue ahead to Kensington Palace. At the road barrier turn R and enter Kensington Gardens. Continue ahead following the south facade of Kensington Palace L.*

Location 13

KENSINGTON PALACE *Wren 1702*

Kensington Gardens (937 9561)

State Apartments open, Monday–Saturday 09.00–17.00, Sunday 11.00–17.00. Admission charge. Guided Tours. The State Apartments will be closed Autumn 1995 to 1997 for restoration.

Court Dress Collection open as for the State Apartments.

Orangery open April–September. Admission free.

Kensington Palace was the birthplace and early residence of Queen Victoria; mementos of the Queen are displayed within. There is much fine carving by *Gibbons* and décor by *Kent*.

As Whitehall Palace was too damp for the asthmatic William III the King sought a new residence, not too far from London but away from the river. He eventually purchased Nottingham House in 1689. William immediately commissioned *Wren* to adapt and extend the Jacobean building. Three courtyards were built but, although William and Mary were soon in residence, work was not completed until 1702. Three other monarchs later resided at Kensington – Anne, George I and George II. The palace is renowned for its non-palatial appearance and was simply known as Kensington House until the 19C.

Queen Victoria was born, baptized and lived here for eighteen years but left for Buckingham Palace three weeks after her accession to the throne in 1837. Although George II was the last reigning monarch to live at Kensington it remains a royal palace and both the Prince of Wales and Princess Margaret occupy apartments on the west side behind the State Rooms.

The State Rooms were opened to the public by Queen Victoria to commemorate her 80th birthday in 1899.

The south front by *Hawksmoor* c.1695 is the most impressive facade of the palace.

In front of this, the statue of William III by *Baucke* 1907 was presented by Kaiser Wilhelm II to his uncle, Edward VII, 'for the British nation'. Sadly, within seven years, the British nation were to forget this pleasant gesture due to the First World War.

Turn first L and follow the east front.

The higher section of the palace, seen immediately L, was added for George I by *Benson* 1718–21 probably to designs by *Campbell* (?). It accommodates the Privy Chamber, King's Drawing Room and Cupola Room. The original core of Nottingham House had stood here but required rebuilding.

Facing the path L is the statue of Queen Victoria, the work of her daughter *Princess Louise* 1887.

First L pass the sunken gardens and proceed to the State Apartments entrance in the north-east corner.

Above the doorway is the William and Mary cypher.

Enter, turn immediately L and proceed to the shop for admission tickets.

The **Queen's Staircase** was constructed by *Wren* 1691 to give public access to the royal apartments.

The Queen's Apartments are seen first. Queen Anne rebuilt little at Kensington and as George I only redecorated the King's Apartments, these rooms appear much as they did when completed by *Wren* for William and Mary.

Queen's Gallery. Fine 17C. carving includes the cornice and doorheads by *W. Emmett* and gilded mirror surrounds above the fireplaces by *Gibbons*.

In the **Queen's Closet** Queen Anne and Sarah, Duchess of Marlborough, had their great quarrel in

1710. They had been the closest of friends referring to each other as 'Mrs Morley' (the Queen) and 'Mrs Freeman' (the Duchess).

Queen's Dining Room. The 17C panelling is original.

Queen's Drawing Room. This was damaged by bombs but the cornice, with its 'W&M' cypher, survived.

The **Queen's Bedroom** leads off the Queen's Drawing Room; the bed belonged to James II's second wife Mary of Modena.

The **Privy Chamber** is one of the three State Rooms, added for George I *c.*1720. The other two rooms, the King's Drawing Room and Cupola Room are seen later. All their ceilings are much higher than elsewhere in the palace and they interconnect in a straight line from east to west. The decor throughout is the work of *Kent.*

The ceiling painting depicts Mars wearing the Order of the Garter.

The Mortlake Tapestries, illustrating the seasons, were added later. They were woven in 1623 for Charles I when Prince of Wales.

Presence Chamber. Although the room was designed by *Wren,* the ceiling painting of Apollo by *Kent* was added later. It was the first in London to be painted in the Pompeian style.

The overmantel by *Gibbons* (?) was brought from the King's Gallery.

Designed by *Wren* in 1689, the **King's Grand Staircase** was altered in 1693 when the wrought-iron balustrades were added by *Tijou*. The walls and ceiling were painted later by *Kent.*

The **King's Gallery** was originally created by *Wren* to display important paintings. The ceiling painting, by *Kent*, illustrates scenes from 'The Odyssey'.

The wind-dial above the fireplace was made by *Norden* in 1694. William III sailed frequently to Holland and he learned from this if the wind was favourable before journeying to the coast.

This gallery was once sub-divided by Victoria's mother the Duchess of Kent. At the far end, in her sitting room, Victoria learnt from the Archbishop of Canterbury and Lord Chamberlain of her accession to the throne at two o'clock in the morning, 20 June 1837.

Duchess of Kent's Dressing Room. The Duchess of Kent, much to the annoyance of William IV, extended her ground floor apartment in 1836 to include some of the State Rooms on the first floor. This room had been the King's Dressing Room.

The present wallpaper, curtains and carpeting are reproductions of those which were here during the Duchess's occupancy. Most of the furnishings and fittings belonged to Queen Victoria.

Ante Room. Some of Victoria's perfectly kept toys are displayed in this room.

Queen Victoria's Bedroom. Victoria shared this bedroom, once the King's State Bedchamber, with her domineering mother. So closely was Victoria guarded by her mother that they allegedly shared the same bed (?). Princess Mary of Teck, later the consort of George V, was born in this room in 1867.

Most of the furnishings belonged to Queen Victoria and came from Buckingham Palace.

King's Drawing Room. The decor, including the ceiling painting 'Jupiter before Semele', is by *Kent*.

Displayed is a clock surmounted by bronze figures by *Roubiliac* 1750. The silver reliefs are by *Rysbrack*.

The chimney piece was carved by *Richards* in 1724.

Council Chamber. The ivory throne was made for The Great Exhibition of 1851.

Return to the King's Drawing Room and turn R to the **Cupola Room.**

This is the grandest room in the palace. Victoria was baptized here, Alexandrina Victoria, by the Archbishop of Canterbury in 1819.

The relief above the chimney piece is by *Rysbrack*.

The decor, including the vaulted ceiling, is by *Kent*.

Return to the ground floor by the Queen's Staircase and proceed to the **Court Dress Collection**.

This was opened in 1984 following restoration work. Many of the rooms originally formed the Duke and Duchess of Kent's apartment. The young Queen held her first Privy Council in 1837 in the Red Saloon which has now been restored to its Victorian appearance. This later became part of the apartment occupied by the Duke and Duchess of Teck 1867–83.

The **North Drawing Room,** seen next, has been restored to its 1820 appearance. It is believed that Victoria was born in this room on 24 May 1819 (?).

Uniforms and costumes worn by those attending Court, from the 18C to the 20C, are displayed throughout. Many of the following rooms are decorated and furnished in the appropriate style.

Exit from the palace. Turn L.

The Orangery *Hawksmoor* and *Vanbrugh* (?) 1705. This is rarely open, due to 'staff shortages'. When it is, enter from the south side. The Orangery was built as a summer Supper House for Queen Anne.

The 17C. statues by *Francavilla* and vases were brought from Hampton Court.

The two vases were presented by Elizabeth II. That in the West Room is by *Cibber* and that in the East Room by *Pearce*.

Exit from the palace grounds R. Follow the main path, then take the diagonal path R to the south-west corner of Kensington Gardens. Proceed R along Kensington Gore to Kensington High St. Cross the road to High Street Kensington Station, Circle and District lines.

Outer London

For practical reasons, the scope of this book has had to be limited to the inner city. Unlike most capitals, however, many of London's outer areas have a great deal to offer the visitor. Their royal palaces, great houses, parks, gardens and ancient villages are easily accessible, although fine weather is essential for most of them. The following summary briefly describes the most interesting.

Barnes Waterloo BR (British Rail) to Barnes Bridge. Riverside terraces lead to a village green with its ancient pub, the Sun.

Blackheath Charing Cross BR to Blackheath (or walk from Greenwich). The heath is surrounded by Georgian terraces and great houses.

Chiswick Turnham Green, District Line. Chiswick Mall is an 18C riverside village. Hogarth's House and Chiswick House are nearby.

Dulwich Charing Cross BR to North Dulwich. Dulwich Picture Gallery includes great Rembrandts amongst its vast collection of 'Old Masters'.

East End Liverpool Street, Central, Circle or Metropolitan lines. Sunday street markets include 'Petticoat Lane'. There are three great Hawksmoor churches Christchurch, St Anne Limehouse and St George-in-the-East. The Prospect of Whitby is one of many riverside pubs.

Eltham Charing Cross BR to Mottingham. The royal palace of Eltham, with its great hall and moat is a unique Plantagenet survivor in London. A great Tudor barn and a 17C mansion, Eltham Place, are nearby.

Enfield Liverpool Street BR to Enfield Town. Many 18C buildings survive; Gentleman's Row is one of London's finest period streets.

Greenwich Boat from Charing Cross or Westminster Piers to Greenwich or Charing Cross BR to Greenwich. Wren's great naval hospital, now the Royal Naval College, together with the National Maritime Museum provides one of England's greatest riverside vistas.

Hammersmith Hammersmith, District and Piccadilly lines. Upper and Lower Mall, like Chiswick's, with which they link, are 18C riverside villages. Their fine pubs include the ancient Dove.

Hampstead Hampstead, Northern line. London's most rural village is set on a hillside. Great views of the metropolis are gained from its bucolic heath. Fenton House, a William and Mary mansion, plus winding 18C streets are additional attractions.

Hampton Court Waterloo BR to Hampton Court or Green Line bus 718 from Ecclesston Bridge (Victoria) or boat from Westminster Pier. Henry VIII's great Tudor palace, with William and Mary additions by Wren, stands in extensive grounds which include the famous maze.

Harrow Harrow-on-the-Hill, Metropolitan line. Harrow School, where Churchill and Byron studied, is perched on a green hilltop and surrounded by the old village. Pinner village is nearby.

Highgate Highgate, Northern line. Adam's great Kenwood House and Highgate's Georgian village are also easily reached from Hampstead Heath.

Islington Angel, Northern line. Late Georgian streets and squares dominate Islington more than any other London borough. Canonbury Tower possesses a rare Elizabethan interior.

Kew Kew Gardens, District line, or boat from Westminster Pier. Kew's botanical gardens are the world's most famous. Its Georgian village surrounds the adjacent green.

Osterley Osterley, Piccadilly line. This great Elizabethan mansion set in its park was remodelled by Adam in the 18C at the same time as Syon.

Petersham Approached from Richmond Station by bus 65. Ham House, with London's finest Jacobean domestic interiors, is the grandest of the many fine houses that comprise 'England's grandest village'.

Richmond Richmond, District line or Waterloo BR to Richmond or boat from Westminster Pier. Remnants of Henry VII's palace survive overlooking Richmond Green which is surrounded by some of England's first Georgian terraces. Sylvan riverside scenes include the famous view from Richmond Hill, with the great deer park stretching behind.

Syon Park Waterloo BR to Syon Lane. Protector Somerset's Tudor mansion, like Osterley, was remodelled by Adam in the 18C. Old Isleworth's riverside village nearby is dominated by the ancient London Apprentice pub.

Twickenham Approach from Richmond or Waterloo BR to Twickenham. Riverside properties include Gibbs's 18C Octagon at Orleans House and Marble Hill Park. Past the old village lies Strawberry Hill, Hugh Walpole's 18C residence that inspired the Neo-Gothic style.

Waltham Liverpool Street BR to Waltham Cross or bus (many) from Enfield. Waltham's 13C Eleanor Cross is the nearest to London that survives. Remains of Waltham's great Norman abbey are nearby.

Wimbledon Southfields, District line. The famous Centre Court can be seen when visiting the All England Tennis Club's Museum. Wimbledon Village's High Street (Wimbledon, District line) leads to a great open common.

Windsor and Eton Paddington BR to Windsor and Eton Central or Waterloo BR to Windsor and Eton Riverside or Green Line bus from Victoria to Windsor. The State Apartments of Windsor Castle, still the sovereign's residence, are open most of the year. It is surrounded by the ancient town and Windsor Great Park. On the opposite side of the river is Eton with its historic public school.

Woolwich Charing Cross BR to Woolwich Arsenal. The Royal Artillery barracks has the largest classical facade in England (¼ mile long). Nearby is the regiment's museum, Nash's Rotunda, and the new Thames Barrier.

All these locations are fully described in Christopher Turner's *Outer London Step by Step* and *Windsor and Eton Step by Step*.

English architectural styles

Experts disagree on the precise definitions of some styles and periods, and as this affects their time spans, alternative dates are shown in brackets where applicable. It should be remembered that architectural styles always overlap by several years and no precise dividing line can generally be drawn. Dominant styles are shown in bold type.

Period ruled and ruler	Architectural style	Important London examples and their completion dates
Romans	**Roman** 43–410	London Wall *c.*200 Temple of Mithras *c.*190
Anglo-Saxons and Danes	**Romanesque** 500–1200	
	Pre-Conquest Romanesque or Saxon 500–1066	All Hallows-by-the-Tower/arch 7C
Normans 1066 William I 1087 William II 1100 Henry I 1135 Stephen	Post-Conquest Romanesque or Norman 1066–1200	Westminster Abbey/undercroft 1090 Tower of London/White Tower 1097 St-Mary-le-Bow/crypt late 11C St Bartholomew-the-Great *c.*1125 Westminster Abbey/St Katherine's Chapel (ruins) *c.*1170
	Transitional 1145–90	Temple Church/nave *c.*1185
Angevins 1154 Henry II 1189 Richard I 1199 John		
	Gothic 1190–1550 (or 1630)	
	Early English 1190–1310	St Helen Bishopsgate/south transept and walls (part) *c.*1215
Plantagenets 1216 Henry III 1272 Edward I		Southwark Cathedral/chancel and retrochoir *c.*1220 Temple Church/chancel 1240 Westminster Abbey/chancel, transepts, chapter house, nave (part) and cloisters (part) 1258
	Decorated 1290–1360	St Etheldreda *c.*1300 Winchester House (ruins) *c.*1350
1307 Edward II 1327 Edward III		Westminster Abbey/cloisters (part) *c.*1350
	Perpendicular 1330–1550 (or 1630)	Tower of London/Bloody Tower (part) 1362 The Charterhouse (part) 1371
1377 Richard II *House of Lancaster* 1399 Henry IV 1413 Henry V 1422 Henry VI *House of York* 1461 Edward IV 1483 Edward V 1483 Richard III		Westminster Abbey/west front (part) late 14C Merchant Taylors Hall/crypt and livery hall (part) late 14C Westminster Hall 1400 Westminster Abbey/Henry V Chapel 1430 Guildhall/porch interior, walls (part) *c.*1440 Crosby Hall 1466 St Helen Bishopsgate (part) 1475
Tudors 1485 Henry VII 1509 Henry VIII		St Olave Hart Street 15C Merchant Taylors Hall/kitchen 15C Lincoln's Inn Hall 1492

		Westminster Abbey/Henry VII Chapel 1512 Tower of London/St Peter-ad-Vincula 1520 St James's Palace/Gatehouse, Chapel Royal and Friary Court (part) *c.*1535 St Giles Cripplegate 1550
1547 Edward VI 1553 Lady Jane Grey 1553 Mary I 1558 Elizabeth I *Stuarts* 1603 James I (Jacobean period)	**English Renaissance** 1528 (or 1550)–1650 (or 1830)	Chelsea Old Church/Thomas More Chapel (part) 1528 Middle Temple Hall 1570 Holland House (ruins) 1605 York Water Gate 1626 St Katherine Cree 1630 St Helen Bishopsgate/fixtures and fittings (part) *c.*1635
1625 Charles I (Carolean period)	**Classical** 1622–1847 Palladian 1622–1700	Banqueting House 1622 St James's Palace/Queen's Chapel 1623 St Paul Covent Garden 1630 Lindsey House, Lincolns Inn Fields 1640
1649 Cromwell (Commonwealth period) 1660 Charles II (Restoration period)	Wren Style 1670–1730	St Magnus 1676 St Stephen Walbrook 1679 St Martin-within-Ludgate 1684 Royal Hospital (Chelsea) 1692 St Vedast 1697 St Paul's Cathedral 1710
1685 James II 1689 William III/Mary II 1702 Anne	Dutch Style 1680–1710	St Benet 1683 Kensington Square (part) 1685 Kensington Palace (part) *c.*1691 Schomberg House (exterior) 1698 Laurence Pountney Hill Nos 1 & 2 1703 Queen Anne's Gate (part) 1704
	English Baroque 1705–1731	St Paul's Cathedral/towers 1708 St Michael Paternoster Royal/tower 1713 St Mary-le-Strand 1717 St Mary Woolnoth 1727 St John's Smith Square 1728 St George Bloomsbury 1731
House of Hanover 1714 George I 1714 (or 1702)–1830 Georgian period		
	Neo-Gothic, or Georgian Gothic 1720 (or 1682)–1780	St Michael Cornhill/tower 1722 Westminster Abbey/towers 1745
1727 George II	Palladian Revival 1720–1830	Burlington House (part) 1720 Westminster School/College *c.*1724 Spencer House 1754 Horse Guards 1760 Somerset House *c.*1776 Brooks's Club 1778 Carlton Club 1827
1760 George III	Adam Style 1760–90	Admiralty Screen 1761 Chandos House 1770

Period ruled and rulers	Architectural style	Important London examples and their completion dates
		Adelphi (remnants) 1774 Stratford House 1775 Boodles Club 1775 Apsley House (part) 1778
1811–20 Regency period 1820 George IV	Greek Revival 1766–1847	No 15 St James's Square 1766 St Pancras Church 1822 Regent's Park Terraces *c.*1825 Buckingham Palace (part) *c.*1830 Athenaeum Club 1830 Carlton House Terrace 1832 National Gallery 1838 British Museum 1847
1830 William IV	Gothic Revival 1824–1900	St Luke Chelsea 1824 Holy Trinity Brompton 1829 Houses of Parliament 1852 All Saints Margaret Street 1859 St Pancras Chambers 1869 Royal Courts of Justice 1882 Prudential Assurance 1900
	Tudor Revival 1800–1850	Lincoln's Inn/New Hall and Library *c.*1845
	Italian Renaissance Revival 1830-50	Travellers Club 1832 Reform Club 1841
1837 Victoria	Romanesque Revival 1860–1900	Natural History Museum 1880
	Neo-Wren (or Neo-Queen Anne or Neo-Georgian) 1880–1960	Old Bailey 1907 Piccadilly Hotel 1908 Selfridges 1909 County Hall 1922
	Arts & Crafts 1900–14	Michelin House 1910 The Black Friar/interior 1910
House of Saxe Coburg and Gotha 1901 Edward VII (Edwardian period) *House of Windsor* 1910 George V 1936 Edward VIII 1936 George VI		
	Modernism (or *Functionalism*) 1950–82	Royal Festival Hall 1951
1952 Elizabeth II	*Brutalism* 1960–82	Barbican 1960–82 National Theatre 1976
	Post-Modernism from 1980	
	Hi-Tech from 1984	Lloyds 1986

Vernacular architecture

London's domestic buildings before the Classical period varied little with the prevailing architectural styles adopted for more important buildings and cannot, therefore, be tabulated with them. The oldest examples are as follows: Westminster Abbey precincts – Jerusalem Chamber and Deans Yard (part) 14C, Jericho Parlour 16C, Queen's House (Tower of London) *c.* 1540, No 30 Borough High St *c.*1542, Old Curiosity Shop 1567, Staple Inn 1586, Inner Temple Gateway (Prince Henry's Room) 1611, Wig and Pen Club (part) 1625, Nos 41–42 Cloth Fair *c.*1670.

Architectural terms

Only the lesser-known terms in the book are generally included.
Altar (or *Communion) rail* Low structure enclosing the sanctuary.
Ambulatory Passageway in a church formed by continuing the aisles behind the high altar.
Apse Semi-circular or octagonal extension to a building.
Architrave Internal or external moulding surrounding an opening.
Ashlar Large blocks of smoothed stone laid in level courses.
Attic Low top storey of a building.

Baroque Exuberant continental development of the Classical style.
Barrel or tunnel vault A continuous arch forming a semi-circular roof.
Bay Compartment of a building divided by repeated elements.
Bay window A straight-sided window projecting at ground level.
Blind A structure without openings.
Boss Ornamental projection covering the intersection of ribs in a roof.
Bow window Curved bay window.
Box pew Bench seat in a church or chapel enclosed by high partitions.
Buttress Structure attached to a wall to counter an outward thrust.

Capital Top section of a column or pilaster, usually carved in the distinctive style of a classical order.
Cartouche Decorative panel painted or carved to resemble a scroll.
Casement window Window that is hinged and generally opens horizontally as opposed to a sash that slides and generally opens vertically.
Chancel Section of a church or chapel that houses the high altar and is reserved for the choir and clergy. It is an extension of the nave.
Chantry chapel Small chapel in or attached to a church. Built for the chanting of mass for the soul of an individual, usually the benefactor.
Cladding Material added to a structure to provide an external surface.
Classical Styles following those of ancient Greece or Rome.
Clerestory Upper section of a wall, usually of the nave of a church, which is pierced with windows to provide additional light.
Coade stone Artificial, hard-wearing material resembling stone; cast in the 18C to provide statues or decorative features for buildings.
Coffering Recessed ceiling panelling.
Corbel Wall bracket, generally of stone, supporting e.g., a beam.
Corinthian Greek Classical order. Columns are slender and their capitals intricately decorated with carved leaves and small spiral scrolls (volutes).
Cornice A projecting decorative feature running horizontally at high level.
Coved Concave shaped ceiling.
Crossing Where the nave, transepts and chancel intersect in a church.
Cupola Small domed roof generally surmounting a turret.
Curtain wall Non-loadbearing material providing an external surface.

Dais Raised platform at the end of a large room, generally a hall.
Decorated Second period of English Gothic *c.*1290–*c.*1360. Remarkable for ornate window tracery, pinnacles and porches.
Doric Classical order, the oldest and sturdiest. The capitals of Doric columns are virtually undecorated.
Dormer window Window protruding from a sloping roof.

Early English First phase of Gothic architecture in England *c.*1190–*c.*1310. Characterized by narrow pointed arches and windows (lancet).
Eave Horizontal edge of a roof overhanging the wall.

Fanlight Oblong or semi-circular window above a door.
Fan vaulting Ribs of the vault make a pattern resembling a fan.
Festoon Carved hanging garland of fruit and flowers.
Fluted Vertical grooving.
Flying buttress Semi-archlike structure that directly transfers the weight of the wall to a vertical pier.

Gable Upper section of wall at each end of a building.
Gallery Storey added to an upper level, always open on one side, and usually arcaded. Alternatively, a long room for displaying works of art.
Gothic Style of architecture from 12C-17C employing the pointed arch.
Gothic Revival Serious 19C attempt to reproduce the Gothic style.
Greek Revival Buildings designed *c.*1770–1840 in Greek style.

Groin vault Intersection of two tunnel (or barrel) vaults.

Hammerbeam roof Form of roof construction late 14C–16C.

Ionic Classical order. Columns are slenderer than those in the Doric order and capitals are decorated at corners with spiral scrolls (volutes).

Jamb Straight, vertical side of a door, arch or window.
Joinery Woodwork that is fitted in but not structural to a building.

Lady chapel Chapel dedicated to the Virgin Mary.
Lancet window Slender window with a sharply pointed arch *c.*1190–*c.*1310.
Lantern Small turret pierced with openings and crowning a roof.
Light Section of a window filled with glass.

Majolica Glazed earthenware generally used as decorative tiling. Also known as faience.
Mansard roof A roof where each side is composed of two angled sections. The lower has a steep pitch and is usually pierced with dormer windows. The upper is of a lower pitch.
Moulding Decorative addition to a projecting feature such as a cornice, door frame, etc.
Mullions Vertical bars dividing a window into 'lights'.

Nave Body of the church housing the congregation.
Neo-Gothic Gothic features used in a light-hearted manner in the mid 18C.
Norman Romanesque architecture distinguished by semi-circular arches and massive walls *c.*1060–*c.*1200.

Order Classical architecture where the design and proportions of the columns and entablatures are standardized.
Oriel window Window projecting as a bay but at an upper level.

Palladian Style of architecture based on the 16C work of the Italian Andrea Palladio which itself derived from ancient Rome.
Parapet Low, solid wall surmounting a structure.
Pedestal Base between a column or statue and its plinth.
Pediment Low-pitched triangular gable above a portico, door or window.
Pendant Elongated, hanging feature decorating a roof or stairway.
Perpendicular Architectural style peculiar to England. The last and longest phase of Gothic, 1360–1550 (or 1660). Distinguished by large windows divided by horizontal transomes as well as mullions.
Pier Solid structure supporting a great load, frequently square in shape.
Pilaster Shallow, flat column attached to a wall.
Pinnacle Vertical decorative feature surmounting a Gothic structure.
Plinth Projecting base of a wall, column or statue.
Podium Lowest stage of a pedestal for a column or statue.
Portal Important doorway.
Portcullis Gate that can be raised and lowered vertically for defence.
Portico Classical porch of columns supporting a roof usually pedimented.
Priory Monastic establishment under the authority of a prior or prioress.

Quoin stones Dressed stones fitted externally at the angles of a wall to give added strength. Popular in the late 17C and early 18C.

Refectory Dining hall, also known as a frater when situated in a monastery.
Reredos Decorative structure usually standing behind the altar in a church or chapel. Generally made of wood but occasionally stone.
Retable Raised shelf behind the altar in a church or chapel. Often decorated.
Retrochoir Section of a church behind the sanctuary.
Rib Protruding band supporting a vault. Occasionally purely decorative.
Rococo Last phase of the Baroque style in the mid-18C with widespread use of detailed ornamentation. Few examples are found in England.
Romanesque Style of architecture featuring semi-circular arches. Popular from the 9C to *c.*1200. Saxon and Norman buildings were Romanesque.
Rose window Circular window used in Gothic architecture. Its tracery pattern resembles a rose. Introduced in the mid-13C.
Rotunda Circular building, generally domed.
Roundel Circular decorative panel, e.g., of glass in a window.
Rustication Use of stonework on the exterior of a building to give an impression of strength. The jointing is always deep.

Sacristy Room in a church for storage or sacred vessels and vestments. Generally used for robing. Also known as a vestry.
Sanctuary Area behind the altar rail in which the high altar stands.
Sarcophagus Carved coffin.
Sash window A window of two separate panes that slides and generally opens vertically as opposed to a casement that is hinged and generally opens horizontally. Introduced into England *c.*1680.
Saxon English architecture in Romanesque style pre-dating the Norman Conquest of 1066.
Scissor beam Roof construction in which secondary beams cross each other diagonally in support of the main beams.
Sounding board Canopy above a pulpit. Also known as a tester. Introduced to improve acoustics.
Spire Tall pointed structure with flat or rounded sides surmounting a tower.
Steeple Tower together with its crowning structure e.g., lantern, spire.
Stoup Basin for holy water, usually of stone and situated near a door.
Stucco Plaster applied to the external face of a wall and painted.
Swag Carved representation of a piece of hanging cloth. Generally incorporates festoons of flowers, fruit, etc.

Terracotta Unglazed earthenware used as tiling.
Tessellated pavement Mosaic flooring.
Tie beam Horizontal main beam in a timber roof.
Tracery Intersecting bars that create a decorative pattern in Gothic architecture.
Transept The area that runs on either side of the nave of a large church forming the cruciform (cross) plan.
Transitional The merging of Gothic with Norman architecture *c.*1150–*c.*1200.
Transomes Horizontal bars dividing a window into 'lights'.
Triforium Blind passage that runs above the roof of an aisle in a church.
Trophy Decorative sculptured arms or armour.
Tunnel vault Alternative name for barrel vault.
Tuscan Classical order. Roman adaptation of the Greek Doric order.

Undercroft Vaulted room or area at ground floor level.

Vault Underground room frequently reserved for interment. Alternatively, an arched structure forming a roof.
Venetian window Window of three openings. The central, large section having a semi-circular arch.
Vestibule Entrance hall or anteroom.
Vestry Alternative name for sacristy.

Wainscotting Timber-lining on the lower section of an internal wall.
Weatherboarding Timber strips fixed to an internal or external wall for protection or decoration. Also known as clapboarding.

Annual events in London

January
25 Burns Night. Celebration in pubs and clubs of the birth of Robert Burns, Scotland's national poet.
30 Laying of wreaths by the Royal Stuart Society at the Charles I monument in Trafalgar Square.
Late January or early February: Chinese New Year celebrations in Soho's 'Chinatown' include a dragon dance on the Sunday.
March
Shrove Tuesday: Pancake races at Lincoln's Inn Fields.
Late March or early April: The Boat Race between Oxford and Cambridge Universities from Putney to Mortlake.
Easter Period (March or April)
Thursday before Good Friday: The Queen distributes 'Maundy' money at a selected church – often Westminster Abbey.

Good Friday: Distribution of hot cross buns at St Bartholomew-the-Great, 11.00.
Easter Sunday: Procession of floats and bands in Battersea Park.
April
21 Gun salute to honour the Queen's birthday at Hyde Park and Tower Wharf.
25 Anzac Day memorial service Westminster Abbey.
April: St Andrew Undershaft John Stow memorial service.
May
Late May: The Chelsea Flower Show at the Royal Hospital.
24 Commonwealth Day. Ceremonies at the Cenotaph, Westminster Abbey and Parliament Square.
End May or early June: Oak Apple Day parade service, commemorating the birthday and restoration to the throne of Charles II, takes place at Royal Hospital, Chelsea.
June
Saturday nearest 11 June: Trooping the Colour Ceremony to mark the Queen's official birthday, Horse Guards Parade.
Late June to early July: All England Lawn Tennis Championships at Wimbledon.
July
City of London Festival
Mid July: Royal Regatta at Henley, Berkshire.
Late July to mid September: Henry Wood Promenade concerts at the Royal Albert Hall.
Last Friday: Doggett's Coat and Badge rowing race between London Bridge and Cadogan Pier, Chelsea.
August
Bank Holiday: Caribbean Carnival in Notting Hill.
September
15 Battle of Britain Day. Fly-past over London.
Late September: Admission of Sheriffs at Guildhall.
October
First Monday: Michaelmas Law Term opens and Judges in State robes proceed from their service at Westminster Abbey to the House of Lords.
November
First Sunday: Veteran Car Run to Brighton from Hyde Park Corner.
First week: State opening of Parliament.
Sunday nearest to 11 November: Remembrance Day ceremony at the Cenotaph, Whitehall.
Saturday nearest 12 November: Lord Mayor's Show from Guildhall to the Royal Courts of Justice.

Designers

Outstanding architects, sculptors and decorators whose work is featured in this book.

Adam, James 1730–94
Adam, Robert 1728–92
Archer, Thomas 1668(?)–1743
Bacon, John the Elder 1740–99
Bacon, John the Younger 1778–1859
Baily, Edward Hodges 1788–1867
Baker, Sir Herbert 1862–1946
Barry, Sir Charles 1795–1860
Barry, Edward Middleton 1830–80
Basevi, George 1794–1845
Bird, Francis 1667–1731
Blomfield, Sir Arthur William 1829–99
Blomfield, Sir Reginald Theodore 1856–1942
Blore, Edward 1787–1879
Boyle, Richard, Third Earl of Burlington 1695–1753
Burne-Jones, Sir Edward Coley 1833–98
Burton, Decimus 1800–81
Butterfield, William 1814–1900
Campbell, Colen 1676(?)–1729
Chambers, Sir William 1723–96
Chantrey, Sir Francis 1781–1841
Cheere, Sir Henry 1703–81
Cibber, Caius Gabriel 1630–1700
Cockerell, Samuel Pepys 1754–1827

Index of locations

To help choose a specific type of location the index is divided into six sections as follows: Buildings of architectural and historic interest; Places of worship, Museums/art galleries/art dealers/ auction rooms; Public monuments/statues/street furniture; Pubs/ Restaurants/Hotels; Shops/markets; Theatres/cinemas/operas/concert halls; Parks/ gardens/waterways; Thoroughfares/areas.

Buildings of architectural and historic interest

O =The interior is open to visitors.
OA=The interior is only open to visitors by appointment.

Places of worship

Museums/art galleries/art dealers/auction rooms

Public monuments/statues/street furniture

Pubs/Restaurants/Hotels
R=Restaurant. *H*=Hotel

Parks/gardens/waterways